Dependant Brethren

of

Sussex and Surrey

A History of the Cokelers

Roger Nash

Weyhurst Publishing

To the memory of my great uncle, Walter John Nash, leader and an elder of the 'Cokelers' of Loxwood, 1930-1960, without whom I doubt I would ever have considered this book a worthwhile project, and to David Gumbrill, without whose enthusiasm, help and photograph collection this book would be the poorer.

Distributor: Lulu, www.lulu.com

Contents

Tables

Illustrations

Introduction

"In a peculiar world, they seem reasonably sane."

This sentence was the conclusion to Chapter 13 of *"Abodes of Love",* by John Montgomery, written in 1962. There is no denying the pun on the Plumstead Peculiars out of which movement the Dependants came, and of its ironic truth in the mid-20th century. In about 1850, a preacher and his wife came down from London to several Sussex and Surrey villages, intent on working with the poor and labouring folk, beginning at Loxwood in Sussex, and Shamley Green in Surrey. He was John Sirgood, a shoemaker, and she was Harriet Sirgood. Their unusual surname marks them out, but it is John's preaching of the gospel and the many conversions to his form of Christianity in these villages that form the starting point of his mission. Inevitably, there was some localised opposition.

Beginning in houses and barns, the numbers and enthusiasm of the Brethren soon led to the building of small meeting houses or churches, usually called chapels, in each community, often built with the skills and with the savings of members. Of these, Loxwood Chapel became in several ways pre-eminent, for example in having the only burial ground, and as the most frequently used for the several Big Meetings held each year.

The Dependants considered themselves Dependant on Christ, hence the name. "With God's help we can conquer sin" in the afterlife, said one. Sometimes they are referred to as the Dependant Brethren, sometimes as the Society of Dependants. 'Dependant' is usually, but not exclusively, spelt with an 'a' in their own writings. Confusion is not surprising as in the initial phase of conversion most were illiterate, and much of their later literacy came from studying the Bible, and little else. I have a feeling the less thoughtful spelling with an 'e' became more common over time. Outsiders, however, came to call them Cokelers, which also manifested itself in many spellings, and as many explanations, and across all parishes where they had a presence. Two will suffice here.

It is frequently asserted, with no evidence other than the re-telling, that John Sirgood and/or his followers foreswore alcohol and only drank cocoa, not commonly drunk in those days. It has also been noted that the field next to where the Loxwood Combination Stores was built was known as Cokkes Field, hence those "of Cokkes" became the Cokelers. Who knows! As the name was not liked by the Brethren, I shall, out of respect, and because this will, I hope, be a genuine search for truth about this rural folk, call them the Dependants in what follows. However, this is not intended to be a study of their beliefs, which will only be dwelt on as needed to make sense of their story. An attempt is made at the end of this Introduction to elaborate on all the names used for the Dependants.

No history of the Dependants can omit the retail shops they established, in "combination" between those, mainly female and single, who not only worked behind the counters but also lived literally and communally over the shop. This and other observations of their practices over the years led many observers to conclude Dependants were against marriage and procreation. This is at best only three-quarters true, as although it was undoubtedly common to remain single and committed to the tenets of their bible-based Christianity there were not only numerous families among early converts, but right through to recently, there were families who worshipped in chapel, and constituted a wider Brethren community. Ben Piper of Warnham wrote about his parents choosing not to bring any more souls into the world, and Sirgood preached how we could be more useful to Christ if free of entanglements, leading later Dependants to use the refrain "to keep free for Christ's sake" (q.v. Reed, Mick, *'The Lord Does Combination Love': Religion and Co-operation Amongst a Peculiar People*, in Yeo, Stephen (Ed.), *New Views of Co-operation, 1988.*

Particularly in Loxwood, but also elsewhere, land was acquired for farming, partly to provide basic needs and shop sales, but also providing work for single men, who also ran stables, later garage services, for the Brethren's vehicles. These activities together with the combination stores, had the benefit of integrating the Brethren into their local communities, so they were not seen as monastically inward looking. On the contrary, many observers comment on their kindness in dealing with the wider community.

It is astonishing how the Brethren spread the Word in only a few years across other parishes, such as in Warnham and Northchapel, to the coast at Hove, Chichester and Felpham, and back into south London, most notably in South Norwood. My experience is mainly of Loxwood, where my family lived, and so like everyone else locally we shopped in their shops. But my experience was slightly more personal in that my father and his brother worked on their farms for my great uncle Walter Nash who was their leader or elder from 1930 until his death in 1960. Research has also revealed that numerous members of my wider family tree were once Dependants. My immediate family were never directly involved, being stalwart members of the parish church. I therefore have insights and, in particular, contacts with others who still carry the flame of memory and research. I feel confident I can add to and improve on what has been written about the Dependants over the past 160 years. This is particularly important now as all the adherents of what one recent and accurate writer called "John Sirgood's Way" have died or have long left the Brethren on becoming adults. (q.v. Jerrome, Peter, *John Sirgood's Way, The Story of the Loxwood Dependants*, 1998). It is perhaps appropriate therefore that the first sentence of Chapter 1 opens with the death of the founder.

One source needs to be singled out as essential in my research. There are in circulation several photocopied versions of both the death register and burial register of Loxwood Chapel (now also deposited and transcribed into their website by the Sussex Family History Group). See Plate A1.1. This enables research to be accurate in referring to individuals and their families, something denied to all previous research. it is now possible to add considerably to the knowledge and understanding of the Dependants. There is available a wealth of photographs, personal memorabilia and histories of individuals, assorted newspaper and magazine articles of varying and repetitive veracity. There are several original documents no one has hitherto studied or written about, deposited in West Sussex Record Office. There are also in existence scores of letters written both by and to John Sirgood, and by others of both sexes, but these are of limited use in my quest as they are predominantly religious tracts. The major omission for any researcher, not uncommon with a group of this nature, is that countless documents were destroyed by elderly members as the end time approached. What we have, is, literally, a rescue mission, and my thanks go to all those who have provided help whether deliberately or inadvertently.

Names Given to John Sirgood's Sect

Official Names
The Dependants [as registered by John Sirgood; perhaps abbreviated form for the Dependant Brethren and/or Society of Dependants]
Society (or Body) of Dependants [Dependant, a noun; no documentary origin found]
The Dependant Brethren [Dependant, an adjective; no documentary origin found]
Nicknames
The Cocoalers [earlier spelling of the term Cokelers]; often used to emphasise the supposed link to cocoa drinking, a) by Sirgood, or b) by Brethren.
The Cokelers [generally accepted modern spelling]; disliked and never used by the Dependants.
The Copelers [earliest dated form used, West Sussex Gazette, 1862, contemporary with Loxwood Chapel]; has been speculated about with no evidence whatsoever for existence of "The Book of Copel", a Mormon style book of divine revelations. It has also been suggested to mean *'Couplers'*, with sexual innuendo (Jerome, op. cit.) See also Cuckolders, below.

The Cocklers [West Sussex Gazette, 1864]; if this is an early form of 'Cokeler', it may lend weight to the possibility of the name coming from *'Cokkes Field'* (later *'Pond Field'*) behind the Combination Stores, Loxwood (Plate 5.1). This field belonged for centuries to Loxwood C of E chapel-of-ease. It may have been the location of some of the early open-air meetings in the village, held by the Overingtons (a couple who were Sirgoods closest Loxwood disciples), who lived in Hall House opposite.

Could the word "Cock" have come from Warnham, where the name of the property on which Warnham Stores was built is "Cocks" (see Chapter 9)? This, however, seems just an unlikely coincidence as the land was not transferred until 1879, years after the nickname had stuck.

The Coglers [form used consistently in Leconfield Estate documents]; similar pronunciation to 'Cocklers' also used by the Ordnance Survey in the 1870s.

The Cuckolders [West Sussex Gazette, 1864, as alternative to above]; Jerrome refers to this in its literal sense of sexual impropriety with other men's wives – dissenters were commonly accused of variations on the theme of free love. However, there was a pair of cottages long since demolished called *'Cuckolders Corner'* in nineteenth century censuses, near New Songhurst Farm, north of Loxwood, and close to other Overington homes in Spy Lane and Four Houses, and close to the newly erected chapel. The tentative implication here is a gathering of potential converts in that locality for preaching events.

Dependant Dress and Appearance

Many articles on the Dependants over the past century have naturally highlighted their dress and the way they wore their hair and beards. Many of the brethren, particularly in the first half of the 20th century, did grow a heavy beard, sometimes in a style which wrapped their face in a horseshoe of hair, leaving the moustache and cheeks shaven – a style used by John Sirgood, and presumably copied. Tom Rugman at Loxwood had a splendid example, as did Michael Woolgar at Chichester, Ben Piper and William Booker at Warnham, William Cumber (Northchapel and Norwood) and William Hampshire at Lordshill Common. Henry Aylward, however, was always photographed between the wars clean shaven. In the author's lifetime, beards had gone out of fashion altogether. Male dress was conservative, without being as attention-drawing as that of the ladies. Bearing in mind how formally even labourers dressed until the 1950s, the Brethren were not so out of line. Even those beards were seen on many Victorian men.

Photographs of the sisters give an immediate sense of extreme modesty and lack of any flamboyance, or of fashion, except that of their grandparents. The walking out dress on the way to chapel was, even in the 1950s and 1960s, an eye-catching sight, as a group walked along from the Combination Stores to the little path that led them more privately to the chapel. Dressed all in black or very dark colours in jackets with dresses of ankle length, little black bonnets atop their tightly combed and parted hair with backbun, many with wire rim glasses perched on the nose, black gloves in winter and a hand-knitted black bible bag (perhaps containing a lunch pack), they might have walked straight out of a Victorian film set. Funerals, the most joyous occasions, and Big Meetings at holidays, were large turnouts of similarly dressed sisters and besuited and waistcoated Brethren, dark coats in winter for both sexes.

Having said that, on weekdays, the dress in the shops would be a white apron for the women, and a similar cotton coat for the men in white or brown, not so different from other such shops in a pre-supermarket age. The demure and not particularly colourful dress underneath and their severe hair styles, however, reflected the mindset of these hardworking and puritanical men and women. Even in leisure, such as visits to the beach, dress code was strict, even if the top layer was judiciously removed to waistcoat level or lightweight dress.

Geography

The Dependants existed in communities and outliers across Sussex and Surrey. This book examines these communities in some detail, but for the reader to find a route through the book's locations, it is necessary to provide some introductory detail. Loxwood, the central place in both worship and community alike is a village just within West Sussex on an 18th century turnpike road which would have brought a traveller from Guildford, so not entirely off the beaten track. Not far to the north in Surrey, with Cranleigh lying in between, is the village of Shamley Green, and its adjunct hamlet at Lordshill Common where Sirgood was living in 1851. Both Loxwood and Lordshill became important communities over subsequent decades. Railway stations opened in Rudgwick (4 miles from Loxwood) and Bramley (2 miles from Shamley Green) some 15 years later.

Both were part of bigger parishes: Loxwood in Wisborough Green, Shamley Green in Wonersh, and so distancing themselves from the established church: there was an ancient chapel-of-ease in Loxwood, but no church in Shamley Green until 1864. This pattern of finding the interstices of the Christian map was also to be found in Plaistow (chapel-of-ease again) and neighbouring hamlets of Kirdford parish to the west, in Northchapel further west still where the adherents also came from small hamlets and set up their chapel on the southern fringes of the village. Northchapel had become a parish separate from Petworth in 1717, so retained a sense of remoteness, similar to Loxwood, Plaistow and Shamley Green. In Warnham, near Horsham, on the eastern side of Rudgwick the pattern described holds too, the chapel being in countryside near Friday Street. The latter's stores it should be said were right in the heart of the villages where trade was good. With no centre in or near larger villages like Cranleigh or Rudgwick, there seems to have been a tendency, perhaps an unconscious one, to disperse the communities within considerable walking distances of each other. Plaistow only developed much later. See Appendix A3 for maps.

The dispersal of the population of the Low Weald in numerous hamlets based on agriculture and/or rural industry, the latter particularly true of Northchapel, provided fertile ground for preachers among poor mostly illiterate people with little connection to or from the established church at a time of rising population in large families. This is brought home by the extension to communities further south where chapels in Chichester, and later daughter chapels in Hove/Portslade and in Felpham near Bognor, did not just serve the small proportion of the urban population but also those scattered adherents in parishes across the South Downs who walked huge distances every Sunday. In moving back to south London, the choice was made to set up in South Norwood, again for an initially scattered membership, but the chapel was built on the very edge of the then growing suburbs, soon to become surrounded by houses, but among people with no roots in the community.

CHAPTER 1

"Our Dear Elder Brother"

PLATE 1.1

Sirgood Family

Fig 1 -
John Sirgood,
1821-1885.

Fig 2 -
Harriet Sirgood,
1811-1876.

Fig 3 – Avening Gloucestershire, an old photograph. *Ack: ukphotoarchive.org.uk.*

Fig - 4, John and Harriet's Marriage Certificate, March 1845. *Ack: ancestry.co.uk.*

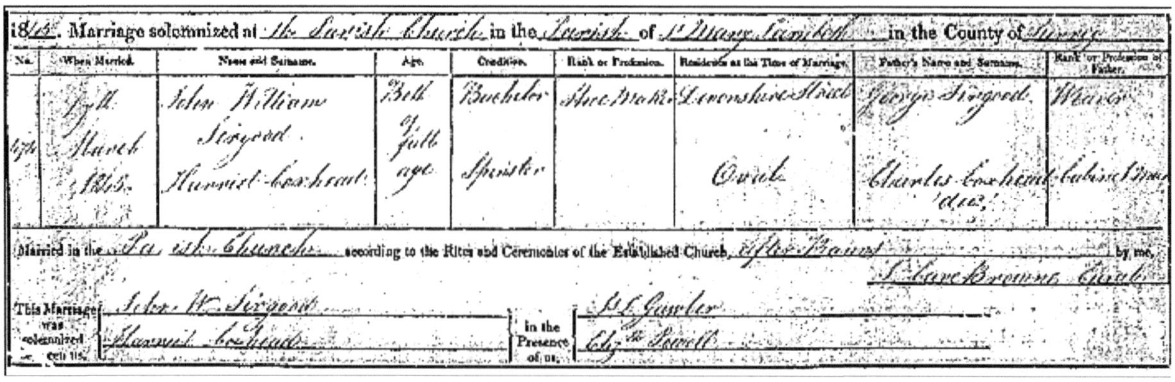

John Sirgood, 1821-1885

The death of John William Sirgood, the generally accepted founder of the Dependants, was recorded at Loxwood Chapel in Spy Lane. It was on 19 October 1885 at Loxwood Stores, and his burial in the graveyard alongside the chapel in Spy Lane on 24 October was in grave plot 108. He was aged 63. His date of birth was given as 23 August 1821. The West Surrey Times and County Express published a brief obituary on the day of his funeral.

At the inquest, reported by the Brighton Observer on 26 October, some medical background emerged. Although he had died in Loxwood, he was just visiting, as he had many times before. He may well have walked there or come on a cart. His body was identified by Catherine Enticknap, an assistant in the Combination Stores in Loxwood. She stated his address, Lordshill Common, Shamley Green, Surrey, and his occupation of bootmaker. Further details are given later in this chapter. The text image is in Plate 5.2.

He had been a widow for nine years, his wife Harriet having pre-deceased him in 1876. John had officiated at her funeral, as he had at seven others in the early years of the Dependants. However, the Sirgoods were buried in separate plots, as was normal. The role of officiating Elder for John's funeral fell to brother William Hampshire of Lordshill Common, Shamley Green, the only one he ever undertook. Hampshire, a single man born in Bramley, Surrey and a farm labourer, had provided a home for Sirgood at Lordshill Common after his wife had died (1881 census); he was one of the early converts there. Sirgood is first recorded at Shamley Green in the 1851 census. Some sources, including the Post Office, use 'Lords Hill' as the address. I will use the older, and current Ordnance Survey, single word.

The 1881 census gives Sirgood's age as 59 and tells us he was born in Gloucestershire but not where in the county. In 1871, "Gloucester, Gloucestershire" was given, but whether this has any significance is open to question. The 1861 census agreed his age, 39, and stated "Gloucestershire, place unknown". In 1851, his age was 30, and his place of birth unknown. He was described as a shoemaker, except in 1881 when he was a draper in the Lordshill Stores. In 1841, he and any family seem to have evaded the enumerator altogether. The literature on the Dependants however refers to his birth in the parish of Avening in the Gloucestershire Cotswolds. Is there any proof? The short answer is 'No'. Documentary proof of his birth is lacking. A cottage on Lordshill Common is named Avening Cottage, purely circumstantial evidence as is much else. There seems no reason to doubt the link, or the oral history within the Dependants.

Joseph Sirgood, a Younger Brother

A thorough search of the records available on the Ancestry website, on the Findmypast website and the Mormons' Family Search has been undertaken by the author. Records include both censuses, and births, marriages and deaths, some from original parish records. Joseph Sirgood was baptised at Upper Forest Green Independent Chapel, Avening, 11 September 1826. He looks to be a good candidate for younger brother, and possible confirmation that John was also brought up in the village. Forest Green is one of the hamlets of the parish of Avening. Joseph's father was stated to be George Sirgood.

Joseph Sirgood and Caroline Gregory were married in Kennington, Lambeth in 1850, where they raised a family, in contrast to John and Harriet, who as far as can be ascertained never had any children. By 1861, Joseph had changed his work from coal merchant to become a bookseller and stationer in Kennington Lane, and this time he remembered to tell the census enumerator he was born in Forest Green, Avening. His occupation, and the religious life led by John, shows that somewhere along the line the boys had gained enough education to get on in life. Joseph then moved nearby to 8 Windmill Row, where he ran his business for the remainder of his life. He died in 1877. Caroline continued the business for a few more years. There is no evidence this family was ever attracted to Brother John's faith, especially as Joseph had worked in a pub (1841) and later his eldest son, also named Joseph, in a distillery (1871). The Dependants would not have approved. As explained below, there remained a brotherly attachment. Joseph, even after his marriage, was closer to his father, living with him in 1851, when he had been widowed.

John's Marriage to Harriet Coxhead

Who was the father, George? There is no evidence whatsoever of his birth in the usual sources. The picture is made a little clearer if we fast forward to John's marriage to Harriet Coxhead, which took place in the parish church of St Mary, Lambeth in south London on the 17th March 1845, when Sirgood was 24, and his wife ten years his senior. Banns had been called there too; John lived then in Devonshire Street, Kennington, and Harriet at The Oval, nearby, not as stated repeatedly in the literature as already married by the age of 20 and living in Clapham! At his marriage, John was stated to be the son of George Sirgood, a weaver – which was of course a trade much in demand in Gloucestershire and gives us the same name as Joseph's father. John was already a shoemaker, but no apprenticeship is known. Devonshire Street, which is no longer there, was off Upper Kennington Lane (so not far north of The Oval cricket ground). This by the way confirms the sources which say that Sirgood spent his formative years in the capital. Where he was in 1841, we do not know, possibly apprenticed somewhere in London. His presumed brother Joseph was in London by then, in service in the household of a Mr William Ball who kept a pub in Chancery Lane. John's bride, Harriet, was the daughter of the late Charles Coxhead (born about 1776 in Hungerford, Berks, died about 1825 in Godalming, Surrey). Charles had married Ann Chitty at Godalming in 1803 and was a cabinet maker. Harriet was born in 1811, the third child, and baptised an Anglican, as were all their children, at St Peter & St Paul, Godalming. The family moved to Farnham, Surrey in about 1813 for a few years (two brothers were born there, in 1814 and 1816), so she would have spent her younger years in Farnham. They then went to Winchester, where two more children were born, a sister in 1819 and a brother in 1821, returning to Godalming between 1821 and 1825. She was 14 at the time her father died in Godalming. In the same year as he died, Ann gave birth to another child, George. Intriguingly George was living in Bramley, Surrey in 1841 and 1851. Might this have influenced the Sirgoods to travel south to the Surrey border villages just beyond Bramley? There is no doubt, from Harriet's letters, that she was fervently committed to her husband's work and mission.

Two brothers became wheelwrights or in the case of James, a coachsmith. Another became a bootmaker, and was also married in Kennington in 1850, living just ½ mile from where

Harriet had previously lived. There is no evidence any of her siblings followed her into the Dependants. Most lived in the south London suburbs.

Mary Meredeth, an Older Sister

Mary Sirgood, born 1818, a possible older sister, is known to have married Charles Meredeth in Swanscombe, Kent in 1837. They are listed in the 1841 census, with two children and Mary's mother Sarah Sirgood, née Emmery (see below), living together in the village of Twerton, Somerset, near Bath, where, according to the 1851 census, Mary was born. Grandma Sarah, presumed wife of George Sirgood, was probably helping to look after the younger child, a daughter aged 7 months. By 1851, like the rest of the Sirgood clan (except John), the Meredeths were in Lambeth (Charles a labourer), their two younger children born in Vauxhall. What's more, the 1841 Meredith baby, called Sarah, was wrongly stated in 1861 as born in Gloucestershire (not Somerset) and is to be found visiting Tom Pacy, a known Dependant in Skiff Lane, near Loxwood, aged 20, an interesting mistake and an interesting link.

George and Sarah Sirgood, Parents of Sarah, John, and Joseph, and possibly Mary

Records show that George Sirgood (John's supposed father) had married Sarah Emmery on 25th February 1816 in Hilperton, Wiltshire (not far from the Gloucestershire border, and a weaving centre). Was Sarah mother of John and Joseph Sirgood? This spelling of the name Emmery is so rare, I believe she was. Sarah died and was buried in Kennington in March 1851, aged 59. In the census of the same year, George is to be found, as indicated above, a widower, living with his son, Joseph, and his new wife, Caroline. George was now a bill sticker, and was aged 63, birthplace given as unknown, but his son Joseph gave his birthplace as Twerton, and his wife's at Paulton, also in Somerset! This is a family which had moved around and like many others was confused as to its origins; confusion to the extent that Joseph's marriage entry in Kennington parish church gives his father as Charles, an auctioneer – no trace of whom have I found. Either it was an error, or there are elements of these relationships still unknown.

In summary, John Sirgood's father, George, a weaver from Axminster, Devon, moved around the West Country, where he could find work in the mills and weaving sheds. in 1816 he married Sarah Emmery in the mill village of Hilperton, Wiltshire. In 1818, when Sarah was born, they were in Twerton, near Bath, where there were mills on the River Avon. In 1821, they were in Avening, Gloucestershire, another weaving area in the Cotswolds, where John William Sirgood is said to have been born. They were still there when Joseph was born in 1826.

There is also a record of William Sergood *(sic)* baptised in Twerton, the son of George and Sarah Sergood on Christmas Day, 1827. This George is described as a "milman" (millman). Had they returned there? There are, however, no further records of William. A Robert Sirgood, aged 1 year 10 months, died in Twerton in 1828. These leads do not shed much light.

A few years later, in 1853, John Sirgood's widowed father went back to Somerset, to the Bath area, possibly Twerton, to marry Mary Branan from Wiltshire, his second wife. Was this in Twerton? There is no church record, only a civil record. The 1861 census finds them back in Lambeth visiting his first wife's relative, Joseph Emmery. George now gives his birthplace as "Axminster, Somerset" (actually it is just over the border in Devon) so the evidence mounts for a West Country origin. The best estimate of his birth is 1788, from census ages. There are a number of families in the Devon-Somerset-Wiltshire-Oxfordshire area who spell their name Sargood, which fits the West Country burr quite nicely. Of course, Axminster is famous for its carpets, so there would have been plenty of weavers in and around the area. George, died in 1865, and his second wife Mary in 1870, both in Lambeth.

John's Whereabouts, 1840s to 1885

It is now possible to conjecture that the entire family had moved to London by the 1840s, but John is a step ahead, as by 1851 he was in Shamley Green, having begun his religious work in the Surrey-Sussex border parishes. At some point, he may have made moves to distance himself from his family. Two letters dated 1849, both to Brother Banyard, are transcribed into an unattributed notebook lodged in West Sussex Record Office. Both give off a touch of insecurity, of a young convert seeking the truth about how to judge and advise someone working on a Sunday. Banyard is clearly seen as an adviser, and Sirgood is put out by a small disagreement in the first letter. A one line note at the end tells the reader "written about four years after Br John believed." This places his conversion and his marriage in the same year, 1845.

John Sirgood's movements are hard to reconstruct. It is known he moved about, preaching and staying with his followers. To reiterate, his address on his marriage in 1845 was Devonshire Street, Kennington. What do the censuses tell us? From his initial sighting in Lordshill, Shamley Green in 1851, he is then confirmed in Spy Lane, Loxwood in 1861, around the time the community was commencing to build a chapel there. He lived in one part of a house occupied by Thomas Overington's family. Like William Hampshire at Lordshill, previously mentioned, Tom Overington was one of the first converts in Loxwood, and one of the elders of the community for many years.

Peter Jerrome (*John Sirgood's Way*, op.cit.) has examined directories which show that John practiced his trade as boot and shoemaker at 4, Bromell's Road, Clapham, in 1864 and 1865 (Plate 1.2). An advertisement in the South London Chronicle appeared in several issues in 1864: *"For strong made boots and shoes go to Sirgood's boot and shoe manufacturer and Lancashire clog warehouse, 9 Market Place, Bromell's Road, Clapham. All kinds of repairs done at the shortest notice on the premises"*. There are interesting differences of address here. In 1869 he was at No 34. In 1871, however, he was listed at 48 Bromell's Road, with his wife and a young servant, trading as a leather seller (ironically next door to a pub!). Jerrome suggests there was some house re-numbering in the mid-1860s. It was a period of change and development in Clapham. Clapham High Street Railway Station was built in 1862. Clapham Junction Railway Station opened in 1863. There is no evidence of his apprenticeship in the shoemaking trade, whether in Gloucestershire or in London. Likewise, there is no evidence of a Dependant community, still less a chapel, in Clapham. There is no certainty how much time he spent in Clapham, or how often he came and went from the Sussex and Surrey villages.

A young James Reeves, 20, from Loxwood, also a shoemaker, with a teenaged German as assistant, was trading at No 34 Bromell's Road by 1871. Reeves was a farm labourer's son from Brewhurst Mill, Loxwood. Is this period in his life the one frequently associated by earlier writers with Clapham Common, or is it true, as many have asserted, with no evidence, that he began his preaching there in the late 1840s? He was, of course closer to his family, but perhaps contact was limited as they did not share his sense of mission.

Bromell's Road is at the eastern end of Clapham Common, leading directly to The Pavement, along its north eastern edge, so it is very likely he did preach in the open there. Much of the early preaching of men like Sirgood was on common land whether in town or country parish. Sirgood walked or rode in any available cart or carriage covering great distances and preaching wherever he was. He is also known to have travelled by train on occasions, so he may well have moved frequently village to village and back to south London as the need arose. He had been in Loxwood for a funeral in 1869. He returned to the Surrey-Sussex borders, leading another funeral in 1872.

Harriet died in Shamley Green in 1876, her funeral unsurprisingly led by John. She had been ill and very deaf for some time, as John's and her letters testify. By 1881, four years a widow, he is found with his old friend William Hampshire at Lordshill in Shamley Green. Incidentally, at this time the modern parish of Shamley Green was part of the parish of Wonersh, and Lordshill just a small common with a cluster of (mainly Dependant) cottages. Sirgood's own death at Loxwood Stores in 1885, aged only 63, reflected a hard life of travel and service, a contrast with many of his adherents who lived particularly long lives.

Origins of his Faith and his Mission

So, what of John Sirgood's faith and his Christian mission? He is apocryphally said to have taken his goods and his wife on a handcart to Sussex in about 1850, having had enough of preaching to an unreceptive semi-urban population on Clapham Common. It has been shown above that he and Harriet were in Shamley Green in 1851, so there is truth in the destination, if not the exact origins in south London, though whether he had also reached Loxwood by then is simply not known.

He is also said to have been a disciple, from early in the 1840s, of William Bridges, who founded the Plumstead Peculiars in 1838, active mainly in Southwark, and who believed in Christian healing, rather than medicine, perhaps not so foolish then as it might seem today with our advances in both inoculation and medical care. Bridges is said to have himself been a disciple of Robert Aitkin, a charismatic preacher, who he heard preaching about 1836/7. Another Aitkin disciple was James Banyard, who met Bridges in 1837. He was to become founder of the Peculiar People in Essex, an offshoot from Methodism. Here we are on stronger ground as the link between them and the Loxwood Brethren has always been strong. "Peculiar" in this context and timeframe meant a people of God's own persuasion, not in the sense of "unusual", and certainly not eccentric or unwell. The word has, it must be said, never been used of the Dependants, who were dependant on Christ. Sirgood is remembered for having preached against the excesses of alcohol, using his own experience of enjoying a drink before his conversion. He did not rule it out altogether, just excess. Sirgood said, "I always wanted to serve God, but I did not know how till I had heard Brother Bridges." Was this in 1845, as the letter transcriber tells us?

Later, when chapels were built, and regular long services became the norm, there was no Holy Communion. Sirgood taught that the bread and wine were given only to the Disciples by Jesus himself as a remembrance after the crucifixion. Similarly, there was no use of the Lord's Prayer as this was His prayer, not ours. Sirgood did not accept the Trinity, believing there was no Holy Spirit. Brethren did not need such an outward sign to bring Him to mind. He believed Christ himself was the substance of faith, and that there was no need to remember someone who was always with you anyway. Sirgood's belief that we are all born in sin meant repentance was a major part of faith in order to receive remission from sins and in order to live a holy life free from sin, a righteous life waiting for the Lord to come at the final reckoning. The Bible was his inspiration. 1. John.ch3.v7 has been given as a key verse: *"My little children, let no man lead you astray: he that doeth righteousness is righteous, even as he is righteous."* We should prove our faith by action, not just listen to others, and that by joining the Dependants.

Alfred Goodwin (the beliefs above reported by him) was the last elder of the Loxwood Dependants. He also described Sirgood's great propensity to write letters, which grew longer as he grew older, some of which have survived. They were copied into copybooks for later use and re-use by many devoted followers. Like many Dependants, Alf did not want this handwritten evidence to survive, but some have. Goodwin also told how Sirgood was an itinerant leader and preacher, never settling in one place, but appointing elders of the chapels, writing copiously to the communities, and visiting them often on foot. Early on, elders were "anointed" (as they were in Essex), and both William Hampshire (Lordshill) and John Overington (Loxwood, Tom's brother) became elders in this way, but later the elders were simply appointed. Both the building of seven chapels and the beginnings of the community Combination Stores, of which there were five, date from before Sirgood's death. By 1958, late in the day, a hymn book was considered desirable – most of the hymns were written by Sirgood, and passed on individually, orally or in letters. These have therefore survived, but as might be expected give negligible historical information. Some were sung to traditional tunes, all without musical accompaniment.

In his first Surrey-Sussex border period, Sirgood endured considerable objections to his own dissenting voice. Not only were meetings disrupted and assaults made by the mob, but also one local gentleman, a magistrate and Member of Parliament, on finding his men had held a meeting in a house he owned, had banned meetings forthwith. A solicitor was instructed in 1861 to threaten Sirgood with litigation if he persisted in holding supposedly unlawful congregations.

This episode led Sirgood to publish his *"Working Man's Reply to a Notice from a Magistrate"*, which he entitled *"Religious Intolerance in the Rural Districts of Sussex"* (Plate 1.2). Intriguingly, it was printed by "James Sirgood", 8 Windmill Row, Kennington, the address of his stationer brother Joseph. Did Joseph feel he had to disguise himself as James? If so, his address was plain enough! There was no James! The suggestion another brother

James emigrated to North America has been made, but there is no mention of him in US or Canadian censuses.

Sirgood addressed his reply from Clapham, although in the same year (1861) he was in Loxwood for the census. Sirgood's defence was naturally to fall back on the word of God in the Bible, whose word he preached, so that he felt compelled to tell it as it is written, and that the magistrate could not oppose him without admitting he did not believe in the Scriptures. "I thank God that He is on my side." Sirgood comes across as forceful, a fundamentalist, and highly literate.

An extract here plays to the reality of Loxwood chapel-at-ease's location, remote from Wisborough Green:

"You must know that in this village up to the time we had the meetings, there was nothing that ever bore the name of religion, except that once in a fortnight, and that on a Sunday morning, but even then the service was nothing better than a school boy may be able to perform, and that is all the village now has, except the meeting now complained of, and for holding these you wish to punish me with penalties. Now even if that fortnightly cold and formal service was such as would feed a hungry and thirsty soul, do you think one service in two weeks sufficient to maintain life in the true Christian? Does not God's word command us to meeting daily?"

From Brother John

An analysis of the letters is difficult. Apart from their simple but impenetrable religious content, the copyists did not have exact dates or even recipients for many of them. The vast majority were written by John Sirgood, signing himself "Brother John". Many were written to a number of female adherents, "Dear sister", usually adding a more effusive salutation. Some were to named individuals, or to entire groups of brethren at a church or stores. Some were dated by the copyist with just the year or a note saying before or about a particular year. Others had exact dates. Some had none.

The earliest two letters in a collection acquired by Marion May, a researcher living in Shamley Green, and author of a useful booklet, were dated 5 May 1858 and "about 1859", both to Tom and Ann Overington (née Reeves), in Loxwood. These are significant letters written much earlier than all the rest. It is not clear, however, where they were written, but both are signed "J & H Sirgood". These are all that survive dateable from Sirgood's "early Surrey-Sussex border period", 1850-1864, a period when it seems likely that oral communication was dominant among a largely illiterate labouring class, who flocked to his preaching on commons and in houses and barns, most to listen respectfully, some to heckle and create a nuisance.

Others in her collection of copybooks written by Sirgood include one written on New Year's Day 1870 in Clapham, one in 1873 from Brixton, and in 1874 two from Battersea, another in 1877 from New Kent Road. These were all written in Sirgood's "London period" between about 1864-1877, as noted above, when he may have been based in Clapham. Visits to Clapham have been authenticated as early as 1861. No known Dependant community survived this period of proselytising on the open spaces of London's inner suburbs. The nearest chapels known to have been built later were for an important community that grew in South Norwood, near Croydon, and for a short-lived one in Peckham, four miles north-east of Clapham.

Several letters clearly point to a group of adherents in Bath, which has been speculatively suggested by Peter Jerrome to be related to those in the service of masters who visited the spa city. The first of these was in 1874. Most likely he made several visits by train from London. Other letters point to a community around Headcorn in Kent. Other Kent locations noted from censuses were Sevenoaks with Sundridge, Maidstone, Canterbury and Margate (see Table A2.1). Letters show also that Sirgood visited Lincolnshire, visiting as late in his life as 1883, just two years before his death.

Assuming the Sirgoods had retreated to Shamley Green before Harriet's death in 1876, he may then have given up on Clapham. In 1878 he wrote one each from Warnham and Loxwood. From 1878, a "late Surrey-Sussex border period" is dominant, with letters in 1880, 1881, 1883, 1884 and 1885 all datelined Warnham (this may reflect survival of the letters rather than any long stay there, and one is dubiously dated after his death), with others from Loxwood in 1882 and 1885, Northchapel 1883 and also South Norwood that year, making 1883 the most prolific year. This is co-incident with the work he did developing combination stores in the main communities. There are numerous other letters to and from these localities with no certain date. The tone of letters would suggest they were a rallying cry for the faithful, and it was anticipated they would in the manner of social media today be shared around. Perhaps less like ephemeral social media, their lifetime was more or less unending so long as there were readers to read them. Further letters and copybooks are preserved in the archive of the Petworth Society, and analysed thoroughly by Jerrome in "John Sirgood's Way". Many of these letters duplicate those held by Mrs May.

The Kitchener Primary Sources

A 1914 letter (original shown to me by Don Kitchener of Hillgrove, Loxwood) from "one who knew Br John" to May Kenward, a dressmaker at Brown, Durant, the stores in Northchapel, survives in which the writer tells the following story. He and three other men, all labourers, who finding themselves lodging in Long Ditton for work, set out to walk the 10-12 miles to Clapham, where late in the evening they find Sirgood's corner shop. The Sirgoods agree to let them stay the night and accompany Bro. John to the meeting next day (Sunday) at Deacon Street in Walworth, Southwark. The message to May in this letter is twofold, firstly Sirgood's kindness to humble labourers, and secondly the gentle way he admonishes them, successfully, to keep off beer and porter, which he describes as poorly nourishing and "maltwash", with the food value grains going to livestock. It also clearly identifies a house meeting at the house of Joseph Learls(?). A second letter, with little content worthy of note dated Clapham, 6 September 1861 is verified as in John Sirgood's own hand.

A third is a set of documents from the same year, two respectively dated 14 and 16 March, the original Notice regarding unlawful assembly for religious worship incurring a penalty of £20 for each one, and a letter to John Sirgood from H.F. Napper (the magistrate) suggesting he could "without difficulty procure your conviction", having himself witnessed two "unlawful meetings"... "which have been allowed to go far enough, and that it is quite time they should be controlled."

Mr Sirgood

Sir

I went to your home on Thursday evening for the purpose of giving you the enclosed Notice, but found you were holding one of your unlawful meetings. I am glad I did this because I have now myself witnessed two of these unlawful assemblages. These could without difficulty procure your conviction in two penalties – and these two could probably be easily multiplied.

It is a very general opinion that your illegal proceedings have been allowed to go far enough, & that it is quite time they should be controlled.

I am your obed^t ser^t

H F Napper

16 Mar 1861

The signatories of the Notice were:

Henry Frederick Napper, 77, landowner, Lakers Lodge, Loxwood

John Thornton, 75, vicar of Wisborough Green

Henry Botting, 68, miller, Brewhurst Mill

John Botting, his son, 44, miller, grocer & draper, The Stores, Loxwood (now The Old Stores)

James Woods, 59, farmer, Drungewick,

William Challen, 50, farmer, Newpound Common

Richard John Sparkes, 53, rector of Alfold.

A third lengthy document from HF Napper written on 14 June was in response to both a reply from John Sirgood (and another from Henry Rogers). It may be the only copy to survive. The content of this will be found in Appendix 1. The letter from Rev Rogers, Congregational Minister in Petworth and hence legally responsible for religious meetings of dissenters in his area, has not survived, as far as is known, but a copy is included in the pamphlet Sirgood published entitled *"Intolerance in the Rural Districts of West Sussex, etc."*, dated 27 March 1861. Notes attached to the bundle of documents refer to "Letters from Henry Rogers from 1862 to 1865". These are missing.

On 18 April, Sirgood wrote at length to Mr Napper, a letter which takes up the bulk of the pamphlet, which does not, for obvious reasons, include the reply which has now come to light. The latter reflects the exasperation of local feeling among the land owning, farming, and established church-going classes. Napper's reply is a cutting and sneering letter, damning with faint praise in the formal style of Victorian letter writing. Rogers's letter is *"in a style to which I am not accustomed"*, making reference to *"so much of the law as he thinks is in his favour"*. Sirgood's letter is *"lengthy and frothy"*, which he had *"the honour of receiving"*. He castigates Sirgood for not knowing the difference between religion and worship. *"Religion does not consist of frequent attendance at public worship." "At present you are only a blind guide (Matt XXIII)."* Napper pushes harder with the assertion that attendance at his meetings is "a grand delusion". *"You ask, what I think is the reason why the multitude come to your meetings – I will tell you – I believe it is because you preach to them a doctrine from which they 'find comfort and confidence' (to use your own words) now, and hope eventually also to find Heaven – but I believe it to be a present comfort based upon an unfounded confidence – probably like Popery, a very comfortable faith to live in, but not to die in – the good they get for their souls is very questionable."* He goes on to question the fruit of Dependant teaching, that *"having the Holy Spirit they cannot sin"*, another delusion as having broken any or every Commandment (which he admits Sirgood will say, having the Holy Spirit they will do none of those things), they will be tempted, and sin under the delusion that it is the Holy Spirit, *"and there are many, nay most, of your (untaught) hearers to discern the difference if they are misled by their preacher"*. Napper was unaware that Sirgood denied the Trinity!

At the end of the letter Napper explains why no charges will be brought, something that has puzzled the author hitherto. He explains that not having the most recent Statutes to refer to at Loxwood, he was *"under the impression that the most recent law on the subject was the Act for Certifying and Registering Places of Worship, but he now understands another would be passed only a fortnight afterwards to exempt altogether the most objectionable meetings from the necessity of Registration"* [his underlining]. This was the Places of Worship Registration Act, 1855, which applied retrospectively to existing places of worship. The Church of England was exempt. Wikipedia states: *"Registration is not mandatory, but an unregistered place of worship cannot be used for the solemnisation of marriages."* The Act is still in force.

John Sirgood's Death

The Brighton Gazette (26 October 1885) covered the death and inquest of John Sirgood, who died 19 October 1885. Miss Powell, it reported, was manageress of the Combination Stores, then in its infancy. Catherine Enticknap, her assistant, reported to the coroner that Sirgood had been ill for several days, having come to visit (from his home at Lordshill) on 10 October in apparent good health, but reporting illness that night. He refused a doctor, and was much better the following Sunday, but was up and down subsequently, until at 5.00 pm on 19 October he was greatly changed.

Miss Enticknap, born 1860 in Northchapel, so only about 25, seems to have been close to Sirgood, as it was she he woke when his condition deteriorated, and who provided all the evidence at the inquest. By 1891 she was recorded as draper's manageress at the Combination Stores, Loxwood. Doctor Humphries arrived from Wisborough Green at 7 o'clock. Sirgood was sinking fast. His post-mortem examination revealed a diseased kidney and bladder, with peritonitis. The medical verdict was degenerated kidneys and cystitis of long standing, accepted by the court.

PLATE 1.2   John Sirgood, Clapham, and the 'Intolerance' Dispute

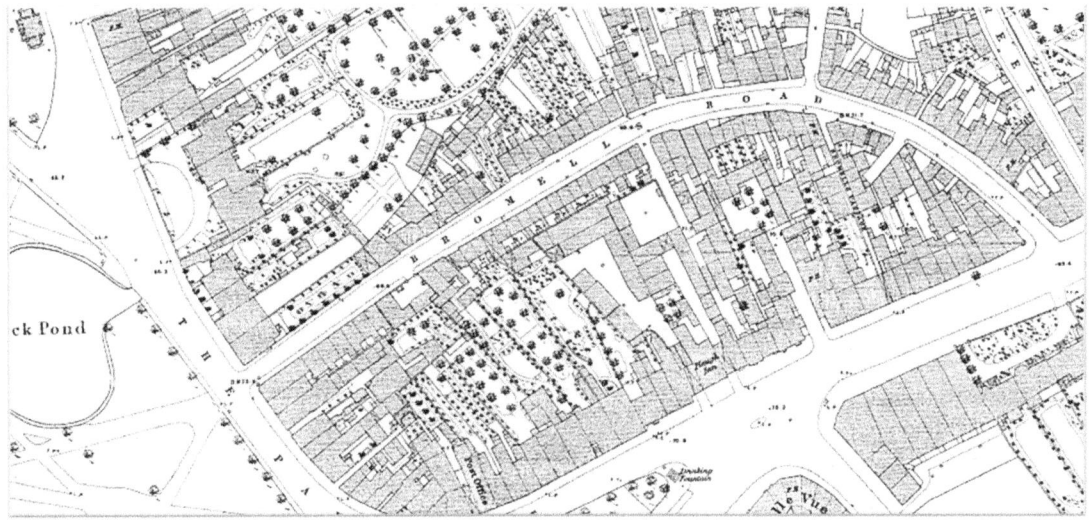

Fig 1 – Bromell's Road, Clapham Common, John Sirgood's abode in the 1860s.

Fig 2 – The Shoemaker's Reply, dated 16 March 1861, cover.

Fig 3 – A Working Man's Reply, undated, pub. James Sirgood, Kennington, cover.

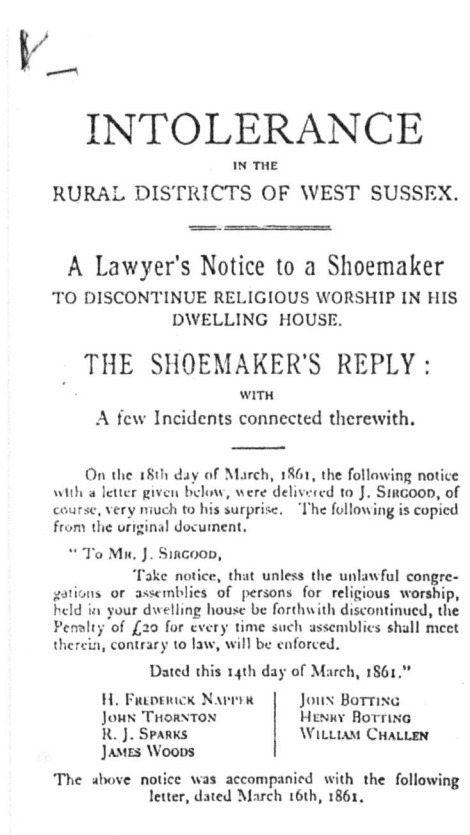

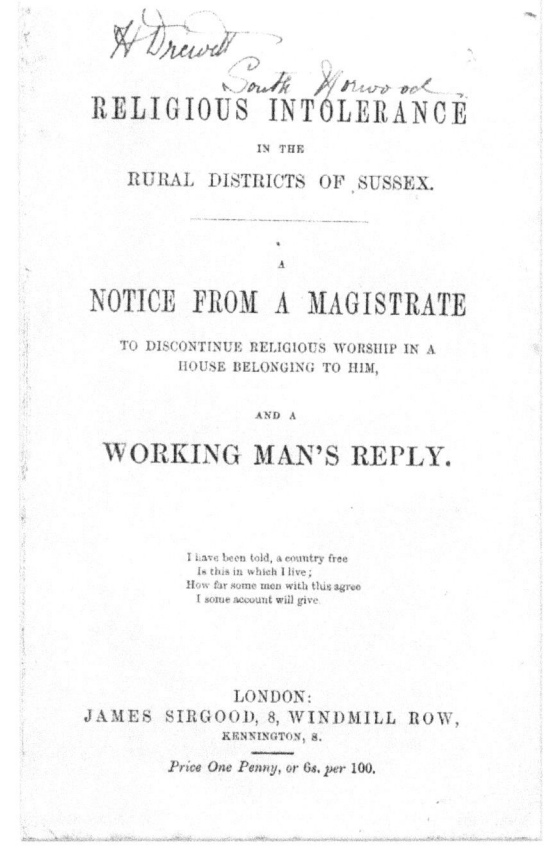

CHAPTER 2

Becoming a Dependant

By Sirgood's death in 1885, it is estimated there were about 2000 followers, but this was no more than a guess by Earl Winterton, who wrote about them much later in 1904. He also said, with slightly more likelihood of accuracy, that there were only 900 at the time of writing. Henry Aylward, an elder at Loxwood, claimed 600 in 1916. Donald MacAndrew of Pallinghurst (in Rudgwick) claimed there were only 200 left more recently in 1942, possibly restricting himself to Loxwood. Nevertheless, their impact through their Combination Stores over nearly a century of trading was profound. The late 19th century was a time of large families and rural poverty, and a generation that had missed out on compulsory education and felt neglected by the established church was ripe for any way out of its desperate struggle. Sirgood's simple message was seductive and liberating and offered an escape from a life of degradation. The message was seldom heard by the better off or the yeoman farmer but was received well by many labourers and by a few skilled artisans.

Family of James Denyer, Plaistow, Sussex

The example of one family is illuminating. In *"A Short Account of The Life and Experiences of James Denyer"* by his daughter Elizabeth Denyer, a handwritten manuscript, she describes Sirgood as arriving in Sussex about 1854 [from Shamley Green?], to preach the gospel of truth as it is in Jesus and having to preach in a very direct and simple way as most of his followers were very poor and illiterate. James was born in Plaistow in 1843 and died there in 1931. His daughter lived from 1882 to 1975 and died in Northchapel aged 93. Theirs was one of many families who lived long lives and spanned the whole history of the brethren in two generations. She says that Sirgood "had much pains in trying" to bring them to a more cultivated state and with gentleness and carefulness by degrees he succeeded. Although he agreed that certain things were lawful and allowable, as said by St Paul, he nevertheless taught that marriage, partaking of intoxicating drink, fashionable attire and other so called innocent pleasures should be dispensed with [note, not forbidden] - marriage for example interfering with the individual's relationship with God. The meetings allowed for those who felt inclined, even if illiterate, to give a testimony to the honour and glory of God if they were moved by the spirit and often, they spoke with power so that many were converted.

James Denyer was one of these early illiterate converts. The memoir does not say when he first heard Sirgood, but he would have been a teenager when Sirgood was preaching locally. It was not long before he was travelling to other villages himself, leading small meetings after labouring on the farm. They lived, as did many an agricultural labourer on large estates, in the farmhouse of one of the constituent farms. Their home was Quennell House, just outside Plaistow on the road to Loxwood, and he held meetings in this house. He remembered the opposition from local men who would waylay the Dependants walking home, and how they would bang saucepans and other utensils, but James remembered too how they always overcame these people with speaking and a hand on the shoulder. At other times they had to stop locals from breaking up their house meetings (incidentally, the last recorded entry of provocateurs I can find was at Northchapel's chapel in 1895). James's wife Martha, from Warnham, was also a convert, and so Elizabeth, Martha, Annie, Alfred and George were brought up in the Dependant ways, this meant straight to school and straight home, playing only in their Plaistow garden among each other. They were not able to go on the annual school treat but taken as a family to the seaside on one day each year,

2. Becoming a Dependant

where each was given only a penny to spend – in line with the strict economy taught by Sirgood. No one (it was about 1890) was ever allowed any fashionable hat.

Much later, in the late 1940s, the author's family was able, through my great uncle's generosity, to have the key to a beach hut the Dependants owned at Felpham beach, near Bognor Regis. Photographs show the young pre-school Nash playing on the beach. Among the photographs acquired from Dependant sources, are two of the Dependant brethren and sisters relaxing near the same hut before the war, and one, taken years later, by a caravan, possibly at Bracklesham Bay, where there were many caravans in the post-war years. At this time, the Dependants had several cars for their use in the garage next to The Combination Stores. Felpham was the location of a chapel but the community had declined, and it had been closed before the war. This may explain why the Brethren went there, but it also throws light on their very rare occasional leisure time.

Later, Elizabeth admits she was tempted by a life of pleasure, but chose to follow her parents when God, she writes, touched her heart and she yielded to the call before her sixteenth birthday. After three years in service in Horsham, when she tried to attend chapel in Warnham whenever she could, she was asked to go to Northchapel to join the brethren there and stayed the rest of her life - see Chapter 18. This denial of "a life of pleasure" was not so bad, given the security of work, food and companionship in the close-knit community. Tales of self-denial of any pictures, flowers, and so on in their homes are wide of the mark, though cultural, sporting and reading pleasures were rarely indulged in. An elder is quoted in the Daily Mail in 1905 as declaring the brethren to be the holiest people in the world. By their practice of business in the stores, they also eventually gained respect and a reputation for sincerity, cleanliness, work ethic and honest trading.

Plaistow Place

Elizabeth Denyer's older sister, Annie, went to Plaistow Place (Plate 2.1) in the 1880s, a farm rented from the Lee-Steere Estate (Jeyes at Ockley, Surrey), a house of great historical interest, where a Dependant community was growing under the farmer, Richard Nightingale Jr of Warnham (Plate 2.1), and Harriett Enticknap, the 'Mother Sister'. This community, which was unusual in its inclusion of farmers and the sons of farmers, rather than labourers, eventually transferred to Loxwood after the deaths of Richard and Harriett. Is it reading too much into this information to think of it as the crucible out of which came communal living in the various successor communities and stores? Census returns laid out in Table 2.1 also show how the community also welcomed curates in charge of Plaistow's chapel-of-ease as lodgers, maintaining a good relationship with the established church.

Nightingale Family

The origins of this small community go back to Warnham, where two census households (Table 2.1 below) for Betchetts Farm and Stone Farm in 1861 and 1871 respectively include not only Nightingales but also Sayers and Killner family members, all related to each other (and co-incidentally also to the author!). Richard Nightingale Sr of Warnham was an early convert.

PLATE 2.1   **Plaistow Place**

Fig 1 – top, Plaistow Place today.

Fig 2 – Plaistow Place in 1954, when the Horsham stone roof was still there.

Fig 3 – (top right) Richard Nightingale, 1854-

1916, at Plaistow Place.

Fig 4 (right) Elizabeth Holden, 1869-1953.

Fig 5 (right) - Walter John Nash, 1871-1960 (outside Loxwood Stores).

Fig 6 (left) - John Holden, 1855-1933.

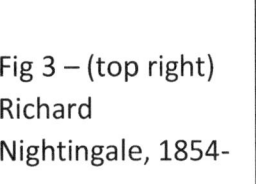

Richard Nightingale Sr married the widowed Emily Sayers (née Killner), the author's great great grandmother. Richard Jr was their only son. Betchetts Farm, where Emily already lived, was near the hamlet of Rowhook, and quite off the beaten track – indeed it is now demolished. Soon, Richard Nightingale Sr moved his family to Stone Farm where, Ron Muggeridge and Henry Piper (both Warnham writers) tell us Dependant meetings took place. Richard Sr, his wife, and Richard Jr were joined by Dependants Henry Killner (related to Emily) and John Cock. Piper confirms that Richard Sr (not necessarily Emily) was a Dependant. Richard Sr held meetings at his house, and perhaps attended the new chapel in his final years, though both he and Emily were buried at St Margaret's churchyard at Warnham parish church. He died in 1876, aged 54, Emily a year later, aged 62. The author's father told Peter Jerrome that Nightingale Jr had at first moved to Plaistow to work on the farm there, and was then persuaded, despite his lack of capital, to take it on in the hard agricultural depression of the 1870s. Financial backing came from the Lee-Steeres who recognised his abilities, and labour came from his loyal band of Dependants. The community lasted until his death in 1916.

Table 2.1.   Censuses at Betchetts Farm, Stone Farm and Plaistow Place Farm

Betchetts Farm, Warnham, 1861
1st Part

Richard Nightingale (Sr)	39	head, farmer of 100 acres	Warnham Sx
Emily Nightingale	46	wife	Southwater Sx
Daniel Sayers	20	stepson, ag lab	Southwater Sx
Walter Sayers	16	stepson	Nuthurst Sx
Martha Nightingale	13	niece serv't (dau of Frank)	Warnham Sx
Richard Nightingale (Jr)	6	son, scholar	Warnham Sx
Benjamin Nightingale	30	brother ag lab	Warnham Sx

2nd part

Francis Nightingale	47	head, ag lab (bro of Rd Sr)	Warnham Sx
Martha Nightingale	38	wife	Warnham Sx
Mary Nightingale	11	daughter	Warnham Sx

Stone Farm, Warnham, 1871

Richard Nightingale	49	head, farmer of 360 acres	Warnham Sx
Emily Nightingale	56	wife	Horsham Sx
Richard Nightingale (Jr)	16	son, ag lab	Warnham Sx
Harriett Fuller	14	general servant	Warnham Sx
Henry Killner	30	carter	Southwater Sx
John Cock	18	ag lab	Warnham Sx

Plaistow Place Farm, Plaistow 1881

Richard Nightingale (Jr)	26	head, farmer of 600 acres	Warnham Sx
Walter Sayers	36	farmer	Nuthurst Sx
George Franks	39	farmer	Rudgwick Sx
Louise Franks	39	farmer's wife	Nuthurst Sx
Louisa Franks	3	daughter	Wisborough Green Sx
Harriett Enticknap	28	general servant	Chiddingfold Sy
Ann Baker	14	nursemaid	Kirdford Sx
John Holden	26	milkman	Slinfold Sx
Frederick Reeves	19	carter	Wisborough Green Sx
David Thayers	13	boy	Wisborough Green Sx

Plaistow Place Farmhouse, 1891

Richard Nightingale	36	head, farmer (employer)	Warnham Sx
Harriett Enticknap	37	housekeeper	Haslemere Sy
John Holden	35	cowman	Slinfold Sx
Mary Heather	29	general servant	Bramley Sy
Elizabeth Holden	22	general servant	Warnham Sx
Walter Nash	20	shepherd	Rudgwick Sx
Henry Killner	18	carter	Rudgwick sx
Clonard Hildebrand	28	lodger, curate of Kirdford	Leicestershire

Oakhurst Cottage, Plaistow, 1891

George Luff	40	head, ag lab	Wisborough Green Sx
Mary Ann Luff	44	wife	Wisborough Green Sx
Ellen Luff	12	scholar	Wisborough Green Sx
Lucy Luff	10	scholar	Wisborough Green Sx
George Luff	8	scholar	Wisborough Green Sx
Caroline Luff	6	scholar	Wisborough Green Sx
Ethel Luff	4		Wisborough Green Sx
Fanny Luff	80	mother	Wisborough Green Sx

Plaistow Place Farmhouse, 1901

Richard Nightingale	46	head, farmer (employer)	Warnham Sx
Harriett Enticknap	48	housekeeper	Haslemere Sy
John Holden	45	cowman	Slinfold Sx
Mary Heather	39	housework	Bramley Sy
Lucy Enticknap	35	housework	Lurgashall Sx
Henry Killner	29	carter on farm	Rudgwick Sx
Annie Denyer	29	housework	Kirdford (Plaistow) Sx
Harry Garman	25	shepherd on farm	Warnham Sx
Samuel Rugman	20	stockman cattle	Kirdford Sx
Dewi Douglas Kirby	28	lodger, clergyman (CofE)	Suffolk

Oakhurst Cottage, Plaistow, 1901

George Luff	50	head, carter on farm	Wisborough Green Sx
Mary Ann Luff	54	wife	Wisborough Green Sx
John Hansell	63	cousin, Naval Pensioner	Hampshire
Arthur Reeves	11	schoolboy	Warnham Sx

Plaistow Place, Plaistow, 1911

Richard Nightingale	58	head, farmer (employer)	Warnham Sx
Henry Killner	36	carter on farm	Rudgwick Sx
Harry Garman	35	stockman on farm	Warnham Sx
Lucy Enticknap	45	housekeeper	Lurgashall Sx
Annie Denyer	38	servant	Kirdford (Plaistow) Sx
Sybilla Smithers	22	servant	Kirdford (Plaistow) Sx
Lucy Pannell	19	servant	Petworth Sx

Oakhurst Cottage, Plaistow, 1911

George Luff	60	carter on farm	Wisborough Green Sx
Mary Ann Luff	64		Wisborough Green Sx
John Reeves	21	farm labourer	Warnham Sx

Photos: Plate 2.1, John Holden. Plate 2.1 Elizabeth Holden. Plate 2.1 Richard Nightingale Jr. Plate 2.1 Walter Nash. Harry Garman. Sybilla Smithers. Lucy Luff.

2. Becoming a Dependant

Denyer Family

Returning to the young Elizabeth Denyer, her mother was Martha Nightingale (married to James Denyer of Plaistow in Brighton, 1870). Martha was a daughter of Richard Nightingale Sr's eldest brother Francis, and his wife, also Martha (the second family at Betchetts in 1861). Francis (Frank) was born in 1814. In 1869 he was the first from Warnham to be buried in the new graveyard in Loxwood, the funeral led by Loxwood elder Tom Overington.

Elizabeth's father, James, was likewise born into a Dependant family. George Denyer, born in 1804, must have been one of the older converts. When he died in 1870, he too was buried at Loxwood with Tom Overington leading the service. As explained in a later chapter, the first ever burial was in 1866. Did the young James and Martha wait until after Frank and George's deaths to feel free to marry? Elizabeth makes clear her father James knew "Brother John" Sirgood personally. Both sets of grandparents are highly likely to have heard him preach too. Sirgood will have attended and spoken at house meetings at Quennells in Plaistow and at Stone in Warnham.

Elizabeth came therefore from two Dependant families, the Nightingales and the Denyers, and settled in Plaistow. A characteristic of any faith is marriage within its community – even in one like the Dependants where marriage is, to a large degree, discouraged. A marriage within the community maintains that community; a marriage outside on the other hand sows the seeds of its destruction. That is one reason why there were a minority of Dependants who married throughout their history. In the long run, it did not happen often enough to maintain the sect, that is, through the children of married Dependants, and, as will become clear, Sirgood's concept of 'combination' allowed and encouraged single women to have a role as workers.

The Plaistow Place community was established sometime in the 1870s, perhaps soon after Richard Sr's death in 1876. Richard Nightingale Jr pioneered a communal and religious life and was clearly determined to build on it. By 1891, the Luff family had joined him living in Oakhurst Cottage next door to the isolated farm. They remained there until after 1911 and raised their children in the community and at Plaistow School, where they would have been in classes with the Denyer children. Lucy, Ellen and George would go on to be significant members of the Warnham community. The Reeves boys who lodged with them also came from a Dependant family in Warnham.

Sayers Family

Richard Nightingale Jr's mother, Emily, remained at Stones but died in 1877. She was the widow of George Sayers, and three of her five children by him, Daniel, Walter, and Louisa were Dependants. Walter Sayers joined the Plaistow Place community, as did Louisa, who had married Rudgwick born George Franks, whose siblings, and parents John and Ann Franks were also early Dependants at Exfold Farm in Tismans Common, Rudgwick. Significantly John Franks had employed Loxwood born John Overington, and possibly his brother Tom around the time they were among the very first to be converted by John Sirgood.

George and Louisa Franks brought up their daughter, also Louisa (known as Louie), at Plaistow for a while, but George died in 1883 (see below). His wife, Louisa, subsequently

PLATE 2.2   **Killner Family**

Fig 1 – believed to be Sally Killner 1843-1925, daughter of Michael (born 1827) unverified image and believed to be the oldest to show Dependant dress.

Fig 2 - Kate Killner, née Spooner, 1874-1948 (centre), wife of Michael (born 1870), with Kate Rugman, 1878-1977, and Elizabeth Holden, 1869-1973.

Fig 3 - Alfold House Farm, home of the Killners, 1920s – 1940s.

Fig 4 – funeral of Freda Killner, 1941-1957, died aged 15. Great granddaughter of Michael Killner (1817), grand-daughter of Michael (1870), daughter of Gilbert and Ethel from Loxwood, later Alfold. Alf Goodwin, tall man centre, worked for Michael Killner (standing in doorway) in the war). Freda's grandmother Ethel, far left. Her unmarried Killner aunts line the right side.

joined her brother, Walter Sayers, at Pawlies Farm, Loxwood (1891 census); ironically much later to become one of the farms owned by the Dependants under Walter Nash's leadership (Plate 2, Fig 6). Walter Sayers began his Dependant life in the Plaistow community. He was Richard Nightingale Jr's stepbrother. Walter Sayers was married late in life to another Dependant, Emily Luff. By 1901, they were farming at Willetts, a smallholding in Loxwood. Meanwhile young Louie married Ernest Rugman and had several children in Cranleigh. Walter joined them after being widowed. Several Rugmans were Dependants, but neither Ernest nor Louie nor any of their three children were recorded in the Loxwood registers. It would be interesting to find out if it was common for the third or fourth generation to leave the Brethren, but it is also likely that those who moved away to another parish, even one as close as Cranleigh, became spiritually as well as physically distanced.

Killner Family

Henry Killner who joined Richard Nightingale Jr at Plaistow Place in the 1880s was a nephew of the Henry who had been with him at Stone. The Killners, like the Sayers, had originally come from Southwater. Emily Sayers/Nightingale was born a Killner, at College Farm. She married George Sayers in 1840. George was brought up at Easteds Farm, before moving to Raylands on the border of Nuthurst. The older Henry was Emily's nephew, the younger one was her great nephew. Emily's brother Michael Killner was a Dependant by the time he lived in Warnham in the 1880s and was buried at Loxwood in 1895. Five of his seven children were known Dependants, as were nine grandchildren and ten great grandchildren. The Killners produced many Dependant children over four generations, well confounding the myth of universal celibacy.

Michael's son, also Michael, moved around from farm to farm in Rudgwick, Warnham and Kirdford. He was buried at Loxwood in 1916. A daughter, Sally, who kept house for her uncle Henry until his death at Headfoldswood Farm, Loxwood, where he lived after he left Plaistow Place (1911 census), may be the subject of a photograph said to be the earliest photo of a Dependant woman in her Victorian clothing, commonly worn to chapel (Plate 2.2). Both were buried at Loxwood.

A third generation Michael married Loxwood Dependant Kate Spooner (Plate 2.2), and farmed at Denhams Farm, Billingshurst, where their seven children were born between 1899 and 1912. In the late 1920s they settled at Alfold House Farm, Alfold (Plate 2.2), where Michael and Kate lived until their deaths in the 1940s. They became prominent members of the Loxwood community, all the children remaining Dependants throughout their lives, in birth order: Gertrude, Gladys, Hilda (all unmarried), Gilbert (who married Ethel Pullen, had five children, was a market gardener in Rosemary Lane, Alfold, and a trombonist in local bands), Cyril (unmarried), Leslie (who married Elsie Williams and lived at Elsmere in Spy Lane, Loxwood. Elsie was one of the last to give testimony regularly before the chapel closed in 1984. Lastly, Winifred married Ron Parsons, and lived in Guildford Road, Loxwood. All three who married wed Dependants. Gertrude, Gladys, Hilda and Cyril lived together at Merry Hills (Pinetree Lodge, over the garages in the old stable block), Loxwood. Altogether, 25 Killners are buried at Loxwood, all descended from Michael who was born in Southwater in 1817.

And it was to the Killners that Alfred Goodwin, the last elder at Loxwood, came, from South Norwood, to work at Alfold House Farm in 1941. He was a young Conscientious Objector who had never lived in the countryside. The farm business was continued by Cyril after Michael's death the following year. Alf, as one might imagine, left as soon as he was free of his wartime obligations, to work at The Combination Stores in Loxwood. Cyril was one of the last Dependant trustees of the Loxwood chapel (Plate 2.2). Leslie was one of the few Dependants to survive into the 1990s. He died in 1998, aged 92, still at Elsmere. It is therefore possible to trace a line of descent and numerous complex family relationships across the entire period of the Dependants' existence. The same would be true of other families less well known to the author.

Walter Nash

Elizabeth Denyer's sister Annie had met and got to know, rather too well, another of the Brethren at Plaistow Place. Walter Nash, the author's great uncle, had joined the community some years earlier. In 1901, Annie was quietly shipped off to Hove for the birth of a son, who was subsequently wet nursed by a Mrs Boardman, not known as a Dependant herself. In the census of 1911, Mrs Boardman referred to this son Alfred, who was still living with her, as her adopted son.

Were such unacceptable liaisons common? I do not know, and perhaps I only know of this because the son, named Alfred Nash Denyer, was accepted into our family as a teenager. He lived with one of Walter's sisters in Crawley, later working in the family shop, inheriting half the business. In adult life, he adopted the name Alfred Denyer Nash. The Nash family have always been very open about his birth, but Elizabeth Denyer, in her manuscript, airbrushes Walter and the baby out of the story altogether, even though there are substantial sections describing her sister's life history. Annie came to Loxwood, and spent most of her life in Hall House, opposite the stores, where Walter lived, and where he led the Dependants as elder for thirty years.

I subsequently discovered Walter had briefly attended Warnham School in 1877 when his father managed Stone Farm probably when Richard Nightingale left to go to Plaistow. My father, Jim Nash, was interviewed by Peter Jerrome for the Petworth Society about his uncle Walter, who he says, after leaving school in Ellens Green, Surrey (the family farmed in nearby Rowhook across the border in Sussex), was sent down to Brighton to get a job on the railway, but on arrival was told he was too small! On his return he found a letter addressed to him by Richard Nightingale, his uncle, inviting him to Plaistow for a holiday. Well, it was a long holiday, as he never returned, becoming a Dependant.

When Walter eventually left Plaistow to join the Loxwood Dependants, it was to deliver bread – described then as a 'carman' – by horse and trap to the area he knew, over Plaistow and Box Green way. In another interview, Alfred Goodwin remembered Walter had gone to Lordshill (Shamley Green) where he heard John Rugman's testimomy. In later years, Walter frequently referred to the secret that ran through the lives of those who lived in Biblical times, as referred to by Rugman. On a walk from Plaistow to Loxwood Chapel, it dawned on Walter that the secret was obedience to the will of God. Nevertheless, in researching the Dependants, I am left wondering whether Walter's family were as far removed from the

Dependant ways as I was brought up to assume. After all, Walter came from an extended family containing many Dependants.

The Dependants were not against looking after relatives of their brethren. I have come across this with the Killners where one girl brought her mother along to stay at Lordshill. The most notable for me is how Walter Nash looked after two of his sisters. One, Emmie Nash had spent her life as a lady's maid, travelling the world, including several trips to Hawaii. The other Lil Herrington had emigrated to Australia with her husband and son. After her husband's death she left Australia. Both women came to live in a flat in Loxwood Place farmhouse, provided for them by the Dependants. Neither were Dependants but accepted their largesse and died there in the late 1950s. It must have been a comfort to Walter for them all to live so close in their final years.

Rugman Family

John Rugman, whose testimony influenced the young Walter Nash, died in 1904, another of that generation of first adherents. He was born in Wisborough Green and was one of several in the family who became Dependants. His younger brother Tom was among the Loxwood brethren, living in Alfold on a small farm. He ended his life at The Myrtles in Loxwood. Tom's daughter Kate Rugman (Plate 4.3) lived and worked at The Combination Stores for much of her life, and her brother George of Northchapel Dependants had a daughter Edith Rugman who was one of the first residents in The Retreat in Spy Lane in Loxwood in the 1970s. The Retreat was built by the Dependants for their final years. Edith died in 1965, Kate in 1977. Several photographs of the family survive.

Conscientious Objection in the Great War

The beliefs of the early converts, and those of their children's generation, created a crisis of conscience, belief versus service, in the First World War. The passing of a Conscription Act in 1916 meant that groups such as the Dependants, the Peculiar People, Quakers, and others had to register as conscientious objectors, with all the opprobrium from the wider society that went with it. Accordingly, a letter of petition from a Dependant meeting was sent to Herbert Asquith, the Prime Minister, lobbying for conscientious objection to be included in the Bill before Parliament. It was sent from the Loxwood community, signed by Henry Aylward, Chairman, Eli Herrington, Thomas Rugman, and Richard Nightingale. It was penned by Walter Parr, Hon Secretary (Plate 2.3).

George Denyer, Elizabeth's brother, was one of those exempted as a result. He appeared at a Local Military Tribunal and was permitted to do useful work in lieu of military service, so worked for an agricultural engineer. Elizabeth Denyer wrote that none of the younger Dependant Brethren were made to fight. However, in Northchapel, Frank Talbot did join up, and left the sect, whilst Fred Greenfield did "time" in prison (Plate 2.3).

Greenfield's personal account is in the West Sussex Record Office. He was a member of the Hove community. It recounts how he had to go through a hierarchy of appeals. The first was a Local Appeals Tribunal in Hove. He was supported by Walter Hart, the local elder, and William Booker and George Denyer, both from Warnham. His appeal was for exemption as a market gardener. When that failed, he had to appear before a Military Appeal Tribunal, then an East Sussex Appeal Tribunal in Brighton. On the third occasion he was supported by Walter Hart, William Booker, George Denyer, Frank Weller, William Russell (Hove), Edwin Elliott, Chris Hale and William Powell. Still facing a blank wall in seeking a Non-Combatant Certificate, his leave to appeal to the Central Tribunal was refused. He also sought the help of Miss Fry, a noted Guildford Quaker, to no avail.

Next, he faced call-up, a Military Notice to report to a barracks in Brighton. When he did not attend, he received a police warning, before being arrested. In court, his sister and parents, together with brothers Hart, Booker, Russell (and his sister) and Joseph Lindfield of Warnham supported him. He was fined 40/- as an absentee under the Military Service Act. He had no option but to remain in custody and was sent to Chichester Barracks, where he refused to sign papers, and, to use his own word, was "humiliated" by the officers and NCOs. He asserts he gave no trouble while in custody. Eventually, he was allowed out, and met his supporters in Chichester, Michael Woolgar, and Fred and Fanny Hughes. On another occasion he met up with Harry Hart (Walter's brother) and John Slade. Fred was serious about his protest – he refused to wear uniform. He was then sent to Seaford (Plate 2.3), to a unit of a non-combatant corps, the 4th Eastern Camp NCC, for unarmed military support duties. Here the Conscientious Objector either accepted the rules or was sent to France where they could be shot. This CO decided to continue to refuse to wear his uniform, he was therefore sent to the guardroom, where he had to sleep on the hard floor for nearly 4 weeks in considerable discomfort. Then came the Court-Martial, with yet again the brethren in attendance – brothers Hart, Booker and Lindfield – but he was found guilty and received 112 days of hard labour. Eventually, he was transferred to Wormwood Scrubs, avoiding France, to serve out his sentence. At the end, he eventually got his Central Tribunal hearing, and was freed with conditions: to work in an Aberdeen quarry. He was finally discharged on 28 February 1918. Greenfield lived in Hove until 1959, aged 69. He had been one of nearly 6,000 who reached the stage of Court-Martial.

"The NCC may have been a shock to the COs who agreed to join it. But for the absolutists and alternativists who were forcibly enlisted into the NCC it was much worse. They immediately faced the question of whether to agree to wearing uniform. The men who decided to refuse were formally charged and court-martialled. Often, they were treated harshly, bullied, deprived of basic needs and rights, and imprisoned in inhumane conditions. So were the men who refused to perform duties like handling munitions or building rifle ranges. Some broke down, physically or mentally, as a result of their ill-treatment." (Peace Pledge Union website)

In February 1916, an article about Ralph Arnold appeared in the Surrey Advertiser (Plate 2.3) He had appeared at the Hambledon Rural Tribunal which met in Guildford under the chairmanship of James H Renton, a barrister living in Shalford. In this case, it was a member of the Shamley Green community at Lordshill named Ralph Edgar Arnold, a baker aged 28. He was from a Cambridgeshire family which moved to Worthing to run a nursery. How he got to Shamley Green is a mystery, but he was working in the Dependants' bakery. He died in Worthing in 1970. His service record has survived, and it is not a good ending. Having been exempted from combatant service, and narrowly missing a posting to 16th Royal Fusiliers on his call up 5 May, he was 'accepted', not enlisted, to be transferred to 4th

Eastern Coy, NCC, as a private on 13 June. However, like Fred Greenfield, he was arrested even before that, on 18 May, to await trial. On 30 May he was sentenced to 112 days for "disobeying a lawful command given by his superior officer as to show wilful defiances *(sic)* of authority whilst in the execution of his office". He was sent to Lewes Prison, 5 June until September. Sometime after his release, and unbroken, he was re-arrested 22 December, and held over Christmas. At his trial on 2 January, he was sentenced to two years hard labour, one year remitted for confirming authority. What happened to him in 1918 is unknown.

On 29 March 1916, the Surrey Advertiser had a short article headed *"The Gentleman at Guildford"* regarding an Appeals Tribunal. This referred to the person unnamed who had written the submission on behalf of three Cokelers of the *"Registered Dependants at Petworth"*. *"You supplied the conscience and the gentleman supplied the language. Is that right?"* to which the answer from one was *"Yes, I had a little assistance."* the unnamed men were exempted from combatant service only. A similar case had been heard in Horsham by the Horsham Rural Tribunal which covered the Warnham area on 4 March 1916. Here too a man was granted relief from combatant service only, that is he would be called upon to do his duty in other directions of service.

In May 1916, the case of Raymond Croucher, aged 30 from Lordshill, where he was described as foreman bread maker, was before the Hambledon Rural Tribunal. There is no record of service. Ray went on to be the last person to run the Lordshill Stores in 1935.

… and in the Second World War

The same applied in the Second War, and this time debate was recorded in the Minute Book of Aylward, Smith & Co. at a meeting chaired by Benjamin Piper, an elder at Warnham, above the names of William Booker (Warnham), Samuel Rugman (Northchapel), Fred Hughes (Chichester), Fred Greenfield (Hove), and written by Walter Nash (Loxwood), Secretary. A Committee was appointed to study the interests of "our young men". The decision to send the petition was proposed by Walter Nash and seconded by Harry Garman (Loxwood).

Fred Greenfield, who knew all about the consequences of being a CO in the 1st War, stated "it was in the tenets of our faith that no Dependant should take part in Military Service…in the unwritten letter of the heart, our conscience, which is a true Dependant's guide". Alfred Goodwin was one of the successful conscientious objectors in the South Norwood community.

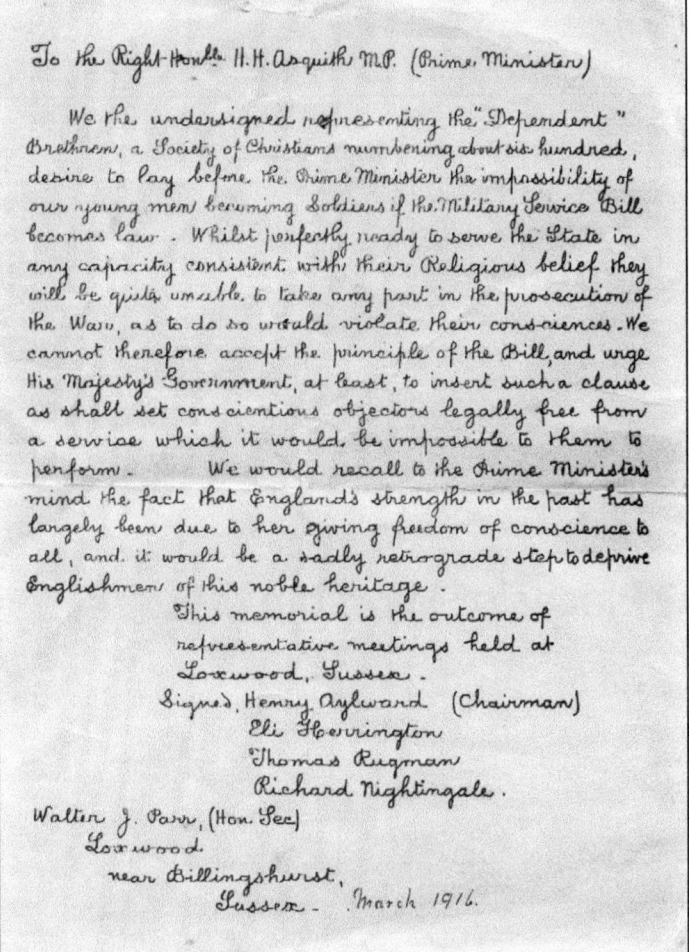

To the Right-Hon'ble H. H. Asquith M.P. (Prime Minister)

We the undersigned representing the "Dependent" Brethren, a Society of Christians numbering about six hundred, desire to lay before the Prime Minister the impossibility of our young men becoming Soldiers if the Military Service Bill becomes law. Whilst perfectly ready to serve the State in any capacity consistent with their Religious belief they will be quite unable to take any part in the prosecution of the War, as to do so would violate their consciences. We cannot therefore accept the principle of the Bill, and urge His Majesty's Government, at least, to insert such a clause as shall set conscientious objectors legally free from a service which it would be impossible to them to perform. We would recall to the Prime Minister's mind the fact that England's strength in the past has largely been due to her giving freedom of conscience to all, and it would be a sadly retrograde step to deprive Englishmen of this noble heritage.

This memorial is the outcome of representative meetings held at Loxwood, Sussex.

Signed, Henry Aylward (Chairman)
Eli Herrington
Thomas Rugman
Richard Nightingale.

Walter J. Parr, (Hon. Sec)
Loxwood.
near Billingshurst,
Sussex. March 1916.

HAMBLEDON TRIBUNAL.

SHAMLEY GREEN CONSCIENTIOUS OBJECTION.

STRONG ATTENDANCE OF COKELERS.

One of the religious community at Shamley Green, known as the Cokelers, or the Society of Dependents, was the only conscientious objector to claim exemption from military service at the meeting of the Hambledon Rural Tribunal, held at the Guildhall, Guildford, on Wednesday. He was Ralph Edgar Arnold, aged 23, a journeyman baker, of Shamley Green, and there were a number of Cokelers present during the hearing of the case.

The members of the tribunal present were Mr. J. H. Renton (chairman), Sir Josceline Wodehouse, Colonel Bullock (acting for the military representatives), Messrs. P. W. Burdock, W. T. Mitchell, A. Mitchell and C. Musgrave, with the Clerk (Mr. F. F. Smallpeice)

Arnold stated that he asked for total exemption on conscientious grounds on a divine standpoint. By accepting the teaching of Jesus Christ as the only true way of life, and believing human life to be sacred, he could not assume the possibility or liability of inflicting death.

The Chairman questioned applicant at considerable length, and the man said if his life were in danger, and he had the means of preserving it by killing another man, he would stand by his convictions, and allow the other man to kill him. He would consider his own life less sacred than that of the other man. If his wife and children or the honour of his family were in danger, he would have to live up to his convictions. He had only belonged to the Dependent Brethren for a year and three months, but held those convictions before that period.

Do you agree that it is very important that England should be victorious in this war?— That is outside my convictions. I cannot answer for any country. I am bound to stand by my convictions; you cannot make a soldier of me.

Further cross-examined, he said so far as he was concerned it was of no importance to him whether England or Germany won the war. He would rather have England invaded by Germans than that he should assist in killing Germans in order to prevent that invasion.

Applicant objected to going into the R.A.M.C. as his work there would be making this nation more efficient to win the war.

The tribunal decided to exempt applicant from combatant service only.

PLATE 2.3   Conscientious Objection

Fig 1 - Letter to Prime Minister, March 1916.

Fig 2 - Surrey Advertiser, February 1916, Ralph Arnold, Shamley Green
(Ack: findmypast.co.uk, © TNA).

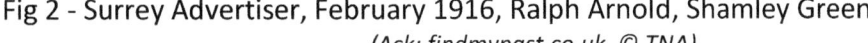

Fig 3 - Fred Greenfield, 1890-1959, Hove with his wife, Bessie.

Fig 4 - Seaford Camp, November 1916
(Ack: BBC WW1 At Home; Seaford Museum).

Chapter 3

Dependant Places of Worship

PLATE 3.1 - Loxwood, 1876 1:2500 OS Maps of Early Dependant Locations in the Text

Fig 1 - Spy Lane, Old Cottage is opposite the "Coglers" Chapel, built in the 1860s.

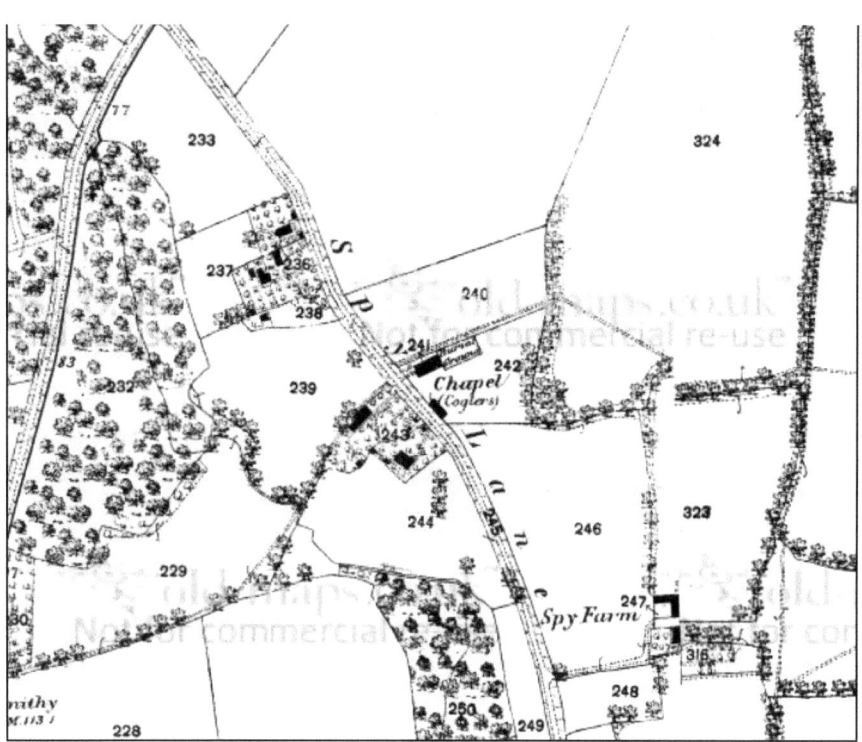

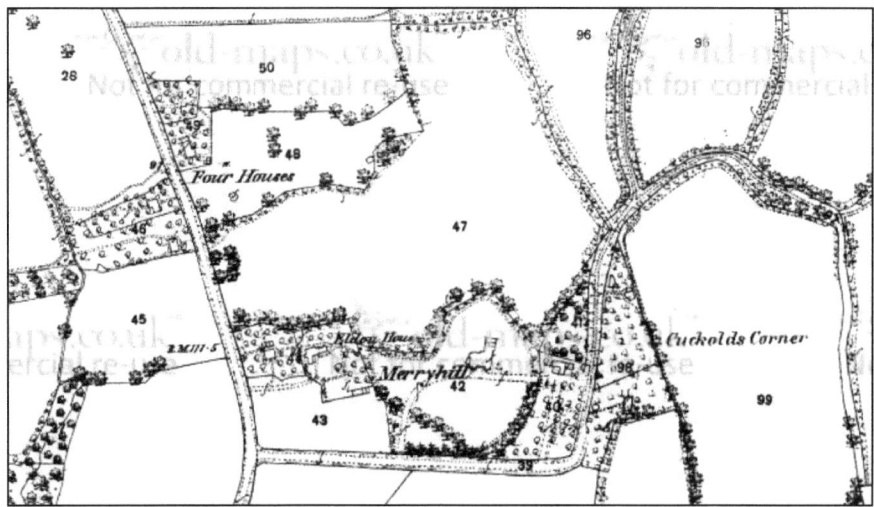

Fig 2 - A little further north is Four Houses and Cuckolds Corner, all cottages of early adherents of John Sirgood.

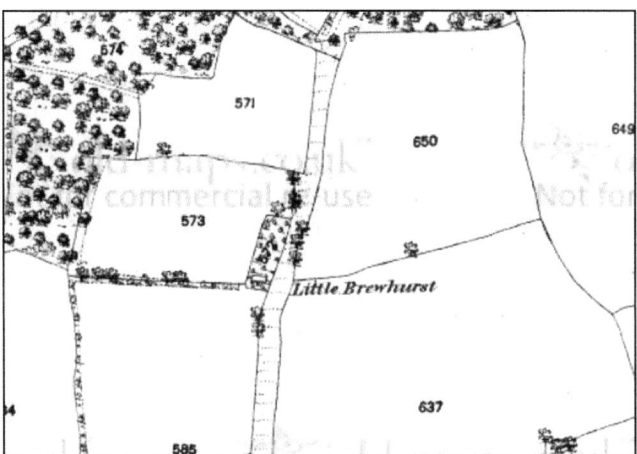

Fig 3 - Little Brewhurst, a very remote cottage near Roundstreet Common, long demolished, located south of Loxwood, was cited as a Dependant house.
Ack: all maps, © old-maps.co.uk.

Almost always referred to as chapels, there are also primary sources which refer to Dependant places of worship as churches. For clarity I shall call them chapels. In all cases, they replaced meetings held in followers' homes, which themselves gradually took on more importance than the open-air sermons and testimonies favoured by John Sirgood and his first cohort of elders. Preaching outdoors or in houses continued in outlying areas long after the chapels were built, for example in Newpound and Gunshot Commons near Wisborough Green, Balls Cross near Petworth and Roundhurst (west of Northchapel), Southwater Street near Horsham, and at Gate Street, Bramley. The house in Southwater was described in an 1873 newspaper as a "registered place of worship, where on this day 10-12 worshippers were gathered". Details are in Chapter 13. Dependants in outlying villages such as Lodsworth, Fernhurst, Graffham, and Funtington would walk or ride miles to chapel meetings but may also have met on open land or in houses to proselytise their faith, or to hear itinerant preachers, perhaps John Sirgood himself.

The First Meeting House in Loxwood

An anonymous undated typescript (the worst kind of source!) suggests some details of the meeting places in Loxwood. Is there any truth in what it states? It begins by saying the Sirgoods lodged initially with Tom & Ann Overington in Little Brewhurst, a remote cottage south of Loxwood, said correctly to have been taken down (it disappears from maps), and more apocryphally that it was shipped to America (Plate 3.1). Taking these points one at a time, Sirgood did lodge with Tom and Ann Overington, but in Spy Lane in Loxwood village (1861 census, Plate 3.1). No Overingtons lived at Little Brewhurst. In 1841 and 1851 this cottage, lying south of the river, on what is now the bridleway between a timber business near Malkinsons Farm and Drungewick Lane, was occupied by William and Mary Wells. It is true that their sons Joseph and William became Dependants. William married Hannah, also a Dependant, and their daughter Sarah (married to George Baverstock) became the last sister to be "put behind the desk" in chapel at Loxwood by Sirgood himself. Another son, Thomas, married Elizabeth who was also a Dependant. It is therefore very possible that John Sirgood did take lodgings here but with the Wells family, very early in his time in Sussex. Quite possibly he held open air meetings in nearby Roundstreet Common whilst there. By 1861, however, this family had moved into Loxwood village, and a family called Tickner had moved into Little Brewhurst. Although there were other Tickner Dependants, this family were not.

The writer of this typescript goes on to say that the *first* meeting was held at Four Houses (Plate 4.1), at the north end of Loxwood, "in the little cottage nearest the walnut tree, which [the cottage] has since been pulled down". The walnut was blown down in about 1945-6. Obadiah and Ruth Overington (the parents of the Dependant Overington brothers) lived at nearby Cuckolds Corner, not at Four Houses. One son, Obed, his wife Caroline (née Thayre), and their children did live at Four Houses from their marriage in 1858 right through to Obed's death in 1906. However, 1858 may be too late for a first meeting place.

Nevertheless, a Stephen and Charlotte Overington did live at Four Houses, earlier than Obed, certainly from before 1851 to their deaths in 1868. If they were related to the 'Cuckolds Corner family' as they may have been, it was not a close relationship, but crucially they were both Dependants. Moreover, in 1861 another Dependant family, that of Samuel and Elizabeth Etherington also lived at Four Houses. Even more interesting is a fourth family, the elderly James and Elizabeth Sandford. James was a Dependant too and was the very first person ever to be buried in the Loxwood graveyard, the service taken by Rev Henry Rogers from Petworth in 1866. There were four cottages at 'Four Houses' until the nineteenth century, two each side of the turnpike road. Today there is only one each side, Four Houses itself and Chestnut Mead. With three Dependant families, Four Houses was indeed significant in Dependant history, and, yes, it may have been the location of the earliest indoor meeting, in the home of Stephen and Charlotte, but there is no way of knowing which cottage was theirs, or if it is still there! We may also infer John Sirgood's presence and perhaps his lodging there on occasion.

The Beginnings of a Spy Lane Presence

The above useful little document goes on to say that meetings were also held at the little cottage in Spy Lane "where Mr & Mrs Webb are now living". This is probably The Old Cottage, now behind New Cottages, which the Dependants built much later, alongside the path (Lovers Lane to some). The Dependants later walked this path from the Combination Stores to their chapel. The Old Cottage used to be a pair of dwellings. In 1852, Tom Overington had married Ann Reeves and sometime before 1861 they moved into one of these, right next door to John and Harriet Sirgood. Other Spy Lane Dependants in the 1861 census, in a significant cluster at about the time when the chapel is thought to have been built (as the next section explains), were George and Harriett Denyer, originally from Plaistow, Charles and Mary Kitchener and Martha Marriner.

The Chapel Indentures 1865 and 1880/83

An indenture for Loxwood of 1865 records the transfer of the land on which the chapel stands from Mary Bonsey of Worthing to the trustees, on whose behalf Rev Henry Rogers of Petworth Congregational church acted. The very first trustees were James Reeves, Felix Foster, Charles Denyer, Alfred Jenner, Peter Pacy and Obed Overington, several of whom were still trustees fifteen years later. Mary Bonsey, born in 1800 in Loxwood, became a lodging house keeper in London. She did well, described as a fundholder in 1861, when she had moved to Montague Street, Worthing, where she died in 1866, very soon after this indenture was signed. Intriguingly, a newspaper article dated 5 January 1864, was found in the National Newspaper Archive (available on the Findmypast website). The Petworth, Midhurst and Steyning Express reported that Frederick Standen of Flitchfold Farm, Loxwood was charged and found guilty of riotous, violent and indecent behaviour at Loxwood Chapel on 27 December 1863. Testifying against him were James Hampshire, James Reeves (trustee) and Charles Kitchener. All three men are known from the registers. Mention was made of Sirgood's presence. PC William Tribe declared that he had had numerous complaints of disturbances "during the last two years". This strongly suggests that the chapel dates from 1861, and that the 1865 indenture was not dated at the time of building and opening of the first Dependant chapel. Other sources corroborate this (see below)

Fortunately, an important Dependant document survives as a notebook copy of an Indenture (*WSRO Acc 11283 Box 3/3)*, dated 24 May 1880 (signed 2 March 1883) establishing the legal title to all the chapels existing at the time. All these chapels were built some years earlier. For example, Alf Goodwin says Loxwood was the first to be completed in 1865, and South Norwood the last (of the seven in the notebook). As an elder and chapel trustee, he must have been familiar with this document, perhaps in its original parchment, since sadly presumed destroyed. He was not to know the date was 1861.

The Indenture lists the Chapel Trustees, in 1883, for Lordshill, Northchapel, Warnham, Loxwood, Chichester, Peckham (Radnor Street) and South Norwood (Cobden Road). Peckham is a surprise inclusion, as no reference to it can be found in any other Dependant source, article or interview. However, exist it did, and the Peckham Society have corresponded with me on the subject, and photographs have been exchanged. The building still exists, which is more than can be said for Norwood, Chichester and Lordshill chapels. Other chapels will be examined later in this chapter.

Loxwood Chapel

The 1883 Trustees of Loxwood were, occupation/addresses as in document, with ages added (all married except the last two):

Charles Denyer of Loxwood, labourer, Spy Lane, 47

Peter Pacy of Loxwood, labourer, Foxbridge, 54

Obed Overington of Loxwood, labourer, Gunshot, 48

David Thayre of Loxwood, brickmaker, Brickyard (Roundstreet), 48

James Randall of Loxwood, carpenter, Crabtree (Drungewick), 61

Owen Puttick of Loxwood, labourer, Black Hall, Loxwood Street (lodging with Foster family, see below), 39

Richard Nightingale of Loxwood *(sic)*, farmer, Plaistow Place, 28.

In addition, Loxwood witnesses subscribing to the indenture (other than referred to above) were:

Felix Foster of Loxwood, carpenter, Black Hall, Loxwood Street, 23

James Pannell of Alfold, carpenter, Plaistow, (later of Weavers, next to Combination Stores, Loxwood), 61.

For Loxwood, the indenture states: "Charles Denyer, Peter Pacy, Obed Overington, David Thayre, Owen Puttick and Richard Nightingale convey to Loxwood a field or close of land, one acre, west of Spye Lane." This was the largest plot of any chapel, large enough for a graveyard. The adjoining landowner to the plot on which the Loxwood chapel was built was Henry Hemming, an auctioneer living at Alfold Bars, probable owner of Spy Farm, occupied by James Puttock. General Onslow was the lord of the manors of Loxwood and Drungewick, so owner and absentee landlord of Loxwood Common, which included the waste on the east side of Spy Lane at the time. Presumably, the land was acquired from one of these gentlemen *(Plate 3.2)*.

Given what seems a discrepancy in exactly who conveyed what to whom, one possibility might be that Mary Bonsey had the status to obtain the land on behalf of the named Dependants, who then pooled their meagre resources and the donations of others to reimburse her generosity.

PLATE 3.2   Loxwood Chapel

Fig 1 – Left, an early 20th century photo of Spy Lane, viewed from the east, the chapel right

Fig 2 – Right, much the same streetscape viewed from the west

Both photos show the cottages opposite, built later and owned by the Dependants, apparently for the elderly, despite the stairs.

Fig 3 – Left, originally a colour washed photo, taken from the cottages opposite

Fig 4 – Right, first of three photos by Loxwood professional photographer Harry Sopp, whose former studio, now a showroom, is still on the verge in Loxwood High Street.
Figs 5 and 6 - the interior, and the graveyard, respectively. The latter is now levelled. All three probably taken pre-war.

There are several names listed above whose occupations will have made them suitable as builders of Loxwood Chapel. There is no record of who might have contributed labour, but from what is known of Warnham and Northchapel, it seems likely the chapel was a wholly Dependant project. A good candidate to manage the project was Henry Spooner, a Dependant from Northchapel, a builder by trade (and brother of William Spooner who built the chapel at Northchapel), who moved to Alfold Bars sometime after the April 1861 census and remained there until his death in 1928. He and his carpenter son Albert were in business locally for many years and may have built the Combination Stores in Loxwood as well as the chapel. The Spooners' involvement, or the date of his move, cannot be verified.

The 1883 Indenture concludes by stating that all the chapels are *"to be fit and needed for the purpose or may by erection thereon or otherwise become or for the time being to be fit for the purpose to be used occupied and enjoyed as a place for the Public Worship of God according to the usages of the Protestant Dissenters of Congregational Denomination now registered as and commonly called Dependants…, assembling for worship therein and for the instruction of children and adults and for Church meetings and for the promotion of such other religious and philanthropic purposes…."*

There is no history of the chapels having any special services for children. They were expected to attend worship with their parents. Note the absence of any reference to baptism, marriage or funerals. Loxwood Chapel of course conducted numerous funerals and burials over time. Other chapels might have a meeting to celebrate someone's life, particularly if the body was to be buried in the parish churchyard.

At a Special Church Meeting convened of Members of the Congregations of the seven* churches or chapels, all trustees were appointed. Others in attendance were exhorted "to execute these presents [statements]". We do not know where or when this took place.

The Indenture was signed sealed and delivered by **Charles Heather.** He is referred to elsewhere in the document as of Grafham Surrey, a sawyer.
In the presence of   **Thomas H Stubbs**, Gent, of Phoenix Wharf Lambeth SE
                         Thomas Bonson of Ventnor IoW, brickmaker

*Felpham, although included in the document as an eighth chapel, had no trustees of its own.

Other Chapels Listed in the 1883 Indenture

At **Lordshill**, William Hampshire conveyed a cottage and land of ¾ acre on Stanards Lane; John Sirgood was one of the Trustees; "already built" (Plate 3.3).

At **Northchapel**, William Spooner conveyed his own cottage and its land and garden; "already erected" (Plate 3.4).

Near **Warnham**, Henry Piper, conveyed a garden and orchard of ¼ acre; "built thereon" (Plate 3.5).

In **Chichester**, Michael Woolgar conveyed part of a field (100ft x 50ft) called Joyes Croft on St Pancras Street; "already built" (plate 3.7).

At **South Norwood,** George Tate and five others conveyed (to the Northchapel Trustees) an unexpired 90-year lease from 25 December 1878, with mortgage of £350 dated 17 March 1880, rental £9 10s, £200 and arrears of interest still owing, on land and premises at Cobden Road. John Enmore Jones and two others took a lease, dated 19 December 1879, subject to a mortgage of £350; "erected" (Plate 3.6).

In **Peckham,** James Light and three others conveyed a 41¾-year lease on land to the west side of Radnor Road, dated 2 January 1883; no chapel mentioned (Plate 3.7).

In the manor and parish of **Felpham**, Charles Heather conveyed a 1000-year lease (dated 1795) to Northchapel, a piece of land, formerly waste, on the road to Middleton, on which no rent has been paid since 1868; Felpham seems to have been only at an early stage of planning (Plate 3.7)

Numerous followers of John Sirgood were prepared to put up enough money required to purchase land, no mean feat when most were labouring or skilled men and women. The conveyors of these plots of land were all members of the Dependants, not original owners, and so were legal go-betweens to facilitate the conveyances to the trustees. The rôle Sirgood played is uncertain. *A fuller text of the indenture is in Appendix 2, page 305.*

Dating the Chapels

Combining all sources, indicated in italics, both primary and secondary (from which the dates of the erection and closure of chapels are not equally verifiable) the following is an attempt to catalogue confusing conjecture and bring order to the fog of history.

Loxwood – Sirgood was in Loxwood in 1861. The chapel is said to have opened 1861 *(sources: newspaper article, see above, also in Wikipedia)*. The 1865 indenture cited above confirms it was built _by_ 1865, supported by the commencement of funerals the following year. The first funeral was reliably documented in September 1866 (that of James Sandford of Four Houses, Loxwood, a retired hoopshaver, aged 86), led by Revd Henry Rogers, Congregational Minister in Petworth, legal sponsor of the chapel.

Loxwood closed in 1974 *(source: Mrs Marion May, talk to Petworth Society 1991)*, but some claim a later closure: Loxwood was cited as open in 1976 *(Sussex Life)*, and closed 1982, when 32 members were still alive *(source: Evening Argus, confirmed by oral tape by Alf Goodwin)*. Whatever the official date of closure for regular meetings, the last funeral taken by the last elder, Alf Goodwin, was in 1991, that of Annie Matthews, aged 80, who had died in Crawley Hospital. Alf himself was laid to rest in 1996, and the last funeral recorded in the register was in 2002, that of Elsie Piper, aged 104.

Loxwood Chapel in Spy Lane was and still is in regular use by the Emmanuel Fellowship, who took over the Chapel Trust in 1984; the date of their first service was 26 August 1984. The later funerals were conducted under their auspices. 1982 looks to be the most likely year for the last meeting.

Lordshill – Sirgood was already in Shamley Green in 1851 and became a chapel trustee. By 1855, the "community [was] set up" *(source: Winterton, 1904)*, including meetings at Gate Street Farm, Bramley. This seems an acceptable date.

The chapel however was not built until 1870 *(source: Alfred Goodwin)*, at a cost of £110-£120. William Hampshire who conveyed the land was a labourer from Bramley, and in no way could he have found such a sum without donations from the Dependants in the south of Surrey. The 1871 OS map shows a chapel, with no ancillary buildings.

Its closure is well documented in several sources. The last meeting was in August 1967, the building closed the next year. This followed the death of housekeeper Nellie Franks, daughter of former elder Stephen Franks, and niece of George Franks of Plaistow Place. She had looked after Alfred Kelsey who lived until 1970. The two featured in *The People, 8 Dec 1963* with a photo and article. Located by Lordshill Stores on Lordshill Common, it was demolished after becoming dilapidated and a house built on the site about 1973/4.

Northchapel – opened 1860-62 (*source: "The Dependants, Peculiar to Sussex", Sussex Life*, date not known – perhaps a misprint for 1870-72); 1870 (*source: Wikipedia, Montgomery*); 1872 (*Secret Sussex, Chapter 14 The Dependants at Northchapel, H Scott, 1949*). Consensus seems to settle on early 1870s. William Spooner, a bricklayer, lived at Common House, aka Green Cottage, close to the site of the chapel and stores. Spooner and Thomas Street, both bricklayers, were the builders, and first elders. William's brother Henry moved to Alfold Bars, Loxwood after 1861. Was he the builder of Loxwood chapel?

It was still open 1976 *(source: Sussex Life)* but closed in 1988 *(source: Wikipedia)*. Others say 1986. Located behind the Northchapel Stores, it is now a private home.

Warnham – a "community [was] set up" in 1876 *(source: Winterton, 1904, repeated in Sussex Life, Wikipedia and Montgomery)*. Before the chapel was built, meetings had been held, as elsewhere, on farms, and preaching was also done in the open air. Muggeridge names Stone, Old Denne and Chatfield Mayes Farms and the cottages next to where the chapel was to be built. The chapel opened on the last Sunday in August 1874 *(sources: Ron Muggeridge, Henry Piper Jr, and Wikipedia)*. Ron Muggeridge, who provides the precise Sunday, relates that the young Richard Nightingale used his father's horses to haul stones, presumably from Stone Farm, for the building of the chapel in Byfleets Lane, Warnham, the furthest away from a settlement of any chapel, completed in 1874 for £150.

Muggeridge's father, though not a Dependant himself, worked at Warnham Stores, and his grandfather married a Nightingale. Whilst Muggeridge names John Nightingale, his cousin, as the principal builder, Benjamin Piper's testimony, below, in this chapter, which confirms the story of the stones, names Alfred Tickner, a carpenter from Plaistow, Henry Piper, Amos Garman, James Garman, Joseph Lindfield, and "one hired man of the world". Henry Piper, an agricultural labourer, moved into one of the neighbouring cottages in Byfleets Lane around the time the chapel was built in the mid-1870s. Henry Piper Sr was influential in getting the chapel built, and was the first elder, anointed by John Sirgood. He was succeeded by his son, Benjamin, and then Ellen Luff *(Plate 9.2)*.

PLATE 3.3   Lords Hill Chapel, Shamley Green

Fig 1 - William Hampshire, 1833-1900, who conveyed the land for the chapel, and who was a close associate of John Sirgood. This may be a photo of the chapel - the building at the rear.

Fig 2 - A recent view, cf Fig 1. The middle house conversion retains the beam for lifting goods to the storeroom, faintly visible in Fig 1. A new house may just be discerned on the chapel site behind.

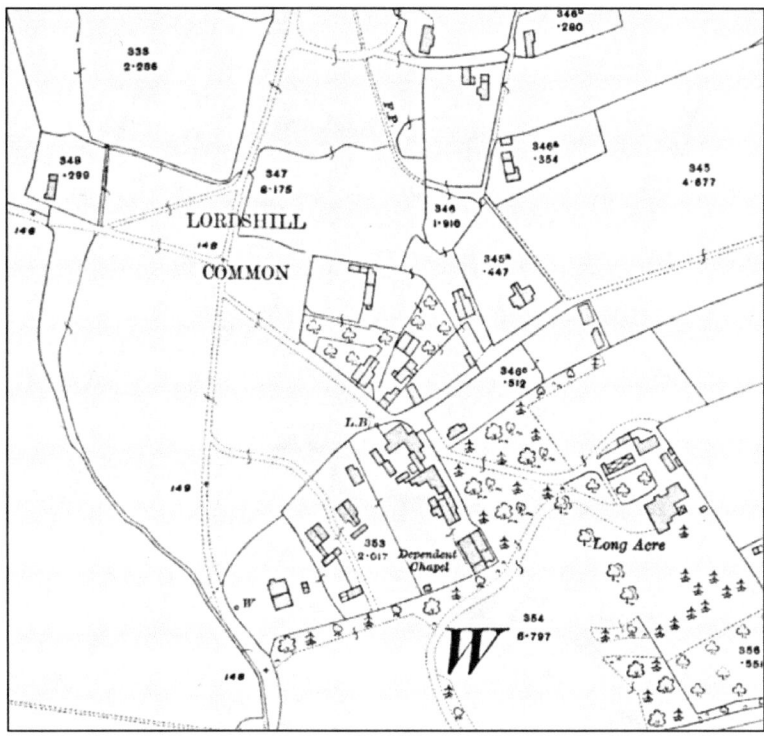

Fig 3 - This 1913 map of the Lordshill hamlet, a short walk west of Shamley Green, shows the chapel to be at the back of the plot which also has the shop and other buildings for the Dependant's business, matching the photos in Figs 1 and 2.

47

PLATE 3.4   The Dependants' Chapel at Northchapel

Fig 1 - The chapel has been converted into a house. Uniquely, this chapel is built of local greensand.

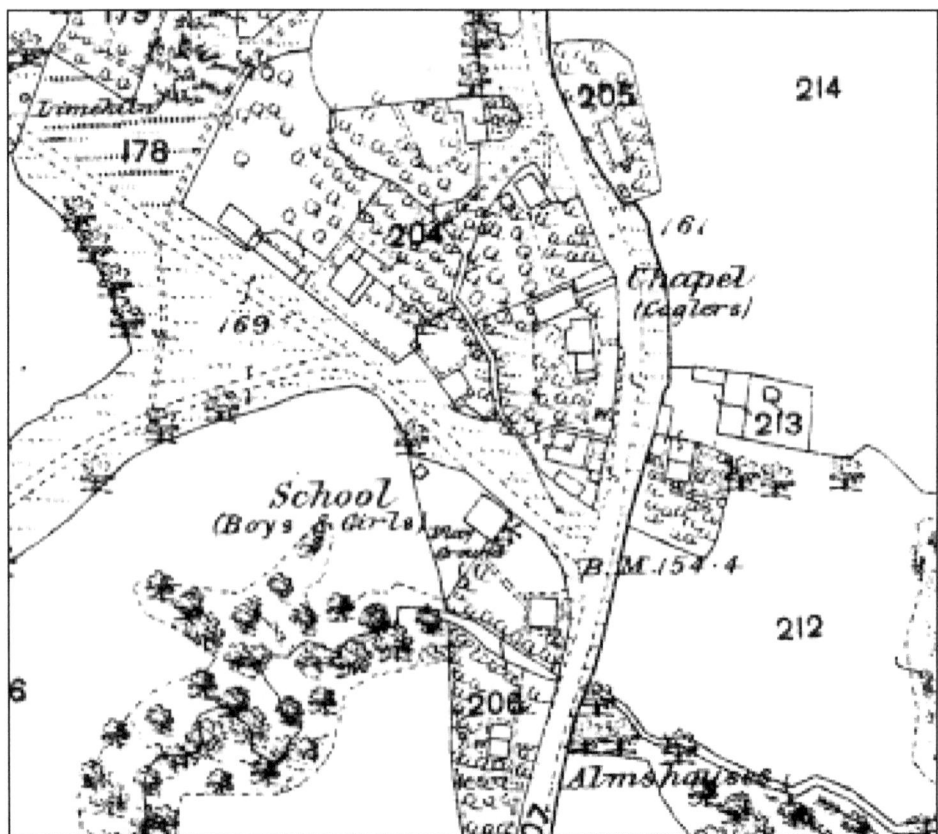

Fig 2 - The 1875 map shows the chapel, and a path to the road, next to Laurel Cottage. Northchapel village centre is to the north.

The last service was in April 1976 *(source: Sussex Life)*. On 13 July 1977, King & Chasemore auctioned the property belonging to the Trustees of the Warnham Chapel with planning permission for conversion to a dwelling, initially with Mr HAE Redford (9, Chapel Cottages) showing potential purchasers around, then Miss K Etheridge (Friday Street). It was described as brick and stone construction with a slate roof, pine panelled inside with a partition (for the tearoom), outside WC, garage, garden, sharing a cesspit with 9 & 11 Chapel Cottages (owned previously by the Dependants). Title commenced with a Deed of Trust dated 24 May 1883, probably the one transcribed and referred to numerous times in this history, dated 24 May 1880, signed 4 March 1883, so not the date the chapel was built, "already erected" in 1883.

South Norwood – the significant community established here "split from Southwark" about 1875, and a chapel opened before 1882, possibly before 1880 *(source: private correspondence, John Hickman)*, and, as stated in the 1883 indenture, mortgages were taken out in 1879 and 1880 on two leases of 1878 and 1879. It was in 1885 that John Sirgood made his last visit to Norwood, only weeks before his death *(Plate 11)*. A split from Southwark presupposes a community in Southwark. There is however no other evidence for this, except that Sirgood's early years were spent there.

The 1883 indenture merely says "erected", not by whom. Alf Goodwin stated that Norwood was the "last of seven" to be built, but was he including Peckham (see below?) John Hickman, a local historian, discovered a "mission house", the fourth building in Cobden Road from the junction with Portland Road in Ward's Croydon Directory, 1880. A c1880 chapel in Cobden Road, if correct, was a short-lived structure. A local man, formerly a delivery boy for Randall, Slade (the Norwood Stores), was adamant, telling John Hickman that a building facing Woodside Road, was the chapel, which is confirmed by all maps from 1896 onwards. By then, the retail side of the community was well developed. The chapel was set within the site of the grocery and drapery stores, occupying a corner of the site, but unlike the stores, it fronted Woodside Avenue. It had seats for 200. It took until the OS 1966-70 1:1250 scale map for it to be recognised as a Dependant Chapel, by which time it is likely to have closed! By 1976, the building was no longer named, and is no longer there. The site is now modern premises for manufacturing.

About 1890, Woodside Road was renamed Woodside Avenue. Ward's Directory and Kelly's Directory referred to a chapel/mission room at 2 Woodside Avenue in 1893. By the next edition in 1896, the chapel is clearly listed in Woodside Avenue. When the replacement larger chapel was built in the early 1890s, the built-up area by then extended south to Woodside Station, but was still very much on the metropolitan fringe, with farms and a golf club in the countryside around, including east of the main thoroughfare, South Portland Road.

The Cobden Road building immediately behind it on the Dependants' corner plot was incorporated into the expanding Dependants business activity as a garage. No date has been found for the closure of the building. Charles Taylor was the first elder at Norwood (died 1935). He was recipient of many letters from John Sirgood and was a trustee of the Cobden Road chapel. In an urban area subject to much development over the past 130 years, Norwood is a complex location.

PLATE 3.5   Warnham Chapel, Byfleets Lane

Fig 1 and 2 - Two photographs from 1977.
Fig 1 is from a brochure for the auction of the chapel held on 13 July.
Fig 2 is from the West Sussex Gazette, 17 November, in an article about the chapel's closure.
Three pictures show the timber-framed Chapel Cottage next door, itself having been home to Dependants.

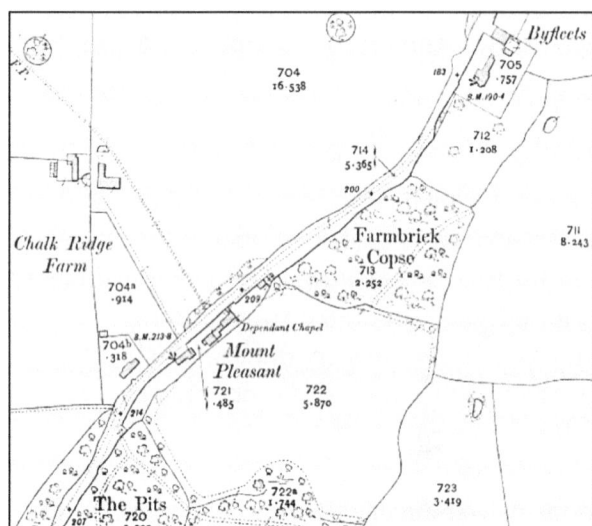

Fig 3 - The chapel mapped in 1912. Warnham village is to the north-east. In 1912, the chapel was described as Dependant, but on earlier maps, the Ordnance Survey incorrectly described it as Plymouth Brethen, then more accurately as Nonconformist.

Fig 4 - A recent photo of the house conversion, much extended, but still with a paling fence, as marketed by Henry Adams, estate agents, © Henry Adams.

PLATE 3.6   South Norwood Chapels

Fig 1 - the site of the chapel in Woodside Avenue, redeveloped for commercial use.
Photo taken looking towards Portland Road.

Fig 2 - the OS map, top, is dated 1879-80. The supposed Cobden Road 'mission house' in Ward's Directory 1880, the one in the indenture which specifically mentions Cobden Road, may be the fourth property near the sharp left-hand bend, on the junction with Denmark Road.

Fig 3 – right, the 1896 map, names the replacement chapel fronting Woodside Avenue. The retail business is on this triangular corner site between Cobden Rd and Woodside Ave.

Fig 4 - This October 1983 photo is of the chapel local people remember. At the time it was occupied by a company, Bensons Lifts. Note the steam bakery chimney behind.
Acknowledgement: Dr Bruce Osborne, great grandson of Isaac Steer.

PLATE 3.7

Outlying Places of Worship

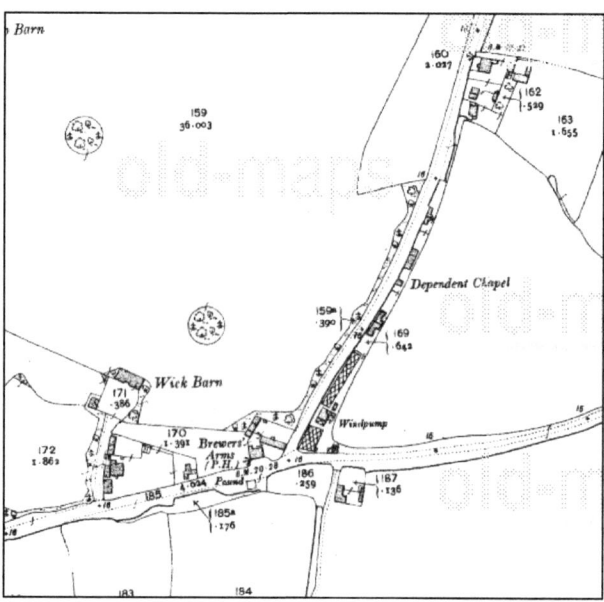

Fig 1 a & b - Felpham Chapel, Flansham Lane. This short-lived place of worship appears on the 1912 OS map, labelled as 'Dependent Chapel'. The site is now a rather uninspiring house. *Ack: photo, Marion Woolgar*

Fig 2 a & b - Peckham Chapel, Radnor Street

A chapel, which may be the one used by Dependants for a while, can be seen on the 1893-6 OS map, near the angle in Radnor Street, now a small block of flats.

Ack: photo Google Streetview

Fig 3 a & b - Chichester Chapel, Adelaide Road

The Chichester chapel in the St Pancras area of the city has given way to Chapel Cottages on the same footprint.

Felpham – opened 1898 *(source: Wikipedia)*, an iron building on Flansham Lane. Services latterly were held on Wednesdays only. For a time in the 1930s the chapel was shared with Methodists. It closed in 1939 *(source; Wikipedia)*, and has since been demolished).

Peckham – on land leased in January 1883. This site was still undeveloped when the indenture was signed in March. The Peckham Trustees were from Bermondsey, Rotherhithe, and Streatham, one from Peckham itself; other witnesses were from Camberwell and Peckham. Perhaps any chapel here served a wider community in east and southeast London. The Peckham Society only knows of a "Gospel Hall" on Radnor Road (now Radnor Street) from 1888 to 1922. 1888 seems a likely date of opening. It may then have become a Methodist chapel, as one in Radnor Road has been noted. Radnor Road was otherwise residential but was comprehensively redeveloped after the Second World War. This chapel must have been handed over to the Methodists at an early date. The Loxwood death register records the death of Joseph Elliott, a listed Peckham trustee, "of London" in 1909. There were other short-lived meeting houses in London, such as on New Kent Road, Yelverton Road, Battersea, and in Brixton, but these may have just been private rooms.

Chichester – opened before 1883; still open in 1949 *(source: Sussex Life)* closed in 1975 *(Wikipedia)*. Michael Woolgar (died 1927) was influential at Chichester, as was Selsey-born Walter Hart (died 1945). Walter moved to the new Hove community as an elder, possibly in 1905, certainly by 1911. Both were married men, seldom the case for elders of core communities inland. The building is now unrecognisable as a pair of cottages, Chapel Cottages, on the corner of Adelaide Road and Jays Croft. Maps of 1898 to 1974 show the chapel. There is evidence the group met in a hall before this (see Chapter 12).

Plaistow – said to have opened about 1883/4, but not included in the indenture of March 1883. However, it appears neither on the 1897-8 Ordnance Survey map, nor (the attached house) in the 1901 census. This was Zion House, lived in by Dependants in 1911 and it was clearly shown as a non-conformist chapel and house on the OS map of 1912. It seems likely that this substantial brick-built chapel and unique attached house was a short-lived place of worship. Alf Goodwin remembers attending in about 1920. His recollection is that it was never "official" and catered for the elderly brethren in Plaistow, who met there in the weekday evenings, travelling to Loxwood on Sundays in a Model-T Ford van. Closed before 1942 *(source: Sussex Life)*. More authoritatively, it was bought by Arthur Wooldridge, owner of the neighbouring builder's yard, in 1931 *(source: Dr Elizabeth Brockhurst, correspondence with Marion May, 1991)*, the chapel converted and divided into two dwellings, later known as Zion Cottage and Marazion. In 1939, the Wooldridge family were in the house, Zion Cottages likewise occupied by non-Dependants. Located on Rickmans Lane, the road to Kirdford, the old chapel and attached house are now in private hands, making three dwellings on the site today. It looks like a chapel to this day (Plate 3.8).

Hove – a late addition, opened 1905/6 in Aldrington, on the corner of Linton Road and Payne Road, probably an off-shoot of Chichester, from where Walter Hart moved to be the elder. Still open in 1976 *(source: Sussex Life)*. Some have suggested there were previously meetings in nearby Portslade, possibly house meetings. Directories refer to it as a Mission Hall until 1936 when it was called the Christians' Meeting Room until 1951. The now white painted building still stands, converted to a rather unusual house (Plate 3.8) after closure in 1978.

Haslemere – there was a chapel on King's Road, also attended by Dependants living in Fernhurst. William Newman, aged 60, of Valewood Farm had his funeral there, conducted by Jesse Puttock (Loxwood) and William Spooner (Northchapel), in 1915, reported in the Surrey Advertiser of 29 May (Plate 3.8), as did Ellen Moore the same year (same elders). She and her husband John, a coal merchant in King's Road, had been "largely responsible" for building the chapel "about 10 years ago" (W Sussex Gazette, 30 Sep 1915). Ellen died on a visit to Lordshill. Mrs Moorey of King's Road was caretaker in the early 1920s (there were two families there of this name).

Newpound Common, Wisborough Green – Sirgood is known to have preached here, but Alfred Goodwin told Marion May in a taped conversation that old Mrs Carter (of the family which owned the engineering works at Newpound, and a good friend to the Dependants – her family were longstanding members of the former General Baptist community in Billingshurst) had provided a meeting room on their premises or in a house owned by them for an unknown period of time, attended among others by the Luff family, who lived nearby. George Luff, Alf Goodwin recalled, was an habitué of the Bat and Ball. He went into the pub one day and walked out again, never to go back, saying, "You will never hear my voice in here again". This is likely to have been quite early in the history of the Dependants, possibly before the chapel was built at Loxwood. George and his wife Mary Ann were at Oakhurst, next to Plaistow Place, farming with Richard Nightingale, by 1891. It was their children, Ellen, Lucy, George and Caroline who featured strongly in the Warnham, Northchapel and Loxwood communities.

There are also stories of Sirgood having preached in Kent, at a place called 'Harden', which may have been near Sevenoaks, where there were Dependants, or perhaps Kent dialect pronounced Headcorn village as 'Harden', another documented birthplace of Dependants. The latter seems more likely (see Table A2.1). Sirgood wrote letters from as far away as Lincoln and Bath.
It is curious that his alleged preaching on Clapham Common never led to a community there. After all, he is known to have taken a house and shoemaker's shop there in the 1860s.

Descriptions of the Chapels

The chapels at Lordshill, Northchapel and South Norwood were adjacent to the stores, but in Loxwood the location was a short walk away in Spy Lane, and in Warnham, a longer walk from Church Street to Byfleets Lane. Some have become private houses: Chichester, Hove, Warnham and Plaistow. South Norwood has been turned into a stationery factory and looks nothing like it did. Northchapel was of Petworth stone, with brick dressings, and a porthole window in the gable. The only image of Lordshill chapel is a tiny grainy newspaper advert for the adjacent house, in which it resembles Loxwood. Brick-built Hove is now rendered in white. The chapels, or meeting houses, were all very plain, and quite small, but each held a good-sized congregation in tightly packed pews, Loxwood 300 at a pinch, compared to South Norwood only 100. There was no cross on the altar table, but a raised dais provided seating for up to three elders.

The meetings in the chapels could be 3 hours long. There were two on Sundays, one, or two, on a weekday. The Dependants had no Communion service. The chapels were not licensed

3. Dependant Places of Worship

PLATE 3.8   Later Chapels in Hove and Plaistow

Fig 1 – Hove Chapel, corner site Linton Road and Payne Avenue. There is no mistaking its origin, even after conversion to residential use, and white render. It was originally red brick.

Fig 2 – 1951 OS map (1:1,250) showing Hove's L-shaped 'Dependents Chapel', located south of the coastal railway line, located between Hove Aldrington, the first to name it.

Fig 3 – Plaistow Chapel (left, now residential) with attached Zion House (originally accommodation)

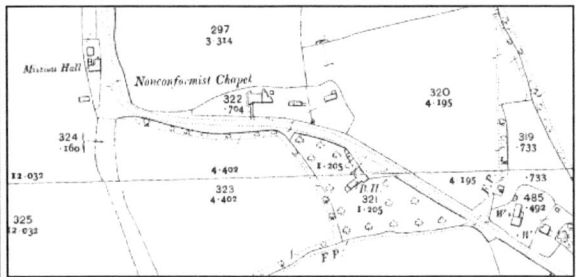

Fig 4 – The OS map indicates the Plaistow Chapel as a 'non-conformist chapel'. Not he Mission Hall; Plaistow had several places of worship in addition to the Anglican church.

Fig 5 – Confirmation that a chapel existed in King's Road, Haslemere in 1915. Left, funeral, William Newman; right, funeral, Ellen Moore.
Left, Surrey Advertiser 29 May 1915; Right, West Sussex Gazette 30 Sep 1915. ©Findmypast.

DEATH OF A COKELER

Mr. William Newman, a farmer, of Valewood Farm, Haslemere, who died on Saturday at the age of 60, was a member of the sect known as Dependents, or Cokelers which has a considerable following on the Surrey and Sussex borders, though unknown in many other districts. The funeral took place on Wednesday in the chapel belonging to the sect, and situate in King's-road, Haslemere. Mr. Jesse Puttock, of Loxwood, and Mr. Wm. Spooner (Northchapel) conducted the service.

Two well-known inhabitants of Haslemere who passed away last week were buried in the Parish Churchyard on Friday afternoon. Mrs. Moore, of Kings-road, was the widow of Mr. John Joseph Moore, a local coal merchant, who died just nine years ago. She was on a visit to Shamley Green, when she was suddenly taken ill and died in an hour or so. She was prominently associated with the sect known as Cokelers or Dependents, which flourish in various parts of Sussex, notably at Northchapel and Loxwood, and with her husband was largely responsible for building the meeting house at Haslemere about ten years ago. The denomination was largely represented at the funeral, which was conducted by Mr. Jesse Puttick and Mr. William Spooner, of Northchapel. Mrs. Moore was 69 years of age.—Mr. James Talbot, who passed away in for baptism or marriage. Only Loxwood held funerals with burial, and had a graveyard for the entire membership, though some, particularly in the distant communities, chose to be buried (usually with no headstone) in their local parish churchyard, following a service in the chapel. Funerals, however, were not a time for mourning, rather an exuberant celebration of life. There was also a tearoom for refreshments. Usually, worshippers would stay for a meal they had brought with them, and drink hot tea, in between the two Sunday services, or even sleep there if from another community.

Loxwood Chapel was at the centre of activities as not only did people travel there for funerals, but they also came for five three-day Big Meetings held at Christmas, Easter, Whitsun, early August Bank Holiday and late September. On each day, meetings were from 10.30 – 1.00, 2.30 – 4.00, 5.30 – 8.00. So many wished to give testimony. It made sense to have get-togethers which provided more than just spiritual nourishment but brotherhood too. Although in the early days travel was as often as not on foot, later the community came to own vehicles which could be garaged next to Loxwood Chapel, a building that began life as stables, and still exists.

A Big Meeting, 1884

The letter that is described below suggests that sometimes the Big Meeting might be spread not only over more than one day, but also more than one chapel, and included those from small far away communities. The letter was written to Charlie, 3 June 1884, Whitsun Big Meeting, from "your wife Louie" (Charles and Louie Taylor; other names in brackets are best guesses). It was sent from Northchapel Stores. The following is a précis. It refers to "Carrie [Luff] and I" walking to Loxwood, setting out at 6.30 Saturday, arriving after 9; Bro John took them to Warnham, Sunday, i.e., Carrie, Hannah, Louie, & Eliza Luff from Northchapel, Bro [Henry] Brett and his wife from Brighton, Bro Downing from Bath, Bro [John] Hemmings [Hove] & Bro Fisher from Cambridge. John, Eliza and Louie herself walked back to Loxwood, *"there being so many to stop [sleep] at Warnham who could not very well walk"*. On Monday, Michael [Woolgar], Fanny [Hart], John Carter, Walter Hart & more from Chichester, John Slade, Bro Harper, Bro [Harry] Hart & others from Brighton [Hove] were there; we had the booth out to make the place larger. Bro Michael had a dance down the aisle, *"as though he was flying. In the evening, Bro John gave out the hymn 'There's a city of gold', when he got to the words 'He has promised that we shall be there', … he lifted up his hands & looked upon us all. Oh, it was heavenly; we left off singing and continued praising God for some time; we then went on again, and when he got to the words 'Oh Lord Jesus come quickly' he again lifted up his hands, and we all went on praising God for a long time, and although there was so much shouting I could hear his voice praising God above all the rest, and such a sweet sound. He leaned over his desk and took hold of Sister Steele's hand and they shouted together."* Brother John must be presumed to be John Sirgood. It is a unique insight into the power of Sirgood's evangelism, and this very close to the end of his life.

Another on the New Year Bank Holiday 1 January 1885 was reported in the press, referring to Rev John Sirgood and Rev John Overington. It is rare to see elders given this title, as they would never have sanctioned it themselves. Upwards of 300 attended.

Hymns and Other Writings

Services opened with a hymn, then a prayer and testimony, alternating with further hymns. For many years, an elder would read the verse of a hymn from a large book before the brethren sang it. As well as the copious correspondence that survives in the handwritten notebooks of a number of Dependants, there are a very large number of hymns. Many of those which are attributed to a named individual are by John Sirgood. Many others are by Charles Taylor of Norwood. However, it was not until 1958 that a printed book was produced. Most stalwarts of the chapels knew the words by heart anyway. They sang (unaccompanied) to known tunes but with different words. They did not use the canon of hymns used by most other denominations. Peter Jerrome has counted over 1000 hymns, of which only 461 appear in the book. The main handwritten source is the book started by Charlie Circus in Norwood in 1887, continued by his son Ephraim, a bulky written record including another 221 which never made it in print.

As well as hymns, there were meditations used in testaments made by individuals standing up to speak from the heart and from their experience, and there were poems too. Here is one allegorical story written in Elsie Piper's notebook from another member's testament, perhaps that of Harry Aylward. Elsie was one of the last Dependants to pass away, at a Worthing nursing home, in 2002, at the ripe age of 104.

"Brother Harry told us of an experience of a little girl that he heard about when he was a little boy.
This little girl was sent on an errand by her Mother.
Her Mother told her not to turn to the right hand or to the left but come straight home. The little girl set out on her journey & she met such a lot of persuaders with all sorts of things which wanted her to turn out of her path, but she kept to what her Mother told her and said I cannot leave this narrow path. I'm going home. We can all take this for a lesson on our spiritual journey."

The Piper Family of Warnham

Henry Piper had conveyed the land on which the chapel at Warnham was built. He held meetings at his house at Chatsfold Mayes (aka Chaffields) before the chapel was built, as did the Nightingales at Stone Farm. Henry's son Benjamin Piper was also very prominent from a young age, leading his first funeral meeting at Loxwood at the age of 20. Benjamin (Plate 3.9) left a revealing lengthy personal testimony from which the following is an extract.

"I Benjamin Piper, do take in hand to write what I remember. I was born in the year of Our Lord 1868. Now I do remember, my father, Henry Piper was turned out of house, for Christ's sake, our furniture was put in a barn Cider Mill Farm, but we children went to a place called Butlers [now demolished, near Monks Farm] with our Aunt Mary Wells. Father [and] mother had two weeks around with Brethren and God so helped them that it took all their care away....

"On the day that we were moving from the old house Chaffieds [sic, Chaffields] Farm they had no more a Meeting Place, but to their surprise, God had worked beyond what they could have thought. Brother Richard Nightingale, only a lad, had given place to the truth, therefore

attended these meetings at Chaffieds Farm …. Therefore, He worked upon Brother Richard Nightingale['s] father who was a farmer and had a large house. He came and said we have a place to meet in, and that was his own house, in the kitchen where they lived themselves. Only consider what joy for the poor Saints at Warnham. Then shortly after, he let my father and mother with us three boys one bedroom to live in and sleep also. But God was with us. After a space of time, the parlour under our bedroom was vacant. Then the meeting was held in there. While being there in this house, Stone Farm, our chapel that is was built in the year 1874.

"While this was going on our circumstances were very poor. Father was not well with a bad hand, and we three boys had measles and whooping cough. Only think all in one room but God was with us. We were very poor nothing coming in from any source. Then it was God worked. We had a pig and of course no money coming in, could not afford to keep it, therefore killed it. Although it was not fat, but God multiplied. My dear mother made some lard, and had to borrow vessels to put it in, as she had not enough. But God blessed it, and there was enough lard out of that pig which was not fat to last over two years…. Also at this time of poverty, my mother had been out in the harvest field gleaning up the wheat ears and this was thrashed [sic] by Moses Muggeridge's thrashing machine, when at Stone Farm to work. The wheat was taken to Shiremark Windmill and our need was great. The wind did not blow for some time to turn the mill, therefore could not grind the wheat to make flour but at this time my father prayed to the Almighty God and asked Him to make the wind to blow. After he had prayed, he met a Brother and told him the wind would blow before night, and so it did. God answered his prayer. The wheat was ground and dressed made into flour and thank our Almighty father we ate it with gratitude to Him who had not [only] done wonders in days gone by but also in our day. Oh, Halleluia to God who rules everything right for those who trust in him.

"Now our chapel was being built. The Brothers that helped to build were Brother Alfred Tickner, a carpenter from Plaistow, Henry Piper, Amos Garman and James Garman, Brother Joseph Lindfield, and one hired man of the world, but the dear Brothers worked with such interest and pleasure, also such small wages, it being for God's children to meet together to worship God. It only cost £150. Now Brother Richard Nightingale's father sent his team of horses and wagon to fetch stone free of charge, and I wish to say that before he left this world he looked to God. Brother John Sirgood and my father went to see him and prayed with him, which caused them much joy on his behalf for God had used him very much for the benefit of his people. The chapel was opened the last Sunday in August 1874. From this time God's work went on and God very much prospered the Brethren's labours both physically and spiritually. Brother James Mitchell was one whom God helped to do much to improve the chapel and property, not for money, but out of love to God, and I may say I had much pleasure sometimes late at night in only handing our Brother nails and screws that he wanted.

"The chapel was built but not fully paid for. The money was borrowed from my mother's brother free from interest, whom also God used for His own cause. This had to be paid off. The Brethren did all strive very much with their little, which was very small, ten or twelve shillings weekly wages. But thank God it was paid off. Once I remember in the harvest time my dear father and mother's desire to help, which they did. Brother John Nightingale

finished the daily labour about 5.30, so came evenings when it was very hot, working night[s] in the harvest field to earn a little more to help pay off, although I was very young at this time. I remember one dinner time when it was very hot in the harvest field, it was very pleasant to sit a little longer but my dear father said, 'Now come on boys, we want to earn a little extra to help pay off the chapel debt'. So up we got and I do remember that God got up with us. My dear father took the scythe and my dear brother Henry and I took out the wheat sheaves. My brother George who was very small drew the bonds and my dear mother tied them up, and oh the joy and pleasure we had together. It was I am sure a real taste of Heaven. Whenever I think upon, it brings joy to my heart.

"Now the debt that I have spoken of was quickly paid off, and God blessed the labour of our Brethren very much, that I am sure what they had done, God more than made up to them. I should like to go back now to what I have heard my father say, that when he was coming home from work one night, God taught him what a deal more freedom and liberty both he and my mother would have for Christ's sake, if they remained as they were, and not bring souls into the world, which if not born again is very sad. Now the very next Sunday, Brother John Sirgood came down from London and taught the very same that how much more useful we could be for Christ's sake, by keeping free from entanglements, which by the grace of God can be avoided. This very much strengthened their faith in God and in each other. For this time unknown to my father, Brother John Sirgood had met with very much [the same] position about this line of things. Therefore, they were able to strengthen each other's (sic) in God. This line has always been taught at Warnham that the more free we are the more useful we can be for God's work....

Plate 3.9
Benjamin Piper of Warnham, a Portrait Photograph.

"My dear mother passed away in the year 1909. My brother George passed away in the year 1911. My brother Henry passed away in the year 1919. My father Henry passed away in the year 1921. I Benjamin Piper the only one living in the year 1936."

Note, written by whoever transcribed the document: "Benjamin Piper passed away in 1948. The stores were sold in the year 1948. The chapel was closed April 4th, 1976".

A Common Situation?

The sites of chapels tell us much about the way in which outdoor meeting locations were changed to permanent buildings in which to preach the gospel and provide a sheltered home for lengthy meetings, away from the catcalls and objects thrown at the brethren. Can a correlation be found with the commons and wastes on which much of the preaching had taken place? The requirement was to be close to existing settlements, but not central to them, which is true of all chapels. Only Lordshill was a major move from one parish (Bramley) to another (Wonersh). It is not known if there was much of a community in South Norwood prior to its chapel being built (or whether this involved any re-siting from either Southwark, or Clapham, or Peckham). Later sites followed the same trend on the south coast and smaller centres inland such as on Rickman's Lane in Plaistow.

To answer the question posed about commons and roadside wastes, which were or had been linked to local manors, it is clear that Spy Lane, Loxwood adjoined manorial land, that Northchapel had roadside waste behind the site on the track to Diddlesfold Farm, which the Dependants also ran for many years *(see Chapter 10),* that Lordshill was fringing common land, that Warnham was built on a rural roadside, as was Plaistow. South Norwood, however, was built on land right on the fringe of London, next to a brickfield, although the streets were already laid out, as they were the streets in Chichester and Hove, where corner sites were obtained. Peckham, Felpham and Haslemere were the only ones built along a longer street. Unsurprisingly, it was the rural heartland chapels which conform to this model. Of all these, only Lordshill and Northchapel had the later combination stores built on an adjoining site.

Chapter 4

The Loxwood Death and Burial Register,

and Dependant Funerals

PLATE 4.1

Some Loxwood Dependant Elders

Fig 1 – right, Tom Rugman, 1851-1935, a studio portrait)

Fig 2 – below, Henry Aylward, 1864-1937 (photo Harry Sopp), in the road near The Combination Stores.

Fig 3 – left, an elderly Walter Nash, 1871-1960, outside The Combination Stores.

Fig 4 – below, Alfred Goodwin, 1906-1996, with his mother, Edith, aged 87.

Funerals, and the Reverend Rogers of Petworth

The first recorded funeral was at Loxwood in 1866. Perhaps the 1861 building was not registered for funerals until then. The Revd Henry Rogers, Congregational Minister in Petworth, not only took this first funeral meeting but also supported Sirgood by fielding the issues arising from the persecution of the Dependants by local landowners around 1861.

Rogers was himself minister of a relatively new church, as the following, from The London Gazette, 17 Oct 1851, states:

"NOTICE is hereby given, that a separate building, named the Petworth Congregational Church, situated in Golden-square, in the town and parish of Petworth, in the county of Sussex, in the district of Petworth, being a building certified according to law as a place of religious worship, was, on the 8th day of October 1851, duly substituted and registered for solemnizing marriages therein, pursuant to the Act of 6th and 7th Wm. IV., cap. 85, in lieu of Petworth Independent Chapel [dated 1819], the registry of which had been cancelled in consequence of the same having been disused as a place of worship by the Congregation on whose behalf it had been previously registered. Witness my hand this 11th day of October 1851. Arthur Daintry, Superintendent Registrar."

An Overview of the Death and Burial Registers

Keeping a register of burial is a legal requirement; keeping a death register is an additional resource, of great value to the historian as it lists additional names and details of those who were buried elsewhere. The Dependants showed their loyalty to their brethren and sisters, and their "dependancy on Christ", through this death register, and through often short but revealing comments squeezed into the foolscap sheets. It would be foolish to assume it is a complete register. Many of those who attended other chapels are not recorded here, for example, if they were not well known in Loxwood. Others, even those from Loxwood, may have been omitted, for reasons unknown. Some details are absent, such as age or first name, suggesting they were not that well known. Having sorted the data in an Excel spreadsheet, it has been easy for the author to utilise this rich seam of evidence, but the sheer number of names precludes some possible lines of analysis.

From the start, locations where the deceased lived were given. The first 24 of these were from Loxwood, Wisborough Green, Plaistow and Alfold, with the sad exception of Sarah Jane Varndell, a babe of 6 weeks, from Haslemere. The first from elsewhere was Warnham Dependant, Francis (Frank) Nightingale in 1869, who featured in Chapter 2. There were 61 funerals in the first ten years, an average of six a year. Life was often cut short then, and some were older converts. However, within these first ten years, a lot of children, infants and babies were buried, bringing the average age down. This may well have reflected the age of conversion, there being many young Dependant families, but it may also indicate the precariousness of life, with few medical cures available, and epidemics of diseases like scarlet fever and typhoid in the late 1860s and smallpox in the early 1870s taking away both children and young adults.

John Sirgood presided at only eight of these, perhaps because he was in Clapham, or "on circuit" much of the time. He clearly gave independence to each of the elders of the chapels, Loxwood being no exception. By the end of the 19th century, 542 burials had been recorded, averaging 16 per year. Numbers rose as the Brethren aged. Table 4.1, below, gives a breakdown of the numbers.

The Overington Family of Loxwood

It is interesting to note the dominance of one family at Loxwood Chapel. Thomas Overington and his wife Ann (plate 4.3) lived in Spy Lane, and in 1861, John and Harriet Sirgood were lodging with them, whilst Tom's brother John was working at Exfold in Tismans Common. They lived in The Old Cottage that now lies behind the row known as New Cottages. The brothers, both agricultural labourers, were the dominant elders in the Loxwood Dependant community for the remainder of the 19th century, John and probably Tom, anointed by Sirgood himself. Tom led funerals until three years before his death in 1896, 81 in total.

John, who outlived him, carried on until two years before his death in 1909, having officiated at 74 funerals. John and their sister Jane lived at Hall House in the centre of the village where he farmed the small 10-acre smallholding adjacent to it, house and land that later would be bought by the Dependants for their own use.

Tom and Ann lived in Spy Lane for the rest of Tom's life. Ann was as active in the Dependants as anyone, and probably received more letters from John Sirgood than any other recipient, some the earliest known. By 1871, Ann had become a school mistress, with influence over the young of the village, some say a dame school. Was it held in the chapel room, or perhaps in her home? This venture may well have not outlasted the building of the new Board school in the village soon after. She died aged 77 at the Dependants' Beulah House, South Norwood, where perhaps she was visiting. At her funeral she was described as "mother of Loxwood church". Ann is the only woman to have led a funeral – that of a child, Alfred Ayling, in 1888.

The third brother, Obed, seems not to have been an elder, but has been noted in Chapter 2 as a trustee of Loxwood chapel. He married Charlotte and they raised a family, perhaps a barrier to being an elder. He worked on farms. They later lived in Alfold. Another brother, James, was keeper of the tollgate next to the Onslow Arms in 1881 and continued to live there after the tolls were abolished. All were Dependants, and like so many others, were buried in Loxwood chapel graveyard. See also Chapter 12, Thomas Overington of Hove.

Peter Pacy, Renowned Preacher from Plaistow

Another preacher at Loxwood is worthy of note at this point. Peter Pacy (plate 4.3) became one of the chapel trustees, but he only took one funeral. He had been head gardener at Ifold House for Mr Napper, but lost his job as a result of his preaching activities, which had annoyed Napper as his fellow gentry and farmers at hunt meets "had donged his ears" about the annoying house meetings on their estates, forcing Napper to get rid of him. Napper clearly regarded Pacy as a good worker as rather than sack him he sent him off to do copse cutting and farming, as piece work. Pacy had earned 12/- a week as gardener, and by his hard work he now earned £1. However, the "rhiners" (oak bark strippers) refused to work with him, so he went wood cutting by himself, upping his work rate to earn 24/- a week. He was by all accounts a busy itinerant preacher, as was Tom Overington. Jerrome quotes from James Brightman's Life Story in which he tells of Pacy, one of the founding fathers, coming to Norwood for a week of meetings, at the end of which Peter told him "he spoke in the power". Brightman was an elder and trustee in Norwood.

Table 4.1   Loxwood Chapel Burials in the First Decade, 1866-1875

	At Loxwood	average age at death	Total No. in Petworth R. D.*
1866 (part year)	3	37	183
1867	9	35	153
1868	9	37	192
1869	5	47	189
1870	**10**	36	**246**
1871	4	**26**	189
1872	4	**14**	172
1873	2	75	176
1874	3	51	187
1875	6	33	188

* R. D. = Registration District, including Loxwood – figures from www.ancestry.co.uk.

Note the small 1870 peak in deaths in both Loxwood (from a very small sample, to be treated with caution), and especially in Petworth District, in which Loxwood is a constituent parish, and the lower age at death, which continued locally to 1872. Infant and youth mortality was significant component of the data, except in 1869, See also Table 4.2 below.

Table 4.2   Loxwood Chapel Burials, Age at Death 1866-1875

1866	86, 0, 25 - **37**
1867	75, 30, 7, 37, 25, 14, 0, 82, 46 - **35**
1868	44, 29, 55, 3, 68, 0, 1, 59, 72 - **37**
1869	6, 57, 55, 29, 85 - **47**
1870	79, 10, 55, 24, 17, 66, 24, 4, 44, one unknown - **36**
1871	77, 27, 0, 1 - **26**
1872	0, 11, 30, 15 - **14**
1873	83, 67 - **75**
1874	72, 52, 28 - **51**
1875	57, 85, 1, 16, 23, 15 – **33**

Average in bold

Table 4.3   Dependant Surnames, Burials 1866-1875

Sandford, Pollard, Woods, Foster, Jenner, Pannell, Marriner, Manville, Etherington, Varndell, Smithers, Pacy, Wells, Overington, Baverstock, Covey, Thayre, Nightingale, Sopp, Garland, Denyer, Durant, Ayling, Reeves, Spooner, Haslett, Killner, Baker, Randall, Raymond, Batchelor, Hard, Greenfield, Knight, Bonsey, Booker, Wood, Boxall.

The Unfortunate Marriner Family, 1867-1871

Many of the names in table 4.3 will become familiar to anyone reading this book from cover to cover. Almost all were from Loxwood, some from Kirdford/Plaistow, some from Alfold. They also included some elderly parents, and noticeably young children of those newly converted young adults who would have formed the backbone of the community. Among them were six members of the Marriner family, who it seems were an early example of migration within the Dependant community, in this case from Northchapel. The six were from more than one family. Two were infants, two young adults and two middle aged, all dead in the late 1860s. It looks as though an infectious disease may have spread through them, and investigating this, it turned out that another person living with one of the Marriner families, on Chapel Green (Station Road) also died. However, one should be cautious about such a conclusion as life expectancy was so much lower than today, for a whole host of reasons. These were largely working-class men and women, whose lives were blighted by poor housing, poor sanitation, poor hygiene, poor nutrition and lack of education.

One possible explanation of the deaths in the Marriner family, and of others at the time is a smallpox epidemic. The strain circulating in the 1860s was particularly virulent, for example in London in 1862-3, with higher mortality in under-fives than previously. The 1870 pandemic in Europe was triggered by the Franco-Prussian War. The population was still largely unvaccinated despite its encouragement by the government since the 1850s. *(sources: JD Rollaston, 1933; A Hardy, 1983).* Might the pandemic have reached Loxwood and Petworth in 1870?

Longevity Among Later Dependants

The data below is inclusive of both the burial and death registers, except where stated. There is good reason to think that as time went on, the security and quality of a simple lifestyle particularly of those who lived at The Combination Stores (Chapter 5), combined with increasingly modern medical care, which they did not shun, meant Dependants had a longer life expectancy than the population as a whole. However, meaningful comparison is difficult because of the natural ageing of the Dependant population sample, especially in the 20th century, and its skew towards females during the later years. In the 1860s and 70s there was a small male majority in the adult burials. In 1900-1909, the numbers were exactly 50% of each sex. However, of the 169 deaths in the 1960s, only 18% were male (including several from Germany who were recorded as brethren). Many of these women were childless; women generally were outliving men in the 20th century; the stores had more successfully attracted young women converts, now reaching old age. Table 4.4 shows that these 169 men and women died at an average age of 84.

The first to reach 90 was Hannah Percy in 1891, followed by Thomas Hills in 1909, then Martha Tickner in 1922, Henry Spooner, 1928, George Baverstock, 1933 and Eliza Stemp, 1939. In the 1940s, seven reach 90 or over; in the 1950s five (some well over 90); in the 1960s ten; then six in the shrinking pool of mainly Sisters in the 1970s (including one centenarian, Edith Bradshaw, 103, and Kate Rugman, 99, plate 4.3); six in the 1980s (including Christopher Hale, 100). Of those who survived to the very end (from 1990) six out of nine lived to over 90, with Elsie Piper reaching 104 in 2002 (plate 4.3). These figures are taken from the Loxwood Chapel burials register, so do not include those buried elsewhere.

Table 4.4   Age at Death, Dependant Burials and Other Deaths for Selected Decades

1866-1875	36	(54 in sample, burials only)
1900-1909	69	(86 in sample, burials, and other recorded deaths)
1960-1969	84	(104 in sample, burials, and other recorded deaths)

The death register, which includes both duplicate and additional names to the statutory burial register, was only commenced with the death of John Sirgood himself in 1885. The span of years during which John Sirgood was alive, and leading the Dependants, was from 1866 to 1885, nineteen years. Table 4.5 shows numbers who were buried, in decadal periods.

Table 4.5   Loxwood Chapel Burials, 1866-1885, by Decadal Age Groups

0-10 years   20
of which seven were under 1; five were aged 1; four were aged 2-4; four were aged 5-10

11-20	12		
21-30	15		
31-40	6		
41-50	8		
51-60	13		
61-70	11 (includes John and Harriet Sirgood)		
71-80	10		
81-90	9	**Total**	**104**

Table 4.5 highlights three peaks, children up to 10 years, young adults and those in their fifties. Child deaths became rarer after 1885. It marks not just an improving life expectancy for the young, but also a growing belief in the community that marriage and procreation should be discouraged. Nevertheless, the large proportion of child funerals, of which a third are of infants under one year old, casts the early Dependants in a very different light from those in living memory. It has been speculated that smallpox took a toll in the 1860s and 1870s. In 1880, infectious and parasitic diseases still caused one third of all England & Wales deaths. Many adults succumbed to TB in their 20s to 50s. The survivors of these young families were the backbone of the community as it entered the 20th century. Moreover, an unknown number must have left to make a life outside the community, probably, like their non-Dependant peers moving to work in towns and to London. Of the older deaths, it is a salutary reminder that those who lived longest had been born before 1800, over 50 years before Sirgood first came to Loxwood. Table 4.6 examines these remarkable 18th century survivors more carefully.

Loxwood's Sphere of Influence

As has been mentioned above, the early burials were almost all local to Loxwood Chapel. There were several who might have attended meetings in Mrs Carter's Newpound house, including the Luffs. Benjamin Hayler may have moved from there to Warnham in the 1870s

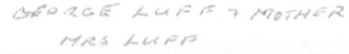

PLATE 4.2

Dependant Funerals – Rare Images

Fig 1 – Lucy Luff's mother Frances 'Fanny' (or 'Granny') Luff, 1813-1901) with her son George Luff, Lucy's brother, a baker at Northchapel. George died 1930.

Fig 2 – Lucy Luff (1853-1937) whose funeral is depicted here. Lucy and her younger sister, Ellen, were Warnham stalwarts, directors of Lindfield Luff & Co, Warnham Stores. No photo of Ellen survives but she was one of the mourners at Lucy's funeral. Ellen died 1949.

Fig 3 and 4 – Sombre scenes at the grave will have contrasted with joyous thanksgiving inside the chapel. Lucy died 4 February and was buried on 10 February 1937. Note the heavy Sussex clay!

about the time the chapel there opened. However, it can be inferred from table 4.6 that even elderly folk travelled quite a distance to Loxwood services in the early days.

Table 4.6   Births and Residence of Oldest Dependants Buried at Loxwood between 1866 and 1885

	Birth	Death	Age	Place of birth	Place of death	Address at death
(Loxwood unless stated)						
James Sandford	1783	1866	83	Wisb Gn	Loxwood	Four Houses
Mary Ayling	1783	1869	85	Kirdford	Plaistow	White Acre, K'ford
George Smithers	1785	1867	82	Kirdford	Loxwood	Little Songhurst
Charlotte Smart	1790	1879	89	Lurgashall	Wisb Gn	Rickmans, Wisb Gn
Elizabeth Smithers	1790	1875	85	Kirdford	Loxwood	Little Songhurst
James Etherton	1790	1873	83	Wisb Gn	Loxwood	Skiff, prev Barnfold
Hannah Sopp	1791	1870	79	Kirdford	Wisb Gn	Holdens Cott, K'fd
Harriett Foster	1792	1867	75	Pulboro	Loxwood	Four Houses
Mary Etherton	1793	1869	79	Kirdford	Loxwood	Skiff, prev Barnfold
William Randall	1794	1871	77	Kirdford	Loxwood	Parish Cott, K'fd
Benjamin Hayler	1795	1877	81	Pulboro	Warnham	Wellers, Np'd Comn
Stephen Overington	1796	1868	72	Wisb Gn	Loxwood	Four Houses
Hannah Covey	1799	1880	81	Wisb Gn	Wisb Gn	Lunns, Wisb Gn
Samuel Etherton	1799	1883	83	Wisb Gn	Wisb Gn	Bittles, Wisb Gn
Charlotte Overington	1800	1868	68	Wisb Gn	Loxwood	Four Houses

Note: it has proved impossible to verify some of these dates in other sources. The burial register, however, has proved to be accurate.

Jerrome quotes from Frank Talbot, *"Within a short space of time, Sirgood had a congregation of 200 people within a three-mile radius of Loxwood. Meetings were held of say 12 to 15 persons or less in the cottage homes of his followers Sunday afternoons and on summer evenings open-air meetings to preach the Gospel on Roundstreet Common, Newpound, Wisborough Green, Kirdford, Mackerels Common, Plaistow, Tismans Common and Alfold"*.

The existence of a number of worshippers from Kirdford and Wisborough village and farms at this stage is interesting if only because no chapel was erected later, the preference being for sites remote from the Anglican churches in these two parishes, at Loxwood and later Plaistow. As described in Chapter 2, the hamlet of Four Houses in Loxwood was an early cluster.

Religion was a family matter. This small sample has three married couples and two Etherton brothers (in some sources Etherington, as also Overton for Overington). It might be expected that some Dependant families had attended other non-conformist places of worship before joining. One such family was that of James and Mary Etherton, who had two children baptised at the Calvinist Chapel in Wisborough Green in 1826 and 1828, though they used St Peter's (the parish church in Wisborough) later. It may well have been the case that some of those who occasionally attended Dependant meetings strayed away. Data is, unsurprisingly, lacking on this, but there are hints. Another unrelated Loxwood Etherton family buried their 14-year old daughter Eliza in 1867 in the chapel graveyard, but they themselves were not buried there when their time came.

Table 4.7   Years in which Elders Officiated at Funerals in Loxwood, 19ᵗʰ Century

Henry Rogers	1866	(Congregational Minister in Petworth, born in Gloucestershire)
Thomas Overington	**1866-1893***	**Loxwood**
John Sirgood	1866-1881	
Peter Pacy	1867	Plaistow
John Overington	**1867-1907***	**Loxwood**
James Overington	1867	Loxwood
William Spooner	1887	Northchapel
William Hampshire	1888	Lordshill
Benjamin Piper	1888-1943	Warnham
Ann Overington	1888 (with Benjamin Piper) Loxwood	
Jesse Puttock	1889-1919	Loxwood
Stephen Franks	1891-1898	Lordshill
Henry Piper	1894-1907	Warnham
Eli Herrington	1896-1916	Loxwood
Thomas Rugman	1896-1928	Loxwood
James Pannell	1897	Loxwood
Mark Covey	1899	Loxwood

* Periods of dominance in bold indicate the recognised senior elder.
No attempt has been made to show the number of funerals led by any elder. Location is where they lived.

Table 4.8   Funerals Led by John Sirgood

John Sirgood led eight funerals.

Ann Woods	1866
William Durant	1869
William Raymond	1872
Caroline Booker	1875
Harriet Sirgood	1876
Felix Foster	1880
Jane Holden	1881
Alfred Pannell	1884

The Role of Elders, Exemplified in the Leading of 19ᵗʰ Century Funeral Meetings

Leadership was concentrated in one or two individuals, who may have been anointed by Sirgood, yet was also shared much more widely when appropriate by others who sat "behind the desk" in services. The Burial Registers always named the person officiating. Whilst the Overington brothers dominated chapel life as elders in Loxwood, William Hampshire (died 1900) and John Rugman (died 1904) did the same at Lordshill. At Warnham, Henry Piper (died 1921) was described as the "father of Warnham Church" (Dependants sometimes referred to their places of worship as churches).

Many Dependants became involved in their 20s, so, inevitably, those with vision and drive would quickly lead their peers. An appreciation (author unknown) of Samuel Rugman, elder

PLATE 4.3

Portraits of Loxwood

Fig 1 – Ann Overington, 1833-1910, sister to Tom, Loxwood's first elder, a teacher and prominent Dependant sister in her own right. The only woman ever to take a funeral, and then jointly with Benjamin Piper in 1888.

Fig 2 – Peter Pacy, 1828-1905, preacher and early chapel trustee, head gardener and woodsman at Ifold estate, Plaistow. He only ever took one funeral in 1867.

Fig 3 – right, Kate Rugman, 1878-1977, a long life to 99. Became manager of the drapery department at The Combination Stores, having joined at 13 in 1891. Later the residents' cook. Daughter of Tom (Plate 4.1).

Fig 4 – left, Elsie Piper, 1898-2002, photographed on her 104th birthday. Married to George, originally from Kent, Elsie, née Randall, was born in Plaistow. They lived much of their lives in S Norwood, where George was the baker's roundsman at Northchapel, and one of the second generation of elders (died 1949), illustrates this, *"Some 40 years ago, Mr Rugman came to assist on the Business side, and he showed great integrity of character and gifts of leadership. Some 20 years ago he was elected to be thespiritual leader as well as the business manager."* By the 20th century, it was more likely that the elder of the chapel would also be business manager, or director, of the community's stores trading company. The evidence is necessarily circumstantial as the Society of Dependants was decidedly not hierarchical. Combination stores are dealt with in later chapters.

Funerals in the 20th century

Dependant funerals, when Brethren were "called home", were not supposed to be sad occasions, but the Dependant dress inevitably lends photographs a mournful appearance. That of Lucy Luff of Warnham illustrates this, as it is the only one where photographs survive, to the author's knowledge (Plate 4.2). Lucy had been at Warnham Stores (Lindfield, Luff & Co Ltd) since its beginning in the 1870s. Her funeral was on a cold early February day in 1937. She was 83. William Booker, also of Warnham, led the meeting. The first photograph shows a large gathering around the grave, after the coffin has been lowered into the stiff Sussex clay. A second photograph appeared in a local newspaper, which seems to show six pallbearers and a conventional coffin. Rowland Leswell wrote that he often measured up for a coffin and sent to the Horsham undertaker for it to be delivered. Lucy may well have first heard Sirgood preach at Gunshot Common, where her father was working on a farm. She remained unmarried and was survived by her Dependant siblings George and Ellen.

Table 4.9   Years in which Elders Officiated at Funerals in Loxwood, 20th Century

Henry Aylward	**1905-1938***	**Loxwood**
William Newman	1908	Haslemere
William Booker	1909-1949	Warnham
James Brightman	1911	South Norwood
Samuel Rugman	1935-46	Northchapel
Walter Nash	**1936-1960***	**Loxwood**
Walter Hart	1938	Hove
Frederick Greenfield	1947	Hove
N Piper	1948	
J Stevens	1949	
Rowland Leswell	1958-1980	Loxwood
Alfred Goodwin	**1960-1991***	**Loxwood**
Cyril Killner	1961-1966	Loxwood
Mr JM Coombs	1986	
Roy P Barbour	1992-2002	Emmanuel Fellowship
Mr Bonsey	1992	
John Crocombe	1996	

* Periods of dominance in bold indicate the recognised senior elder.
No attempt has been made to show the number of funerals led by any elder. Location is where they lived.

A photograph in Muggeridge's book about the history of Warnham purports to be of a Dependant funeral, but the same photo is in Diana Chatwin's book, *Slinfold Street*, 2000. Chatwin has positively identified the house in the background, and it is doubtful a Dependant would have had the wreaths shown. As there were no burials in Warnham, Muggeridge should have realised it could not be correct – perhaps the Victorian dress fooled him. Burials were in unmarked (but recorded) graves with mounds in serried rows. The mounds were later flattened when there was no one left to tend them by hand. The burial ground remains to this day a sheltered, peaceful and sacred spot.

The evidence in Tables 4.7 and 4.9 for officiating at funerals gives strong clues to the leadership by elders at Loxwood. Table 4.9 clearly highlights three elders who were the effective leaders of community worship during the 20th century. Henry Aylward (died 1939, Plate 4.1) came from Sevenoaks, soon to become chairman of Aylward, Smith & Co (the trading company of Loxwood Dependants). He had commenced in the male dominated bakery by 1891. He was the "employer" in the 1901 census, and emerged as elder from about 1909, following the death of John Overington two years before. Walter Nash (died 1960, Plate 4.1) took on the leadership in the late 1930s through to the end of the 50s. At his death, a rare personal tribute was minuted by the Secretary of Aylward, Smith & Co (Bessie Hempstead), *"A tribute was paid to our deceased Director Walter Nash to whom we owe so much, for his life of unselfishness, and all his efforts for the benefit of all, for his steadfast example, and Quiet Spirit. His absence was much felt but the same bond of love and concern still remains. Thanks was rendered to God for every blessing."*

Alfred Goodwin (died 1996, Plate 4.1), who had come to Loxwood many years before from the Norwood community, was the main officiator at funerals for the remainder of the time the dwindling band of Brethren met at the chapel. He said he took over 70, including those of both his sisters, Bessie and May. Alfred became a Director of Aylward, Smith at the same time, 1960. He was assisted in his chapel duties by Rowland Leswell (died 1984), who had joined the Dependants from the Peculiars in Essex in 1940. Leswell became Secretary to the Trustees of Loxwood Dependant Church and other funds, including the trust for The Retreat (the home for older members) in 1979, when Bessie Hempstead (Company Secretary of Aylward, Smith) was in ill health. He arranged for local non-Dependants to become trustees of The Retreat so that it could function long-term as a Memorial Home of the Dependants. *"I feel that I have achieved a little during my life and hope that the work of the Lord will continue in Loxwood, and many may find Jesus as their Saviour and Redeemer"*, he wrote.

Such was the power of a Dependant funeral meeting for its participants, Elsie Piper (who died 2002 aged 104), when 17 years old wrote a 13-page description of a meeting following the death on 13th February 1917 of Charlie Hackman [not buried in Loxwood, probably Shamley Green], in her notebook. She entitled it *"A brief account of a very glorious meeting at Lord's Hill on the 19th Feb., after putting away the remains of our dear Br. C. Hackman One of the most beautiful times ever spent in God's house was that Monday evening."* See Chapter 8 for a full account.

The Final Years at Loxwood

Alf Goodwin has spoken on tape about the final years. Among the last to give testimony other than himself was Elsie, wife of Leslie Killner. However, when she fell and broke her hip, he had to ask himself, "How will we survive?". Asked on tape how the community would survive, Alf thought for a while, clearly uncomfortable, but his answer was that all members had been "edified", all comforted. Inevitability of closure was a distressing reality. He added, sadly, "latterly they did not come, there was a lack of desire (his emphasis)." Rowland Leswell, chapel trustee, died the same year. There were others attending services with Alf, but not giving testimony (including three members of the Killner family who were described in Chapter 2). Others were too frail to attend. Both Elsie and Leslie Killner lived on into the 1990s at their bungalow in Spy Lane, and Alf also, at Rose Cottage, but from 1982 there was no future for the chapel as a Dependant place of worship. The chapel closed in 1982 when Alf was away visiting a sister community in Germany. He went on to take another 10 funerals, but it would fall to the pastor of the Emmanuel Fellowship, Roy Barbour, to continue after that, and to take Alf Goodwin's in 1996. It is fortunate that Roy's group are willing to continue worship in this small but historic building. It has even become something of a meeting place for the community in Loxwood. The Spy Café is open every Thursday, 10.00 to 4.30. Its reach is well beyond the Sunday congregation.

How Many Dependants Were There?

Sirgood could claim the attention, if not the allegiance, of nearly half the agricultural working class by the 1860s, it was said. There were 543 burials at Loxwood between 1876 and 2002, but this greatly underestimates the total number as an unknown number were buried in local parish churches, mostly those from other communities, especially those at a distance. A total of 851 deaths were recorded, thus including some of those buried elsewhere, and a tiny handful of close relatives. This is still well below the total one would like to know! One undated estimate of those from the south of Surrey (i.e., in the sphere of influence of Lordshill), made by an unknown hand, was 60 named and located individuals. Such numbers are subject to difficulties such as movement from one community to another.

The Times reported on the 1904 election, suggested there might be 400-500 Dependant men who might not cast their votes in the Horsham Division. As women did not have the franchise, the number was, in reality, double that. Alf Goodwin claims there were 200-300 at the first Big Meeting he attended in 1915, when he cycled from Norwood to Loxwood to attend. In 1926, it was reported in The News Chronicle that 100 attended a Big Meeting at Loxwood, and the next year the Derby Telegraph estimated it could be double that. In 1931, the Sunday Express suggested 1000 members in total; an Australian newspaper also estimated 1000 members in the same year, perhaps taking information from the Express. A more recent magazine article The Gentle Folk, late 1980s, quoted a higher figure of 2000-3000 in the 1930s. P Cooney, from Lordshill, 1983, suggested that around the year 1900 total estimates ranged from 1,500 to 3,000, but Viscount Turnour (Later Earl Winterton) wrote in 1904 in his oft-quoted National Review article (reprinted 1931 in Sussex County Magazine) that there were by then only 900. The fog of war is as nothing compared to the fog of religious observance! There is, moreover, a discrepancy between the interwar numbers and the 19th century ones, if the accepted view of slow decline is accepted. The real question, which cannot be accurately answered, is when did decline commence and from what peak?

A question also worth consideration is what proportion of the communities joined the brethren? The villages may have had populations under 1000, so a couple of hundred members might be 20% or more, a not inconsiderable proportion, higher if children are omitted. No wonder some Anglicans felt under threat in the early days. In 1871, Wisborough Green and Loxwood together had 1,756 people. Loxwood would have had only about one-third of this. Warnham had 1,007. Wonersh, including Shamley Green and Lordshill had 1,561, again with only the smaller proportion in Shamley Green. South Norwood, on the other hand had 3,634 people. Here, the Dependants had to exist alongside a wide selection of churches, and a fast-growing London suburban population at that.

In 1957, Charles Wickens of Henfield wrote in an authoritative tone suggesting that at Sirgood's death there were 2000-3000, in 1957, 400-500. Marion May, in *The Story of the Dependants,* suggested at John Sirgood's death in 1885, it had been said there were 2000 followers, in 1916, 600, in 1942, 200 and in 1983 just 30. The vicar of Warnham reported a peak membership in his village of 100-200 but did not venture a date. Rowland Leswell was quoted in the Argus newspaper in 1982 saying that Loxwood had 200 members at the peak (he only came to Loxwood in the 1940s, so his figure may date from then), by 1982 down to 32. He is also quoted saying the stores would have employed 35. This is a similar number to other stores, such as Warnham in the Edwardian period.

After the Second World War, numbers were easier to compute as the total shrank. A reliable figure for Loxwood came in 1947, when Sarah Woods wrote a short memoir on her life. She reckoned attendance at the Loxwood chapel at the time was between 50 and 60 each service. Several sources refer to numbers barely in double figures attending chapel services post-war in smaller communities like Hove. The pathetic story in The People, December 1963, of just two at a Lordshill service underlines the total collapse of the Dependants as a credible faith group in the 1960s and 70s.

Loxwood Dependants, 1861 and 1911

An attempt has been made using the burial and death registers and census information from 1861 and 1911, the latter the most recent census available, to compute numbers of Loxwood Dependants. Family members not so recorded are excluded.

One insurmountable research obstacle was the impossibility of verifying when an individual or family was first converted to the Dependant way. It seems very likely that a majority of those who were adults, and many who were teenagers, in 1861, would have joined in the initial phase of preaching in the 1850s. The validity of the data must therefore take into account possible later conversion. The burial of some as early as the 1860s, the known importance of some as elders or preachers of the church, or their relatives, the identification of addresses at known locations where preaching took place at the time, and the likely enthusiasm of many joining in their teens or twenties all point to early take up. Some caution must, however, be noted.

In 1861, the parish of Wisborough Green included Loxwood, and the parish of Kirdford included Plaistow. It was thought sensible, and indeed more accurate in terms of the sphere of influence of Loxwood as a nodal location (and residence of the Sirgoods) to include all

4. Loxwood Registers and Funerals

those with clear links to Loxwood in both parishes, as well as a small number in Rudgwick, together with Surrey parishes Alfold, Cranleigh and Dunsfold. During the process of extracting names from the registers, the view of Jerrome and others was reinforced. Numerous converts were recruited and were meeting at this time in house groups and on common land across the district, and that once Loxwood chapel was up and running after 1861, were likely to visit this chapel, often having family connections in Loxwood too.

In Wisborough parish 116 names emerged from the analysis, including some who were still children in 1861. In Kirdford, there were another 62 (including four who were then in Warnham but moved to Plaistow Place later). In other parishes, there were eight in Rudgwick, seven in Alfold, seven in Cranleigh, and six in Dunsfold. This gives a total of over 200 possible Dependants, a figure not dissimilar to that in 1911. There may be others who did not remain long in the sect and drifted away long before the end of their life, when the registers confirm membership. The likelihood is that numbers peaked sometime in the period between these dates as younger converts swelled the congregations, and the chapels and combination stores provided increasing nodality. In 1861, however, there was, one imagines, a raw intensity of newfound faith and comradeship in these rural backwaters. It was at exactly this time that local clergy, landowners and other pillars of the community were becoming alarmed, as has been described in Chapter 1.

Wisborough Green and Loxwood, 1861

In Wisborough parish only 14 could be said to be living in Wisborough village or farms in the vicinity; another 15 were living in Newpound, a significant number in this hamlet, known to have been a centre of preaching, together with four at Bittles, just north of Newpound. In the modern Loxwood parish, outlying southern areas were also significant: nine at or close to Roundstreet Common on the road to Newpound, and on Skiff Lane a significant cluster of 19, most of whom were living around Gunshot Common. To the east of the village there were families at Barnfold, Crabtree and Drungewick Hill. To the north, as has been noted elsewhere, Four Houses, Cuckolds Corner and Songhurst had a few. To the west there were some at Ifold Kennels.

It was in the village of Loxwood that most were found. Unsurprisingly, Spy Lane, where the Sirgoods lived, and where the new chapel was built, had the largest cluster. As well as fourteen living on the short length of Spy Lane, and one in Pancake Lane, there were six on Chapel Green (now Station Road) and another eight on the village street at Willetts, Blackwool, and the turnpike toll house. Another couple were in the Brewhurst Mill locality.

Spy Lane is of special significance. The fourteen known Dependants who lived here in 1861 included both the Sirgoods and the Overingtons. Starting from the end now opposite North Hall, two timber-framed cottages are the first pre-1861 houses to be seen, Pound Cottage and Little Pound Farm. Two non-Dependant families are followed by George and Harriett Denyer, and Charles and Emily Denyer. Emily's husband appears not to have been a Dependant at the end of his life. Probable non-Dependants William and Sarah Heather are next, but their daughter Catherine would later be a Dependant, married to Tom Rugman. Another large family follows. Thus, six families could have occupied these two cottages, suggesting there may have been another cottage. Next, Tom and Ann Overington and their children Lucy and Thomas lived in The Old Cottage opposite the site of the chapel, confirmed by a later census. The Sirgoods also lodged here. Furthermore, the Overington grandparents, Obadiah and Ruth, with Tom's brother, Dependant Obed, were at Cuckolds Corner across the fields. Charles and Mary Kitchener follow next and then Thomas and Martha Marriner. Martha was a Dependant, but probably not her husband. There were a couple of cottages here which have subsequently been lost. Around the corner in Pancake Lane were William Bonsey, a Dependant, and his wife Mary, and on Chapel Green, the Foster, Pacy and Marriner families, whilst at Willetts were the Hamshire family. However, there were no Dependants living on the site of the future Combination Stores in 1861.

The surnames involved are those of the labouring class. Among the most frequently occurring are Covey, Denyer, Etherington, Foster, Greenfield, Jenner, Kitchener, Luff, Overington, Pacy, Randall, Reeves and Thayre. Relatively few can be identified as two-generation adult members at this stage. Forty altogether are agricultural labourers. The next most numerous were brickmakers, just three of them. There are also five other males with occupations including shoemaker (Sirgood himself) and grocer (Felix Foster). Very few women have occupations, there being only five in service at this stage, two laundresses, and the great majority married women of no occupation. There was no sign of the later trend to singleton status. Ten-year old George Luxford of Orfold Farm Wisborough was the only identified schoolboy. We may assume all but a few of the Dependants were illiterate. 24 married couples can be identified, 15 without dependent offspring at home in 1861 (though this needs further analysis as older and future children are not included). A further four were widowed. The overwhelming majority remained in Loxwood (or Wisborough) until the end of their lives. Two notable exceptions were the Luff and Reeves families who went on to become stalwarts of the Warnham community and are both featured in other chapters.

Kirdford and Plaistow, 1861

Kirdford village, like Wisborough, was home to fewer than were living further north. Plaistow was without doubt an important location of Dependant growth, remote from the mother parish church in Kirdford. Sixteen of those identified lived in the hamlet itself, but the census is bleak territory to identify the exact cottages. However, Rickmans Lane, where the chapel would briefly thrive later, was an already identifiable location. Also close to Plaistow hamlet were Quennells House and Common House, both to the east and, nearer Loxwood, Little Wephurst and Ifold New Lodge (home of Peter Pacy, whose preaching in Plaistow may have contributed as much as Sirgood himself to this community). To the north and north-west were others at Shorts, Lyons, Parkgate and Kings Park, in the direction of Shillinglee. To the south, closer to Kirdford, there were, thinly spread, Dependants at Mackerels, Pound and Steers Commons, as well as a few in the village. Surprisingly, two families lived way south in Strood Common. West of Kirdford and Plaistow, allegiances might be expected to be more towards Northchapel, and this is indeed the case in the remote wooded country of Ebernoe, Colhook and west of Balls Cross, but some of the local inhabitants of these areas had stronger links to Plaistow. Some Kirdford families such as the Spooners moved to Northchapel during the 1860s. These are excluded from the numbers.

As in Wisborough, Kirdford resonates with local Sussex family names: Bentley, Denyer, Eames, Herrington, Marriner, Pacy, Pannell, Puttock, Randall and Tickner to name the most frequently occurring. Some of these also occur in Wisborough. As might be expected, there is considerable cross-marriage within and around these parishes. One irritant to research was that no marriage could be found for several men who clearly had wives. Perhaps the difficulty of getting to church to marry was a factor. Two were brothers: James and Eli Herrington and their wives Ellen and Esther. Twenty-two of the 26 men and older boys were agricultural labourers, of whom one had a second occupation of wood dealer. There was also one small-scale farmer, Alfred Tickner, with 50 acres at Lyons Farm. Two men were carpenters, one a farrier. Six women were in service, one other a schoolteacher, Sarah Eames, originally from Leicestershire, wife of John in Rickmans Lane. There was not one school child in the parish. One 'scholar', Richard Nightingale, still only six, who was still at home in Warnham, would soon move to Plaistow Place (see Chapter 2) where he would emerge as a leader of the Plaistow Dependants. The occupations in Kirdford were therefore broadly similar to those in Wisborough. One significant difference between the two parishes is that the Kirdford residents may be divided between those who stayed and those who left for Loxwood. As many as 27 individuals are recorded in the registers as dying in Wisborough parish, most of them in Loxwood. As described elsewhere, Plaistow chapel was not long-lived, and the Plaistow Place community dispersed even earlier.

Wisborough Green, Kirdford and Other Neighbouring Parishes, 1861

Taking both parishes and the other parishes referred to above together, seventeen were aged over 60, all except one or two, therefore, born in the 18th century in 1801 or earlier. Fourteen were born in the 1802-1811 decade, so in their fifties in 1861. The numbers are rising among the 40-50 age group, 37 in total, with most born towards the end of the 1812-1821 period. 35 were aged 30-40, being born 1822-1831. Another 35 were aged 20-30, born 1832-41. Finally, 39 of the 10-20 generation were either Dependants or soon-to-be Dependants. Clearly the faith taught by John Sirgood had appeal for young and old alike, and as each generation came of age his charisma and Christian message were accepted eagerly. Only six 30 years old and over were single, and another six aged 25-29: the widely held view of Dependant singledom had not yet taken hold.

Finally, analysis of place of birth shows that the overwhelming majority were born in either Wisborough (77) or Kirdford (64). When compared to the ratio of 116 (Wisborough) to 62 (Kirdford) in parish of residence, this indicates an astonishing lack of recognition in all the literature known to the author of the importance of Kirdford, and Plaistow in particular, in the history of the Dependant sect. To be fair, Jerrome referred to numerous locations known to have been important for outdoor preaching right across the parishes of Wisborough, Kirdford and Northchapel and so this finding should not be as surprising as it may seem.

When movement was very much harder than today it made geographical sense that Warnham, Loxwood and Northchapel, rather than Rudgwick and Kirdford/Plaistow located in between, would become meeting centres. Rudgwick, however, has always been the odd one out in that far fewer Dependants had any connection – only eleven born there, only eight living there in 1861. A similar picture emerges from the data when examining the Surrey names. Only eight were born in Alfold, one in Cranleigh, one in Ewhurst, five in Dunsfold, and one in Chiddingfold. There was a clear geographical separation between the

Lordshill community and the Sussex ones to the south. Of course, female birth places range more widely as marriage brought people together, and a few couples were noted as in-migrants from other nearby parishes.

It is probably true to say that the great migrations of rural folk across a wide swathe of southern England, particularly pulled by urban work, was only just picking up steam in 1861. The intended pun in that statement reminds us that the LB&SC railway from Guildford to Horsham did not arrive at Rudgwick, Cranleigh and Bramley stations until 1865. Without the rail connections, John Sirgood could not have accomplished his travels, and the converts in Kent, for example, could never have moved across to the Sussex and Surrey communities as they did in later decades. Not long after, Chapel Green in Loxwood would become Station Road!

Loxwood and Plaistow, 1911

Table 6.3 (1911 census, Loxwood) includes about 200 persons, both individuals and families, many the last of their kind, as very few are included who were born *after* 1911, and many of the younger brethren and sisters in 1911 died single or, if married, without children or with children who left the Dependants. Within the 200 are a considerable number who, putting it plainly, came to Loxwood to die. As arguably the most sustainable community in the 1960s and 70s and later years, there was a steady trickle of Dependants from other communities, and from nearby parishes (Alfold and Plaistow especially) to Loxwood.

In some cases, they lived in Dependant properties: The Combination Stores, Hall House, Jubilee Villas, The Old Cottage (Noah's Ark) and Rose Cottage all neighbouring the Combination Stores; Old Cottage and New Cottages in Spy Lane, or later The Retreat, also Spy Lane, all neighbouring the chapel. In some other cases they joined forces with other brethren or sisters occupying private houses. There are some houses in Loxwood that are repeatedly mentioned, both in the 1911 census and as final homes at the time of death which seem to have been occupied continuously by Dependants for perhaps 70 to 100 years. A few of these were: Hill Grove on Pancake Lane; Oak Grove on Spy Lane; Tollgate House, Canal Villa and Penfold House in the High Street near the river. In Station Road, among other houses, were Church Cottage and another Rose Cottage.

In 1911, more outlying houses in Loxwood had Dependant families than was the case later: at Alfold Bars, Pawlies Farm, New Songhurst Farm, Roundstreet, and Newpound. There were also seven in Alfold. Michael Killner Jr. and family were in Billingshurst, soon to move to Alfold House. Michael Sr. was in Kirdford. The Killners were easily the largest extended Dependant family in Loxwood and Alfold in the mid-20th century.

At Plaistow, for which there is more detail in Chapter 2, there were about 30 in 1911 (Table 4.10). As well as Plaistow Place (Richard Nightingale's community) and Oakhurst (George Luff's family) there were the Denyers in the village, possibly at Melbourne House, the Baverstocks at Barkfold, the Herringtons and Durrants at Shorts. But of most interest are three families living in Rickmans Lane. The Randalls were at Chapel Cottage adjoining another mission room; the Britts were at Zion House, the cottage attached to Plaistow

Dependant Chapel, still called this today; the Belchambers were at Rose Cottage. There was no community as such, just individual families, and a chapel.

Table 4.10   1911 census, Plaistow Community, (excluding Plaistow Place)

Zion House, Rickmans Lane Plaistow			Place of birth
Henry Britt	62	labourer	Preston Brighton
Harriett Britt	61		West Grinstead Sx
Herbert Kidby	52	house painter	Tenterden Kt
Rickmans Lane Plaistow			
William Belchamber	66	labourer	Kirdford Sx
Eliza Belchamber	64		Kirdford Sx
Chapel Cottage Rickmans Lane Plaistow			
George Randall	54	farm labourer	Kirdford Sx
Ellen Randall	56		Kirdford Sx
Plaistow village			
George Denyer	73	farm labourer	Kirdford Sx
Harriett Denyer	76		Kirdford Sx
Plaistow village			
Alfred Tickner	85	pensioner	Plaistow Sx
Annie Buck	33	housekeeper	Warnham Sx
Plaistow Street			
Martha Denyer	63		Warnham Sx
Martha Mugridge	39	assistant (dau)	Plaistow Sx
Barkfold Farm Plaistow			
George Baverstock	67	farmer	Wisborough Green Sx
Sarah Baverstock	67		Wisborough Green Sx
Maryann Puttock	49	servant	Petworth Sx
Shorts Farm Plaistow			
Charles Durrant	41	hoopmaker	Kirdford Sx
Emily Durrant	39		Kirdford Sx
Shorts Farm Cottage Plaistow			
William Herrington	74	farm labourer	Kirdford Sx
Caroline Herrington	66	tailoress	Kirdford Sx
Clarks Strood Green Plaistow			
Maria Foster	81		Kirdford Sx

Another trend was for Norwood Dependants to move to Loxwood after 1911, notably the Goodwins, together with the Manns, the Pykes, the Butchers and the Walls, together with Helen Gifford and Christopher Hale from Norwood Stores and Alice Carpenter from a subsidiary Dependant grocer's in Croydon. Very few from nearer communities made this transition, some exceptions being Elsie Street from Wonersh Mill, Edith Bradshaw from Lordshill Stores, Sarah Kennard from Northchapel Stores and the Kennards who came to Loxwood from Brighton. Later, there was a Norwood drift to Loxwood for end of life care.

A measure of the spread, albeit very thin, of Dependants migrating from other nearby places is: the Garmans from Broadbridge Heath, Manns and Francis from Cranleigh, Franks from Epsom, Kitcheners from Hardham, near Pulborough, Phillips from near Haslemere, Pullens from Horsham, and Boxalls from near Petworth. Then, there are the continuing migrants from Kent: two Cronk families, and from the Peculiars in Essex: the Hempsteads and Leswells.

There is no doubt that these migrations to the centre strengthened the Loxwood community in the middle of the 20th century. The names Hempstead, Leswell, Phillips, Goodwin and Killner are particularly represented as elders and/or company directors.

A German Connection

For a close-knit mainly rural community the brethren made an astonishing leap in fostering international links with Germany between the 1930s and 1970s. No other such links emerge from research, not even with dominions of the Empire or the United States. It has been suggested the Germans made the first contact, having heard of a community not unlike their own. Certainly, Harry Aylward and Walter Nash were enthusiastic, and Alf Goodwin states that Nash went to Germany first in 1950, and twice more, the last in 1957; Alf himself went in 1949. The first communication was in 1935 in a letter to Henry Aylward. Soon, two came over to Warnham, and two Dependants (Sydney Croucher, Norwood, and Ben Piper, Warnham) returned to Germany for a month. Who spoke whose language is not remembered! The 1935, or perhaps 1936, visit is validated by a group photo taken at Warnham, with the two Germans identified but unnamed, also by a letter sent by William Garrett from Ealing (an unknown brother) to Sister Göthe in Hamburg, 25 September 1935. Translation of the dense biblical references and discussion must have been a challenge.

The Loxwood death register includes several often misspelt or incompletely named German brethren. The seventeen in Table 4.11, below, are an attempt to rationalise the spelling and to show any connections (author's suggested corrections in brackets).

Table 4.11   The German Connection (listed by recorded date of death)

1950	Annie	BYER [BEYER], Schwerin Sister, "mother" [her mother?]
1950	Gretel	WEBER, Neustadt [Neustadt, Bavaria or Neustadt, Mecklenburg]
1955	-	GÖTHE, "mother"
1957	Fritz	SCHUE [SCHEU], Bruckberge [Bruckberg]
1961		BRUNO [BRUNOW], Schwerin, bro Bruno suddenly called home, Rowland's father [Roland]
1962	-	HELDAGARD [HILDEGARD, a first name], "mother"
1962	George MEYER, 75 [Georg]	
1962	-	RENN [REHN]
1963	Henry	EDLEAMAN [EDELMAN], 78
1964	Otto	SIEGMEYER
1965	Maria	HUTTONER [HUTTNER], Shobdach [Shabdach is a surname]
1966	Hedi	CONRAD [Heidi], Steinburg [??] Steinberg, Bavaria
1966	Leia	SCHU [SCHEU], Fritz's wife, Bruckberge [Bruckberg]
1966	Erika	GÖTHE, 79, Schwerin
1967	Hellen	GÖTHE, Schwerin
1973	Marie	HUTTNER
1973	Herman VOGEL [Hermann]	

This is an intriguing list, as it confirms Schwerin in northern Germany as a location. It also raises the possibility of other places, including in Bavaria. Three sources confirm that the town the German Brethren came from was Schwerin, a town of nearly 100,000 people today, east of Lübeck in the state of Mecklenburg. The town is situated alongside a large lake in an attractive setting, with a castle, both of which attract tourists. Loxwood and Warnham visitors must have enjoyed their visits. By 1945, Schwerin, once the seat of the Grand Duchy of Mecklenburg, was in the Soviet zone, and so became part of East Germany. Schwerin is overwhelmingly Protestant. One other link with Schwerin has been found. Walter Nash's sister, Emily, received a postcard of Schwerin from Anni [?Beyer] and Erika [?Göthe] in 1937, showing the town and high school (Stadt und Lyzeum).

In the list above, the place name Bruckberg also occurs. Bruckberg, is a small village near Ansbach, south west of Nürnburg in the Franconia region of Bavaria. In Emily Nash's postcard collection there are two cards written in German from "M & M", both received in 1954, both a photo of a tourist destination near Ansbach: Rothenburg ob der Tauber and Wassertrüdingen.

There is as far as can be judged, just one church, St Martin's, in Bruckberg, built coincidentally in 1935, for the Evangelical Mission in Bavaria (Franconia is largely Protestant). This organisation had strong mission origins not only in Germany but in Australia, USA, and particularly Papua in the Far East. Its leader also developed relations with the Nazis by support for the NSDAP, although the church did not. Could this organisation have made a link with Sussex? It is a step too far to say it was.

Another, larger settlement called Bruckberg, near Landshut in Lower Bavaria, north of Munich, is a less likely candidate, in the author's opinion, as it is much further away from the two towns featured in the postcards.

Jerrome quotes from an anonymous detailed account of the first of the three meetings held on 12 January 1936, when Germans from Bavaria were present. It was, he asserts, these Germans, no mention of Schwerin, who had written to Harry Aylward, having read about the Dependants in a newspaper. Reference is made to the testimony, and a prayer (in German), of Brother Poppe. From this he reasonably infers that the Bavarian link was the one continued after the war. Schwerin was by then behind the Iron Curtain.

There were, therefore, two communities which the Dependants developed links with, a city in the north and a village in the south. Contacts were kept up from 1935 to 1973, only broken, and surprisingly, the Nazi years and the war, followed by the division of Germany, but then neither would have bothered the Dependants.

A further Brighton (Hove) Brother was referred to in the death register as "1929, Henry Hunny [Huny or Hunne], 79, German Brother". There is no record of his death in England, so might this represent earlier contact than we have other evidence for?

PLATE 4.4   The German Connection

Fig 1 - A Warnham group photo taken when two unnamed German visitors were present in 1935 or 1936:
Germans: lady, back row, 5th from left; gentleman, back row, right.
Warnham Dependants;
(back L to R):
Mollie
Farquhar, Nellie
Lindfield, Gwen
Bradshaw,
Bessie Booker,
German, Kate
Etherington,
May Madgwick,
May Mills,
German;
(front L to R):
Polly, Annie,
Sally Baker,
Lucy Miles,
Mary Booker.

Fig 2 – Location of Schwerin, south east of Lübeck.

Fig 3 - Location of Bruckberg, west of Nürnberg (Nurenburg), also locating Rothenburg ob der Tauber and Wassertrüdingen.

Maps © viamichelin.co.uk.

Chapter 5

Community Life and Combination Stores

From Benjamin Piper's Testimony (Warnham)

"There was a good number of Sisters in service who were serving worldly masters and mistresses, therefore they had not much liberty to be at the meetings. There was such a desire in Brother John Sirgood for the Sisters' welfare that he wanted them to have liberty, to be at the house of God to all be able to worship together, so he began to work on their behalf. He said to my father Henry Piper what he had in his mind, to be able to free the Sisters and they both helped each other in this wonderful work of love, and God also worked with them, and many Brethren also. This was the starting of our stores which now is. Note there was also much opposition but that did not stop God from working. There were very many earnest prayers delivered to God to bless and prosper the labour of the Saints' hands. This God answered and worked on behalf of the Sisters. Satan worked against it but God turned all his working into profit for his Saints who were striving together in love for each other and although this was started in the year 1879 it is still going on, the same love ruling, which is the love of Jesus that will last for ever.

In the Beginning....

Mick Reed, who has, uniquely, written an academic essay on Dependant co-operation, suggests that the origins of combination go back to the 1870s, quoting from hymns written at this time such as Hymn 64 in the Dependant Hymn Book:

Christ's combination stores for me / Where I can be so well supplied, / Where I can one with Brethren be / Where competition is defied.

Another has the refrain "Now combine" four times in each verse. It also exhorts, *"It makes us all in one complete, then combine"*. This concept of "spiritual one-ness" is also the case in a hymn written on Sirgood's death, quoted in Chapter 6. Reed ascribes this to St Paul, and points out that, as in dependance on Christ, one-ness is a millennial kind of belief in the Second Coming, and that "combination is achieved in spiritual devotions, prayer, scriptural awareness, and frequent collective worship". He then argues that *"the stores were the distinctive economic characteristic of the Dependent (sic) movement, and with their associated farms and other undertakings, were the physical manifestation of 'one-ness' or combination"*. Yet, combination is not a biblical ideal. It has more in common with earlier dissenting traditions, from the American Puritans to the Quakers, and to nineteenth century industrial and social pioneers such as Robert Owen at New Lanark Mills near Glasgow, or possibly to communism in its pure form. The word even had risky overtones from Pitt's 1799/80 anti-trade union Combination Acts forbidding combination for political reform, (though they had been repealed in 1824). Government, in living memory, had been afraid of commercial and social democracy.

It is striking that Sirgood seems to have promoted the good of the young women who came to believe his version of Christianity. The late 19th century saw a huge increase in opportunity for domestic service in households of the *nouveau riches*. However, this often took young girls barely out of puberty many miles away from home, with little money to return home, little time off, and daily drudgery "below stairs". Once sent into the outside community, getting to a Dependant meeting was difficult, but Sirgood reasoned that if they could be provided with service opportunities in their own or nearby communities, he could provide them with secure homes, keep them in the faith, and provide for the daily needs of their Brethren and the wider community.

As Peter Jerrome says, *"combination is in some ways the most enduring of John Sirgood's ideas"*. He regards it as a social, not a religious concept, which is not to say that religious groups do not espouse commerce. The Quakers are one group who certainly did. It is often said that it was contemporaneous with chapel building, but the evidence does not stack up. Loxwood Chapel was built in 1861. One might therefore expect to find a community created at the Combination Stores by the 1871 census, but this is not the case until 15 years later. However, retailing, as will be demonstrated, did have an early presence before 1880.

Stories of commerce in Northchapel date from 1881, possibly a spontaneous event beginning with the sale of lardy rolls and coal, as told later by Alf Goodwin. In a 1920s letter from Bert Newing at Warnham to his cousins Ethel and Nellie Gifford at South Norwood, he wrote that eggs and kettle holders were early trade goods, sold door to door. This may possibly refer to early trading in Warnham, where Bert was an upholsterer in the stores, arriving there in the 1890s. Jerrome tells the story in full, and he has also identified a reference to a letter written to "Warnham Stores" on 21st June 1879. George Piper's notebook contains another, the letter written by Sirgood to the stores in 1881. As Tables 5.4 on page 92 and 9.1 on page 173 demonstrate, Warnham had the only stores to be identifiable in the 1881 census. Another letter was written to "Northchapel Stores" on 3 June 1884. These indicate communities active enough and large enough to be living communally. There were, as in Loxwood, Dependant *families* running shops from the late 1850s or earlier. As such, some retail expertise was therefore available in the community. Nevertheless, Loxwood did not pave the way as did Warnham.

The generally quoted commencement date for retail communality as a Dependant experiment, project or concept is 1879. Sirgood is said to have "retired" in 1878. Perhaps the concept was very much in his dreams, until taking a back seat in religious terms enabled him to give full rein to developing his next project. The idea took root slowly at first, as and when funds and willing volunteers (as participants in either construction or living in at the store) emerged in each community. Leaders, mainly, but not exclusively, women, had to be found with the necessary business experience. Funds largely came from small shares purchased by members. Later, these were left to other Dependants in people's Wills, so that the purchase of new shares became rare.

Jerrome goes on to quote from a letter written by Sirgood in which he describes his busy life buying for the stores in London, and his zeal for combination *"I am so very busy getting combination goods ready.... I feel my zeal for combination is on the increase having had such proof from God that He loves it"*, but that he will rid the church of any *"that is not one with us"*. The move to set up stores was not universally approved of. He continued, *"... hard at it from four o'clock yesterday morning and was so strong and well till eleven that night and packed up twenty baskets of goods and sent them away"*. Moreover, he and his successors, were always on the lookout for those who might better serve the Dependants in a different community, and this accounts for many of those who were born in one locality but served much of their working life in another.

The Origins of Combination in a Dependant Family Business, the Example of Loxwood

Felix Foster lived in a cottage called Sheppards, one of the older houses in Spy Lane. Close by were the Pacy and Bonsey families. Peter Pacy's son, also Peter, became one of the most remembered preacher-disciples of John Sirgood. Foster, Pacy and William Bonsey were probably early Spy Lane converts in the 1850s, soon to be joined there by Tom Overington. Felix was an agricultural labourer born in Loxwood. He became a prominent Dependant. In the 1850s, he had taken shop premises then called Black Hole [Blackwool, now Black Hall] where there was also a blacksmith (Plot 249, Fig 1, Plate 6.1). This is only 100 yards or so north of the later site of the Combination Stores. Felix was recorded as the shopkeeper at Black Hall until his death, still only in his 50s, in 1880. His funeral taken by John Sirgood, perhaps a mark of his significance to the Brethren.

He and his wife Sarah (née Etherton) had had several children. Sarah, and Caroline, two of their daughters (Plate 5.1), continued to run the grocer's together, with a son Felix also at home, a carpenter by trade, and an indenture witness in 1883 (as his father had been in 1865). Another young Dependant, Owen Puttick, an agricultural labourer, was lodging there by 1881. Owen Puttick had been brought up at Orfold near Wisborough Green. He was a trustee of the chapel.

Another daughter, Mary, left home as a servant girl at ten (or younger) to live with William and Hannah Wells in Roundstreet Common, perhaps with free board and lodging to look after an elderly mother or a one-year-old toddler, either of whom may have been in her charge. It is unlikely therefore she had any schooling. William Wells was an ag lab, so unlikely to be able to afford domestic service. The Wells family were another Dependant family, born in the early 1820s, probably converts from the 1850s, as were the Fosters. Mary then had a spell in service in Lambeth before returning to Loxwood.

She returned from Lambeth, perhaps with new skills, to set up as a draper in the village. Her shop is listed in 1878 and again in 1882. Sarah Woods also remembers this shop, locating it at Loxwood Post Office and Stores. The building was then in the curtilage of Hall House (Plot 247, Fig 1, Plate 6.1). The 1881 census shows that she was joined by Hannah Osborne, another young, more experienced, draper, visiting from Northchapel (see section on Northchapel in this chapter).

By 1882, Foster's, grocers, was replaced by "Puttock and Co, grocers", whilst the drapers continued as "Foster & Co, drapers". Was Owen Puttick (the spelling was interchangeable) now nominally in charge? More realistically, one or more of the Fosters still ran the grocers. Sarah Woods, born in 1869, remembers Foster's shop in what later became the kitchen at Black Hall. This was before the Foster-Puttick marriage. In 1885, Mary Foster married Owen Puttick, who was also born in Wisborough parish in 1843, a little older than her. in 1897, the two shops were no longer listed in Kelly's Directory. In 1891 Owen, Mary and Amy were living at Black Hall, confirmed as no longer a shop, and no longer her mother's home. The Combination Stores had opened down the road, and Owen had obtained new work as a workman on the council roads. Curiously, a few months before his death at Jubilee Villas, he filled in the 1911 census form as 'labourer on farm', but in the next column incorrectly wrote 'butcher', then crossed it out. Well, somebody must have had to prepare meat for sale in the stores, and Dependants were notable jacks of all trades. If Mary worked in the stores' drapery department she did not let on in the censuses (a normal thing for married women to remain silent).

Returning to the 1881 census, it shows how the enumerator's 'walk' took in Station Road (Chapel Green, 14 households) to visit Loxwood Place Farm, then down to the Onslow Arms, taking in a number of cottages and houses, then returning to the Station Road junction heading northwards to Weavers (now Rose Cottage, photo Plate 5.2), where the Combination Stores would soon be built, crossing to Hall House next, before reaching Black Hall (Plate 5.2) and Penlands (Linden House). There being no names to identify the houses, it is left to research to unravel the geography, so I use modern names.

In 1876, the Ordnance Survey map of Loxwood has Rose Cottage and a further rectangular building nearer the pond (the pond is still a landmark on the corner today), probably a barn (Plot 225, Fig 1, Plate 5.1). The site would become the Combination Stores. Incidentally, the Post Office was then at another grocers, later called Hilltop Stores, which would be their only competitor for the public's attention until 1944, when it too was bought by the Dependants. Locations referred to above are also shown on the map in Plate A3.9.

To understand the location of the two Foster shops, and the homes of other Dependants, it helps to list the heads of household in "enumerator's order" in Table 5.1.

Table 5.1   1881 Census, Heads of Household in Loxwood Street

From Chapel Green south

Loxwood Place Farm	Charles Lovegrove, farm foreman
Willetts	**James Hampshire, woodman**
Loxwood Street	John & Edwin Elliott, grocers (Hilltop Stores, now Alameda & The Old Stores)
	William Wooldridge, shoemaker (Cherry Cottage)
	William Tickner, lath bender (Cherry Villa)
	James Hard, ag lab (Box Cottage)
	Daniel Puttock, sawyer (Ryley Cottage)
	Henry Heather, gardener (Ryley Cottage)
	George Standen, bootmaker (Finches)
	John Sopp, butcher (Mellow)
	Thomas Pratchett, grocer & baker (Garton)
	George Standen, farmer (Garton)
Onslow Arms Inn	Robert Knowles, innkeeper

From Chapel Green north

Loxwood Street	**James Overington, wood dealer** (Rose Cottage)
	Mary Foster, draper (Post Office and Store)
	John Overington, farmer of 10 acres (Hall House)
	Thomas Pacy, carpenter (Black Hall)
	Sarah Foster, grocer (Black Hall)
Penlands	George Goodwin, retired builder (Linden House)

Note: Dependant families in bold; modern property names in brackets.

Within a year of the census, the Foster's grocers' shop had become Puttick's, as described above. Table 5.1, with the drapers next to Hall House, indicates that James Overington, widower and Dependant, owned, leased, or rented the site of the future Combination Stores in 1881. Weavers, Rose Cottage, is still standing today, the same footprint as in 1876.

Overingtons, both in the other part of Rose Cottage and in Hall House, are significant Dependant neighbours. James was another of the Overington siblings who had become the backbone of the Dependants in Loxwood. His brother John and sister Jane lived opposite. A dame school was held in Hall House, under Elizabeth Carter, who lodged there; ten years earlier, Ann Overington, wife of Tom in Spy Lane, had been the schoolmistress. Thomas Pacy was brother of Peter, the preacher. George Standen later moved into Jubilee Villas when they were newly built next to the stores in the 1890s. James Hampshire died at Willetts in 1888. There was a strong sense of community among these neighbours, as there was in Spy Lane. There were numerous Puttocks and Putticks in Wisborough Green and Loxwood, but none was a grocer. Likewise, the Fosters: there was no previous tradition of running shops.

Armed with this information, it is possible to deduce that Puttick and Co and Foster & Co, soon joined by marriage, became the seed corn of 'combination', from which Aylward, Smith & Co. Ltd would grow, families in 1881, a communal store by 1891.

It has been said that the adoption of the limited liability company conveniently and sensibly offset the unlimited liability of share owning by the Brethren and their heirs which was far too risky for such poor folk. There was no place in the new set-up at the Combination Stores for Sarah Foster. She and her daughter Caroline moved to Spy Lane.

In 1885, the inquest into John Sirgood's death reveals that he died at The Combination Stores (Plate 5.2). This, and the evidence above, persuade me that the building of the Combination Stores was at least partly completed, in business, and habitable then, maybe even earlier by a year or two, coinciding with the evidence above for the two small shops which preceded it. The report in October 1885 names Ann Powell manageress and Catherine Enticknap, her assistant. He died knowing his second big contribution of his life's work was under way. In 1891, the Combination Stores were fully occupied by residents, unmarried women, and men (Table 12)

Communal Living Over and Adjacent to the Stores

Table 5.2   Numbers Present* on Census Night at Dependants' Stores

	1881	1891	1901	1911
Loxwood		10 (7f, 3m)	15 (10f, 5m)	11 (8f, 3m)
Warnham	6 (3f, 3m)	13 (10f, 3m)	22 (16f, 6m)	29 (22f, 7m)
Lordshill		12 (7f, 5m)	11 (8f, 3m)	11 (9f, 2m)
Northchapel		13 (10f, 3m)	18 (13f, 5m)	24 (18f, 4m)
South Norwood		6 (4f, 2m)	19 (11f, 8m)	30 (19f, 11m)
Average size	-	**11**	**17**	**21**

Note: Sex ratio in brackets
* Persons visiting another community have been included in the numbers for their usual home.

PLATE 5.1

Pre-Combination Stores Loxwood

Fig 1 – 1870s OS map, 25" to 1 mile

Plot 227 – Black Hall: smithy and grocers

Plot 225 – Rose Cottage: drapers (site of Combination Stores)

Plot 222 – pond

Plot 224 – Cokkes Field (see Intoduction)

The path to the chapel in Spy Lane is on the north side of plot 228.

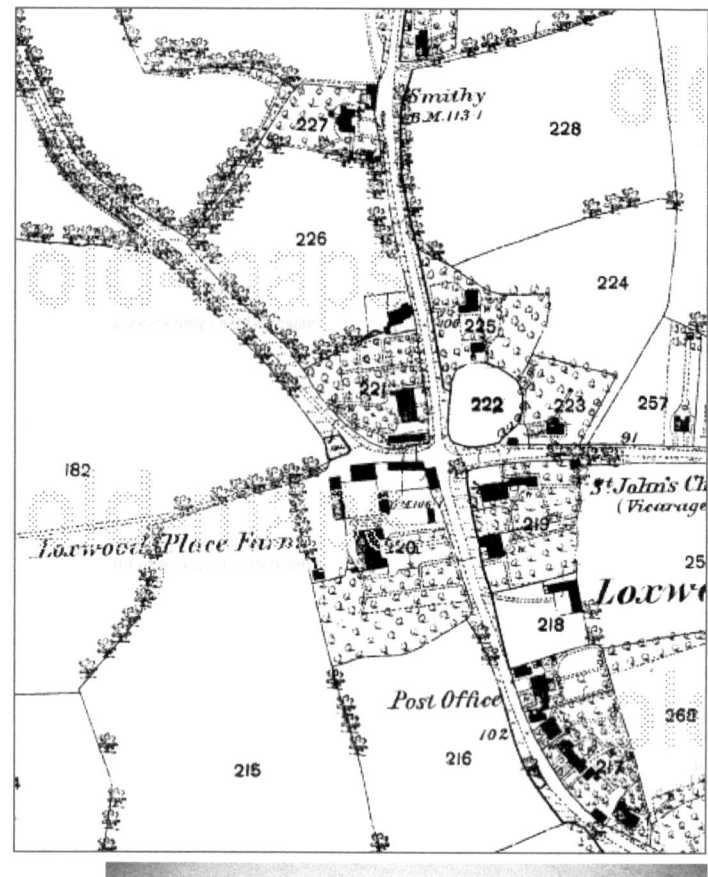

Fig 2 – Caroline (Carrie) Foster's sampler, 1866. See her entry in Fig 3 below.

Fig 3 – 1881 Census page

90 – Rose Cottage (part)

91 – Rose Cottage (second part) drapers

96 – Black Hall grocers

Acknowledgement: ancestry .com

90	Do	1		James Overington	[illegible]	Widr	56		Wood Dealer	Do , Loxwood
				Eliza Parsons	Serv	W		57	Housekeeper	Do . Do
				Miriam Overington	Daur	Daur		10	Scholar	Do . Do
				John Do	Nephew	[illegible]	17		Labourer . Carter	London
91	Do	1		Mary Foster	Head	Unm		50	Draper	Sussex . Loxwood
				Hannah Osborn	Visitor	Unm		[illegible]	Do	Cambs . Girton
92	Do	1		John Overington	Head	Unm	47		Farmer of 10 Acres	Sussex . Wisboro' Green
				Jane Do	Sister	[illegible]		42	Housekeeper	Do . Do
93	Do			Elizabeth Carter	Lodger	Mar		[illegible]	School Mistress	Surrey . Bramley
94	Do	1		Thomas Pacy	Head	Mar	55		Carpenter	Sussex . Kirdford
				Louisa Do	Wife	Mar		48		Do . Do
				Mary C Bowen	Visitor			9	Scholar	Surrey . Alfold
				Kate Do	Do			6	Do	Do . Do
				William Do	Do		4		Do	Do . Do
				William Do	Do	Widr	32		Bricklayer	Do . Dunsfold
95	Do			Thomas Puttock	Lodger	Unm	34		Carpenter	Sussex . Wisboro' Green
96	Do	1		Sarah Foster	Head	W		[illegible]	Grocer	Do . Do
				Caroline Do	Daur	Unm		24		Do . Do
				Felix Do	Son	Unm	21		Carpenter	Do . Do

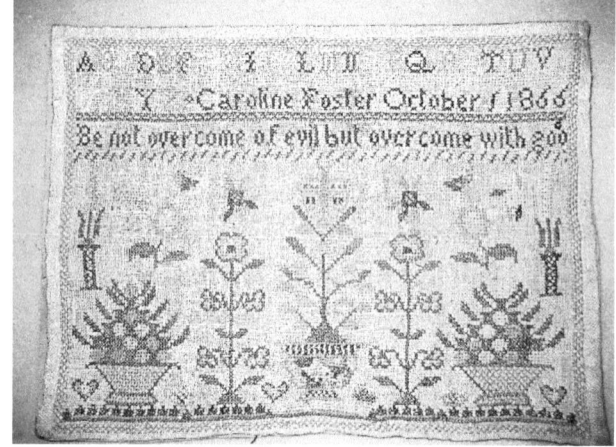

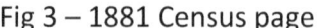

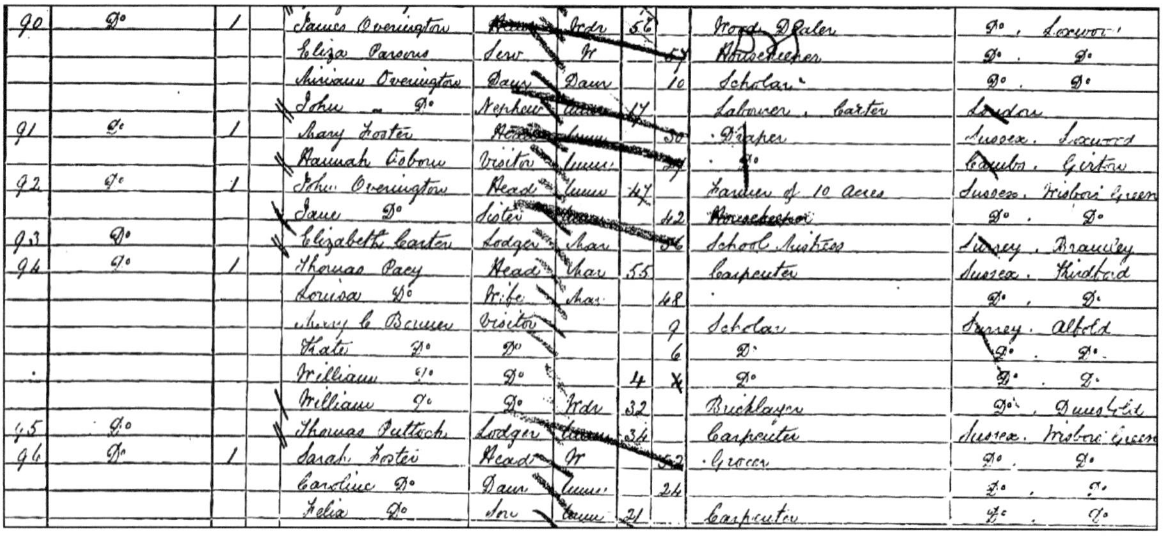

At all the stores, Loxwood, Warnham, Northchapel, Lordshill and South Norwood, there were wide variations in size of the live-in community, and numbers steadily increased, except at Loxwood and Lordshill. The numbers are further complicated by the existence of adjacent annexe households (not included in Table 5.2), such as Hall House in Loxwood, The Cross (Plate 9.5) in Warnham, and Beulah Cottage in South Norwood. In South Norwood, the stores are separated into several households. These numbers are not the whole story, by any means. The wider communities included numerous families or sibling, households, households that mixed family or unrelated individuals. However, increasingly these communal households over and adjacent to the stores came to represent a core, but open, community, one that had more dealings with the whole village by serving the public. Visits to other such groups are often mentioned in the literature, and the censuses back this up, occasionally catching a visitor. Further fascinating analysis reveals the balance between the sexes – the dominance of women (Table 5.2), and the wide variation in place of origin of the members of these fluid communities, e.g., Loxwood, Table 6.1). "Closed", they were not. Another form of openness was that some employees did not live in the communal facilities, some not even Dependants. For example, in table 5.2, Warnham had 22 living in, in 1901, but it is said that it employed 31 workers in 1904. As time went by, some of these were not Dependants, men or women whose skills were valuable. In serving anyone who chose to deal with them, the wider village was never excluded. Indeed, in the depressed years between the wars, prices remained low, and groceries were even given away to the needy.

Using the 1911 census sheets, which were filled in by the head of the household, it is possible to find how much space there was in each community building. The results only reveal the space available at the time, but it is fair to say that the communities were well established by this time and in their mature phase. Thus, South Norwood is very overcrowded, but Loxwood and Lordshill are not. Rooms were, where possible, private refuges for what has been called "secret time", that is, prayer, reading the bible and contemplation.

Table 5.3 **1911 Census, Occupancy Rate**

Loxwood	12 rooms	11 persons	Hall House*	10 rooms	7 persons
Warnham	16 rooms	20 persons	The Cross	10 rooms	9 persons
Lordshill	12 rooms	11 persons			
Northchapel	16 rooms	24 persons			
S Norwood	16 rooms	30 persons	Beulah Cottage	6 rooms	9 persons

Hall House was not yet owned by Aylward, Smith & Co, even though the occupants are Dependants.

Business Organisation

The stores were all set up as limited companies, using the names of the chairman and secretary (who may or may not have been managers of departments, grocery and drapery, sometimes bakery) to create a double surnamed company, which one imagines they felt reflected the communal nature of the enterprise. The first named was more likely to have been chairman. Most of the named individuals were female, one suspects better educated. Bringing talent into the business was important, always by converts to the faith, many born in diverse locations. Later, anyone not of the faith would invariably live outside the community. It is difficult to know their history in most cases. Only Northchapel, as far as is known, held the same name throughout its existence as a company. Later, for example in Loxwood, where there was no name change after 1896, some chief officers were never reflected in the name of the business. Had this occurred, there could have been Nash, Hempstead & Co in Loxwood from the late 1930s!

Table 5.4   Dependant Limited Companies, Named Joint Managers/Directors

Names	Place of birth	Vital dates *(first occurrence)*
Loxwood - Puttick & Co grocers, **Mary Foster**, drapers [1878 to c1885],		
Owen Puttick	Wisborough Green Sx	1843-1911
Mary Foster (later Puttick)	Wisborough Green Sx	1851-1922
Loxwood – Powell & Co, grocers, **Enticknap & Co**, linen drapers [1885 to 1896]		
[Note: John Sirgood died at 'Loxwood Stores', Oct 1885; obituary named 'Combination Stores']		
Catherine Enticknap	Northchapel Sx	1859-1932
Ann Powell	Itchingfield Sx	1849-n/k
Loxwood - Aylward, Smith & Co Ltd [1896 to 1973]		
Henry Aylward	Sevenoaks Kt	1866-1939
Ethel M Smith	Corton, Suffolk	1863-1939
Warnham – Linfield, Potter & Co Ltd [1879 to 1887]		
Joseph Lin(d)field	Shipley Sx	1853-1933
George Potter	Alfold Sy	1854-1913
Warnham - Joseph Lindfield & Co Ltd [1888 to c1895]		
Joseph Lindfield		
Warnham - Lindfield, Luff & Co Ltd [c1895 to 1948]		
Joseph Lindfield		
Lucy Luff	Wisborough Green Sx	1853-1937
Ellen Luff	Wisborough Green Sx	1855-1949
Lordshill - Earle, Franks & Co [to c1911]		
Jacob Harry Earle	Bramley Sy	1863-1948
Stephen Franks	Rudgwick Sx	1849-1909
Lordshill – Bradshaw, Foster & Co [1912 to c1918]		
Edith Bradshaw	Tetbury Glos	1873-1977
Mary Foster	Bramley Sy	1855-1932
Lordshill - Bradshaw, Foster, Street & Co Ltd [c1918 to 1934]		
Edith Bradshaw		
Mary Foster		
Leslie Street	Cranleigh Sy	1868-1937
Lordshill – Smith & Croucher [1935 to 1951]		
Henry F Smith	Strood, Kt	1887-nk
Wallace J Smith	Marden, Kt	1904-1965
Raymond Croucher [1937-48]	Headcorn, Kt	1886-1977

Northchapel – Osborne & Spooner [c1882 to c1887]
     Hannah Osborne   Girton, Cambs   1852-1887
     Harriett Spooner [to 1884]   Kirdford Sx   1850-1919

Northchapel - Brown, Durant & Co Ltd [c1887 to c1969]
     Caroline Brown   Streatham Sy   1841-1931
     Elizabeth Durant   Shebbear, Devon   1858-1932

South Norwood - Ford, Randall & Co Ltd [1882 to 1895]
     Julia Ford   Cheltenham, Glos   born c1857
     George Randall   Hammersmith Mdsx 1847-1915
     [A Slade & Co, drapers traded from 1890]

South Norwood - Randall, Slade & Co Ltd [1895 to 1969]
     George Randall,
     Alice Slade   Dorchester, Dorset   1857-1932

Dependant Family Businesses Elsewhere

The details of the main combination stores will be dealt with in the chapter on each community. In some communities, there was no equivalent of this family model of Dependant shopkeeping. For example, among known Dependants, Michael Woolgar kept shop (grocers, dairy) in The Hornet, Chichester, James Randall did so in the Lodsworth village store, and Ezra Varns the family "department store" (a combination store by trade but a family-run business) in Fernhurst, all in Sussex. The latter two, of course, were not in Dependant communities. No evidence has come to light so far of a Dependant business in Hove.

The Fernhurst Historical Society describes the Varns business, a little later in time, *"The [Chapel Street] shop was staffed by Ezra Varns, his wife and the family of four girls and one boy – Florrie, Nellie, Bertha, Edith and Ernie. Ernie baked the bread and delivered the groceries. The family were Cokelers, a nonconformist religious sect and the women always wore long black skirts and black blouses. They used to go off in their black bonnets on a Sunday morning and go to Northchapel to attend services. They were particularly known for their kindness and courtesy. They also baked particularly good lardy rolls! A bill from 1939 describes their business as Grocer and Draper, Household Furnisher, China, Earthenware, Boot & Shoe Stores. At one time there was an entire bedroom suite in the window.*

PLATE 5.2   Loxwood's Retail Development

Fig 1 – (left) a later photo of Loxwood Post Office, the original Foster's drapers shop next to Hall House (right). It bacame a saddlers and post office by 1900.

Fig 2 – (right) a later photo of Black Hall, the former Foster's, then Puttick's, grocers shop. The smithy, front right, was Tom Pacy's carpenter's workshop in 1881.

WISBOROUGH GREEN.

INQUEST.—On Saturday, an inquest was held by Mr A. W. Rawlison, coroner for the Western Division, touching the death of John William Sirgood, aged 68.— Catherine Enticknap, the first witness, said she was an assistant to Miss Powell, the manageress of the Combination Stores, at Loxwood. She identified the body of the deceased as that of John William Sirgood, of Lords Hill, Shamley Green, Surrey, a bootmaker, 68 years of age. She had known him for about 25 years. He came to stay at the stores on Saturday last, and did not complain of anything. About twelve that night he came to her room and said he felt very poorly. She asked him if he could do anything. He said "no," and she then went to bed again. About half-past one he came again and ask her if she would get the others up as he felt so ill. She called up a young man named Puttock a friend of deceased's, and offered to send for a doctor, but he did not wish it as he said he should be better presently as he had been like it before, and had suffered similarly for ten years. He got better on the Sunday following, but was afterwards worse, and continued to alternate during the week. She ask him several times to let her send for a doctor, but he would not allow her, as he said he should be better. On Monday she noticed a change in him about five p.m., and sent for a doctor who got there in about two hours, and deceased died about twenty past ten the same night.—Mr Reginald Humphrey, surgeon, Wisborough Green, said he was sent for on Monday last about 6 p.m., and saw deceased a little after 7. He was then dying. He gave him a little whisky and milk, but he could not swallow it. He stopped till a few minutes after nine. He was then sinking fast. He had since made a post mortem examination, and found that deceased had a diseased bladder, and the left kidney was dilated and nearly decomposed, and had about a table spoon full of matter in the lower part. The right kidney was also diseased, but there the disease was not so far advanced. There was also general peritonitis or inflammation of the covering of the bowels. The cause of the death was degenerated kidneys and cystitis. The disease was of long standing, and his life could not have been saved had he been called in when he first taken ill on the 10th inst.— The jury returned a verdict of "Death from natural causes."

Fig 3 – Brighton Gazette, 26 October 1885, the inquest into the death of John Sirgood. This article confirms the prior existence of The Combination Stores and its two managers, Misses Powell and Enticknap.

Fig 4 – Weavers, later Rose Cottage, was the house on the site chosen for the Combination Stores. Esther Thayre at the gate. The cottage still stands.

Chapter 6

The Combination Stores, Loxwood

PLATE 6.1

Combination Stores Loxwood
1890 to 1915

Note: field plot numbers have changed since the previous edition of the map. size in acres is now shown.

Fig 1 – (right) 1896 OS 25" to 1 mile map

Note the plethora of buildings in 252, a plot of 1.259 acres. The large building on the road frontage is the store. The rectangular building behind is the bakery. Weavers has a path to the door. Jubilee Villas are shown as a a pair in the northern corner.

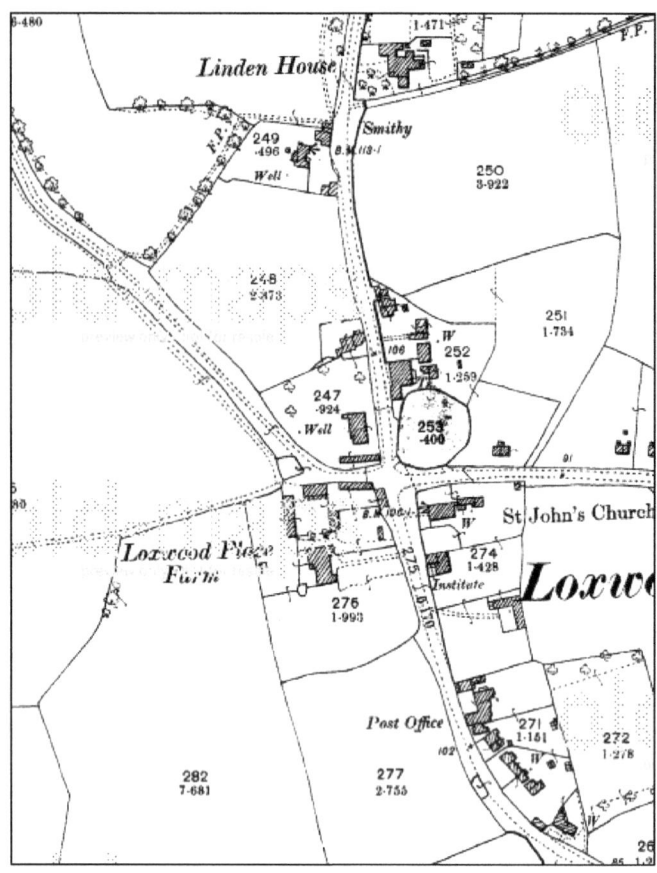

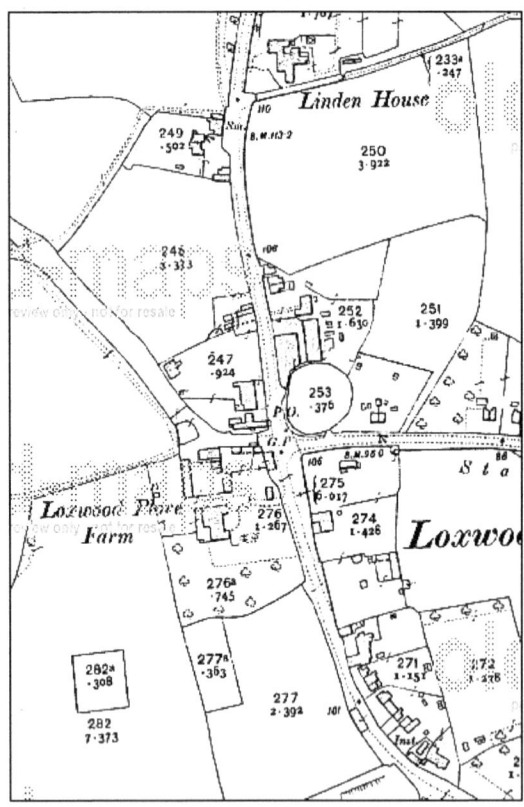

Fig 2 – (left) 1912 OS 25" to 1 mile map

Compare the size of the enlarged and combined buildings at the rear with Fig 1. The store seems to be shaped around the pond, but this may be just a mapping change. The plot has a revised acreage of 1.63 acres, with no apparent change in boundary.

Note too that St John's CofE church has been demolished. A new church was constructed in 1902.

Ack: both maps, old-maps.co.uk

96

The Arrival of Combination in Loxwood

Loxwood was the only store that explicitly took the title 'Combination Stores', used in print as early as John Sirgood's West Surrey Times and County Express obituary and Brighton Gazette inquest report, both 1885. As already explained in Chapter 5 and Plate 5.1, the 1878 edition of the Ordnance Survey map, at a scale of 1:2500, shows the plot then numbered 225 with a house called Weavers (as named in censuses, now Rose Cottage), and another building, probably a barn, nearer the pond. Weavers later became, in one part, Noah's Ark (known occupants Etherington 1911 and Stovold 1934), and in the other part, Rose Cottage, not to be confused with Rose Cottage in Station Road, where the Jenners lived 1877-1960. It was occupied by Dependants from its purchase until becoming, appropriately, the home of the Goodwin family. The last leader in Loxwood, Alfred Goodwin, who died in 1996, ended more than a century of the community on plot 225. There is no evidence to say from whom plot 225 was purchased, or when, but it almost certainly included plot 224, the field behind.

By 1887 in Kelly's Directory, and confirmed in the 1891 census and the 1885 inquest (Plate 5.2), the managers of the new store were both female, Catherine Enticknap and Ann Powell. The directory shows how the initial structure of two separate companies continued under Anne (Powell & Co, grocers), and Catherine (Enticknap & Co, linen drapers). Nevertheless, the census used the then established term, Combination Stores, reflecting an economic merger as well as a communal experiment, as envisaged by Sirgood near the end of his life. A hymn composed at the time of his death refers to this, and informs the reader that combination refers to human or social combination, 'one-ness', not economic as in a modern department store. One might be forgiven for thinking the latter as in time there were more than two retail departments.

"He brought forth combination / And did its virtues tell. / We see the work he's left behind, / For you and I to do, / In one-ness for to be combined, / His footsteps to pursue."

Table 6.1   1891 Census, Combination Stores, Loxwood, *(Enticknap & Co; Powell & Co)*

First Household (Enticknap & Co) / Place of Birth

Name	Age	Occupation	Place of Birth
Catherine Enticknap	31	draper's manageress (employer)	Northchapel Sx
Esther Cumber	20	general servant	Guildford Sy
Jesse Puttock	37	carman	Kirdford Sx

Second household (Powell & Co)

Name	Age	Occupation	Place of Birth
Ann Powell	43	manageress grocers (employer)	Itchingfield Sx
Jane Knight	56	housekeeper	Kirdford Sx
Mary Denyer	24	grocer's assistant	Wisborough Green Sx
Jane Whetton	33	general servant	Lower Heyford Oxon
Caroline Pullen	33	baker's assistant	Petworth Sx
Albert Maple	32	carman	Sellindge Kt
Henry Aylward	25	baker	Sundridge Kt

Table 6.1 names all the sisters, and two brethren, living communally in 1891. It is very much part of a wider pattern in all the communities that those who resided together were seldom born in the community they then served. Indeed, some are converts from a much wider geographical range, reflecting Sirgood's extensive travels. Henry Aylward, who had learnt

the bakery trade, was a future chairman and elder in Loxwood. Esther Cumber, the youngest, was destined one day to be Company Secretary, and eventually Chairman, of Brown, Durant in Northchapel.

In the 1891 census there were six discrete households within the plot. Two were named Combination Stores (Table 6.1); another, also apparently in the curtilage, was a family headed by Edwin Tapner, a coachman, but not listed as a Dependant in death or burial registers. He worked for the Dependants as their coachman/groom. He soon moved on to Putney in Surrey. The next two entries are for "Combination Stores, Weavers". Weavers as previously explained was the old name for Rose Cottage. Here lived George Standen, a shoemaker, and James Pannell, a carpenter, both in married Dependant families.

Building the Combination Stores and Jubilee Cottages

By the time of the next edition of the OS map in 1896 (Plate 6.1), the plot had been transformed. The shop, its façade alongside Loxwood Street, was a large building which would have appeared from the road much as it does today, but its depth was shallower. A separate building lying further back and towards Rose Cottage was probably the bakery, built in the former cottage garden. This building was enlarged before 1912, replacing outbuildings, towards the pond. It survives today as The Old Bakery, at that time with accommodation above, and later joined to the store as one building. Accommodation must have been more rudimentary in these early days when the buildings were smaller. On the roadside further north, but still in the old curtilage of Rose Cottage, was a pair of new cottages and associated outbuildings, at first named Jubilee Cottages. Loxwood Street had itself been transformed. The effect on the whole village was profound, not only in the streetscape (cover photograph) but also in the services provided.

By 1901, the families of Owen Puttick and George Standen occupied 1 and 2 Jubilee Villas (no longer called cottages). The families of James Pannell and James Etherington occupy Rose Cottage. All four are Dependant headed households. Owen and Mary Puttick were the subject of extensive comment in Chapter 5. Owen died soon after the census in 1911 (Mary not until 1922; see Plate A4.3). Both Puttick and Standen families had moved from Rose Cottage to Jubilee Villas probably when new. In 1904, George and Elizabeth Standen died on Christmas Eve and Christmas Day respectively, and were buried in a joint funeral a few days later. Jubilee Villas were for older Dependants. The elderly did not retire as we know the term. Both Jubilee cottages had outbuildings. Could they have been workshops respectively for the shoemaker and a carpenter who lived there, both providing a necessary part of the complete package the stores were designed to offer? George Standen's son was a coalman and would have needed a coal yard for his business, another possibility. Eponymously named William Cole (one of several Dependants from Kent) was also a coalman. He lived at Jubilee Villas in 1911, by which time coal deliveries were a strong component of the business. The larger outbuilding at No 2 would, if it had survived, have been in the front garden of a later house, Walcot (where the Goodwins lived before moving to Rose Cottage). Jubilee Villas will have been named in honour of Queen Victoria's Diamond Jubilee (1897), though they seem to have been completed a year or two earlier as they were marked on the Ordnance Survey map of 1896. Confusingly, the 1901 census lists all four households as "Weavers".

First Managers of the Combination Stores

What of the two managers of the Combination Stores? Catherine Enticknap's parents, Charles, a labourer, and Sarah, were brethren at Northchapel, though they lived in Lurgashall. The reason Catherine (known as Kitty) did not stay in her job for long was because she married Ernest Standen in 1894. No married couple was able to "live in" at the communal stores. The Standens both remained faithful to the community for life, moving to Alfold, where he was a postman, later a fly proprietor, and she ran a laundry next to The Crown Inn, possibly in Jasmine Cottage, employing three workers, rising to seven by 1911. She was clearly a capable businesswoman despite her humble background. There is no evidence any of the seven laundry employees were Dependants. All were single girls aged 18-29 at the time of the census. Kitty died in 1932; Ernest survived her, and died living at Elm View, Loxwood with Alfred and Grace Munday; by coincidence, the property where the author grew up.

Ann Powell is harder to track. She was born in Barns Green, Itchingfield. Her father was born in New Jersey, USA, but was a British Subject. The family then moved to Hayes Cottages Slinfold. By 1871, however, aged 22, she was living in Wisborough Green with her brother-in-law, Mark Holloway, also a Dependant, whilst her parents and siblings had moved to Chiddingfold. In 1881, Ann was in Croydon, a servant in the home of Dependant Brethren, brother and sister Philip and Olive Mann. It was here she also met George Randall (whose name is in that of the Norwood stores, Randall, Slade & Co) and James Brightman. All four are documented as having been close to John Sirgood from the earliest days. Philip Mann was a bootmaker from Northchapel, where he lived close by the Spooners' grocery shop in 1871. Once in Croydon, the Manns stayed there, at 69 Penge Road, and were joined by William, an older brother who lived in Cobden Road, close to the Norwood stores and chapel. Ann had an influential apprenticeship in Norwood.

But where did Ann go after her short spell in Loxwood? With her family history, America, perhaps? Her younger brother Joseph and his wife and son were Dependants in the Lordshill community, running a dairy business in Merrow, later retiring to Wonersh. Their daughter, Ellen Jane, was among the few child burials at Loxwood, aged 4 in 1884. This, and Ann's presence in Penge Road, indicate that the Powells were early converts to the Dependant faith. Interestingly, Ann and Joseph's brother, William, became a member of the Loxwood Stores community by 1901, and was still there in 1911. If Ann married, no certain evidence has emerged from the registers, nor has her death been found.

The Founding of Aylward, Smith & Co, c1896

The 1895 directory still listed the two separate companies. The most likely date for the foundation of Aylward, Smith & Co, named for Henry Aylward and Ethel Smith, was in 1896 (Table 5.4). Henry Aylward was already there as baker in 1891, Ethel by 1894. As dating evidence, a surviving 1897 calendar (which must have gone to the printers in 1896) in the name of Aylward, Smith is rather more important than might at first be thought! Henry Aylward joined the community from Kent. There were several converts from the Sevenoaks area, after visits by John Sirgood to various towns and villages in Kent (named by Mr Frank Talbot as Sevenoaks, Maidstone, Headcorn, Marden, Newbury, Goudhurst and Tonbridge – quite a circuit – see also Table A2.1). Henry's parents, Abraham (an agricultural labourer and quarryman) and Charlotte, were among the converts. The family, including Henry's brothers James and William moved to Loxwood in the 1880s, all except Henry lodging with Ann Overington, by this time a widow, in Spy Lane. The Aylwards were brought up in Sundridge, Kent, before moving into Sevenoaks. Henry, known as Harry, went on to become not only the eponymous Aylward of Aylward, Smith & Co, but also the senior elder of the community from 1905, succeeding John Overington. A big man in physical terms, he was a well-respected leader by those who worked with him. Harry Aylward was an employer in 1901, very much the senior partner, and presumably Managing Director of the company. As the stores evolved alongside the religious aspects of the communities, it became common for the roles of elder and director to be combined. In 1899, Aylward, Smith & Co were listed in Kelly's Post Office Directory as: *"Grocer's, provision merchants, drapers, ironmongers, cycle makers and agents"*.

Ethel Smith came from Warnham in 1894 to replace Catherine Enticknap on the latter's marriage (Autumn 1894 in Steyning Registration District). By 1901, Ethel Smith was an established presence. Catherine's departure may have precipitated the need for a new business structure. Did Sirgood also preach in Suffolk, where Ethel was born? Probably not, as Ethel had been in service in Southwark, so may well have met Sirgood at one of his London meetings. She came first to Warnham Stores (1891 census) as an assistant in the grocery department, but in 1901 she headed the Loxwood household as housekeeper.

Elizabeth Holden was brought in to run the drapers with Clara Fry. Clara Fry came down from South Norwood and ended up marrying Eli Etherington and settling in Warnham. Liz Holden had been at Plaistow Place, described in Chapter 2. She remained in Loxwood Stores until her death in 1953. Smith also remained at Loxwood Stores until her death in 1939, as did Harry Aylward, who died the same year. They left it to a new generation to see the business through the war when significant changes would be made. Table 6.2 names all the Combination Stores residents in 1901.

Table 6.2   **1901 Census, Combination Stores, Loxwood** *(Aylward, Smith & Co Ltd)*

			Place of birth
Henry Aylward *>	56	grocer, draper etc (employer)	Sevenoaks Kt
Ethel Smith >	38	housekeeper	Corton, Suffolk
Jane Knight *>	66	housekeeper	Kirdford Sx
Caroline Pullen *>	42	housemaid	Petworth Sx
Elizabeth Cogger >	37	cook	Maidstone Kt
Deborah Minall	34	pastrycook	Lambeth Sy
Elizabeth Holden >	32	draper's assistant	Warnham Sx
Walter Nash >	32	carman	Rudgwick Sx
Clara Fry	30	draper's assistant	Twickenham Sy
Kate Rugman >	22	grocer's assistant	Wisborough Green Sx
Jesse Puttock *	48	wholesale carman	Kirdford Sx
William Powell	19	baker	Chiddingfold Sy
Caroline Dalman	40	needlewoman	Oving Sx
Sarah Woods >	31	grocer's assistant	Kirdford Sx
Alfred Munday	26	carman	Wootton Sy

* denotes living there 10 years earlier, 1891; > denotes lived in Loxwood Stores for life

PLATE 6.2   Aylward Smith & Co Calendars and Advertising

Fig 1 – 1897. This plain calendar dates from the earliest beginnings of the company.

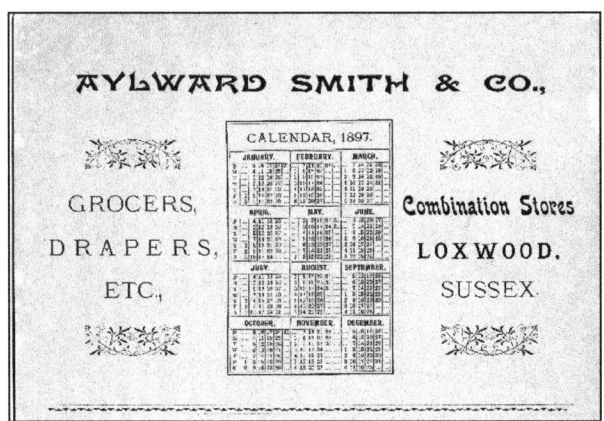

Fig 2 – 1901. This calendar dates from the South African (Boer) War.

Given the Dependants later conscientious objection in 1916, it is perhaps surprising they joined in the jingoism of an image of a Scottish regiment parading through a 'chocolate box' English village! The answer may lie in the company which provided the calendar – Dulcemona Tea Company – who were considered an upmarket purveyor of fine teas suitable as Christmas presents, a 3lb canister for between 5/- and 9/- in 1900. They entitled the image "Home from the War".

Fig 3 – 1904. This year, the sponsoring company was Tower Tea, for which Aylward, Smith were agents. The image is of a castle on high ground overlooking a river, but significantly shows a motor vehicle. Very few customers of the stores would have aspired to this method of leisure transport in 1904.

These calendars would be collector's items if they ever came on the market. The author only possesses the images, not the originals! Ack: Marion May.

Fig 4 – Advertisement 1907-8 (next page). This is taken from a Directory for that date. The company was now able to offer cars and motor bikes for sale or hire, alongside a wide variety of other offerings.

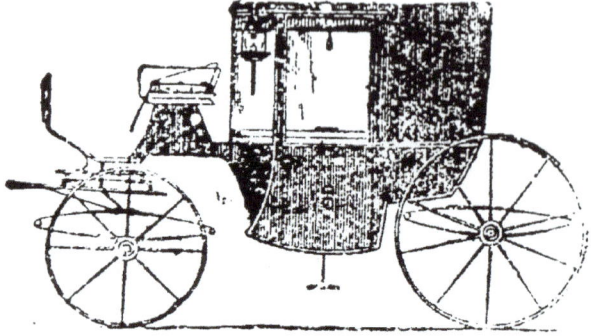

The 1901 grocery assistants, such as Elizabeth Holden, were among the long-term residents. Sarah Woods was a local girl whose parents, Charles and Jane, were also Dependants. Kate Rugman, who switched to the drapery department a few years later, and eventually became its manager, is the subject of a family history in Chapter 2. The Bakehouse was manned by William Powell (Ann Powell's brother), with Deborah Minall as pastrycook, replacing Henry Aylward (who may still have given some time in the bakehouse, as William was only 19).

The welfare of the household under Ethel Smith's watchful eyes was important. There were domestic roles for Jane Knight and Caroline Pullen, who had both been there over 10 years, Elizabeth Cogger (one of the Kent Dependants) and Caroline Dalman, a needlewoman from the Chichester community. Caroline would have made and mended their clothes, including the dresses and aprons worn in the shop, and perhaps worked for drapery customers too.

The growing need for transport and deliveries, both wholesale to other Dependant stores, and locally to those willing to buy, was represented by the role of three carmen. A carman was employed to go out with horse and cart or van, later a motorised van. Walter Nash, having moved in from Plaistow Place, Alfred Munday, and the somewhat older Jesse Puttock, were three of the five men living in. Jesse became a chapel elder. Alfred married, and went to Warnham, though he and Grace returned to Loxwood in the 1930s, living at Elm View, before they moved back again to Warnham for the rest of their lives. Walter Nash would go on to replace Henry Aylward as elder.

Carrie Dalman moved to Byfleets Lane, in a cottage next to Warnham Chapel, as housekeeper to Seth Spooner. Deborah Minall, who was a widow, may have come from Kennington, where John Sirgood had once lived. Most of the people listed remained in Loxwood for life, although Jane Knight and Caroline (Kitty) Pullen were to die before the next census. Loxwood became a very settled community.

The Years of Expansion

In the last years of the 19th century, there were many competing businesses in Loxwood, not only in shops but also in other trades. Of course, virtually no-one was able to go to any local town then, and with disposable income rising for some, the competition must have kept the Dependants on their mettle. The stores needed to compete for business beyond the Dependant community to prosper as a business.

Diversification in the Edwardian years provided for everyone's needs and enabled stronger competition. A full-page advertisement in Pike's Directory, 1907-8 (Plate 6.2) read:
"Aylward Smith & Co. Grocers, Provision Merchants, Bakers, Drapers, Ironmongers, House Furnishers, Coal Merchants. Motor Car Depot, Motor Cycles and Trailers for sale or hire. Horses and Traps for hire. "Combination Stores," Loxwood.
Kelly's Directory of 1909 included further details:
"Grocer's, provision merchants, drapers, ironmongers, cycle makers and agents" and
"coal & coke merchants, broughams, motors and trailers and wagonettes on hire"

Expansion was under way. A large garage was built to the north of the grocery shop, in front of the Bakehouse, but was not completed by the time a new OS map was published in 1912.

A later 1937 map shows it to be a large structure, capable of housing all the vehicles for delivery and for hire, and space for their maintenance, now that cars, vans and trucks were in general use (see the cover photograph).

By the 1911 directory, the word "farmers" was added too. Walter Nash was undoubtedly the farmer, his occupation clearly stated in the census (Table 6.3). William Cole, referred to above, who lived at Jubilee Cottages, was married to Emma Aylward, who was Henry Aylward's sister. Later they moved to Hazelwood, just along Loxwood Street. By 1918, a directory entry for Aylward, Smith & Co reached its longest ever:

"Baker's, grocer's, draper's, ironmonger's, cycle agents, house furnishers, boot stores, china & glass dealers, farmers; cycles & trailers on hire, petrol & motor oils; agents for Northern Assurance Co Ltd".

However, it is not unique to the Dependants to develop a truly "general" village store. Neighbouring villages have contrasting models. In Slinfold, where there was never a Dependant community, the West family ran Slinfold Stores, which in the 1899 Directory were "grocers, provision merchants, drapers, bakers, corn, coal and coke merchants, ironmongers and china and glass dealers". The essential difference was that this was a family-run business, pure and simple. By contrast, in Rudgwick there were a number of different businesses both in the village and nearby hamlets supplying local needs. No single business sold everything, though by 1911 the Cowdery family ran a "baker, draper, grocer and provision merchants and Post Office". No one model fitted all villages, but the Dependants model was universal across all the villages where they had stores. In 1930, Aylward, Smith traded as:

"Grocers, bakers & confectioners, drapers, outfitters & house furnishers; beds & bedding; china, glass; cycle & motor agents; accessories & repairs; motor spirits & oils; combination stores".

Much later, in the 1960s, the garage was reduced in depth to allow a butcher's shop to be placed in front – right behind the petrol pumps! The butcher's business was acquired from the Sopp family whose longstanding business at Fair Maggots (now Mellow) had closed.

Table 6.3   1911 Census, The Stores, Loxwood *(Aylward, Smith & Co)*

			Place of birth
Ethel Smith *>	48	grocery drapery cycle dealer	Corton Suffolk
William John Powell *	29	grocer assistant	Chiddingfold Sy
Walter Nash *>	42	farmer	Rudgwick Sx
Sarah Woods *>	41	shop assistant grocer	Plaistow Sx
Kate Rugman *>	32	drapery assistant	Loxwood Sx
Sarah Ketchell	51	housemaid domestic	Felpham Sx
Elizabeth Cogger *>	46	parlourmaid domestic	Maidstone, Kt
Annie Williams *>	46	housekeeper domestic	Northchapel Sx
Deborah Minall *	43	cook domestic	Lambeth Sy
[The following were visiting South Norwood:			
Henry Aylward *>	66	cycle dealer	Sevenoaks Kt
Elizabeth Holden *>	42	draper's assisatant	Warnham Sx]

* denoted living there 10 years before   > lived at Combination Stores for remainder of life

In 1911, as indicated above, Henry Aylward, cycle dealer, and Elizabeth Holden, draper's assistant, were visiting the brethren in South Norwood, staying with Philip Mann (a Chapel Trustee, and bootmaker dealer) and his sister, an hospitable couple in whose home Ann Powell had lived years before. Henry no doubt found the newly popular cycle department more congenial than the early hours in the bakery. Cycling was fashionable. An account of the life of Ivy Port who lived in Rudgwick cites her joy at walking to Loxwood to buy her first bicycle! From the mid-1890s, there had been a cycling club in Loxwood, and a bicycle hire and agency at the Onslow Arms, whilst Mr Harris was landlord. The cycle department of the stores was where John Murray's butcher's shop is now.

Jesse Puttock (1901 census, Table 6.2, above) moved to Hall House (from 1920, owned by Aylward, Smith; see Chapter 7), where he lived with the Spooners, and worked on the farm. He retired to Canal Villa where he died in 1940, aged 91. Sarah Ketchell also moved to Hall House much later and was at Rose Cottage when she died aged 88. Kate Rugman outlived them all and died when still living at The Stores in 1977, aged 99 (Plate 4.3). She had joined The Stores aged 13 in 1891.

Table 6.4   1911 Census, Some Other Dependant Households in Loxwood

Properties owned by Aylward, Smith, High Street and Spy Lane

Jubilee Cottages	**William Cole**	45	coal porter
	Emma Cole	37	wife
	Charlotte Cole	15	draper's assistant [Aylward, Smith]
	and 1 other child		
	William Aylward	32	general labourer, brother-in-law
Jubilee Cottages	**Owen Puttick**	67	farm labourer
	Mary Puttick	60	wife
Noah's Ark	**Kezia Etherington**	78	farmer's widow, retired
	Jane Whetton	53	housekeeper
Old Cottage	**George Puttick**	41	farm carter
	Mary Puttick	40	wife
	and 1 daughter and mother		
Hall House	**William Spooner**	49	general labourer
	Ann Spooner	46	wife
	Elizabeth Spooner	70	mother
	Mabel Spooner	22	shop assistant
	and 3 other children		
	Jesse Puttock	57	general labourer
New Cottages, Spy Lane	**Charles Denyer**	74	farm labourer
	Emily Denyer	70	wife
New Cottages, Spy Lane	**Eliza Hunt**	68	widow
	Clara Hunt	36	daughter
	Mary Heather	48	charwoman, boarder
New Cottages, Spy Lane	**Fanny Moore**	72	caretaker [chapel?]
New Cottages, Spy Lane	**Annie Batchelor**	53	knitter

Properties not thought to be owned by Aylward, Smith

[Toll] Gate House	**Lucy Reeves**	72	widow
	Alfred Killner	22	farm stockman
1 Canal Villa	**William Thayre**	50	farmer
	Esther Thayre	49	wife

	James Pannell	89	carpenter retired
	George Randall	65	farm labourer
High Street	Charlotte Overington	70	widow
	Eli Harrington	70	wood cutter
Saddler's Shop	Ellen Smith	89	widow, mother
and son-in-law [George Weller], daughter and granddaughter			
	David Thayre	75	farmer, retired
	Mary Ketchell	58	housekeeper
Oak Grove, Spy Lane	Walter Parr	54	draper, retired
	Mary Parr	84	mother
	Caroline Foster	54	housekeeper
Hill Grove, Pancake Lane	Jane Overington	72	private means
	Ann Squelch	70	boarder
Rose Cottage, Station Rd	Harvey Jenner	72	farm labourer
	Phoebe Jenner	55	wife
	Thomas Jenner	22	general labourer, son
	Alfred Jenner	16	shop assistant {Aylward, Smith?]
and 1 other adult son			
Station Road	John Franks	61	bricklayer
	Harriett Franks	61	wife
and 3 others			
Station Road	Louisa Pacy	78	widow
	Mark Steer	54	general labourer, boarder
Station Road	Harriett Randall	58	widow
	Harriett Randall	27	dressmaker
and 1 other adult daughter			
Church Cottage	David Thayre	48	labourer
Station Rd	May Thayre	43	wife
and 1 other			
Penfold House	William Puttock	76	shopkeeper, retired
	William Puttock	64	wood dealer, nephew
	Ann Puttock	62	housekeeper, niece
Four Houses	David Thayre	43	general labourer
	Emily Thayre	35	wife
and 2 children			
Alfold Bars	Henry Spooner	75	builder retired
	Jane Spooner	76	wife
Fernleigh, Alfold Bars	James Garman	40	bricklayer
	Agnes Garman	33	wife
	Sarah Tidy	90	grandmother
Pawlies Farm	James Elliott	68	farmer
	Ann Elliott	64	assisting in business, wife
and 2 adult children and 2 adult grandchildren			
New Songhurst Farm	Alfred Ayling	45	farmer
	Mary Ayling	44	assisting in business, wife
and his father			
New Songhurst Farm	John Carter	69	farm labourer
	Mary Carter	34	wife
Barnfold Cottage	Thomas Puttock	38	mill carman
	Rosina Puttock	34	wife
and 5 children			

	Charles Wadey	63	coppice cutter
Headfoldswood Comn	**Henry Killner**	70	farmer
	Sarah Killner	68	sister
Newpound Common	**William Denyer**	66	farm carter
	and 1 adult daughter and housekeeper		
Newpound Common	**William Fuller**	42	farm labourer
Roundstreet Common	**Mark Covey**	44	farm labourer
	Jesse Covey	54	farm labourer, nephew
	Jane Bentley	55	housekeeper, invalid
	Mary Bentley	77	boarder, Jane's mother
Roundstreet Common	**Jane Woods**	64	widow
	and 1 adult son		

Those included by name and in bold are all listed in the Dependant death/burial registers.

At the beginning of the list are properties known to belong to Aylward, Smith, including those in Spy Lane, followed by others to the south of the village, in Spy Lane, and those in nearby Station Road. They are followed by those to the north, outlying farms and common cottages. Strictly speaking Roundstreet Common is in Wisborough Green.

The names often resonate as part of a wider clan of Dependants or as early and important Brethren or Sisters. In the former group are the Puttocks, Putticks, Spooners, Reeves, Killners, Denyers, Jenners, and Thayres. In the latter group are surnames Cole, Aylward, Overington, Pannell, Franks, Foster and Parr. Some of these names will "die out" in the registers quite soon, others persist.

There are 78 names in Table 6.4. Add to that the eleven in the Combination Stores for a total under 100. It is difficult to say how many of the other members of these households might have been practising members at the time, or if both spouses were committed, or other households are omitted. Scouring the census against the death/burialregisters is time consuming and not without error. It is a low number but does not include some from outside Loxwood in neighbouring villages: Wisborough Green, Rudgwick, Cranleigh, Alfold and Plaistow for example, who are also named in the registers. Of these Plaistow is by far the most significant with at least eleven households, and Alfold with a further five.

Some observations include the following. The number of widows and married couples remind the reader that many were married in the nineteenth century, forming an outer and outlying group from the core where it was normally expected to be single. That said there are some unmarried of both sexes, and it is notable how the Dependants looked after each other with a housekeeper. Some of the singles were adult children, though it is also clear that some of those married and/or may have left the community in due course.

Aspects of Aylward, Smith & Co

The earliest Aylward, Smith calendar (Plate 6.2), as has been said, dates from 1897. It was a simple card sheet, no pictures, but by 1901 pictures were printed, including the one of soldiers returning from the Boer War. Such jingoistic celebration of victory sits uneasily with later pacifism, but the calendar was clearly sponsored by Dulcemona Tea. In 1904, sponsored by Tower Tea, the picture was more innocuous as it had a family in a car passing a castle. It is not known how many more of these were produced. Warnham Stores, and perhaps others, also produced calendars. The Aylward, Smith series of Loxwood postcards, on the other hand, constantly appear on eBay. They were produced over a long period, and depict a variety of Loxwood views, of great use now, particularly for Edwardian local history. By the 1950s a variety of small items such as screwdriver sets, leather stamp books and pottery were made and sold with "Loxwood" printed or stamped on.

Several photos from the 1920s survive, illustrating association of the Combination Stores with Loxwood Fair (Plate 6.3), which was both an agricultural and social event. The village would be *en fête* for the occasion, with wares laid out on the pavement in front of the shop. Kate Rugman, Miss Kennard, Bessie Hempstead, Mabel Spooner, Winnie Cronk and Sarah Woods were in attendance in their white uniforms. The men were to be seen at the cattle fair. Pictures from the 1930s show Walter Nash watching the sale inscrutably, and in one a young John Phillips is seen parading a cow in the ring. The fair was founded in 1868 by Mr Edward Eager, a surveyor and estate agent in Godalming. In the 1920s, I have been told the fair was held in the field north of Black Hall (now a housing estate). In the 1930s, the livestock were shown and changed hands at Lakers Lodge. The show was held in early May.

In 1947, Sarah Woods, then aged 78, who lived at the Combination Stores for over 50 years until her death in 1951, was persuaded to write about her life among the 13 who were there at that time (including three others by then over 70 – Elizabeth Holden, Walter Nash, Kate Rugman). She described the 'secret time' for private prayer between breakfast and the opening of the shop each day, and again before chapel services on Tuesday and Thursday evenings, and of course on Sunday mornings.

She ends, *"We have a nice lawn where we can relax from business (Wednesday afternoons etc). We enjoy the peace and quietness and communion with God. We also have a boat and sometimes have a nice row on the river and enjoy the beauties of nature, the wonderful creations of God, sometimes a motor ride to the sea where we again behold the majesty of God in his beautiful handiwork."* One project that post-dates 1947, was the restoration of gardens and an island in the old manor pond next to the stores. Here too, there was a small boat, which was used for practical gardening tasks and recreation.

After the 1939-45 war, the Dependants bought a beach hut at Felpham, near Bognor Regis. There had of course been a chapel in Felpham, and one in Chichester. It would have seemed only natural to them to head in that direction. As an employee and relative, the author's father was able to use this hut on occasions and remembers these outings as a small child, and the photos in a family album. There are also some of the Dependants, more formally attired, even here at the seaside. Many group photos of brethren and sisters taken at the Combination Stores or in the larger garden of Hall House (and others of Warnham brethren) have survived too.

Loxwood, a 1939 Snapshot

The 1939 register (Table 6.5), made in order to find out the nation's war manpower and readiness, is a treasure trove of basic information on individuals alive then, and not serving in the armed forces. The data were collected in September 1939 very soon after war broke

PLATE 6.3   Loxwood Fair, 1920s

Fig 1 and 2 - 1924. Shop assistants drumming up trade and friendship on the street during the fair.

Fig 3 and 4 – Meanwhile, Henry Aylward attends the fair (year unknown).

Fig 5 – (below right) not known if this photo is the same years as the two above.

Fig 6 – 1920. (below left) Not on a fair day. Note the donkey cart, and the Pratts Spirit lorry.

Fig 7 – 1930s. A young John Phillips (in later life a director of Aylward, Smith & Co) leads the cow in the ring. The Phillips family always had an interest in the farm side of the business.

LOXWOOD Show was held last week and is chronicled on page 4. Here we have a presentation of expressions at the sale of the fat stock by the auctioneers interested. It will not be difficult for agriculturalists to identify Mr. Newland Tom others, caught on this field of pricing and buying. There is little tha any countenance here: good judges at a good case are ever intent. happil pictured?

out. As the only names redacted (unavailable) are those who are still alive and/or under 100 years old today, any gaps are largely irrelevant to Dependant households. The data collected were name, sex, marital status, exact date of birth and occupation. For the last named, "Domestic duties" was used for nearly all women, with interesting exceptions for some Dependants. Other information included roles already taken up in civil defence or previous (or reserve) officer service in the forces, and subsequent name changes on marriage (brackets below), through to the 1950s. Yes, it was in use for that long, and was the basis for National Registration Cards and National Health Cards. There was no census in 1941, and the 1931 census was destroyed by enemy action. The 1921 census will not be made public in time for this publication, perhaps for a second edition.

1939 is about 90 years after John Sirgood burst onto the scene, and just 30 years before the terminal decline of Aylward Smith & Co. "Generation 39" will not have remembered their "dear elder" personally, rather it showed signs of ageing, of a female majority. There were distinct layers to the community from its central core to its married and house sharing wider community, neighbours to each other and to the wider village. The neighbouring Plaistow community no longer existed, but there was an outlier in Alfold.

The register narrowly missed the lives of Ethel Smith and Henry Aylward both of whom died in the first months of the year. It did however capture Bessie Hempstead's, Walter Nash's and Elizabeth Holden's first months in office. Of those voting in the 6 June 1939 AGM (Chapter 7), all can be found in Table 6.5 below. Six lived in the Combination Stores, just one in Hall House, two others also in the central core properties, two in the wider community. Only one was married – Harry Garman. Walter was keener to be described as a farmer in the Register than as chairman of the company.

There was strong continuity from 1911, despite the intervening 28 years. Indeed, there were 24 or more still alive in 1973 to mourn the company's passing. From the 1911 company AGM, the first surviving list, the following were still in the land of the living: Walter Nash, Harry Garman, Elizabeth Holden, Kate Rugman, Sarah Woods, Annie Denyer, Sarah Ketchell, Alfred Ayling, William Spooner. Walter Nash, Kate Rugman and Sarah Woods were still living in the Combination Stores. Hall House had a higher turnover, as so many of the household were elderly.

The list below is not definitive, but the author's best shot, using all the resources available to him, with apologies to anyone who might spot a missing name or family member. Several possible names were excluded as not having been recorded in the death/burial lists, others included as spouses or siblings. A surprising number of them were known to him personally, if fleetingly, as a child, perhaps more accurate to say they knew him. There are omissions of names which later in this chapter will be significant, viz., the Goodwins (still in Norwood) and the Leswells (still in Essex). A number of retirees from other communities, particularly from South Norwood, migrated down to Loxwood, some to become important in the life of the declining community. There are other members of Bessie Hempstead's family present in 1939, many of the widely spread Killners (to which can be added married Killners such as Winnie Parsons), a clutch of Cronks, and numerous members of the Phillips family. Harriett Drewett came from Norwood.

The Combination Stores list, and indeed the whole table, is particularly notable for the lack of many serving staff living in, just three (Sarah Woods, Gwen Bradshaw, Irene Drewett). Already by this time, the company relied on paid employees, many of whom do not feature below. There are employees listed, such as Harriett Drewett (from Norwood), Millie Underwood and Mabel Spooner; there are also several retired from such work. The average age of residents was 54, ranging from Mary Hempstead, 78, Bessie's mother, to Irene Drewett, only 25. Five were over 60. At Hall House the average age was 65, with a range from Ann Stenning, 90, to Florrie Phillips, parlour maid, 28. Of the men, only John and Arthur Phillips stand out, both working on the farm side. Frederick Muggeridge (do I remember him being known as Jack?), sub-postmaster, was not to the author's knowledge a practicing adherent, but recorded in the death register as a valued tenant.

A sign of an ageing community is that 25 of those listed were over 70, born before 1870, but balanced by 24 born in the 20th century. This left half the 100 strong community in their 40s, 50s and 60s. The community was by no means on its way out, but without doubt in decline. Names which resonate from the early days include Emma Coles, widow of coalman William, and Henry Aylward's sister, and Walter Nash, Elizabeth Holden and Harry Garman from Plaistow Place. Kate Rugman, Sarah Woods, Sarah Ketchell, Alfred Munday and Jesse Puttock all lived at the stores in 1901.

Table 6.5   1939 Register, Loxwood

A.   The Stores and other Dependant Properties in Alfold Road (now Guildford Road)

Combination Stores	**Bessie Hempstead***	1896-1980	Gen stores manageress
	Walter Nash*	1877-1960	Dairy farm manager
	Elizabeth Holden*	1869-1953	Draper retired
	Sarah Woods*	1869-1951	Grocer's assistant
	Kate Rugman*	1878-1977	Cook
	Gwendoline (Gwen) Bradshaw*	1898-1989	Grocer's assistant
	Winifrid (Winnie) Cronk*	1902-1985	House parlour maid
	A Irene Drewett*	1914-1970	Grocer's assistant
	Mary Hempstead*	1861-1950	Private means
Hall House (hld 22)	**Ellen Francis***	1857-1951	Domestic duties
Hall House (hld 24)	**Annie Denyer***	1873-1963	Domestic duties
	Sybilla (Si) Smithers*	1889-1969	Cook housekeeper
	Florence (Flo) Phillips (Leswell)*	1911-1992	House parlour maid
	Mary Hanks*	1851-1943	Draper retired
	Harriett Drewett*	1872-1964	Boot shop assistant
	Harriett (Annie) Smith*	1886-1965	Boot shop assistant (invalid)
	Henry South*	1857-1944	Market gardener (invalid)
	Mabel South*	1895-1964	Domestic duties & nurse
	Ann Stenning*	1849-1941	Domestic duties
Ye Olde Cottage	**Sarah Drewett***	1877-1973	Domestic duties
	Henry Beaton	1868-?	Carman, retired
	Thomas Skinner	1884-?	Not capable of work
Rose Cottage	**Esther Thayre***	1864-1949	Domestic duties
1 Jubilee Villas	**Fanny Garman***	1879-1951	Charwoman
2 Jubilee Villas	**William Spooner***	1861-1948	Unpaid garden duties
	Mabel Spooner*	1888-1967	Grocer's assistant & carer

Jubilee Villas	**Sally Mann***	1861-1941	Domestic duties
Post Office	**Frederick Muggeridge**	1910-1961	Sub-postm'r, tob'st & conf'r
	Blodwen Muggeridge	1908-?	Domestic duties

B.   Property in Spy Lane, Dependant (New Cottages - Chapel Trust), and Private

1 New Cottages	**George Reeves**	1909-1982	Farm carter & cowman
	Joan Reeves	1914-?	Domestic duties
	and 3 others		
2 New Cottages	**Samuel Underwood***	1871-1952	Farm labourer
	Eliza Underwood*	1872-1950	Domestic duties
	Millie Underwood (Nash)	1916-1966	Shop assistant grocery
3 New Cottages	**Albert Fuller**	1886-1973	Farm cowman
	Elizabeth Fuller	1889	Domestic duties
	and 6 others *(this family may have come from the Hove community)*		
4 New Cottages	**Edith Annie Cronk***	1874-1966	General nursing ret'd
	Joan Cronk	1919-?	Housemaid
	and 1 other		
Oak Grove	**W George Kennard***	1883-1962	Smallholder
	Amelia Kennard*	1882-1962	Domestic duties
	and 2 others		
Elsmere	**Leslie Killner***	1906-1998	Engineer, cycle repairer
	Elsie Killner*	1898-1994	Domestic duties
Woodvale	**Caroline Baigent***	1852-1947	Domestic duties
	Amy Varns*	1876-1958	None, partly blind
1 Hillgrove	**Gilbert Killner***	1904-1984	Brick & tile maker
	Ethel Killner	1901-1986	Domestic duties
	and 2 others		
2 Hillgrove	**Alfred Ayling***	1865-1944	Dairy farmer, retired
	Annie Pullen*	1866-1948	Housekeeper

C.   Some Other Properties in Loxwood and nearby occupied by Dependants

Canal Villa, High St	**A John Phillips***	1917-1977	Dairy farmer
	Fanny Phillips	1907-1977	Domestic duties
	Arthur Phillips*	1909-1982	Farm labourer
	Jesse Puttock*	1853-1940	Farm labourer
	and 4 others		
River View, do.	**Henney Brown***	1857-1948	Domestic duties
River View, do.	**William Tickner***	1874-1959	Wood fence erector
	Louisa Tickner*	1879-1960	Domestic duties
Tollgate House, do.	**David Thayre***	1867-1946	Haulage contractor, retired
	Percy Thayre	1909-1984	Agric'l contr'r & wood mch't
The Myrtles, Alfold Rd	**David Thayre***	1862-1946	Farm and garden labourer
	Mary (Polly) Thayre*	1867-1945	Domestic duties
Linkholme, do.	**Ebenezer Parsons***	1875-1961	General farm labourer
	Phoebe Parsons*	1876-1948	Domestic duties
	Ronald (Ron) Parsons*	1911-1977	Grocer's deliv' roundsman
Hazelwood, do.	**Emma Cole***	1872-1944	Domestic duties
	Edwin Stovold*	1870-1944	No occupation (mental)
Gaywood Cottage, do.	**H Fred Killner***	1900-1981	Omnibus proprietor
Lindene, do.	**Albert Matthews**	1890-1976	Woodsman

	Grace Matthews*	1890-1962	Domestic duties
	and 3 others		
Goldwedge, do.	**William Franks***	1875-1968	Jobbing builder
	Rose Franks*	1879-1958	Domestic duties
Rose Cottage, do.	**Mary Ketchell***	1852-1940	Housekeeper, retired
	Sarah Ketchell*	1862-1947	Domestic duties
Elm View, do.	**Alfred Munday***	1875-1962	Private gardener
	Grace Munday	1887-1967	Chapel cleaner, dom duties
5 Station Road	**Deborah Minall***	1867-1948	Domestic duties
12 Station Road	**Ephraim Boxall***	1864-1957	Jobbing gardener
	Harriett Boxall*	1867-1968	Domestic duties
4a Station Road	**Phoebe Jenner***	1855-1945	Domestic duties
	Kate Jenner*	1881-1970	Domestic duties
12 Council Cottages,	**William Kitchener***	1860-1942	Old age pensioner
Plaistow Rd and 4 others			
Albury, Vicarage Hill	**Percy Phillips**	1876-1964	Journeyman baker
	Ellen Phillips*	1882-1972	Domestic duties
	and 2 others		
Hillcrest, do.	**Harry Garman***	1875-1966	Head gardener
	Olive Garman*	1891-1979	Domestic duties
	Mary Heather*	1861-1943	Incapacitated
Ivanhoe, Alfold Bars	**Kate Bryson***	1874-1956	Domestic duties
	George Killner	1879-1988	Farm labourer
Alfold			
Alfold House Farm	**Michael Killner***	1870-1942	Farmer
	Kate Killner*	1874-1948	Domestic duties
	Gladys Killner*	1901-1986	Poultry and dom duties
	Hilda Killner*	1906-1977	Poultry and dom duties
	Cyril Killner*	1907-1979	Assisting farmer on farm
Rudgwick			
The Laurels	**W Bernard Hempstead***	1903-1965	Coal merchant
Bucks Green	**Charlotte Hempstead***	1895-1983	Domestic duties
Billingshurst			
Robinses Furze Rd	**James (Jim) Matthews***	1900-1981	Public works labourer
Five Oaks	**K Deborah Matthews***	1903-1976	Domestic duties

*denotes persons named in the death/burial registers; hld = household, Hall house)

A year in the life of the Combination Stores, 1955

Rita Phillips, née Polley, is widow of John Phillips, a director of Aylward, Smith from 1952. She is now married to David Gumbrell, to whom I am indebted for many of the photos in this book. They live just behind The Old Bakery. In 1955, she lived in the stores for one year. Rita remembers:

"It was quite an experience! The residents were very kind and thoughtful. Mabel South was the cook, and she cooked with a coal-fired Aga. Bread pudding was made with the leftovers of bread from the roundsmen and the shop. This is a delicious memory of teas and breakfasts, which all the shop staff and roundsmen could enjoy too. The dining room was next to the kitchen. After every meal, the table was always laid ready for the next meal.

The laundry was across the yard, next to the bakehouse. Washing would be put in to soak Saturday evening ready for the big wash at 4am Monday, using an old-fashioned mangle, then hung to dry on lines in the back garden all round the vegetable plot.
Over the shops were six bedrooms. I was in number 3. Then there were another three bedrooms over the other side of the house above the laundry room. Miss Hempstead had an office overlooking the pond.

The sitting room wasn't used too much, as they used to go to their bedrooms after tea, when it wasn't meeting nights, i.e., Tuesday and Thursday. When it was a Big Meeting (Bank Holidays), many brethren from other chapels used to stay, sleeping in the flour room which was over the bakehouse. There was a shute which sent the flour down straight into the dough mixer. I am sure it is still there in The Old Bakehouse.

I was going to chapel one Sunday morning when Bessie Hempstead stopped the car. She asked whether I was going to chapel like that. I was wearing a pink hat which wasn't approved by the Brethren who were always wearing black or navy or brown. Yes, I did go to chapel in my pink hat!"

PLATE 6.4

A Century of Aylward Smith & Co

Fig 1 – very early photo, posted 1906, before tree was cut back, one of the company postcards.

Fig 2 - better quality maybe a Sunday as all is quiet. Are the cups and saucers on the wall of the single storey building a nod to the china department, a Dependant speciality?

Fig 3 – from the opposite direction, also a company postcard, again posted 1906, a winter scene.

Fig 4 – a 1920s scene: note the K1 design telephone box at the Post Office, left. Kiosk 1 were erected 1921 to 1929. Little has changed.

Fig 5 – 1930s? The Post Office has a red telephone box; the stores remain unchanged. Summer awnings are prominent but can also be seen in Fig 1. Pollarded trees outside Hall House (house not visible) are also a feature from earlier days.

Fig 6 – post-war? A change to the buildings: the creation of a flat roof private balcony (behind modern style signpost). The board facing away from camera is intriguing!

Fig 7 – taken after the creation of the petrol station, with its National Benzole sign visible. This dates the photo to the late 1960s.

Fig 8 – 'cycle accessories' frontage, similar date.

Fig 7 – a busier photo with pedestrians and vehicles. Late 1960s (the car is a C reg). Hall House visible left.

Fig 8 – a late edition Aylward, Smith card with insight into the layout of domestic rooms overlooking the pond and the balcony. Note the advertising wording.

Fig 9 – a clutch of shop employees, not all of whom were Dependants by the 1950s: Winnie Cronk (1902-1985), Grace Skinner, Doreen Holden, Wevie Smith, Tom Hendy, Mabel Spooner (1888-1967).

Fig 10 - a photo of the site after redevelopment for retail and residential use. The architecture of the old buildings has either been preserved or sympathetically merged in.

This view is now obscured by tall vegetation, which no-one has cut back for several years.

Chapter 7

Aylward, Smith & Co Ltd,

the Company

Plate 7.1   Some Loxwood Brethren and Sisters

Aylward, Smith & Co directors (figs 1-5):

Fig 1 - Ethel Smith, 1863-1939, unknown person behind.

Fig 2 - Henry Aylward, 1866-1939

Fig 3 – left, Walter Parr, Company Secretary, 1857-1935

Fig 4 – right, Rowland Leswell 1886-1974, and Lily Leswell, 1897-1971 (photo Harry Sopp)

Fig 5 – John Phillips, director, 1917-1977

Fig 6 – May Winnifred (Winnie) Cronk, 1902-1985

Fig – 7 below left, Alice Irene (Renee) Dewett, Mabel Spooner and Milicent (Millie) Underwood (later Nash)

Fig 8 – right, back row l to r: Winnie Cronk, Bessie Hempstead, Kate Rugman, Fanny Phillips, Edith Holden; front l to r: Sarah Woods, Sarah Ketchell, E Bicknell

Fig 9 – 1950: standing l to r: Ron Parsons, Bessie Goodwin, Sybella (Si) Smithers, Florrie Phillips, Lucy Pannell, Alfred Goodwin, Mabel South, Bessie Hempstead, Mabel Spooner; seated l to r: Mrs Edith Goodwin, Sally Drewett, Mrs Cox, Sarah Woods, K Pannell (visitor S Norwood), Kate Rugman, Edith Holden; on grass l to r: Winnie Cronk, Renee Drewett, May Goodwin, John Phillips.

Fig 10 – left, Annie Denyer, 1873-1963

Fig 11 – right, Mabel Spooner, 1888-1967

1911-1920

There survives a Minute Book for Aylward, Smith & Co, commencing in 1911 and ending in 1973. Any earlier one is lost. The first annual general meeting reported was on 5 May. The Directors all lived at the stores (Table 7.1).

Table 7.1   Attendance, Aylward, Smith & Co Annual General Meeting, 5 May 1911

Directors
Henry Aylward (chairman),
Ethel Smith (company secretary),
Walter Nash
William Powell

Auditor
Walter Parr (Oakgrove, Spy Lane).

The following were also present:

Living at the Stores:
Elizabeth Holden
Kate Rugman
Sarah Woods
Deborah Minall
Elizabeth Cogger
Sarah Ketchell
Annie Williams

Living at Plaistow Place:
Richard Nightingale
Henry Killner
Annie Denyer
Lucy Enticknap
Harry Garman

Elsewhere

Sarah Baverstock	Parkfold Farm, Plaistow
George Luff	Oakhurst Cottage, Plaistow
William Belchamber	Rickman Lane, Plaistow
Mary Heather	New Cottages, Spy Lane, Loxwood
Alfred Ayling	New Songhurst Farm, Loxwood
William Spooner	Hall House, Loxwood
Charles Wadey	Barnfold, Loxwood
Jane Whetton	Noah's Ark, Loxwood
John Holden	Lordshill Stores

25 shareholders turned up; a 2½ % dividend was agreed. Most Dependants would have held a few shares, some rather more, having inherited from deceased Brethren. The Brethren were able to gain in a small way from the activities of the stores and other business ventures. Spread among many it seems unlikely to have amounted to very much, and it was often said that dividends were returned to the business.

The coal business was sold in 1918, no reason given. William & Emma Cole (Plate 7.8) remained in Loxwood, moving to Hazelhurst. In the same year, a pair of cottages and a meadow "near the stores" was purchased (possibly 1 and 2 Station Road with the meadow behind the stores, about 1½ acres). A significant expansion took place in 1920, when the Post Office and Hall House next door were purchased separately.

Acquisition of Hall House and the Post Office, 1920

Hall House (also known as Hall Hurst and reputed to have been an inn), with its 10 acres, had been the home and smallholding of one time elder and farmer John Overington and his sister Jane until John's death in 1909. Jane then moved to Hill Grove in Pancake Lane (Station Road), owned by Dependant Alfred Ayling. The name of her house may have been taken from Hillgrove in Lurgashall, where the Dependant Spooner family lived. Hill Grove later came into the ownership of the Kitchener family (through Ayling's daughter Jane, married to William Kitchener, also a Dependant) whose family still own it today.

William and Ann Spooner, also Dependants, lived in Hall House in 1911 and until the 1920s. James Manville also died there in 1911. Jesse Puttock was boarding with the Spooners at the time of the 1911 census. William Spooner eventually died at Jubilee Villas in 1948. Hall House became an annexe for the stores after 1920. John Franks, formerly of Station Road, moved there, and died there in 1930. Alf Goodwin (who did not himself live in Loxwood until much later) has been quoted as saying the farm belonged to John Overington, who lived there in 1901, and in 1906, when he sold his effects on leaving, three years before his death. The house however was one of the lots in the Loxwood House estate sale in 1905.

Goodwin also stated that Walter Nash had been very loyal to Richard Nightingale at Plaistow, refusing to leave until a successor, Harry Garman, had obtained his father's permission to take on shepherding in the 1890s. As shepherd Walter knew the sheep flock would need constant care. Alf suggested that Walter, once he had moved to Loxwood to work in the bakehouse, also took on the farmland of Hall House for the stores "on the community's behalf".

Until about 1900, John Elliott, grocer, at the top of the little hill beyond Willetts (next to the chapel of ease), also ran the post office in his shop, so named on Plate 6.1, Fig 1. In 1901, John Dennis, a saddler from Devon, had taken on the postal service. His premises were a saddler's workshop, which may explain why today's post office looks like a workshop, narrow and deep. By 1905, saddlers and post office were run by the Weller family. George Weller's daughter Ellen was sub-postmistress, and George was saddler in his narrow-fronted shop. The Edwardian attached house was probably built by the Wellers, and certainly before 1911. They were not themselves known to be Dependants, but George's mother-in-law was. Ellen Ann Smith was buried at the chapel in Spy Lane in 1918, with the epitaph in the register "Dear old lady Smith", which event may have left Weller free to retire. He was by then in his 70s.

There was, one suspects, a tendency by the Dependants to seek to monopolise trade in the village, a tendency which was probably a benign one, providing assured employment for their members. To some extent, this was also true of their farming enterprises. Farms at this time absorbed more labour than the Dependants could muster, but there was a strong tradition of farm management running through the veins of Richard Nightingale at Plaistow Place, and increasingly, at this time, of his protégé and relative, Walter Nash, who as has been said above moved to The Combination Stores from Plaistow in the 1890s. The insertion of the word "farmers" in the directory listing of the company in 1911, together with Nash's description as a farmer in that year's census seems to be the coming together of a collective

PLATE 7.2 Hall House and Hall Hurst Farm

Fig 1 – Hall House (undated, probably 1930s). It is reputed to have once been an inn.

Fig 2 and 3 – Hall Hurst Farm, with John Phillips, left and his sister, Florrie right. This small farm was suitable for piggery, chicken, a little grazing and had the tractor barn for Loxwood Place Farm. all buildings demolished and a housing estate now on the land.

Fig 4 – top left, Florrie Phillips, in Hall House garden, with piggery and tractor bar in background.

Fig 5 – top right, Si Smithers at rear of house, which was used as a dairy, for milk consumed by the community.

Fig 6 – Florrie feeding chicken.

Fig 7 – outside the tractor barn, driver Ron Matthews (not a dependant), with the author atop the straw cart, early 1950s (out of focus).

outlook which legitimised farming as a business which the company should be undertaking "in hand", not leaving to members to undertake individually. No doubt some of the meat, milk and eggs found their way into the stores, but the farms were run as genuine commercial enterprises.

Early Farming Activities

Outsiders have noted the Dependants' "practising of agricultural co-operation long in advance of the rest of England" *(Labour candidate for the Chichester Division, 1918 General Election)*. At the turn of the century, as well as Plaistow Place, which he may have had in mind (also perhaps Lower Diddlesfold at Northchapel – *Chapter 10*), there had been farmers at Hall House (the first, John Overington on his few acres). More significantly, Walter Sayers, another protégé and relative of Nightingale's, from the Plaistow community, had Pawlies Farm, on high ground north of the village, from about 1890 to 1895, and then moved to Willetts, a village centre smallholding, for some years. Pawlies was subsequently farmed by two other Dependant families, headed by John Carter, who was there in 1901, and James Elliott, formerly of Balls Cross, near Kirdford, in 1911. This is beginning to look like long term tenancy. Another Dependant farmer was James Etherington who farmed at Beldhamland, Skiff Lane, Wisborough Green, before retiring to Rose Cottage, next to the stores. Other than these, farmers in the environs of Loxwood were not Dependants, and included landowners who had in the past been vociferous opponents, such as the Bottings, who had farmed at Brewhurst Mill, by the river, and Loxwood Place in the late 19th century. Pawlies, Beldamland, Willetts and Hall House had been part of the Loxwood House estate up until its sale in 1905 *(The Times, 1 July 1905)*. There is no evidence that any of these properties passed into the ownership of the Dependants at that time.

Farms and Property, 1920s and 1930s

Some sources allude to farming, usually with respect to supplying the shops (which is only at best partly true, as much of the output of a mixed farm inevitably goes into national markets one way or another). As Mike Reed wrote, *"the farms astutely provided income and especially security through difficult times in the economy and falling numbers of brethren"*. The directors, who included Walter Nash, were interested in using his talents to bring rundown farms up to scratch and sell on for a small profit, having also taken any profit from the farming activities. These were tough years, especially the 1930s, so there may not have been much profit, but they were worked with zeal and commitment in line with the Protestant work ethic embodied by the Dependants. By this time, farms were not communal as in Richard Nightingale's day. There were not enough men to farm them, so workers were increasingly non-Dependants, and as late as the 1950s it still required 14 men to farm the combined Pawlies and Loxwood Place Farms (Plates 7.3 and 7.4).

That farming was indeed part of the weft and warp of the company is strengthened by the purchase of Pawlies Farm for £3,000 in 1924. This required an overdraft of £2,500 to be negotiated at the bank. Clearly it required faith in Walter's ability and a sympathetic manager at Westminster Bank, Cranleigh. The first thing to do was to sell off parts of the farm of no use, so The Rookery woodland was sold to Lady de la Zouche at Loxwood House and the remainder of the farm's timber to Agates, timber merchants. Was the venture a success? It was sold on after only one year in 1925 to Messrs Funnell & Sons. Did such

PLATE 7.3   Farming at Foxbridge and Loxwood Place

Three Loxwood photos, part of a collection of Dependant photos passed to me, like so many in this book, by David Gumbrill. Remainder from Jack Nash.

Fig 1 – tedding hay, Loxwood Place Farm in 1925. Thought to be Walter Nash using the fork. Notice the sheep hurdle used to guide the hay in a not very efficient tedder.

Fig 2 – turning hay with a swath turner, Foxbridge Farm, Plaistow, in 1943. Fred Day (author's uncle) rides the more modern machine. Charlie Pullen stands with hay fork.

Fig 3 – 1943, Foxbridge Farm, gathering the hay using a Carter Brothers of Billingshurst elevator, and a traditional horse wagon converted to tractor towing – possibly the first tractor on the farm.

Fig 4 – 1953, Loxwood Place Farm, using a stationary Carters elevator to unload to a haystack.

Notice how the first job needs a two-man team, the second three-man team. Farm workers were not usually Dependants.

Fig 5 – left, 1950, Loxwood Place Farm, bringing in the hay. John and Arthur Phillips on top, Bessie Hempstead by tractor, Walter Nash centre. Land girl driving tractor.

Fig 6 - right, c1954, Jack Nash with Violet, record breaking yielding Guernsey, in field next to the river.

Fig 7 – Walter Nash, right, with Jack Nash, his nephew. Left, Sam Underwood, Millie Nash his daughter, & Eliza Underwood. The Underwoods were a Dependant family.

Fig 8 – right, 1791, Loxwood Place, from Grimm's Drawings of Sussex (ack: British Library).

Fig 9 – left, Loxwood Place, early C20th.

Fig 10 – below, 29 June '48, after the fire.

Fig 11 – W Sx C Times 29 June 1948, a 2-hour inferno in the early hours of the same day.

TWO DEAD IN FIRE

FROM OUR CORRESPONDENT
HORSHAM, June 28

Loxwood Place, a sixteenth-century house at Loxwood, near Horsham, was burnt out early to-day. The owners of the house, Mr. and Mrs. Arthur Michael Robinson, were trapped in their bedroom and burned to death. The fire had got a firm hold before it was discovered by people living opposite the house.

Mr. Robinson returned a fortnight ago from Africa, where he had goldmining interests. He and his wife were to have travelled to Paris to-morrow.

trades in land go on earlier? The company minutes have not survived. There is evidence Pawlies returned to the Loxwood House estate as it was included in the sale of 1939.

Also, in 1925, 1, Pancake Cottages (corner of Spy Lane/Station Rd) was sold to Henry Aylward and Ethel Smith "as individuals". Was this intended for their retirement? Was it a ruse for raising capital? It would not have been unusual for single Dependants to share a house, but both died living at the stores. In 1927, Skiff Cottage, Wisborough Green, was sold for £100. Then, in 1928, the goodwill of the corn, meal & cake business was sold to Mr CM Bradley at Brewhurst Mill, Loxwood. As with the coal business, sold in 1918, there are signs that the wide range of business activity was beginning to be scaled back.

The four cottages known as New Cottages, opposite the chapel in Spy Lane, had been erected in the 1890s for the "afflicted aged Brethren". By 1929, the Brethren had created a Trust to administer the chapel. It was agreed the cottages and one other, possibly Oakgrove, should be sold to the Trustees of Loxwood Dependant Church for £100 in December of 1929, eventually signed in 1931, a rational housekeeping move.

Much earlier, in 1898, Col John Constable purchased the Ifold House Estate which lay between Plaistow and Loxwood. Connie Bayley informs us that during Constable's ownership it was Walter Nash who managed the farms up to 1914, when Constable sold the estate, including Ifold House, Headfoldswood and Foxbridge Farms (Plate 7.3). The subsequent owner of Ifold House Farm, Montague Scott (for the consortium Intercontinental Trust), went bankrupt when swine flu wiped out the pig herd in the 1930s. It was after this that the estate was divided into "plotlands" for sale to urban settlers, mostly Londoners, who bought enough land to build on with some spare to give them a real taste of country living – hence the present-day village of Ifold. Walter Nash, according to the author's father, played a part in this process alongside the appointed land agent. After all, he knew the farm better than most.

Changing the Guard

In 1927, there must have been a spot of bother, because the chairman cautioned members to "keep their own council'. The secretary, Ethel Smith, wrote, "Much comfort was felt while singing and in conclusion had much help and blessing in prayer". Mention of their faith was rare in the minutes. Unrelated to this, William Powell resigned as a director, his new address given as Strood Common, near Lordshill. The likely reason is that his mother Emily had died, and his father was left on his own to run a market garden. He had long worked as a grocery assistant in Loxwood. He was a nephew of Ann Powell who had been manager of the grocery department thirty years before. Joining the company and the brethren in about 1924/5, Bessie Hempstead (Plates 7.1, 7.3, 7.4, 7.7, 7.8), from Grays, Essex, was a recruit who would soon become the company secretary. She may have come from the Peculiars, strong in Essex, as did several others from time to time.

As noted elsewhere, the 1930s saw a notable number of elderly brethren deceased through old age. The company auditor, Walter Parr, died in 1935. He had come to Warnham Stores in the 1890s with considerable experience in the retail trade in his family shop in Fairford, Gloucestershire and then in Ledbury, Herefordshire. Whether it is of any significance or not, this family had roots in Somerset, then Gloucestershire, similar to John Sirgood's family – Walter's mother, Mary, also a Dependant, was close in age to Sirgood. Parr and his mother lived at Hillview in Spy Lane, opposite the chapel.

In 1936, a West Country newspaper carried a story which could have ended the career of Bessie Hempstead. As shown elsewhere, she was a keen driver. She was driving in Bath, perhaps on a visit to someone from the city where John Sirgood is known to have preached, and collided with a larger vehicle, hers being completely written off. A passenger Amelia Bright, aged 80, who was born in Bath, from the Warnham group, was the only injured party. A narrow escape. Bessie's other passenger was not named.

Ethel Smith, company secretary, and Harry Aylward, chairman, both died in 1939, in January and March respectively. See Chapter 13 for an account of Ethel's funeral. Fortunately, there were suitable successors: Walter Nash as chairman from the very next day, and almost as soon Bessie Hempstead appointed company secretary. Elizabeth Holden was appointed a director (see 1939 Register, Table 6.5, chapter 6). She had, like Walter, been at Plaistow Place years before. On 6 June 1939, Harry Garman proposed that Walter Nash be confirmed as Chairman. Those present were Walter Nash (chairman), Elizabeth Holden (director), Bessie Hempstead (secretary & director), Albert Ayling, Sibylla Smithers, Mabel Spooner, Kate Rugman, Emma Cole, Sarah Woods, Winnie Cronk, Harry Garman, Sarah Ketchell, and Sarah Drewett. Seven of these were present at the first recorded meeting in 1911. Alf Goodwin describes Walter as a great contrast to Harry, small to Harry's large girth and height, a degree of humility to Harry's commanding presence, but of the same beliefs. Walter was no singer but inspired through his testimony. He loved the community. He was also able to visit the German brethren three times between 1950 and 1957. Alf declared his epitaph was "a good man".

Walter Nash, a Proper Farmer, 1. 1939-1943

It is unsurprising to find Aylward, Smith & Co, under Walter Nash's leadership, buying Tokens Farm, Alfold Bars, from the Loxwood House estate in 1941. Lady Zouche had sold the estate as a whole to Mark Frederick North in 1934. North stayed there just long enough to use his surveying skills to knock heads together in the village to get the "North Hall" (village hall) built – it had been a project that was going nowhere fast – before selling up again in 1939. Tokens, 46 acres, let to Mr Gander, originally the home farm of the estate (before Loxwood Chase was created), had been on the market since that 1939 auction. Also purchased by the Dependants were Lots 5 (18 acres north of Alfold Bars), 13 (11 acres south of Loxwood Chase Farm, next to Four Houses) and 13a (3 acres next to Four Houses to the south). This required a loan, but only £100, from two Dependant companies, Randall, Slade in Norwood and Brown, Durant in Northchapel, and the use of Hall House as surety.

This deal was quickly followed by a further purchase of 163 acres at Foxbridge Farm, off Plaistow Road, from Tom Cooper for £3,000 in 1942. Cooper had been able to buy the farm as a sitting tenant from Lionel Constable's Ifold estate in 1925, when that estate was on the market. Tom Cooper continued to run the farm for a year before he was asked to take on the newly acquired Pawlies (see below). Jack Matthews took on Foxbridge. The author remembers Jack as an old man in the 1950s, living at Newbuildings (now Gennetts Farm) behind Pawlies Farm, north of the village.

Janet Austin, in her book *Kirdford, The Old Parish Discovered*, informs the reader that the timber in Corner Copse, much in demand for the war effort, was sold in 1943 to WJ Francis & Sons. Once the stately oaks had gone, Walter Nash and a group of ladies from the stores came to pick over the ground for wood chips to burn in the bakery. The copse regenerated, and is now looked after by the Woodland Trust, who presumably believe it to be ancient woodland! Cooper, probably not a Dependant, was given the tenancy of Box Cottage in Loxwood in his retirement, yet another cottage in the Dependants' portfolio.

Memories of Lakers Lodge and the Wartime Bakery

Jack Nash the author's uncle and Walter's nephew dictated his memoirs to his wife and the author. The extract that follows, though lengthy, explains a great deal about how Walter and Aylward, Smith operated in the tough years of the 1930s-40s. The Nash brothers, Jack and Jim, came to Loxwood in 1933 (when Jack was 19, Jim 17) from Warnham, following the early death of their father, who had farmed Warnham Court Farm, opposite Warnham Stores. They were not Dependants.

"Between the wars and up to the 1950s, they [the Dependants] seemed to have farmed just about every farm in Loxwood and Plaistow at some time, including Flitchfold, Foxbridge, Walthurst and Loxwood Chase, as well as ones mentioned elsewhere in this account! In the late 30s Walter was manager of Lakers Lodge Farm in Loxwood, rented from Major Guy Horne, and Wephurst Farm in Plaistow, rented from the well-known Wallace Heaton, a widower, who had made money in photography. Walter kept bees and grew sainfoin for them. Heaton's son lived there too, in a bungalow which was the old wooden cricket pavilion from Wisborough Green!

"Walter helped me to get a job at Lakers Lodge on the outskirts of the village, where I continued to learn the dairy trade, looked after cows and made butter, and kept poultry. I volunteered to join the Army, but was told firmly that food distribution was essential, and that I was of far more use where I was. As a worker in food distribution, I was in a Reserved Occupation, and so I remained throughout the war."

Note: Work at Lakers Lodge lasted only until 1937 or 8, when Lakers Lodge (which went on the market) and Wephurst were no longer farmed by the Dependants. In true Walter Nash fashion, the neglected farms had been brought up to scratch and were now fit for profitable farming.

"Jobs weren't easy to get then, there was agricultural depression, and my uncle suggested I go to work for the Dependants. Help was needed in the Bakehouse, and for deliveries, especially as labour shortages were rightly feared as war became more and more inevitable. I did so, unwillingly, thinking it would at least be immediate employment, and that I would get back to farming soon. My future was now firmly associated with the Dependant Brethren, though I was not one myself. One important thing was that it was at the stores that I met my future wife!

"We started at 5am, kneading and weighing the dough. We baked 4 or 5 batches before breakfast, which was around 8.30/9 am – half an hour allowed, so luckily home was just down the road. I went back to load up with boxes of groceries and bread for delivery round Loxwood, Ifold, Plaistow, Kirdford, Wisborough Green and Newpound. Somewhere in between I got home for my main meal, usually about 12.30. I completed the rounds, but often had to go back to the stores for more supplies. Back to the stores about 5 pm to check in money, orders, etc., home to tea, then it was time to set the dough to rise for next day – usually taking half an hour, and I finished around 7.30pm. Early on, I used a Morris van, then I had an old bus, which was easy to load and unload, after that was worn out, I had a newer van. Fred Killner [Plate 7.8] did all the repairs for the stores and kept the vehicles on the road. The other round was towards Alfold and back via Rudgwick which was done by Ron Parsons, and he was assisted by my brother Jim before he went in the army. Their round included daily delivery to Mr Moore's little shop in Alfold. I used to see Doris Harris regularly on my round doing her round for the bakery in Hilltop Stores which her mother Polly ran. Strangely, for wartime, I don't ever remember us running out of flour. In the Bakehouse, I remember there were also two women, Mabel South, and Betty Dudman, who made the agricultural workers' pies which were sold for 4d each, and very good beefy pies they were too (not all were claimed by the workers, so we sometimes were able to buy one).

"In 1943 I married Millie Underwood, who also worked at the stores in the grocery shop, where one of her duties was to deal with the ration coupons, which came from the Food Office in Petworth. Her father, Sam, was a Dependant who had come down from Leicestershire to join the Loxwood group. He and Eliza lived opposite the chapel in New Cottages, Spy Lane."

Walter Nash, a Proper Farmer, 2. 1943-1946

After just two years, Walter was ready to sell Tokens Farm, which he did in 1943, for £3,350 to Mr Hill of Mannings Heath, and Lots 13 and 13a for a further £1000 to Mrs Joyce McDougall. But in 1944, he bought Pawlies Farm – again – from Miss Hartley, this time for £11,000, initially with Tom Cooper as manager, then with Jack Nash as manager to build up the Paulox herd of Guernseys. The first six cows came from John Phillips at Hall House supplemented by Walter's purchases from Guildford market. Jack moved into the farmhouse with his new wife in January 1946, joined by his brother Jim at Elm View as herdsman. Pawlies had, like Tokens, been a Loxwood House estate farm. A very modern dairy parlour (by the standards of the day) now needed renovating as the previous owner had all the farm down to arable (Plate 7.4).

Part of the land was quickly disposed of: a house called Mayfield was immediately sold for £1,360 to Mr Philpott of Thornton Heath; the next year 1/3 acre of Pond Copse was sold to Percy & Kate Gander of Blackhall Cottage, Guildford Road, for £20, and the rest of Pond Copse, 5.8 acres, to Fred Killner of Gaywood (the owner of Sunbeam Coaches, and a Dependant) for £300. Pond Copse was re-purchased from Fred Killner in 1946, along with the North Hall meadow for £725.

After the war, it was time to sell Foxbridge, so after four years, it was sold in 1946 to Mr Bowley of Burton-on-Trent, amount not stated, but finances were clearly tight in 1947 as an overdraft was obtained from the bank, using Pawlies as security. Mr Bowley later sold the farm to Prince Tomislav, a member of the Yugoslav Royal Family. The farm more recently became a golf course (now closed).

Walter Nash, a Proper Farmer, 3. Loxwood Place

A further similar overdraft of £10,000 was sought by Bessie Hempstead in 1949. She was widely credited with having the financial brains of the company. This was to purchase Loxwood Place Farm. Its location in the village centre made it a key purchase (Plate 5.1). At the auction, it was hoped to place a top bid of £8,000, but it was knocked down at £8,400, necessitating further security from the bank. Pawlies already had a charge of £5,000 on it, so the only way she could raise this to £10,000 was by also lodging deeds of Pond Copse and the North Hall meadow. Additionally, ½ acre of Pond Copse was sold to Percy Thayre in 1950. She was flying by the seat of her pants, but all written in the minutes very matter of factly in her own neat hand!

Loxwood Place has a strong pedigree as both a house and a farm, and a strong association with the Dependants in living memory. It was in effect Loxwood's manor farm. By the beginning of the 20th century its manorial history was long past. The farm had been in the hands of the Churchman family from Ellens Green and Rudgwick, then in the hands of the Bottings. William Churchman's estate sold Loxwood Place to Sydney Botting in 1879.

Sydney Botting retired after the death of his wife to live near Chichester with his daughter's family. The farm was sold to James Waller Stevens MA, JP, about 1903-5 (WSRO SP/372, plan for sale catalogue). He appears in subsequent Kelly's Directories through to 1913, but Claude Garrard (a son of the crown jeweller Robert Garrard) appears on the 1911 census, occupation: farmer, and in Kelly's Directory 1909 and 1911. He later lived at Hawkhurst Court in Wisborough Green and may have rented the property from Stevens. An interesting insight on the size of the house is that it had 16 rooms. But in May 1913, The Times reported that Loxwood Place, described as a Tudor mansion with 120 acres, had just been sold by Knight Frank and Rutley. By 1918 Harold Morphew lived and farmed there, so he may well have been the buyer.

Directories are not very helpful in the 1920s, as Loxwood Place had no named resident in three successive issues. Did the Dependants ever own Loxwood Place? The farm made a lot of sense in their farming portfolio. Most importantly it was opposite The Combination Stores and contiguous with both their small Hall Hurst Farm and with Pawlies. Photographic evidence that they farmed it in the 1920s suggests they did, but there is no evidence from the company minute book. A photograph dated 1925 (Plate 7.3) is said to be of Fred Day and Charlie Pullen working a field there with a horse drawn hay turner (tedder), raising the possibility Walter Nash was farming Loxwood Place in the 1920s. In support of this, Henry Killner, who died in 1924, had probate declared giving his address as Loxwood Place. Henry (related to Walter) was also a farmer and was at Plaistow Place with Richard Nightingale around the turn of the century, then at Headfoldswood Common, before moving to Loxwood Place, where he died in his prime, only 52 years old. Nash was then listed in the 1930 Kelly's Directory as "farm bailiff to Messrs Aylward, Smith & Co Ltd, Loxwood Place". Separately listed in 'Private Residents' was a certain Albert Smith, living at Loxwood Place itself. Nash, as far as is known, lived in The Combination Stores for most of his life from the

1890s to his death in 1960. With no property deal involved, the conclusion must be that the farm was rented from an unknown owner, and that the house was lived in by Dependants at least for some of these years. The author's father is quoted in *Petworth Society Magazine, 67, 1992*, saying that Loxwood Place's ownership by the Dependants (the first, most likely a lease) was "repeated" twice.

The same article describes Walter visiting his farms on his Levis motorbike, later his little Austin 7, always prepared to get his hands dirty, but never himself earning anything from his ventures, all finance arranged by the company. He was very good at seeing the opportunity to clear land that was unproductive, or even wooded, and to remove shaws and trees to let the light in – not always popular locally, but necessary for efficient farming at the dawn of the mechanised age. He insisted on ditch clearance, on hand weeding and on laying good hedges. He was a notable cattle dealer and a good judge of horses, not bad for a former sheep man. He was among the first to have a tractor, and at one time the Dependants had their own threshing machine, but he was no mechanic. His view of combine harvesters was not so positive, as he thought they threw too much seed back on the land.

Several of those close to him remember his expression, when things were not done right, or he was getting stick for his religion, "Massey-oh man"! He was never confrontational, preferring to walk away from a dispute. His was a quiet authority, and he was respected for his knowledge and understanding.

The documented owner in the 1930s was John Turpin of Beldhamland Farm, Skiff Lane, who had in 1930 also been listed as farming Gunshot and Hurst Farms, also in Skiff Lane. He had been at Beldhamland since at least 1927, according to telephone records. By 1938, with Walter Nash still listed as bailiff, the directory now has John Turpin as farmer at Loxwood Place and Headfoldswood Farm alongside his other holdings. It is possible that this double entry is because Aylward, Smith continued to work land which Turpin had now purchased.

Tragedy struck on 28 June 1948. The historic manor house burnt down, ablaze for two hours in the night. Its non-farming owners since about 1938, Arthur Robinson, 55, a mining engineer with interests in Africa, and his wife Doris, 38, died in the fire. They had just returned from abroad. The brethren at the stores rallied round and provided refreshments for the police and fire brigade, even laying out the bodies of the deceased in the back of the stores. A letter of thanks was received from the police at Petworth (Plate 7.3).

The farmland, still owned by John Turpin, went under the hammer at the Town Hall, Horsham on 19th August 1949 (auctioneers, John Churchman & Sons, a family that had farmed there for much of the 19th century). Aylward, Smith, intent on a purchase, obtained it for £8,400. The ruined house, ancient granary, surviving washhouse and 10 acres were purchased separately from the agents McDonald Edwards for an extra £3,000, total purchase price £11,400. Completion on the farm was in 1950, the farmhouse in 1951. One condition of purchase was to hand over any jewellery that might be found on the site up to 1970. The Robinsons must have had some valuable jewellery lost in the fire and never recovered. Rebuilding of the house, albeit a very ordinary but large modern house, which would not stand the test of time, was done in-house by Rowland Leswell.

PLATE 7.4   Farming at Pawlies

These photos are from Jack Nash's personal collection.

Fig 1- left, Pawlies farmhouse, where Jack and Millie Nash lived (out of focus).

Fig 2 – below left, in the loose box, 1950: Gluestone Foremost, the Guernsey bull, sire to many in the milking herd.

Fig 3 – below, the modern 1930s milking shed, Jim Nash right. The cows were red- or fawn-and-white Guernseys.

Fig 4 – above right, in the field: the Paulox Guernsey dairy herd grazing west of farmyard barns, most of which still stand today. Note the water tank, left.

Fig 5 – far left, Reg Kitchener & Bill Wells.

Fig 6 – middle left, Ron Matthews, Jack Nash, Ingrid (Swedish land girl) and Jack Matthews.

Fig 7 – left, Rosalind Kitchener among Southdown sheep, folded on winter swedes.

Fig 8 – below, Millie Nash, Ingrid and Bessie Hempstead

Fig 9 – left, 1948, bringing in the hay (see also Figs 5 & 6).

Fig 10 - above, same tractor as Fig 9. Arthur & John Phillips on trailer, with Evelyn Parsons and friend; Jack on tractor, Millie holding dogs.

Fig 11, left, Jack Nash exhibiting Paulox Tulipette at West Grinstead. A perfect pose for a 1st prize winner!

Fig 12 - right, dairy cattle lines at Cranleigh Show, Knowle Park, Cranleigh, Jim Nash under 'Guernsey' sign (right).

Dependant visitors were frequently photographed at Pawlies Farm. See also Fig 8.

Fig 13 – left, Millie and Ingrid with Bessie Hempstead, company managing director, in front of the Dutch barn.

Fig 14 – right, Renee Drewett with visitors including her sister-in-law.

Fig 15 and 16 – Millie and Jack Nash with their much-loved smooth fox terriers, seen also in several other photos in this plate.

SALE FRIDAY NEXT.
PAWLIES FARM,
LOXWOOD, SUSSEX.
Adjoining Loxwood village, Rudgwick 4 miles, Horsham 10 miles, Guildford 11 miles.—Messrs.
WELLER, SON AND GRINSTED.
are instructed by Messrs. Aylward. Smith and Co., Ltd. (who have purchased the farm) to Sell by Auction without reserve, on
FRIDAY, JUNE 2nd, 1944,
the whole of the valuable
LIVE AND DEAD FARMING STOCK,
viz.:
40 HEAD OF CATTLE.
2 PEDIGREE SUFFOLK MARES.
2 PEDIGREE PUNCH GELDINGS.
MODERN FARM IMPLEMENTS AND MACHINERY, including
1938 FORDSON TRACTOR on Cleats, ploughs, harrows, cultivators, rolls, corn and root drills, McCormick and Massey-Harris binders, haymaking machinery, including Carter's and Innes stacking elevators, waggons and carts, small tools, etc.,
9 EXCELLENT POULTRY HOUSES.
Sale to commence at one o'clock.
Catalogues may be obtained from Messrs. Aylward, Smith and Co., Ltd., Loxwood, Sussex, or from the Auctioneers, 86a Woodbridge Road, Guildford (Tel. 3308).

Fig 17 – Pawlies Farm was purchased in 1944, sold in 1952. Neither documents nor news reports survive of the 1952 sale, but a curious sale in 1944 was advertised by auctioneers Weller, Son & Grinsted. It seems the purchase of the farm included all stock live and dead. The cutting indicates what was to be auctioned, specifically by Messrs Aylward Smith and Co Ltd, on 2 June 1944. To get rid of all this valuable stock in the wartime conditions pertaining is unusual; to start again from scratch indicates the company already possessed the means to buy, and ownership of, some livestock and machinery.

Acknowledgement: findmypast.com; Surrey Advertiser, 27 May 1944.

138

Peak Ownership, the 1950s and 1960s

Occasionally, Aylward, Smith bought and sold houses already in Dependant hands, for example, Oakmead (near Four Houses) from George Kennard for £300 in 1944, resold to George and Flora Reeves (not Dependants) of Barnfold Farm in 1945 for £800; its field was bought back again in 1948 from Flora for £460. In 1947, Fred Kennard, a Dependant, was loaned £7000 at 5% interest to build a house in Kent.

The purchase of Hilltop Stores in Loxwood (7 July 1944, £2,750 + £1,250 fixtures, appliances & goodwill) from Mrs Mary (Polly) Harris, the author's maternal grandmother, who had with her late husband bought the shop in 1911, was a significant event in his family's life as she then bought the bungalow, Elm View, where he would later spend most of his childhood. Curiously, Elm View was sold to her by a Dependant, Alfred Munday. Aged nearly 70, she had decided to retire, finding it difficult running the shop in wartime conditions. No doubt Aylward, Smith sought to extend their retail reach. They already had the Post Office, leaving only Sopp's the butcher independent for a few more years. Hilltop Stores, however, was a direct competitor in grocery, provision and motoring needs, including petrol sales. Frank Wall from the Norwood community was installed as manager, later succeeded by Cyril Clow, who married Frank's daughter Enid in 1960.

Although their numbers were in terminal decline, the Dependants were now owners of much of the village farmland, as well as its businesses. At Pawlies, Loxwood Place and Hall House, in addition to Walter's nephews Jack and Jim Nash, who managed the farms for Walter, farm workers included Jack Matthews and his son Ron living at Newbuildings (now Gennets) behind Pawlies, Reg Kitchener, Bill Wells, Jean, a land girl, the Phillips brothers, John and Arthur, and their sister Florrie at Hall House, and a Swedish girl, Ingrid. At this time, the author as a child was frequently to be found on the farms. The Dependants farmed, whether by agreement or ownership, all the land in the Spy Lane Station Road triangle, some land at Flitchfold, Pawlies Farm, and the North Hall/Oakmead fields, as well as Loxwood Place. The author remembers the first combine harvester being used in the North Hall meadow, where cars are parked today, as well as one of the last outings of the tractor-drawn binder in the field opposite Willetts, as farming began its post-war wave of mechanisation.

In 1950, an unprecedented decision was made to pay a bonus to some key individuals, namely:

Walter Nash	£100	director
Elizabeth Holden	£50	director
Kate Rugman	£50	drapery manager
Jack Coleman Nash	£100	farm manager (assistant to Walter)
Eric George (Jim) Nash	£20	head cowman
Frank Wall	£20	manager of Hilltop Stores
Rowland Leswell	£20	builder, carpenter.

The name most obviously missing from this list is Bessie Hempstead herself. The next year, it was decided to remunerate the directors - £150 per annum, payable each quarter, with "maintenance and lodging upon the Company's premises". In 1955, a 10% dividend was paid, also a rarity. A property in Ifold, 3, Hillcroft, with 10 acres, was purchased in 1950 from Mrs Amelia Martin whilst all these bigger decisions were being made.

Then there was another fire, a Dutch barn fire at Pawlies in the early 1950s. Smoke was seen from the village. The author remembers racing up the green lane from Loxwood Place with a friend on our bikes to see the barn ablaze. After the fire was more or less extinguished crates of beer were brought in for the firemen and farm workers (but not for us!). A useful example of how the Dependants improved a farm was the wholesale removal of Pawlies Copse to turn it into agricultural land. The copse was just west of the farm buildings, south of the lane and footpath to Gennetts Farm. Today, there is no trace of it. It is obviously not something that would meet with approval today but in 1950 the mantra was increased production, and such a large woodland close to a dairy unit must have seemed a problem for grassland management.

However, in 1952, to finance much needed updating of the bakery, it was decided to sell Pawlies, to Mrs Helen Naumann of Rudgwick Grange in Tismans Common, for £15,500. A few parcels of land were retained, OS field numbers 197, 203, 213, 213a and Furzen Wood 217. It is difficult to say, with inflation and appreciation of land values, whether these sales were making much money for the company, but the farm had been bought years earlier for £11,000. It seems good business, given that Loxwood Place was acquired for less.

Jack and Jim Nash with other staff, and the author tagging along, were able to walk the Paulox pedigree Guernsey dairy herd down the green lane to Loxwood Place, and so carry on almost uninterrupted. Jack and Millie Nash moved from Pawlies farmhouse into the new house that Rowland Leswell had built, presumably completed quickly in the intervening 17 months. Also, at Loxwood Place, a new Dutch barn was constructed, where terraced houses now stand. Walking the footpath through Pawlies today, the layout of the old partly disused farm buildings are exactly as the Dependants left them, but at Loxwood Place all trace has been obliterated by new housing, except for the historic granary, still in use for its original purpose in the 1950s. The land estate built up in the 1940s and early 50s only lasted a short time. All would be sold by 1955.

Changing the Guard Again

Meanwhile, at the end of 1952, *"owing to advanced age of the two senior directors [Walter Nash and Elizabeth Holden], necessity being realised of strengthening the Board of Directors, Rowland Leswell of 2 Jubilee Villas and John Phillips shall take their place as directors straight away. As R Leswell is married and not living-in, his pay will be £500 per annum at £9 per week and the balance at the end of the year; J Phillips £5 and maintenance and lodgings and £150 at the end of the year."* Miss Holden died in 1953, having given her whole adult life to The Combination Stores, much of it in the drapery department.

Rowland Leswell, a Stalwart of the Final Years

This seems an appropriate point to digress to Rowland Leswell's typescript memoir of his life. As one of the few who moved from the Essex Peculiar People to Loxwood, his is an interesting story. Briefly, he arrived in Loxwood during the war, following his wife, Lily, who had evacuated from Southend to her friend and Dependant Mabel South, another Essex girl recently moved to Loxwood. He had become a conscientious objector, found himself sent all over the country doing war work. He was a carpenter in a Reserved Occupation and when dismissed from a Birmingham job, travelled back to his wife. He then set about getting work in Petworth (to which he cycled daily!), in Portsmouth, then Cranleigh on agricultural work. The couple decided to stay, moved their furniture and set up home in two rooms at Hall House. Lily worked in the stores. At a CO tribunal he declared that none of the work offered was appropriate to his beliefs as he could not even aid or abet the crime of war. He convinced them to allow him to remain in his farm work. Nevertheless, he writes eloquently of the bullying and difficulties with the authorities. It seems from his account that he did more and more work for the Dependant farms. After seven years, they moved into 2 Jubilee Villas, adjacent to the stores.

As time went by, he also turned his hand to working in the bakehouse, grocery, butchers, on the farms, as a roundsman (the author remembers him coming to his parents' house). There were six vans to keep on the road, private car hire to be arranged, and further work as a carpenter-builder. He was a jack of all trades. He listed farms he worked at – Hall House, Pawlies, Tokens, Foxbridge, but he does not mention Loxwood Place.

On the other hand, he does say: *"At one time Brewhurst Mill was owned by the brethren, and the River Authorities gave orders for the weir and floodgates, which control the river on which the mill stood, to be renewed. This was new work for me, but being asked to do it, I agreed that I would try it, so with the help of a man who had been a hospital porter but had come to Loxwood for health reasons, I started. I had to fix up a kind of gantry with wooden scaffold poles, upon which I hung an endless chain and tackle, to lift the old gate out. When I had made the four new gates, they had to be slid into 9 x 9 uprights with grooves in the sides. Each gate had a 5 x 5 upright in the middle on which a cast iron cog plate was fixed, so they could be raised by a winding gear at the top."* He was offered a well-paid job on the strength of this but refused. The mill was then sold [no dates].

Lily brought her skills of nursing to the Loxwood community. She frequently gave help to the sick, as was very normal among the sisters. Unlike many Dependants, they went on holiday, but always took a couple of the others with them. Lily herself, after becoming seriously ill, passed away in 1971. Florrie Phillips, of Hall House, gave them much help as Lily lay dying.

Rowland and Florrie then chose to marry, the following year. He died in 1984 and she in 1992. Meanwhile, as they became the last of the few, he had more to offer as trustee of various parts of the business and chapel, as explained in Chapter 4. For an outsider, he had given much, and been entrusted with much. Indeed, he had led many funeral meetings in the chapel, so should be considered as an elder. Also, this outsider, had brought skills and a mindset which embraced technology and an ability to make things happen, a doer, more than a philosopher. The Dependants were all the better for his time spent in Loxwood, as so many became frail and less able to cope. I suspect Walter Nash found him a useful ally.

PLATE 7.5   Purchase of Loxwood's Retail Assets

Fig 1 and 2 – Hilltop Stores, purchased from Mrs Mary Harris 1944; left in 1935, right in 1949, when owned by Aylward, Smith & Co.

Fig 3 and 4 – Post Office, purchased in 1920 (with Hall House); left, when a saddler's shop c1905, right as a Post Office 1920s, when owned by Aylward, Smith & Co.

Fig 5 – former butcher's shop, now residential. The former stables are on the left, the shop added in post-war years (low wing joining the buildings). Now called Mellow, its historical name was Fair Maggots. Purchased from the Misses Sopp, £600 for goodwill, van, all equipment and occupation of existing shop rent free for 6 months, until new shop built at Combination Stores (no price for premises available).

Fig 6 – left, recent view of the Post Office.

Fig 7 – right, recent view of The Old Stores, formerly Hilltop Stores

The Nash Era Draws to its Natural Close

In 1953, an overdraft of £1,950 was needed to keep the business going, this time using the deeds of Loxwood Place. Decisions had to be made. From 1955, Walter's title was re-designated as managing director, instead of chairman. Walter was 84, and his health was failing. It was decided to pull out of farms altogether, except for Hall House. After only five years, Loxwood Place (Plate 7.6) was put on the market. The 138 acres were offered by the agents for £17,500. In the event, it made only £14,500, and the meadows north of the North Hall £1,200. All was sold to John Naumann of Rudgwick Grange, son of Mrs Helen Naumann, who had bought Pawlies. At the same time, £2,500 was borrowed from the bank to purchase a house for Bernard Hempstead (Plate 7.8, Bessie's brother), to be repaid from sale of farm stock. The farm sale took place on 11 May 1955, with the Paulox herd of 24 Jersey milkers, 37 followers and 3 bulls as the principal draw. The herd included the bull Gluestone Foremost, sire to most of the cows and in the herd for many years, and Violet, born 1939, once the lead yielding Guernsey cow in the south east. The Naumanns only kept the farms for three years before selling them on again, together with Tokens Farm.

During the Loxwood Place years, Walter's sisters, Miss Amy Nash, a retired lady's maid, and Mrs Lilly Herrington, who had returned from Australia, had lodged in a flat in the farmhouse, but after the sale were accorded hospitality in The Combination Stores with Walter. They died in 1957 and 1958 respectively. Lilly was even buried in the chapel graveyard. Neither to my knowledge accepted the Dependant faith.

Subsequently, in 1996, Loxwood Place, new farmhouse, and all farm buildings, except the historic granary, were demolished and a small development built on the site. Many recently arrived residents of Loxwood may be unaware of its history, or that much of the development is aligned on the footprint of former buildings. The ghost of the old, moated, manor house lives on, as 1 and 2 Tithe Barn, a name which does not reflect the site's history.

Later in 1955, this busy year, the butchers in Loxwood, at Fair Maggots (Plate 7.5), came on the market, the end of an era for the Sopp family whose business had begun in the previous century at the Onslow Arms. The final piece of the retail jigsaw came together as the business was snapped up from Misses Marjorie and Gladys Sopp, and soon transferred to new premises created next to the grocers at The Combination Stores. This was achieved by removing the old petrol pumps, demolishing the front of the garage, and creating a new drive in for petrol, with the butchers behind. What was left of the garage was accessed through the forecourt. The company, synonymous with the religious element, and growing increasingly old and female in composition, reverted to its core activities.

A little surprisingly, as he had lived locally since the 1940s, Alfred Goodwin only attended his first AGM in 1958. In 1960, he was appointed assistant secretary with Bessie Hempstead stepping up to be managing director, whilst retaining the post of company secretary. The feeling of an end of an era, perhaps greater even than the one in the 1930s, as the community shrank in numbers, was expressed in a rare prayer at the AGM in 1959. *"Special thanks was rendered to God for sparing every member to us for another year and for all his manifold blessings especially for the prevailing Spirit of Love."*

PLATE 7.6   The Sale of Loxwood Place Farm, 1955

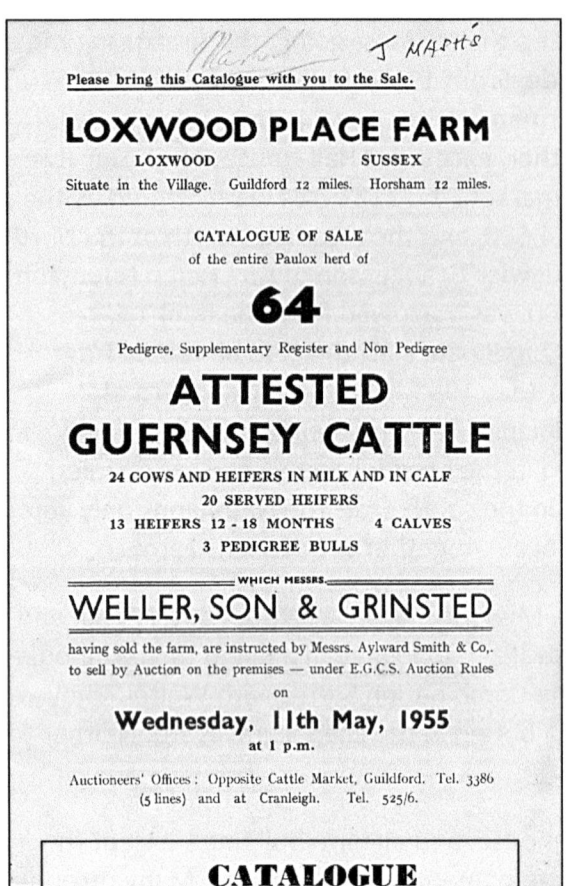

Please bring this Catalogue with you to the Sale.

LOXWOOD PLACE FARM

LOXWOOD   SUSSEX

Situate in the Village. Guildford 12 miles. Horsham 12 miles.

CATALOGUE OF SALE
of the entire Paulox herd of

64

Pedigree, Supplementary Register and Non Pedigree

ATTESTED
GUERNSEY CATTLE

24 COWS AND HEIFERS IN MILK AND IN CALF

20 SERVED HEIFERS

13 HEIFERS 12 - 18 MONTHS   4 CALVES

3 PEDIGREE BULLS

WHICH MESSRS.

WELLER, SON & GRINSTED

having sold the farm, are instructed by Messrs. Aylward Smith & Co,.
to sell by Auction on the premises — under E.G.C.S. Auction Rules
on

Wednesday, 11th May, 1955
at 1 p.m.

Auctioneers' Offices : Opposite Cattle Market, Guildford. Tel. 3386
(5 lines) and at Cranleigh.   Tel. 525/6.

Foreword

The Auctioneers have great pleasure in directing the attention of purchasers to this important dispersal sale of the Paulox herd of pedigree and Grading Register Guernseys, the property of Messrs. Aylward Smith & Co., which arises through the sale of the farm.

The herd as catalogued includes 64 head of which there are 24 cows and heifers in milk and in calf, 20 served heifers, and 13 un-served heifers 12 - 18 mos., 4 calves and three service bulls.

The herd was founded in 1946 with the purchase of a number of females carefully selected for milk and butterfat and the herd sire was the very well bred proven bull Glewstone Foremost A.R. (15) who was by Murrell Golden Tip 14th A.R. (23) D.M., N.M.R. progeny recorded bull, 1952 and out of Rashleigh's Golden Dairy-maid 7th A.R. Now with the exception of four cows every animal is homebred and apart from a few of the older cows all are dehorned.

The performance of the dairy herd is worthy of note and set out hereunder are the averages for the past 7 years :—

1947/48	(3rd West Sussex) ..	8,449 lbs.
1948/49	(2nd West Sussex) ..	9,573 lbs.
1949/50	(4th West Sussex) ..	9,370 lbs.
1950/51	(5th West Sussex) ..	9,495 lbs.—4.91%
1951/52	(10th West Sussex) ..	9,339 lbs.—4.85%
1952/53	(6th West Sussex) ..	9,541 lbs.—4.80%
1953/54	(6th West Sussex) ..	10,003 lbs.—4.73%

The majority of the cows have 1,000 galls. yields at over 4.5% and included in the sale is the foundation cow G.A.702 Violet, who was leading Guernsey in the South Eastern Area and 3rd highest in all England with a yield of 19,980 lbs.—4.34% in 305 days, and that averaged 16,342 lbs.—4.08% with 7 calves.

A number of the dairy stock will be calved or close to calving and of the remainder the majority are due from September to December.

The in-calf heifers are a particularly choice lot well worthy of attention. They have all been served by Holmbury Annas Robert 3rd (Lot 64) and start calving from about mid-September onwards. The unserved heifers range from 18 months down to this year's calves and without exception have been very well reared and show great promise.

3

CATALOGUE

DAIRY COWS AND HEIFERS

LOT

1. *Foundation Cow, Violet G.A.702 (A.V.66407).

Born 1939. Fawn and White.
Last calved Oct. 2nd, 1954.

*Lot 1 gave 11,003 lbs., 3.79%, 320 days—5th calf.
22,108 lbs., 4.48%, 365 days—6th calf.
18,731½lbs., 4.00%, 387 days—7th calf.
16,964 lbs., 4.10%, 337 days—8th calf.
18,320 lbs., 4.04%, 419 days—9th calf.
16,778½lbs., 4.10%, 456 days—10th calf.
and was leading Guernsey in South Eastern Area and 3rd highest in England with a yield of 19,980 lbs. in 305 days, 4.34% butter fat and 867 lbs. fat. 1st Prize Cranleigh Show, 1949 in Recorded Cow Class.

2. *Foundation Cow, G.A.316 Tulip (A.V.62724).

Born 1944. Fawn and Little White.
Last calved 30th Dec., 1954.
Served 14th April, 1955 by †Majestic 2nd of Whistley.

*Lot 2 gave 7,671½lbs., 4.30%, 331 days—1st calf.
8,642½lbs., 5.04%, 310 days—2nd calf.
10,484½lbs., 4.89%, 324 days—3rd calf.
10,036½lbs., 4.60%, 305 days—4th calf.
10,606½lbs., 4.69%, 236 days—5th calf.
9,909½lbs., 4.94%, 325 days—6th calf.
9,408½lbs., 4.60%, 331 days—7th calf.
9,726½lbs., 4.57%, 321 days—8th calf.
and has given 3,175½ lbs. in 83 days.
†See Lot 63.

3. *Foundation Cow, G.A.707 Iris (A.V.66406).

Born 1944. Fawn and White.
Last calved 19th April, 1955.

*Lot 3 gave 6,964½lbs., 3.75%, 328 days—1st calf.
9,578 lbs., 4.38%, 344 days—2nd calf.
10,818½lbs., 4.41%, 325 days—3rd calf.
12,044½lbs., 4.30%, 316 days—4th calf.
11,823 lbs., 4.18%, 307 days—5th calf.
12,423½lbs., 4.46%, 318 days—6th calf.
10,750½lbs., 3.84%, 329 days—7th calf.
9,750 lbs., 4.21%, 319 days—8th calf.

3(a). Her Heifer Calf Paulox Easter Iris.

Born 19th April, 1955.

5

Fig 1 – sale catalogue, front.

Fig 2 – sale catalogue, foreward.

Fig 3 – sample page from dairy stock lots.

Note: lot 1 is Violet, photograph in Plate 7.3. see also Fig 2 above.

Fig 4 – advertisement of auction sale. *Ack: findmypast.com, West Sussex County Times, 16 September 1955.*

SALE WEDNESDAY NEXT
LOXWOOD PLACE FARM,
LOXWOOD SUSSEX

Situate in the Village. Guildford 12 miles. Horsham 12 miles.

MESSRS. WELLER, SON & GRINSTED

having sold the farm, are instructed by Messrs. Aylward Smith and Co. Ltd. to sell by Auction on the premises on

WEDNESDAY, SEPT. 21, 1955

the whole of the valuable LIVE AND DEAD FARMING STOCK

54

ATTESTED STORE CATTLE

1 Aberdeen Angus, 17 Friesian, 36 Shorthorn steers and heifers 12-30 months.

together with the

FARM IMPLEMENTS AND MACHINERY

tractors by Fordson, 3 hydraulic and trailer tractor ploughs, Fordson tool bar, heavy and seed harrows. Cambridge ring rolls, corn and root drills, artificial manure distributor, Massey Harris dung spreader.

HAYMAKING AND HARVESTING MACHINERY

including grass mower, swathe turner, hay rake, hay loader, 2 Albion binders, Carter stacking elevator, MARSHALL 4ft. 6in. THRESHING DRUM, Chevrolet farm truck, trailers, wagons and carts, barn machinery and a quantity of useful farm miscellany.

Sale at 12 noon.

Catalogues from the Auctioneers, Auction Offices, Guildford. Tel. 3386 (5 lines).

At the time, Walter Nash was very sick indeed. He had had both legs amputated. He died in Royal Surrey County Hospital, Guildford, 23 September 1960. The death register records *"Loxwood bro[ther] Walter Nash would have been 90 in March. [He] was a great sufferer, had no legs, but very happy"*.

One immediate consequence was a decision in October not to renew the off license for Hilltop Stores and to cease selling intoxicating drinks s soon as possible. This license had continued from the time of Mrs Harris and had been allowed to continue under Walter Nash's leadership. Miss Hempstead thought differently. In other ways, the loss of Walter was felt deeply. At the AGM in 1961, *"A tribute was paid to our deceased Director Walter Nash to whom we owe so much, for his life of unselfishness, and all his efforts for the benefit of all, for his steadfast example, and Quiet Spirit. His absence was much felt but the same bond of love and concern still remains. Thanks was rendered to God for every blessing."*

Alf Goodwin relinquished his brief appointment as assistant secretary in favour of Irene Drewett. No one was appointed chairman or managing director to replace Walter.

The 1960s and 1970s, the Final Acts

At the post office, a much-loved sub-postmaster, Frederick Muggeridge, died suddenly in 1962 at the age of 52. His loss was widely felt in the village. In those days the post office sold little else, apart from newspapers. The empty space in front of the counter gave it a spacious feel it certainly lacks today, though it is a wonder the business was viable. The company decided in its wisdom that Edwin Carr, the new lessee could continue to sell newspapers, but not toys!

In 1965, a purchase of land would find echoes from the very beginning of combination in Loxwood. The fields that had historically been part of Blackwool, where the Fosters had their grocers' shop in 1860 (Chapter 5), were bought from Major Neil Farmer of Linden House opposite. This was for £3,000. These were added to the land at Hall House (historically Hall Hurst). But in fact, were later sold on for the conifer nursery business that has, older residents might say, blighted this part of the village next to Linden House Hill. Today both Hall Hurst and nursery have been developed for housing.

A re-appraisal of the company's worth was undertaken in 1966 – the authorised capital of the company stood at 2000 shares of £1 each. The issued share capital was 1,212 shares of £1. It was decided to issue the remaining 788 shares at par. All shareholders were invited to apply. In the event of oversubscription shares would be issued in proportion to the number of shares held at 8 Mar 1966. In the event 780 were issued. A high 30% dividend was declared.

In 1970, at the AGM, *"The past year has brought two gaps in our homely little company by the Home call of our dear members Sibylla [Smithers] and Irene [Drewett]. We missed them and consideration was expressed owing to the advancing age of some and the difficulties in the business life in the present age."*

Irene had been appointed assistant company secretary in 1961 and was only 55 when she died. Her loss was felt keenly. In the following 12 months both the taxi service, and more fundamentally, the bakery closed down. This was followed in late 1971 by the sale of both Jubilee Villas to Rowland Leswell (£1,500), and The Olde Cottage (£1,500) to Alfred Goodwin of Rose Cottage (the other half of his cottage). Rowland was a prominent member of the community, as has been described above. Alf had lived at Rose Cottage for many years, and he now had the other portion of the original pair of cottages on the plot that became the site of The Combination Stores over 80 years before. By the time these deals were signed, in 1972, extra land had been added, and the price raised to £2,700 and £2,300, respectively for the villas and the cottage, with the intention that four garages would be built behind, with access from Nicholsfield, on each plot. These garages would form a continuous row when completed and are there today.

Because they had been made over in 1931 to the Chapel Trustees, the sale of New Cottages in Spy Lane was not recorded in these minutes. The author has obtained a copy of the Land Registry title to Nos 1 and 2 which were conveyed in December 1970 by the surviving trustees, namely Bessie Hempstead, Alfred Goodwin and Cyril Killner, No 1 to George Reeves and Joan Ford, and No 2 to Lionel and Irene Watson, for £1,250 each.

Higher sums would be exchanged next as decisions were being made thick and fast. The "amazing sale of assets" was minuted at the 1972 AGM. One imagines everyone was rather shocked. It was in 1972 that Desmond Smithers of Linden House agreed to buy Hall House and the Post Office for £40,000, (the conveyance to Mr & Mrs Smithers was signed that September) and Cyril and Enid Clow agreed to buy Hilltop Stores and the old house attached, Alameda, for £24,000, signed January 1973. Then in February, 1 and 2 Station Road were sold to John Phillips for £1,500, and a small parcel of plot OS203 to the trustees of North Hall and the Parish Council for £500, signed in July. The remainder of this plot was sold to Messrs Hallt, farmers at Songhurst Farm, for £2,000, signed in September. It is to be hoped that the lawyers were being fair to the beleaguered and elderly brethren.

The 1973 AGM was to be the last recorded. It was attended by Bessie Hempstead, Rowland Leswell, John Phillips, Alfred Goodwin, Winnie Cronk, Ronald Parsons, Kate Rugman, Florrie Phillips, May Goodwin, and Mary Farquhar.

Then, recorded retrospectively on 26 March 1973, came the finale. The minutes state it thus (I précis): *Sell to Michael A Slorrick, LLB, solicitor, of Woolspinners, Guildford Road, Loxwood, the freehold property, The Combination Stores, with shops, fittings, fixtures and plant, £40,000, stock at valuation. To take over the business 3 March 1973 so as to work out his trading with VAT system. He would pay on account for stock on that date. Old residents remain as tenants in flat over shops in rooms 1, 2, 3, 4, 5, 6, 7, 8, 9, lounge, bedrooms adjoining and flat roof, entrance by hall door or garage, for 8 years, reducing amount by £8,000 on completion. If tenants desire to give up the flat before, money will be refunded accordingly.*

The contract was signed on 6 July, and the conveyance to Mr Slorrick's company, Fancrest Ltd, for £27,500, and a mortgage signed on 27 November 1973. In pencil underneath is added in Miss Hempstead's hand (she had continued to write the minutes throughout) – *"£12,500 Bessie Hempstead, Mr Slorrick £15,000 Trustees of The Retreat Loxwood".*

Table 7.2   **Dependants Alive in Loxwood, and Elsewhere, in 1973**

Attendees at the last AGM (address from Burial Register):

John Phillips	died 1974, aged 57. living at 1 or 2 Station Road
Ronald Parsons	died 1977, aged 65, living at Linkholme, Guildford Road
Kate Rugman	died 1977, aged 99, living at The Combination Stores
Bessie Hempstead	died 1980, aged 84, living at The Combination Stores
Rowland Leswell	died 1984, aged 78, living at 2, Jubilee Villas
Winnie Cronk	died 1985, aged 83, living at The Retreat, Spy Lane
May Goodwin	died 1985, aged 82, living at Rose Cottage, Guildford Road
Alfred Goodwin	died 1990, aged 96, living at Rose Cottage, Guildford Road
Florrie Leswell (Phillips)	died 1992, aged 80, living at 4, The Court, Guildford Road
Mary Farquhar	died 1999, aged 86, Chartwell, Midhurst, formerly of The Retreat, then Alma

Others in Loxwood

Jack Bradshaw	died 1973, aged 85, at St Luke's Hospital, Guildford (Edith's brother)
John Butchers	died 1974, aged 79, living at The Olde Cottage, Guildford Road
Alice Carpenter	died 1974, aged 86, living at The Retreat, Spy Lane
Helen Gifford	died 1975, aged 91, living at The Retreat, Spy Lane
Alice Goodwin	died 1975, aged 88, living at Walcot, Guildford Road
Alice Mann	died 1976, aged 87, at Worthing Hospital
Ellen Reeves	died 1977, aged 87, living at The Retreat, Spy Lane
Hilda Killner	died 1977, aged 74, living at Pinetree Lodge, Merry Hills
Edith Bradshaw	died 1977, aged 103, living at The Retreat, Spy Lane
Louisa Wall	died 1978, aged 71, living at Alameda, High Street
William Wall	died 1978, aged 78, living at Woodvale, Spy Lane (formerly Alameda)
Cyril Killner	died 1979, aged 71, living at Pinetree Lodge, Merry Hills
Ivy Bridger	died 1979, aged 76, living at Bethel, Guildford Road
Olive Garman	died 1979, aged 87, in Worthing Hospital, living near Petworth
Arthur Phillips	died 1983, aged 73, living at 2, Jubilee Villas
Beatrice Smithers	died 1984, aged 78, living at The Retreat, Spy Lane
Nellie Elliott	died 1985, aged 93, at St Richard's Hospital, Chichester
	(the last entry in the death register)
Christopher Hale	died 1986, aged 100, living at The Retreat, Spy Lane
Edith Goodwin	died 1986, aged 85, living at Rose Cottage
Gladys Killner	died 1986, aged 85, living at Pinetree Lodge, Merry Hills
Gertrude Killner	died 1987, aged 86, living at Pinetree Lodge, Merry Hills
Gwen Bradshaw	died 1989, aged 90, at Dorking General Hospital (Edith's sister)
Memilo Pyke	died 1992, aged 96, formerly The Retreat, living at Petworth Cott Hospital
Elsie Killner	died 1994, aged 95, living at Elsmere, Spy Lane
Leslie Killner	died 1998, aged 92, living at Elsmere, Spy Lane
Elsie Piper	died 2002, aged 104, at a nursing home in Worthing
	(the last entry in the burial register)

Note: those above who died in hospital are assumed to be from Loxwood. Some of those given addresses also died in hospital, but their address was also given or is known to the author. Those listed below are believed to have been members of other communities, or no longer part of their community, at the time of their death. The list is not exhaustive. The author would welcome information on anyone omitted.

<u>Living Elsewhere</u>

Sarah Drewett	died 1973, aged 96, living in Chichester (Loxwood)
Doris Cowell	died 1973, aged 66, living in Chichester
Frederick Kennard	died 1974, aged 81, living in Hove
Doris Johnson	died 1975, aged 61, living at Sutton, Surrey
Elizabeth Denyer	died 1975, aged 93, living at The Norr, Northchapel
Winifred Remnant	died 1975, aged 84, in Worthing
Olive Taylor	died 1976, aged 87, in Worthing
Emily Mitchell	died 1979, aged 68, living in Brighton
Bessie Greenfield	died 1983, aged 82, living in Hove
May Madgwick	died 1984, aged 92, living at Clemsfold House, Slinfold (Warnham)
Kate Candy	died 1985, aged 86, in Brighton
Florence Martin	died 1988, aged 88, living in New Church Road, Hove
Annie Matthews	died 1991, aged 80, at Crawley Hospital
Joseph Hunt	died 1994, aged 88, in Guildford (Loxwood)
Marjorie Polley	died 1999, aged 94, at St Richard's Hospital, Chichester
Gwendoline Earwicker	died 2003, aged 86, living in Chichester
Kathleen Edwards	died 2008, aged 93, living in Bognor Regis (Northchapel)

<u>Total 44</u>

The telephone directory shows that trade continued under the name of Aylward, Smith, Combination Stores to 1980. The company had had a telephone number since 1923, when the line came to Loxwood. Incidentally, at that time numbers were issued as follows:
1 – Post Office; 2 – private; 3 – Aylward, Smith; 4 – JA Harris, The Stores (Hilltop).

PLATE 7.7 Bessie Hempstead

TELEPHONE: LOXWOOD 231

Aylward, Smith & Co. Ltd

Farmers, Grocers, Provision Merchants, Bakers, Drapers, Ironmongers

PETROL & OILS
ACCESSORIES, ETC.

CYCLE AGENTS · HOUSE FURNISHERS, ETC.
TAXI FOR HIRE

AGENTS FOR THE
NORTHERN ASSURANCE CO.,LTD.

Combination Stores

PARCELS TO RUDGWICK STATION

Loxwood, NEAR BILLINGSHURST, SUSSEX

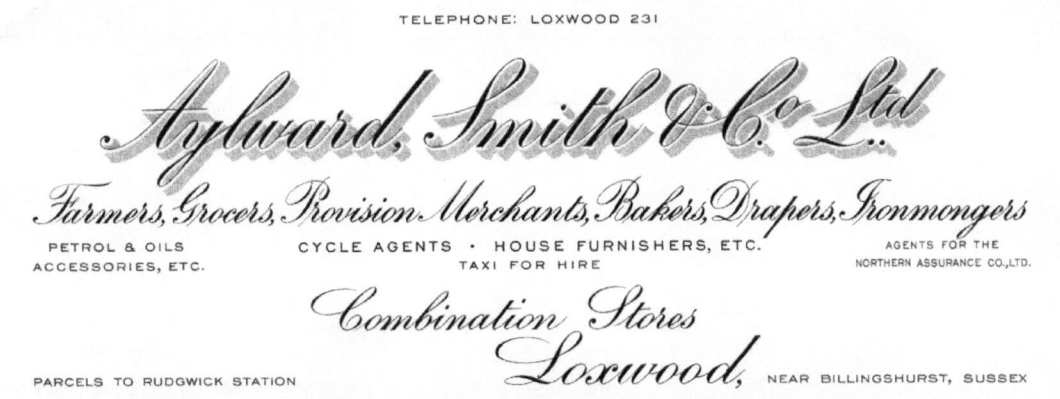

Fig 1 – Letter header found by the author in the demolished petrol station.

Fig 2 - Bessie Hempstead, 1896-1980. Note the photo of Walter Nash.

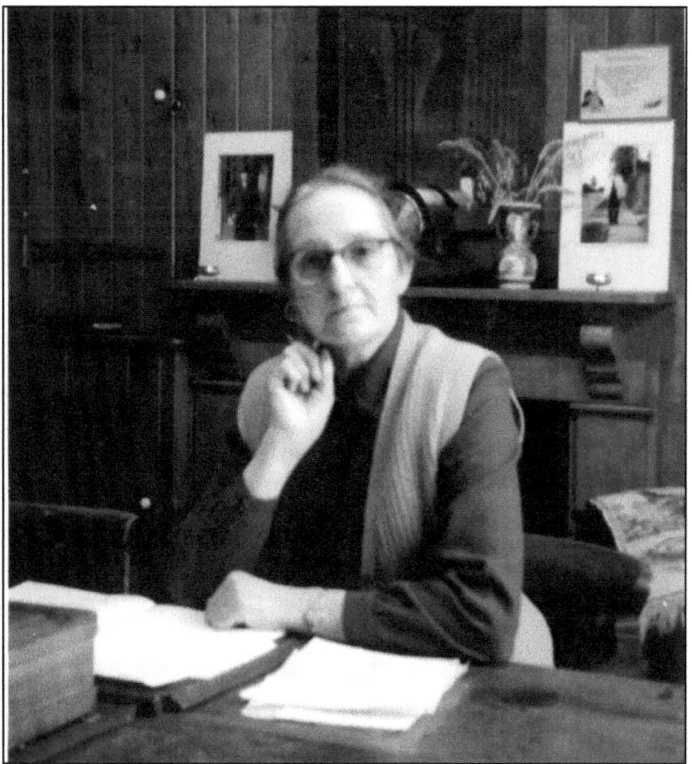

PLATE 7.8   A Male Domain? – Coal, Cars, Vans, Fuel, Butchery, and Buses

Fig 1 – included here primarily for its background barn, a lost landmark of Loxwood's High Street, demolished to make way for a housing estate, appropriately called Hall Hurst, after the name of this small farm. The lady driver is Bessie Hempstead, one of the only female drivers in the Dependant community. The presence of the author's two elderly non-Cokeler aunts (front left) dates this photo c1955. The occasion for the image is unknown.

Fig 2 – left, posted in 1910, an early depiction of a petrol pump for Pratt's petrol. The company advertised itself, "fill here from the golden pump", and eventually became Esso in the 1930s. Note the open topped car parked outside the stores. Two shadowy figures pose one on each sideof the road. The garage behind the pump was for their own vehicles, including horse-drawn ones, their maintenance and that of customers vehicles too.

Fig 3 – above right, the garage remained little altered through to 1955 when this image was taken. Rather than be tied to a petrol brand, the choice of either Shell or BP or National Benzole petrol was offered.

Fig 4 – right, about 1956, the garage is foreshortened after the building of the butcher's behind the pumps, and an office created for petrol sales together with a payment window to the grocer's beyond, thus allowing for regulations separating cash and fuel. The same three petrol brands are on sale. Butcher's shop out of view.

Fig 5 – right, Edwardian Dependant's delivery van for bread or groceries. The number plate BP3183 was for West Sussex.

Fig 6 – below right, a much more modern version, such as the author remembers delivering to his home (poor quality image).

Fig 7 – William Cole, born 1865 in Sundridge, Kent, was coal porter for Aylward, Smith before 1918 when the business was sold. He was married to Emma Aylward, sister of Henry Aylward.

Fig 8 – below right, Wesley Bernard Hempstead, Dependant brother of Bessie, had a coal business in nearby Bucks Green in Rudgwick from 1933 to 1959. He had the coal yard at Rudgwick Station. His business also included removals, haulage, coach hire, and a thrice weekly carrier service to Horsham. He was married to Charlotte, William Cole's daughter.

Fig 8 – below left, Dependant Fred Killner, who married Mary Hempstead, another of the Hempstead siblings, ran Sunbeam Coaches in Loxwood until the 1950s (scheduled bus service to Horsham in The Carfax).

Chapter 8

Lordshill Common

PLATE 8.1 — Lordshill Buildings, Today and Yesterday

Fig 1 – left, Gate Street Farmhouse, Bramley, a recent image. One of the farms where the community first met.

Fig 2 – right, Wonersh Lower Mill, an old image, where Stephen Franks was miller.

Fig 3 – below left, Lordshill Common, an early image. The Lordshill Stores stands proud centre right.

Fig 4 – below right, much the same view in a recent image.

Fig 5 – left, Lordshill Stores, now a 5-bed private house, called Lordshill House, with Partridge Cottage, the former butchers, on the left, and Holly Cottage, right, all within the curtilage of the premises owned from the beginning of Dependant worship here.

Lordshill is a hamlet and common west of Shamley Green, just north of Longacre School. It is in the parish of Wonersh, Surrey. Lordshill is not on the road to anywhere, as it is joined to the main road by a lane that meanders in a near-rectangle off the main road through Shamley Green. As at Loxwood, the Wey & Arun Canal passed close by, but was already closed by the time the Stores opened. The predecessor company to Bradshaw, Foster & Street Ltd, known as Earle, Franks & Co, began trading sometime in the 1880s, about the same time as Loxwood's Combination Stores.

The community originated in both Shamley Green and neighbouring Bramley to the north west. However, John Sirgood was already in Lordshill by 1851, so this is possibly the oldest community. William Hampshire, as has been explained in Chapter 3, was among the earliest converts. A farm labourer, he had no known early link to retail trade, although John Sirgood was staying with him in 1881, interestingly, his occupation draper not shoemaker, emphasising his new focus and enthusiasm on community retailing.

How it all Began

The early years of Lordshill Stores were dominated by Jacob Earle, a labourer's son from Gate Street in Bramley, situated close to Lordshill as the crow flies. Some years later, Edith Bradshaw (whose name was part of the company name) also lived in Gate Street. Numerous individuals involved with Lordshill came from Bramley, and it is known that meetings were held at Gate Street Farm as early as 1855, before the chapel was built c1870. Another of these was William Hampshire, John Sirgood's close associate and who became first elder at Lordshill. Sirgood, Hampshire and John Rugman had shared a home at Lordshill Common before Sirgood's death in 1885. Hampshire and Rugman then moved into the new stores, Hampshire working in the grocery department until his death in 1900. John Rugman (Plate 8.2), a carpenter, also an elder of the chapel, died in 1904 and was buried at Loxwood. He had moved next door to the stores at the end of his life. This 1881 household is the genesis of the business., but it is not possible to locate it accurately from census entries alone. Rugman and George Tickner, also a carpenter, may well have fitted out the shop. Meanwhile Jacob Earle was still living with his parents in Gate Street in 1881, aged just 17.

Eliza Stemp joined Hampshire as an elder, one of the few female elders, along with Ann Overington (1833-1910) at Loxwood (who became an elder many years earlier at a younger age – Chapters 3 and 4). Born in Dunsfold in 1849, brought up in Bramley, Eliza went to London as a servant girl, before returning to Selhurst Common, Bramley, as housekeeper to a widowed wood dealer, with whom she resided for many years. It was not until after 1901 that she became identifiable in the Dependant community as manageress of the dairy at Grist Hill, just south of Shamley Green, where she was joined by her younger sister Polly, who had a similar life story, and Margaret Heather, another confirmed Dependant. The dairy presumably supplied the stores. The sisters both ended their lives in The Retreat in Lordshill, a largely retirement community in a house built on the common. Eliza died there in 1939 aged 90, her sister in 1941 aged 85.

Among those in the wider community were Joseph and Emily Powell (Plate 8.2). He was brother of Ann who was briefly a manager at the Combination Stores in Loxwood. They had moved around frequently in his job as a gardener, but finally settled in Strood Green near

Lordshill (Table 8.3), where he had a market garden. The sphere of influence of both chapel and stores stretched well north into Surrey, including a few individuals in Guildford – the Powells having been in Merrow, for example. Lordshill was notable for relying on Sisters as elders, the Stemps among them, also Carrie Cumber. Carrie was a local Lordshill girl who lived with her blind mother since her father, also a market gardener, had died many years before. She died in 1925 aged 75. Carrie's aunt Mary Ann was also a Dependant. It is interesting to speculate whether the Cumbers had been early devotees of John Sirgood's faith. Lordshill Stores and chapel were however not as commercially or congregationally viable as others. It was off the beaten track, so it is not surprising that the Dependants struggled to keep them going even before the Second World War. Emma White stands out for her presence in all three censuses and in 1939 (see below). She came from near Haslemere, becoming a domestic servant in Guildford, and thus just the kind of girl who might have been taken under the wing of and converted by the Dependants. She died in 1942 at The Retreat.

Lordshill Stores - Earle, Franks & Co

Eight out of the twelve living-in at the stores in 1891 (Table 8.1) were from Surrey, but none had been born in Wonersh or Shamley Green. The other four were from a Sussex Dependant background. Jacob Earle was almost certainly involved with the setting up of the Stores in the 1880s, managing the business until the first few years of the new century. However, in the 1911 census and Directories for 1911, 1913 and 1918, Earle was a farmer/dairyman at The Tanyard (Table 8.2), probably supplying the Stores, which had two possible dairies to call on. He spent his later years in a house named "Peaceful Place" in Shamley Green (Table 8.3), where he shared with Eleanor Franks (this was later the home of Norman Booker, whose grandparents were Dependants).

Lucy Shurlock, co-manager in 1881, had been a servant to a grocer in Cranleigh at the tender age of 14, but switched to drapery on joining the Dependants at Lordshill becoming manager of drapery by 1891 and second manager by 1901. As with other stores, the early managers were mostly in their 20s. What an opportunity, and what an enthusiasm for the movement they must have had. But she then married Charles Miles, a builder, so left the stores, and raised a family. By 1911, they lived in nearby Strood Green. She ended her days at Warnham, still a Dependant, her husband probably not. She therefore joins a small list of those for whom service as a spinster was not right for them. What is more, her parents James and Liza were both Dependants, both buried in Loxwood, 1902 and 1891 respectively, two of the small number of funerals taken by Stephen Franks. James, who had been a lifelong agricultural labourer, lived at Lordshill at his death. They had earlier lived in Wonersh. Her sister Liza was also at the stores (Table 8.1) working as a pastry cook in 1901, assisting in the shop in 1911, and died in 1918, still in Lordshill.

Until sometime before 1911, the company name was Earle, Franks & Co. Stephen Franks, an elder of the Lordshill chapel, was a miller in Wonersh, born in Rudgwick, and buried at Loxwood chapel in 1909. Many of his family were Dependants, his brother George at Plaistow Place, for example. Interestingly, all the brothers were married, and some had children, including Stephen, married to Emma, whose daughters are mentioned below. Stephen was apprenticed by the time he was 12 years old at Gibbons Mill, Rudgwick, under the tutelage of miller William Botting. Of Stephen's daughters, Eleanor had lived in the stores around 1901 working as a draper's assistant and much later was Jacob Earle's housekeeper in 1939, and Henrietta, a little older, had been the first of the family to live in Lordshill by 1881, became a stores housemaid (but who then was married). Both were born in Wimbledon when the newly married family had lived there, Stephen working as a young miller.

Some of Stephen Frank's letters survive in one of the hand-written notebooks the Dependants lovingly compiled. It is likely Stephen milled the wheat for the bakery in the Lordshill Stores. An iron hoist still sits on the gable end of the former stores (now a house) where the sacks would have been unloaded.

Lordshill Stores - Bradshaw, Foster & Co

The company name changed to Bradshaw, Foster & Co. by 1911 (Plate 8.2). Mary (Polly) Foster, who had lived and worked at Lordshill Stores from at least 1891, and died at Lordshill in 1932 aged 77, had been in service locally first in Shalford then in Guildford. Mary was born in Bramley and was not related to the Fosters of Loxwood who were so prominent in the development of combination. However, her mother when widowed was a grocer in Guildford. Mary was grocer's assistant by the 1901 census. By 1911, she was joint manager with Edith Bradshaw, who was quite a few years her junior.

The Bradshaw family may be traced back to Mary Bradshaw, a widow born in 1789 at Uley, Gloucestershire. She became a woollen cloth weaver in Avening, where she might have known the Sirgood family. Her son John married Alice Bowley from Westonbirt in 1847. They had two children, William in 1847, Edward in 1849. When their father died, Alice was left living in Avening, with a small annuity. By 1861, Alice had become a laundress and had not remarried. Edward trained as a carpenter in Westonbirt. In 1873, he married Sarah Bowley from Sherston, Wilts. They set up home in Shipton Moyne, moving to Tetbury, where Edith was born in 1873, then to Dursley, where Florence was born in 1875, presumably their father following the work of a carpenter, before settling in Shipton Moyne where three more boys were born. Sarah supplemented the family income, as her mother-in-law had, as a laundress, assisted by Edith. By the late 1880s the family had moved to Chiddingly, Sussex, where the youngest daughter Gwen was born in 1897. Soon, work took Edward closer to the Dependant heartland as an estate carpenter in Capel, Surrey.

The older children had by now left home. Edith had become a laundress, continuing the work she knew well, in Gate Street Bramley, a long-time centre of Dependants, close to Lordshill. George Rugman was her neighbour. Edith was assisted by her cousin Mary Bowley and her brother Jack, still only 13. Florrie, meanwhile, was still in Chiddingly, in domestic service, where she stayed, rising to the position of housekeeper in 1911. By then, John was in Dorking driving traction engines. Edith joined the staff of Lordshill Stores sometime in the early 1900s, rapidly becoming a director, assisted by Polly Foster. Edith, her brother Jack, and sisters Florrie and Gwen, all became Dependants, each living to a ripe age, Edith reaching 103! The deaths of Edith, her sister Gwen and brother Jack are listed in Chapter 7 having lived to the 1970s in Loxwood. Their parents moved yet again to Wadhurst. Sarah, not Edward, is in the Dependant registers. She died in 1922 at Lordshill. This family may or may not have had a close link or friendship with the Sirgoods of Avening. The chances are they did, way back in the 1820s or 1830s. What might Edith have told us if she were alive!

Table 8.1   **Lordshill Stores, Residents**

1891	1901	1911
Earle, Franks & Co	Earle, Franks & Co	Bradshaw, Foster & Co
Jacob Earle (manager)	**Jacob Earle (manager)**	**Edith Bradshaw (manager)**
Leslie Street (manager)	**Lucy Shurlock (manager)**	**Mary Foster (manager)**
Lucy Shurlock (manager)	Emma White	Emma White
Mary Foster	Mary Foster	Elizabeth (Liza) Shurlock
Emma White	Leah Booker	Leah Booker
Emma Clark	Elizabeth (Liza) Shurlock	Caroline (Carrie) Cumber
Leah Booker	Eleanor Franks	Lily Luxford
Henrietta Franks	George Reeves	Thomas Rapley
William Heather	Alfred Kelsey	John Holden (visitor)
John Rugman	Emma Killner	
Anna Cox	Sarah Killner	
George Tickner		

This was perhaps the smallest community with a maximum of a dozen living in, and only nine present (eight residents) in 1911, but it was also a tight knit and isolated one, with several other houses on the fringe of the common which were also home to Dependants, some from the 1890s. Close by were the Kelsey family, one of whom, Alfred, was destined to feature in a newspaper article at the closure of the chapel, and was the last Brother, as far is known. He died in 1970. Alfred, together with Emma Killner and Sarah, her mother, had been at the stores in 1901. The latter were from the Killner family which had originated in Southwater. He married Emma, by then his much younger housekeeper, in 1912.

George Reeves was from Newpound Common, Wisborough Green (south of Loxwood). His parents John and Sarah were also Dependants. He was in an interesting role in 1891. The Dependants at Warnham set up a branch of Lindfield, Luff & Co in Rowhook, Rudgwick (on the borders of Warnham) for a few years. George was drafted in to manage the shop along with Emma Killner. But both Emma and George then moved to Lordshill, he as a baker, she as a grocery assistant. After a spell in Lordshill George moved to Warnham, where in 1911 he was described at Warnham Stores as "odd job"! He died in Warnham in 1925 aged 76.

Lily Luxford, from a Wisborough Green family which settled in Cranleigh, had moved into the stores by 1911. Both her parents, James, a woodsman, who died in 1938 aged 70, and Emily, were Dependants who had settled in Long Common, adjacent to Lordshill, by 1911. Emily moved to Earlsfield, a Lordshill house perhaps named after Jacob Earle, after her husband's death. Lily's sister Ada moved in with her, and in 1939 was working in the stores as a grocery assistant (Table 8.3). Living with them was Elsie Brackpool, the bookkeeper for the business.

The only man in the small community of eight at Lordshill Stores in 1911 was Tom Rapley, the oldest, aged 61, unmarried, like all the ladies. He was working as an assistant, but it is likely he was responsible for deliveries and transport, as he had been a groom in 1901 and a stableman in 1891, all that time living in Lordshill Common. He died in 1918 aged 68. Who might have succeeded him? Staying as a visitor was another man, John Holden, one of those who had been living at Plaistow Place Farm in 1891 (Chapter 2). He was also helping in the stores in some capacity. He died in Loxwood, living at Hall House, in 1933. His sister Elizabeth was a resident of the Combination Stores.

A little-known Dependant from Lordshill, Ralph Arnold, was involved in a military tribunal case as a conscientious objector in 1916 (Plate 2.3). The story of Dependant conscientious objection in both wars is told in Chapter 2.

Table 8.2   **1911 Census, Dependant Household in Lordshill, Shamley Green and Elsewhere**

Lordshill Stores and Common   Place of birth

Edith Bradshaw	37	grocer, baker & draper	Tetbury Glos
Mary Foster*	55	assistant in shop (joint head)	Bramley Sy
Emma White*	47	assistant in shop	Shottermill Sy
Elizabeth Shurlock*	45	assistant in shop	Shamley Green Sy
Leah Booker*	40	assistant in shop	Northchapel Sx
Caroline Cumber	61	assistant in shop	Wonersh Sy
Lilly Luxford	21	assistant in shop	Wisborough Green Sx
Thomas Rapley	61	assistant in shop	Shamley Green Sy
John Holden	61	assistant in shop (visitor)	Rudgwick Sx
Hannah Cock	60	small private income	Warnham Sx
Elizabeth Smart	77	old age pensioner	Kirdford Sx
George Rugman	58	butcher	Bramley Sy
Mary Rugman	54		Bramley Sy
Joseph Powell	32	foreman baker confectioner	Storrington Sx
Lilian Powell	33		Bramley Sy
Frederick Hitchins	51	journeyman baker	Reading Bks
Sarah Hitchins	39		Northchapel Sx
Stephen Durrant	36	bricklayer	Loxwood Sx
Lydia Durrant	31		Milford Sy
John Booker	63	general estate labourer	Chiddingfold Sy
Betsy Booker	61		Kirdford Sx
Arthur Foster	38	miller's assistant	Bramley Sy
Charles Royal	54	farm labourer	Alton Hants
Emily Royal	54		Shamley Green Sy

Shamley Green (village)

John Kelsey	52	horsekeeper	Wonersh Sy
Alice Kelsey	49		Alfold Sy
Reuben Raggett	49	journeyman baker	Cranleigh Sy
Ellen Raggett	37		Cranleigh Sy
Emma Franks	60	independent	Merton Sy

Long Common

James Luxford	43	journeyman baker	Kirdford Sx
Emily Luxford	41		Ripley Sy
Ivy Luxford	12	school	Ewhurst Sy

Stroud Common

Joseph Powell	55	retired market gardener	Slinfold Sx
Emily Powell	59		West Chiltington Sx
Mary Ether(ing)ton	48	laundry maid	Lower Beeding Sx

Tanyard Farm

Jacob Earle*	47	farmer	Bramley Sy
Caroline Earle	79		Shalford Sy
Harriett Clarke	75		Bramley Sy
Eleanor Franks*	36	housekeeper	Wimbledon Sy

Plunks Farm

James Earle	50	farm carter	Bramley Sy
Alice Earle	48		Godalming Sy

Grist Hill Dairy

Elisa Stemp	62	manageress	Bramley Sy
Mary Stemp	56	domestic work	Bramley Sy
William Lodge	59	farm labourer	Bramley Sy
Margaret Heather	56	domestic work	Bramley Sy
Emily Luxford	20	dairy maid	Wisborough Green Sx

Hullbrook Farm

Ada Luxford	18	servant to a farmer	Wisborough Green Sx

Lower Mill Wonersh

Leslie Street	42	manager of flour mill	Cranleigh Sy
Emma Street	40		Hampshire
Edward Mitchell	52	carman	Shamley Green Sy

Shalford (village)

Alfred Kelsey*	28	carrier	Hambledon Sy
Emma Killner*	44	housekeeper	Southwater Sx

Selhurst Common Bramley

Daniel Edwards	70	carman, wood dealer	Bramley Sy
Susan Edwards	46	housekeeper	Bramley Sy

Godalming

Charles Hackman	58	wood merchant	Godalming Sy
Emily Stovold	53	housekeeper	Puttenham Sy
James Stovold	50	railway clerk	Puttenham Sy
Henry Weale	50	master house painter	Shalford Sy
Charlotte Weale	50		Canterbury Kt

Guildford

Alfred Earle	52	market gardener	Bramley Sy

lived and worked in Lordshill Stores in 1901

Notes from 1911

Much has been explained elsewhere in this chapter, but some things stand out in Table 8.2. firstly, the size of the community is not small – there are additional names that have not been traceable. The shop community as has been pointed out, was small. Not all the houses around Lordshill Common were occupied by Dependants as they seem to have been in 1839, after the stores had become the preserve of the Smith family. There were, however, a preponderance of people in their 50s, 60s and 70s, reflecting the growth of the 19th century community, who would gradually die out over the years to the 1939 Register. George Rugman, Joseph Powell and Stephen Hitchins were respectively a butcher, a confectioner and a baker who each may well have worked at the stores, close to which they lived. The last named had married a younger Sarah Booker, whose parents were in the Northchapel community. Stephen Durrant was father of the Stephen who appears in the 1939 table. That the community looked after its own is a truism often observed. Emma Franks widow of Stephen, Wonersh miller, a founder of Lordshill Stores, and mother of Henrietta and Eleanor, is lodging with another Dependant family. With the mill now in the hands of Leslie Street, Arthur Foster, brother of Mary Foster, who now runs the stores jointly with Edith Bradshaw, is assisting Street in the mill. the network of interlinked families and businesses extends widely through village communities. Other families exemplify this, the Luxfords, the Earles (including an aunt, Harriett Clarke), the Stemps (at Grist Hill Farm Dairy, surely another piece of the producer-retailer jigsaw, which also includes three bakers, not living at the stores) and the Kelseys. The chapel's congregation and store's customers extend beyond Shamley Green to Wonersh, Shalford, Bramley and even to Godalming (including Charlie Hickman, below) and Guildford (an Earle brother). Links with other Dependant centres in Sussex are evident in the birthplaces of many in the census, from Kirdford and Plaistow, Wisborough Green and Loxwood, Northchapel, and elsewhere, as well as from nearby Surrey parishes. There is only one person born in Kent, suggesting virtually no links with the 'diaspora' of Kent converts who flocked to South Norwood, or indeed with Norwood itself, surprising as Lordshill is nearer Norwood than any other community.

A Lordshill Funeral, 1917

Charlie Hackman of Godalming died in February 1917. He was probably buried in Godalming (in the presence of at least some of those who attended the Lordshill evening meeting). There is no recorded funeral at Loxwood. The chapel meeting described below, possibly the same evening, is here recorded by Elsie Piper in her own words, transcribed from one of her books of letters and hymns. Paragraphing has been added for ease of reading. The names of those she refers to are included at the end, with further details on who they were. This account is graphic in its depiction of the way funerals drew the body of Dependants together from across the communities and is notable in referring to a number of the Brethren and Sisters named in this chapter.

"A brief account of a very glorious meeting at Lord's Hill on the 19th Feb., after putting away the remains of our dear Br. C. Hackman. One of the most beautiful times ever spent in God's house was that Monday evening. We commenced by singing, "What do you of Christ Jesus thinks?", we had a beautiful influence all thro' the singing and when we sat down we had such a glorious shout together and sang over and over again, "What think you then of one I

say who has took all our sins away, by being chastised, was ever there such love made known, did ever we know such love such as this exercised."

When the shouting ceased a little, Bro. W. Booker got up and told us that he thought a lot of Him if anyone wanted to know what he thought of Christ Jesus, it was enough that he meant to love him in return all the rest of his days. He also told us how pleased he was with the beautiful day he had spent with the dear ones here, whether it was visiting the Brethren in their homes or at the meal table talking of things eternal, or when we were burying our dear Brother, he enjoyed the sweet love and unity. God very much helped him for our encouragement, he was very brief as he wanted to hear all the others, so sat down with God's blessing upon him. It was such a heavenly atmosphere all the Brethren were praising God.

Our Brother Jesse followed next and exhorted us all to keep on long enough to really feel and know for ourselves, that now in our day God's love is to be enjoyed. He also confirmed Bro. Willie's statement that they had very much enjoyed the day in the company of their Brethren up here.

Bro. S. Croucher was next to tell of God's great goodness. He said with what fulness and with what meaning he had just sung the words, such as this exercised, no other had or ever would exercise such love to die for us, as He had done. He said at times, Satan had wanted him to draw a line just inside of some Brethren and so leave them outside, but he said he had always been careful to draw it just outside and so include all in, like Christ.

Then Bro. W. Cumber rose up to thank God for the many years He had been his helper, and of all the times I ever heard our Bro. have I never enjoyed God in him so much before. He animated him from head to foot he said he was just the right age to enjoy it, it was no mistake but what he made it manifest. He told us some experiences he had had in that house how God had helped him in that seat, God had restored his eyesight and in that seat, He restored his foot to strength when he fell from the ladder and put his great toe out of place, and he would praise Him and he did at the top of his voice. I may add here that the beautiful shout we had as each one sat down no one could really realize what it was like that was not there, we felt we could shout at the top of our voice and laugh in God's Spirit without any shame because we laughed in God's house, then to sum it up it was like heaven on earth. I shall never forget it, and although this is 3 days after I feel it still burning in me as I write it down.

Bro. W. Lee was the next and how the Lord helped him, he said he had never enjoyed so much of God before, and as he often does, he praised His lovely Name and we all felt it was a lovely Name. by this time the fire was got so hot all over the meeting, I hardly know how to describe it, a Sister here clapping her hands, a Bro. there could not keep his feet still, another Sister at the back of the meeting waving both hands at once, yea, yet another clapping hers for very joy, some eyes filled with tears of joy, others filled with joy of laughter, others shouting Glory to God. I should think it lasted quite a ¼ of an hour, but I was too much absorbed in it to think of the time.

My memory is not good enough to tell who spoke next, I believe it was Sister C. Cumber and told us that she would not be like Brother John [Sirgood] wrote once, punish herself quiet when the joy was flowing about so richly, but would give full place to it, and enjoy it to the full, shouting praises to God with the rest. She said when we were asking each other the question what we thought of Christ, she thought He was a darling, and she loved Him better than anyone or anything else, and could say as David did, He has delivered my darling from the power of the dog and from the wild beast and He is alive now to fill us up with joy; also that she was pleased her Brother was just the right age to enjoy the fulness of the joy of God, and as she was only months younger she would soon be there too.

Then Bro. Jacob got up and said we have had the joy from Warnham, Loxwood and Norwood and now we have got it from Lordshill and he so greatly rejoiced, that Bro. Willie clasped his hands and they shouted together, Alleluia to God, it was beautiful, then Willie spoke again and thanked God for the unity he could see and feel amongst us here and in meekness exalted us to go in for more of it.

Sister E. Stemp also spoke how good God had been to her and our Bro. Charlie and God gave her the blessing to impart to us all; it showed plainly to all that God is very pleased with us, when through love we undertake for those that [are] in distress and our Sister's soul was filled with gladness to know that our dear Bro. died among his own people (the people of God). Sister E. Bradshaw told us that soon after she came with us a dear Sister died [Mary Cumber] the Brethren kept saying they expected to have a good time in putting her remains away and she thought how very strange to expect a good time at a funeral, but how glad she was that with all the rest she could say she had spent a good time at a funeral.

Sister L. Shurlock told us how very much she had enjoyed the time spent with the dear ones during the day but especially the time spent in adoration to God in the evening, mentioning all [sic] an especial good time a Bro. and her had had with Bro. Charlie when sitting up with him one night, God was so good to him, that he preached to them for over an hour.

Sister L. Booker got up very much comforted in telling out how good God had been to her in lending a helping hand and how good it was to do all we do to God. One more incident in this remarkable meeting that very much gratified and gave our Brethren joy that was here was to see all the young ones rise and tell how they had enjoyed it, they had never been in a meeting like it before. There were 23 who spoke and more that was longing to do so but as the Norwood Brethren had to catch the train we had to forbear, but after the prayer some remained in their seats shouting others singing and shouting down the aisle and at the supper table we had another shout. The dear Bro. that took them to the station left them on the platform praising God. I shall never forget that parting but now we have all the best to come. Amen."

Names in order of appearing above:
W(illiam) Booker (from Warnham)
Jesse (Puttock, from Loxwood)
S(ydney) Croucher (from South Norwood, but at Lordshill later on)
W(illiam) Cumber (from Northchapel)
W(illiam) Lee (from South Norwood)

and from Lordshill itself:
C(arrie) Cumber
Jacob (Earle)
E(liza) Stemp
E(dith) Bradshaw
L(ucy) Shurlock
L(eah) Booker.

Lordshill Stores - Bradshaw, Foster, Street & Co

In 1918, a directory provides proof of another name change: Bradshaw, Foster, Street & Co, grocers. Leslie Street managed the bakery for the Dependants from as far back as 1891. He had come under the influence of William Puttock, a farmer, and his housekeeper, Ann Squelch. Both were Dependants (later of Loxwood) in Knowle Lane, Cranleigh, before 1881. In 1895, however, Leslie also married, and moved to Woking, where he obtained work as a builder, and raised a family. He was therefore numbered among the live-in Brethren for only a short time. He had worked closely with Jacob Earle, manager of grocery, and Lucy Shurlock, manager of drapery. But, in 1909, he became a director of Bradshaw, Foster, Street & Co, so he had not deserted the Brethren. After Stephen Franks's death, he had taken over the management of Lower Mill, Wonersh, keeping it working (but not ownership, as far as is known) in Dependant hands, and reverting to skills learnt working with flour as a baker in his youth. He now had three children, possibly the only family man to be a senior director of a Dependant company. He was not related to the Streets of Northchapel.

Lordshill Stores – Smith & Croucher

In 1935, the lease was handed over to Henry and Wallace (Wally) Smith (both married and brothers), and their partner, Raymond Croucher who lived next door in Holly Cottage with his wife and family. The business, no longer a combination stores, still a residence, and still in the hands of Dependant adherents, traded under the name of Smith and Croucher. Telephone directories confirm this name from 1935 to 1948 (as does the 1939 Register, Table 8.3). Croucher retired in 1948, but the Smiths continued for a short time before the premises finally closed its doors in 1951. The Smiths were from a Dependant background. The family came from the Headcorn area of Kent where Sirgood is known to have preached. The family settled in Lodsworth for a while around 1911 (also present on census night was May Winter, a 'protégé', aged 18, and a Dependant for life, and in the cottage was Jemima Stevens, a Lodsworth Dependant). All the Smith family present on census night in Lodsworth were Dependants. Wally, a master baker, and his wife worked together in the Northchapel Stores before moving to Surrey (photo Plate 10.5). A third generation, William Smith, ran the ironmongery department. Two members of the family, Henry and May, died in Rochford, Essex, which suggests they moved late in life to join the Essex Peculiers. Others died in Surrey or back in Kent. Ray Croucher was also born in Headcorn, Kent, in 1886. He moved to Croydon in the 1890s, along with his brother Sydney, and by 1911 was baking alongside George Randall in the Norwood Stores. He moved to Lordshill as master baker at the stores, alongside the Smith brothers, and died in Yorkshire 1977, recorded in Loxwood burial register. The premises were sold to a Mr Partridge in 1951. By the 1960s, the building was converted to a private house with a good view across the common.

An advert in the Shamley Green parish magazine in 1924 lists their trade as bakers, grocers, butchers, drapers, outfitters and boots and shoes (Plate 8.2). One notable absence from this list is any mention of a garage. The origins of Embread (Plate 8.2), which they sold, lie with Eustace Miles, a vegetarian food reformer who owned a restaurant near Charing Cross and health food shops. He was an athlete (real tennis) with a keen interest in nutrition. One of his products was Emprote, a protein mix, on which many of his products were based. Was one of the Smiths or Crouchers a follower of this rather eccentric man?

The End Time

Table 8.3	1939 Register, Lordshill, (extracts)		
Peaceful Place	**Jacob H Earle***	1885-1948 S	Old age pensioner
(Shamley Green)	**Eleanor (Nellie) Franks***	1874-1967 S	Housekeeper
Beechcroft	**John H Bradshaw***	1887-1973 M	Steam boiler stoker
(Shamley Green)	**Annie Bradshaw***	1888-1947 M	Domestic duties
Earlsfield (LH)	**Emily Luxford***	1871-1954 W	Domestic duties
	Ada A Luxford*	1892-1959 S	Shop assistant, grocery
	Elsie Brackpool	1902-? M	Head bookkeeper, general stores
Hillside Cottage (LH)	Albert Nash	1914-1996 M	Motor driver, baker & grocery r'ndsman
	Laura Nash	1912-2004 M	Domestic duties
Sherston (LH)	**Ellen Raggett***	1874-1953 W	Domestic duties
	Ronald A Raggett	1909-1977 S	Gardener, private service
	Constance P Raggett	1910-1993 S	Domestic duties
Sherston (LH)	**Edith A Bradshaw***	1873-1977 S	Nurse, housekeeper
	Emma Street*	1870-1942 S	Incapacitated
The Retreat (LH)	**Leah Booker***	1870-1948 S	Housekeeper
	Sarah A Hitchins*	1872-1953 W	Private means
	Emma White*	1862-1942 S	Private means
	Mary (Polly) Stemp*	1865-1941 S	Private means
	Alice L Carpenter*	1888-1974 S	Clerk, general stores
Holly Cottage (LH)	**Raymond Croucher***	1886-1977 M	Master baker, bread & cakes
	Lilian Croucher*	1889-1952 M	Domestic duties
	Mary A Croucher (Capon)*	1920-? S	Grocer's assistant
Lordshill Stores (LH)	**Henry T Smith***	1887-1962 M	Grocer, manager
(Smith & Croucher)	**Ivy E Smith***	1898-1958 M	Domestic duties
	Wallace J Smith*	1904-2001 M	Master baker
	Alice A Smith*	1890-1992 M	Domestic duties
	May R Smith*	1899-1959 M	Domestic duties
	William A Smith*	1922-2000 S	Assistant wks manager, ironmongery
	Lilian M Spooner	1900-1978 S	Domestic daily help
	Robert Ridge	1925-2001 S	At school (evacuee?)
1 Pond Close	**Emma Kelsey***	1866-1942 M	Domestic duties
(Hullbrook Lane)	**Alfred Kelsey***	1882-1970 M	Baker's roundsman
2 Pond Close	**James Earle***	1860-1942 M	Retired farm carter
(Hullbrook Lane)	**Alice Earle**	1862-1940 M	Domestic duties
Wonersh Post Office	**Joseph Powell**	1878-1935 M	Sub-postmaster
`	**Lilian Powell**	1876-1969 M	Domestic duties

LH = Lordshill;   M – married; S – single; W – widowed.
*known Dependant families from other sources (other names included by address and/or occupation).

There is no doubt the community was shrinking by 1939, more so than others. It was commented upon with regard to the 1911 census that there was no element of Kent Dependants here, but the Smith and Croucher families both came from Kent. Many of the older members of the community who were also commented upon as having been born in the mid-19th century had now died, including stores stalwarts such as Mary Foster, 1932, Lizzie Shurlock, 1918, Carrie Cumber, 1925, Tom Rapley, 1918. Others included George Rugman, 1928, Leslie Street, 1937, Frederick Hitchins, 1930 in Norwood, and Charles

Hackman, as has been described above, in 1917. Lordshill Stores were never given as place of death.

An indication of those still alive at the time of the 1939 Register, as near a census as it is possible to be, is in Table 8.3 above. In the late 1930s a few older Lordshill Sisters (Eliza and Polly Stemp, Leah Booker, the housekeeper in 1939) lived at The Retreat, a large square house overlooking the common, built for those who needed accommodation in their old age (Table 8.3). Also accommodated there was Alice Carpenter, doing clerical work at the stores. Later a same-named home was built in Loxwood. Leah Booker had been a Dependant from a young age, born in Northchapel in 1860. Her father, John, was also an adherent, becoming a Lordshill baker's assistant by 1901, the family having moved to Wonersh parish by 1881. Leah had lived in the stores from before 1891 also as a baker's assistant, then servant, then shop assistant. Over its many years of existence, it is thought that fewer of the Lordshill Dependants were buried at Loxwood than was the case with Warnham and Northchapel. For a service in the church at Shamley Green, the Brethren would wait outside, but would also have a meeting to celebrate the deceased in their chapel, as at the funeral of Charlie Hackman, above. Table 8.3 lists evocatively the roll call of house names associated with the Lordhill Dependants, and includes names such as Bradshaw, Earle, Franks, Kelsey, all of which feature in this chapter. Several of those of working age work at the stores, Ada Luxford, Elsie Brackpool, Albert Nash (no relation), Alice Carpenter, and Alfred Kelsey, alongside the Crouchers and Smiths. It may not be too obvious that several achieved a great age, notably Edith Bradshaw (see also Chapters 5 and 7), 103, whose name is synonymous with Lords Hill Stores, but who died in Loxwood, Alice Smith, 102, and over 90, Nellie Franks, Laura Nash, Ray Croucher, Wallace Smith (who was Alice's husband). The stores were closed, as stated above, in 1951, the chapel in 1968.

Today, The Retreat is two private houses, one half called Dursley Cottage, with the pretty Avening Cottage next door, each of the latter named after a place in Gloucestershire, the former associated with the Bradshaw family, and the second, of course, the reputed birthplace of John Sirgood, and a locality where the Bradshaws lived, and their father was born. Neither house is especially old, built in the early 20th century. Sherston (Wiltshire) is another which recalls the Bradshaw family history. In 1911, there had been several Dependant households adjacent to the stores, in recorded order: Hannah Cock (Holly Cottage), George Rugman, butcher, members of the Powell family and Fred Hitchins, but it is not possible to identify which dwellings they occupied. Today, a house called, but misspelt, "Cooklers" stands on the site of the chapel. Partridge Cottage, named after the person who bought the stores, is where the butcher's shop was located, Victoria Cottage was once the bakery. Box Tree Cottage, Pear Tree Cottage, Greenfern Cottage and Holly Cottage are others on the somewhat congested site.

The last to be named in the Loxwood Burial register (or indeed the death register) was Alfred Kelsey who died in 1970 at St Luke's Hospital, Guildford (his final address a Caterham Nursing Home according to probate record). He was 88 years old. Back in 1939, he had lived with his wife Emma in Hullbrooks Lane, very close to Lordshill. At that time, he was the stores baker's roundsman. He and his housekeeper Nellie Franks had also been the last members of the chapel congregation (Plate 8.2). Nellie (Eleanor) was from the Franks family which has been shown above to have been among the first in Lordshill.

Although only tangentially relevant here, Sarah Wells, who is reputed to be the last to be asked by John Sirgood to be an elder in Loxwood, and who married George Baverstock, both becoming prominent in the Plaistow community, was, in 1861, a servant, living alongside the young Stephen Franks at Gibbons Mill, Rudgwick in Sussex, run then by William Botting, Junior. George Baverstock worked for William Botting Senior at Rowner Mill downstream on the Arun, as did Mary Ann Greenfield, who later married George Luff, who farmed at Plaistow Place with Richard Nightingale. These are good examples of young Dependants who met through marriage, rather than remaining single. At the other end of life, by no means all Dependants who were not in Loxwood, had a funeral and burial there. Table 8.4 lists those from Lordshill who did. Only Edith Bradshaw had moved to Loxwood before her death. Moving the bodies of those who died before the age of the motor vehicle must have been a challenge.

A few items from the stores have found their way into Guildford Museum, five spice cans, a steel yard rule, a bacon hook, a 1937 receipt, and a black shawl. Surprisingly, and disappointingly, there is no documentary evidence catalogued here, or indeed at the Surrey History Centre in Woking. The little community at Lordshill, which began in the locality about 1850, has left few traces other than the obvious converted stores and neighbouring houses, with no sign of the chapel itself, the only community to lose all trace, although a modern house exists on the site.

Table 8.4   Lordshill Dependants' Burials at Loxwood

William Hampshire	1900
John Rugman	1904
Stephen Durrant Sr	1906
Harriett Durrant	1909
Stephen Franks	1909
Emily Powell	1922
Hannah Cock	1930
Joseph Powell Sr	1935
Eliza Stemp	1939
Mary Stemp	1941
Emma White	1942
Emma Kelsey	1942
Leah Booker	1948
Edith Bradshaw	1977

PLATE 8.2 Lordshill Stores, its Environs, and People

Fig 1 – 1:25000 scale plan showing the cramped built-up dwellings and gardens on the footprint of the former Dependant properties. Note - + sign indicates a building, e.g. Lords Hill House – the stores, and The Retreat (with Dursley), and Cooklers (site of chapel, actually called Coaklers, both wrong spelling!)

Fig 2 – below left, The Retreat (poor photo) taken some years ago.

Fig 3 – Emily Powell, 1852-1922.

Fig 4 & 5 – left (c1870) & above, John Rugman 1842-1904.

Fig 6 – (poor photo) delivery van, Bradshaw, Foster & Street

Fig 7 - butcher's invoice dated 3 January 1920.

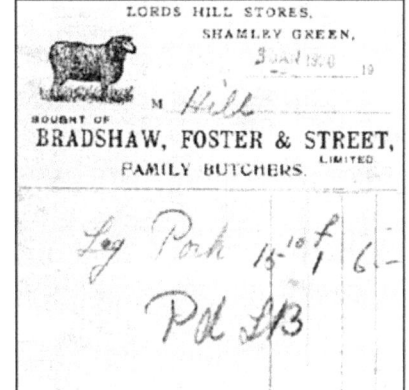

LORDS HILL STORES.
SHAMLEY GREEN,
BRADSHAW, FOSTER & STREET, LIMITED
FAMILY BUTCHERS.

> **BRADSHAW, FOSTER AND STREET, LTD.**
> **Lord's Hill Stores, Shamley Green.**
> BAKERS, GROCERS, BUTCHERS, DRAPERS, OUTFITTERS. BOOTS & SHOES.
>
> **What is "EMBREAD?" It is the Loaf of High Merit!**
> "EMBREAD" is the Eustace Miles' ideal body-building, sustaining, nourishing, and energising Bread. It is the Bread with a delicious flavour. Try a loaf to-day. "Embread" can be obtained from
>
> **Messrs. BRADSHAW, FOSTER & STREET, Ltd., Lord's Hill Stores, SHAMLEY GREEN.**

Fig 8 – an advertisement in 1924. Note the spelling 'Lord's Hill' which was unusual, and historically incorrect. The advert serves to confirm the name of the business at the time.

> TWO OLD PEOPLE WORSHIP ALONE...
>
> **The sad end of a simple faith**
>
> ONE of the strangest church services in the country will be repeated at Shamley Green, Surrey, today.
> The silver-haired preacher will read from the Bible. He will lead the hymn singing. He will deliver the address.
> And it will be heard by a congregation of precisely one, as the picture on the right shows.
> For 81-year-old Mr. Alfred Kelsey and his housekeeper 89-year-old Miss Nellie Franks, are the only surviving members of the Surrey Cokelers left at Shamley Green.
> It is 12 years since Jacob Earle, the Cokelers' last Shamley Green minister...
>
> By MICHAEL DALE
>
> ...rect title is the Society of Dependants – were founded a few miles from Mr. Kelsey's home at the...
>
> *Preacher Kelsey reads from the Bible to his congregation of one*

Fig 9 – an evocative footnote to Dependant worship in Lordshill, Shamley Green. This cutting is from The People, a national Sunday newspaper, in the edition of 8 December 1963. Alfred Kelsey, aged 81, is quoted in the article as saying, *"Ours is a simple religion, and a simple faith. We pledge ourselves to serve God quietly and sincerely to the end of our lives. By holding two services every Sunday, Nellie and I are maintaining our faith."* He told the reporter there were about 100 members left alive across all the communities. The chapel closed the next year, having outlasted Lordshill Stores by 13 years.

Chapter 9

Warnham

Plate 9.1   Warnham Stores

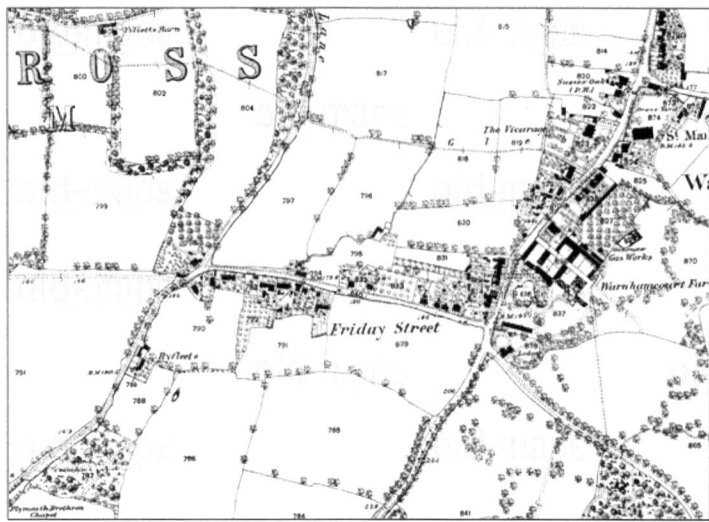

Fig 1 – Warnham in 1876 OS map, just 3 years before the site of the shop, Cocks, was sold to James Etherington. Cocks is just south of The Vicarage on the same side of the street, a Post Office, a small building south of the larger one set at an angle to the street. The location of the chapel is also seen on Byfleets Lane, incorrectly "Plymouth Brethren Chapel"!

The Cross, not yet owned by the Dependants, is located directly opposite the farm pond of Warnham Court Farm, built closer to the street than its neighbours (Fig 1).

Fig 2 – right, inset map from 1897 OS map. The largest set of buildings opening directly to the street is Warnham Stores, attached to the older

Cocks at the rear, with an entrance on the NE side, leading to a yard with numerous outbuildings.

Fig 3 – left, inset map from the 1912 OS map. The site now has a larger building off the yard, reducing the size of the latter.

Fig 4 – right, inset map from 1932 OS map. No changes. Post-1948 closure, there were no changes to the buildings.

Figs 5 and 6 - Cocks, a timber-framed house renamed Cokelers, as the house is today. Fig 5, from the entrance off the street, and Fig 6, in the yard behind. It is separated from the stores by a very narrow passage.

Fig 7 – left Warnham Stores, a recent photo (business left, house right).

Fig 8, 9 & 10, right, and left, recent views of the yard, with commercial and leisure uses.

Warnham Stores, Warnham, Nr. Horsham.

Fig 11 – a graphic image capturing the crowded window displays of this "drapers, hosiers, outfitters, grocery and provision merchants", with residential accommodation above. China seen in the window second from right. The banner across the top probably pre-dates this trade.

Fig 12 – the street view facing south, with a sign on the wall which completes the retail offering, "Household furniture, upholsterers, ironmongers, cycle makers and agents, cycles for hire".

The Origins of Warnham Stores

Warnham Historical Society have claimed *"in 1876 the Dependants were established as Linfield & Potter, in 1887 as Lindfield & Co., and in 1890 or thereabouts, as Lindfield & Luff. At its peak, this company employed 36 staff."* ("Warnham 100-150 Years Ago"). In like manner to Loxwood, as explained in some detail in Chapter 5, it is possible some activity took place on land and buildings unknown in 1876, but the author can find no evidence.

The community at Warnham was nevertheless quick off the mark to occupy premises in Warnham Street (now Church Street), right at the heart of the village, and set up its grocer's business with accommodation for the embryonic community, as Ron Muggeridge and Ben Paper have both asserted, in 1879. This is therefore arguably the earliest confirmed successful attempt at combination (i.e. a community), ahead even of Northchapel and Loxwood, where Combination Stores followed soon after. (the Puttick and Foster businesses were already on the site of the Loxwood Stores in 1879). The 1876 OS map (Plate 9.1, Fig 1) shows buildings known as 'Cocks' on the site, then a pre-existing post office/grocer's shop, albeit back from the road, almost opposite 'Warnhamcourt Farm'. William Tanner kept the Post Office/grocer's then, together with his coal merchant's business, on the site of the Dependant stores. Tanner is not a surname which survives in any Dependant records. In an 1878 directory, there is no sign of any Dependant name or business.

These musings and assertions have been settled by the discovery of the deeds of a property called Cocks. They are in West Sussex Record Office in the documents deposited by Holmes, Campbell & Co of Arundel and Littlehampton (Mss 841-856). Mss 851 is the crucial document in which William Tanner sells his shop to James Etherington, an illiterate farmer and Dependant from Loxwood under a Memorandum of Agreement dated 4 August 1879 (witnessed by George Theyer, farmer, of Tilsey Farm, Bramley, a possible Dependant) followed by a Conveyance on Sale of 30 September, for £600. The displaced Post Office, grocer and draper moved to where the present village shop is located, opposite the Sussex Oak. It was newly built by 1881 by ex-wheelwright Frederick Freeman, who opened a new Post Office there by 1882 or earlier.

Could Cocks possibly be the origin of the name used by others for the Dependants – Cokelers, as has been discussed in the Introduction? The word Cokeler and its many variations was locally in common usage ten or more years earlier, so, no, just a coincidence. Be that as it may, the property descended through members of the Cave family from 1725 or earlier, until sold to William Tanner in 1864. In the 1879 conveyance Cocks (also referred to as Cocks Garden) was described thus: *"the messuage or tenement shop edifices and buildings yard garden and backside thereunto adjoining and belonging situate lying and being in the parish of Warnham aforesaid parcel of a tenement heretofore called Cocks and formerly in the occupation of Stephen Cave deceased late in that of John Cave deceased and now and late in the hands of the said parties to the use of the said William Tanner."* Unfortunately, none of the documents give an area in acres. The sale included the house with its fixtures as per the inventory and premises known as the Post Office, Warnham.

Stephen Cave, the first owner mentioned in the deeds in 1801, was himself a shopkeeper, so the Dependants inherited a long history of retail use of the site. At the time of the Cocks conveyance in 1879, James Etherington had just taken the tenancy of Beldhamland Farm, south of Loxwood, right next door to HF Napper Esq., who had been the scourge of John Sirgood 20 years earlier. James and his wife Kezia had spent some years farming in Cranleigh, then at Thatched House Farm, Bramley (nearer to Dunsfold), before moving to Beldhamland. but his family were from Loxwood, father a labourer at Pephurst, then Barnfold, formerly spelling their name Etherton.

These were experimental years with bold thinking among all Dependants including Sirgood. These Wanham pioneers had started something unique in this area of the country. The small community (six) of 1881 (Table 9.1) was therefore a 'first' for the Dependants, though small enough perhaps to have occupied the existing shop and house at Cocks. Joseph Linfield had arrived in Warnham from Shipley, subsequently changing the spelling of his name to add a 'd', as in the village of that name. His partner, George Potter came from Alfold. Both were 28 years old and running the grocer's shop. With them, were Lucy and Ellen Luff, sisters from Wisborough Green, Lucy (Plate 9.2) behind the counter, Ellen acting as housekeeper, and two others, Elizabeth Caplin from the Northchapel community, and Charles Wadey, likewise, and who was later in Loxwood. The census does not suggest any draper's business, or anything else being sold at this early stage. The extraordinary youthfulness of this little group is astonishing by any comparison with this or any other store in later censuses. But by 1882, the directory lists "Linfield & Potter, grocer's and draper's". George Potter married to Harriett in the mid-1880s, so left to branch out on his own as a butcher, in premises very close by. Married couples were not welcome in the residential community. Warnham Society's description of the business, briefly known as Joseph Lindfield & Co 1887-90, is confirmed in directories of these dates. In the second one, Lindfield's business was "grocer's draper's, ironmongers, etc.". The Dependant style was emerging.

Table 9.1   1881 Census, Warnham Stores *(Linfield and Potter)*

			Place of birth
Joseph Lin(d)field	25	grocer	Shipley Sx
George Potter	25	grocer's assistant	Alfold Sy
Lucy Luff	27	grocer's assistant	Wisborough Green Sx
Ellen Luff	25	grocer's assistant	Wisborough Green Sx
Elizabeth Caplin	29	grocer's assistant	Lurgashall Sx
Charles Wadey	30	lodger	Petworth Sx

Members of two other prominent Dependant families lived almost next door in 1881, Felix Foster and Michael Killner, with their families. Felix was a builder, originally from Loxwood, and a cousin of Felix who had been the first to set up as a grocer there. Was he one of the builders of Warnham Stores? His brothers, James and Harry, as will be explained in Chapter 11, were in Norwood at the time. There seems little doubt the Fosters were very active in three communities simultaneously, Loxwood, Warnham and Norwood. By 1891 even Felix had moved from Warnham to South Norwood. By 1882, Michael Killner and his son Henry, had taken Chaffields Farm, Warnham. Michael's grandson, the third Michael and a Dependant, was in Alfold in 1939. Although the Michael Killners all moved constantly around Sussex, they remained Dependants through the generations. Meanwhile, in Byfleets Lane the Dependant families of Henry Piper, and James Garman (Plate 9.2), with William Booker (Plate 9.2), lodger, were living near the chapel. Perhaps the oldest of this community were William and Maria Cock. He was a Warnham-born labourer living at Little London north of the village (where Walter Killner and his family also lived). He was born in 1807, and died in 1887, when he was buried in Loxwood, as was Maria a year later. One of their daughters, Hannah, also joined the Lordshill community later. Intriguingly, for the story of Dependant trade in the village, his son, another William, was a grocer at the north end of Warnham Street, on School Hill, in 1881, where he lived with his wife, Hannah, and their children.

In 1885, Warnham Stores and its land and buildings, now in the occupation of Joseph Linfield & Co, were conveyed by James Etherington to the Trustees of the Chapel, for the same price, £600, with interest and costs of 10/-, paid in 1879. The trustees were Henry Piper, Byfleets Lane, farmer; Joseph Linfield, Warnham, labourer; Mark Pelling, Warnham, labourer; George Reeves, Slinfold, labourer. The witness was Richard Nightingale of Plaistow Place.

It turned out that this debt was never paid by the trustees, as in 1903 a further document, a Deed of Trust, was drawn up between the same parties, Etherington, now a retired farmer, Piper now being of Bailing Hill Farm, Lindfield now Manager of Warnham Stores, Pelling in Friday Street, Reeves in Warnham Stores, and an additional trustee, Lucy Luff, spinster, Warnham Stores. It was agreed to transfer the debt in exchange for an annuity of £60 per annum, to be paid after Etherington's death to his wife Keziah, and sealed by a Bond, witnessed by Henry Aylward of the Combination Stores, Loxwood, stores manager. James died in 1908, Keziah in 1913 in Loxwood, both buried there.

Warnham Stores - Lindfield, Luff & Co Ltd

Table 9.2 **1891 Census, Warnham Stores, Warnham (Lindfield, Luff & Co)**

			Place of birth
Joseph Lindfield *	37	head of firm, grocer and draper, etc	Shipley Sx
Lucy Luff*	37	housekeeper	Wisborough Green Sx
William Booker	28	grocer's assistant	Rusper Sx
Esther Smith	28	grocer's assistant	Corton, Suffolk
Mary Booker	21``	grocer' assistant	Rusper Sx
Amelia Bright	33	draper's assistant	Bath, Somerset
Mary Wells	33	draper's assistant	Kirdford Sx
Fanny J Durrant	43	baker	Kirdford Sx
Sally Baker	23	baker's assistant	Kirdford Sx
Fanny Carter	27	cook	Nuthurst Sx
Caroline Booker	31	housemaid	Rusper Sx
Elizabeth Booker	30	laundrymaid	Rusper Sx
Benjamin Piper	22	odd man	Warnham Sx
[Ellen Luff*	35	draper's assistant	Wisborough Green Sx
visiting South Norwood]			

*denotes living in Warnham Stores 10 years earlier

PLATE 9.2   Warnham People

Fig 1 - The Luff's were the most significant Dependant family in Warnham, after the Lindfields (the only known photo of Joseph Fig 5 below). 'Granny' Luff, right, born Frances Beer Covey), 1814-1901, was the matriarch.

Fig 2 – below, Ellen Luff, who died at Warnham Stores, at the young age of 31 in 1910, was her eldest granddaughter, by her eldest son George, who was born in 1851, and spent most of his life in the Northchapel community.

Fig 3, below, Lucy Luff, George's sister, 1853-1937, the Luff in Lindfield, Luff & Co (see Plate 4.2). there is no photo of her younger sibling Ellen. Presumed taken at Warnham. (see also Plates 4.2)

Fig 5 - left, a roll call of staff alongside the baker's horse and cart, with the buildings to the rear of the shop behind the yard.
L to R: Jim Garman, Alfred Nuttall?, Joseph Lindfield, George Reeves, (carman not known), Winnie Rose, Sally Baker, Mary Baker, Charlotte Spooner.

Acknowledgement, Ron Muggeridge, A History of Warnham.

Fig 6, unknown gathering of some of the Warnham community. William Booker centre front. Similar date to Fig 7.

Fig 7 – left, William Booker, 1864-1949. Note the underchin beard, hallmark of many Dependant men, and indications of disability. He rose to be a director and furniture buyer.

Fig 8 – below right, George Denyer, cabinet maker, 1884-1979

Fig 9 – bottom, Bert Newing, upholsterer, 1866-1940.

By 1891, the expanding community at Lindfield, Luff's Warnham Stores had four siblings of the Booker family in residence, all born in Rusper, but whose parents (William and Caroline) were from Warnham. Their eldest child was born in Rusper in 1853, so William senior had left Warnham on marriage. How then did the children become Dependants, there being no other known connection with Rusper? William, 28, Mary, 21, both grocer's assistants, Caroline, 31, housemaid, and Elizabeth, 30, laundrymaid, all remained in the stores through 1901, and all except Caroline (who was looking after her elderly father) through 1911 too. William later switched to furniture buyer, and became a director of the company, whilst his sisters remained in the same rôles. The register makes it clear that their mother Caroline, having "much rejoiced in God" in her last few weeks of illness, was in 1910 the first known to die during a chapel service, but was then taken to the parish church for her funeral and burial. The Luff sisters had swapped rôles by 1911, Lucy now housekeeper, Ellen in the drapery department. Ellen, however, was staying in South Norwood with Charles Taylor and his family in Norwood High Street; Charles was a hairdresser and trustee of the Norwood chapel. Fanny Durrant, from Kirdford ran the steam bakery which had by then been built behind the Stores. Sirgood's preaching in Somerset had led to Bath-born Amelia Bright joining Warnham Stores. Fanny Carter from Nuthurst was cook. Benjamin Piper (Plate 9.2) was "odd man", what we now call odd job man. The community, although established, was still relatively young when compared with Loxwood.

Joseph Lindfield was the head of the firm. He was already very experienced, having been part of the company from the outset. George and Ann Linfield were a farm labouring family in Shipley, where Joseph was born in 1853. By 1871, the teenaged Joseph had gone to Oldland Farm in Rudgwick where Michael and Eliza Killner were working, probably on nearby Hermongers Farm. It was almost certainly here that Joseph became a Dependant. Soon after this he is credited with being one of those who helped build the chapel in Warnham, of which he became a trustee. As one of the first to be involved in Warnham Stores he is an important figure until his death in 1933, aged 80. He was not taken to Loxwood for burial.

Likewise, the Luff sisters have a long history within the community. Moreover, they were a local family from Wisborough Green. Their brother George and mother, Fanny Beer Luff, known affectionately in Warnham as Granny Luff (Plate 9.2), were also Dependants. Granny Luff died at Warnham Stores in 1901, at the good old age of 87. She had lived with her son George at Oakhurst, a house next to Plaistow Place, where George (a married man) worked with Richard Nightingale's community. Previously, she had been housekeeper in Gunshot, Wisborough Green, to Charles Greenfield, a Dependant, and before that at Roundstreet, in the long-time family home, Brookland, for her brother-in-law, William Kitchener. He was known as uncle (to Lucy, Ellen & George) in Warnham Stores at the end of his life. Lucy and Ellen were brought up at Brookland. It was a poor household – their brother George was working on the farm by the time he was ten, and their great aunt Sarah Kitchener, living with them, was a pauper (1861 census). Like so many others, their father George was a farm labourer, and like so many other girls Lucy and Ellen went into service, in Pulborough and Portsmouth respectively, Lucy to a miller and Ellen to a drapery master. Perhaps this sealed their future directions as Lucy became grocery manager, Ellen drapery manager by 1901. Both lived to a good age, Lucy died in 1937 aged 83, Ellen, 93 in 1949. Another sister, Jane, died rather young, aged 29, in 1885 at Northchapel. Joseph married and lived in Wisborough

Green, remaining a Dependant. George moved to Northchapel where he was baker at the Stores, finally retiring with his wife to The Old Cottage, adjacent to the Combination Stores, Loxwood. The Luffs were a quintessentially Dependant clan, spanning several communities, married or unmarried, local to Loxwood in origin, and amongst the numbers who first heard Dependant preaching on Gunshot Common between Wisborough and Loxwood.

A branch of Lindfield, Luff & Co was to be found in Rowhook, in Rudgwick parish, at Little Millfields, only a stone's throw from where Loxwood elder Walter Nash was born, and coincidentally the very same house where Walter's grandfather had once lived. They took on an existing shop that was described in 1891 as a co-operative and in an 1899 Directory as Lindfield, Luff & Co, managed in 1891 by Warnham brother George Reeves (Plate 9.2), with Emma Killner and Martha Firman. Emma and George went on to Lordshill, he to be baker, she as grocery assistant. She eventually married Alfred Kelsey there, having been his housekeeper for some years. The Rowhook shop did not survive for long, and no Dependant community took root in Rudgwick after 1899. Martha and George returned to Warnham, both living at The Cross by 1911 (for The Cross, see pages 180 and 187). George Reeves was also one of the Warnham Brethren who was a trustee of the chapel. He had lived in Slinfold as a boy, and when living at The Cross in semi-retirement did odd jobs. His family was from Newpound Common. It has been said there was another branch shop in Broadbridge Heath, but there is no evidence or date to hand. No other company had a branch outlet like Warnham, as far as can be ascertained.

Table 9.3   **Warnham Stores, 1901 *(Lindfield, Luff & Co, Ltd)***

			Place of birth
Joseph Lindfield *	47	manager of grocery and drapery	Shipley Sx
Lucy Luff*	47	grocer & clerk	Wisborough Green Sx
Ellen Luff*	45	draper & clerk	Wisborough Green Sx
Elizabeth Booker*	38	general servant	Rusper Sx SX
Fanny J Durrant*	52	baker	Kirdford
Amelia Bright*	44	draper's assistant	Bath, Somerset
William Booker*	37	cycles and furniture	Rusper Sx
Caroline Booker*	40	housemaid	Rusper Sx
Martha Firman	51	housemaid	Sandon Essex
Fanny Carter*	37	cook	Nuthurst Sx
Mary Booker	31	grocer's assistant	Rusper Sx
Mary Wells*	43	draper's assistant	Alfold, Sy
Benjamin Piper*	32	baker, grocer and carpenter	Warnham Sx
Charlotte Spooner	32	dressmaker	Petworth Sx
Sally Baker*	38	laundrymaid	Plaistow Sx
Francis J (Jim) Munday	27	grocer & carpenter	Wootton, Sy
Herbert Newing	34	upholsterer & cabinetmaker	Maidstone, Kt
Winny Rose	51	upholsterer	Upchurch, Kt
Clara Cuckow	29	grocer's assistant	Boxley, Kt
Alice Carter	26	grocer's assistant	Loxwood Sx
Ellen Luff	22	stockroom maid	Wisborough Green Sx
Walter Parr	44	clerk	Fairford, Glos

denotes living in Warnham Stores 10 years earlier.

By 1901, with Joseph as managing director, three had joined from Kent where Sirgood had also preached: Herbert Newing, Winnie Rose (both Plate 9.2) and Clara Cuckow. Another, Walter Parr, like Sirgood, came from Gloucestershire. He joined the Loxwood Dependants within a few years, serving as auditor to Aylward, Smith & Co. He described himself there, in 1911, as a retired draper, but in Warnham he had been both clerk and grocer, effectively company secretary. He was an experienced shopkeeper. However, both Lucy (grocer) and Ellen (draper), the Luff sisters, were also described as clerks. They may have all been joint secretaries of the company. Three seems excessive! The bakehouse still had Fanny-Jane Durrant and now also Benjamin Piper (son of Henry, above), though the latter was also working in the grocer's and was a carpenter. It is said villagers could bring their own food to be cooked in the bakery ovens. The men had more diverse roles, Francis Munday being a launderer as well as grocer, William Booker ran the cycle department as well as selling furniture (Plate 9.3). The business continued to be known in the village as Warnham Stores, as it did until closure.

Table 9.4   1911 Census, Warnham Stores and The Cross *(Lindfield, Luff & Co Ltd)*

A. Warnham Stores			Place of birth
Lucy Luff*>	57	stores manageress and director	Wisborough Green Sx
William Booker*>	45	furniture buyer and director	Rusper Sx
Ellen Luff*>	55	secretary and director	Wisborough Green SX
Amelia Bright*>	54	draper's assistant	Bath Som
Mary Booker*	51	grocer's assistant	Rusper Sx
Mary Wells*>	53	draper's assistant	Alfold, Sy
Elizabeth Booker*	49	domestic servant	Rusper Sx
Fanny Carter*>	47	cook	Nuthurst Sx
Francis J Munday*	37	baker	Wootton Sy
Winny Rose*>	61	upholstress	Upchurch Kt
Sally Baker*>	48	baker	Plaistow Sx
Alice Carter* >	36	grocer's assistant, widow	Loxwood Sx
Herbert Newing*	44	upholsterer	Maidstone Kt
Fanny Gifford >	63	seamstress, widow	Canterbury Kt
Clara Cuckow*>	39	invalid, rheumatoid arthritis	Boxley Kt
Ellen Lindfield>	19	storeroom maid	Horsham Sx
Ethel Butchers>	19	housemaid	South Norwood Croydon
Lucy Carter	58	nurse to invalid	Loxwood Sx
Florence Pullen	40	dressmaker	South Harting Sx
[Joseph Lindfield*> (visiting Northchapel)]	59	visitor, at Northchapel	Coolham (Shipley) Sx
[Benjamin Piper*>	42	director	Warnham Sx (visiting Hove)]
B. The Cross			
Fanny-Jane Durrant*	63	housekeeper	Kirdford Sx
Charlotte Spooner*>	48	dressmaker	Petworth Sx
Martha Firman>	61	private means	Sandon Essex
Bessie Booker>	25	grocer's assistant	Robertsbridge E Sx
Ethel Mills>	13	domestic servant	Portsmouth Hants
Hannah Rees	14	domestic servant	Tonypandy Glam
George Reeves>	62	odd man	Wisborough Green Sx
George Denyer>	26	cabinet maker	Kirdford Sx
Mark Pelling>	62	boarder	Rudgwick Sx

*denotes living at Warnham Stores in 1901.
> denotes living the remainder of their life in the Warnham community.

The size of the community was surprisingly large, now having risen from six, ten years earlier, to 22. Where did they all sleep is an interesting question to which there is no answer, as no one has troubled to write about it. All we know is that in 1911, there were 16 rooms, including living rooms and communal spaces. There must surely have been some sharing of bedrooms. A notable feature among the places of birth is, a repetitive theme, the continuing link with Kent, an area of preaching by the peripatetic John Sirgood. The 1911 specialisms may explain how Warnham became a centre for furniture making and upholstery.

In the 1911 census, two of the directors were away: Benjamin Piper visited the community in Hove and stayed with Frank and Catherine Walker in Portslade; Joseph Lindfield visited Northchapel Stores. The breakdown of roles or jobs is interesting. Lucy Luff was another director, and manageress, with her sister Ellen as company secretary. Domestic chores were undertaken by Elizabeth Booker, Fanny Carter (cook), Ellen Lindfield and Ethel Butchers. Mary Booker, Alice Carter and Bessie Booker served in the grocery department; Francis Munday and Sally Baker (Plate 9.2) worked in the bakery; Amelia Bright and Mary Wells served in the drapery department, assisted by Florence Pullen and Charlotte Spooner (Plate 9.2), dressmakers, and Fanny Gifford, seamstress. William Booker, a director and salesman, George Denyer (Plate 9.2), cabinet maker, Winney Rose and Bert Newing, both upholsterers, worked in the furniture department (Plate 9.3). Lucy Carter was nurse to Clara Cuckow who was by this time an invalid, but only 39 years old. She is said to have suffered for 16 years before her death in 1917, no doubt lovingly looked after by the community. Several of the longer-term residents had by now changed roles. Undoubtedly, others came in to work in the Stores, including those living in The Cross (Bessie Booker, George Denyer, Charlotte Spooner). The census was neatly completed and signed by Ellen Luff as company secretary.

"Cross Cottage" was in the hands of members of the Lindfield family by 1901, William and Emily, and their children, two of whom then worked at Lindfield, Luff & Co, one as shop assistant and one as a baker. This was not "The Cross", as the address and some of the same Lindfield family still occupied it in 1939, when the addresses were adjacent as they were in 1911.

The author has identified The Cross (Plate 9.5), adjacent to the cottage, explained below. As a mixed residence, The Cross pre-dates Hall House in Loxwood, which served a similar purpose. At The Cross, the 1911 census lists an eclectic mix of ages, both sexes and jobs. Digging down however, the names and the specific jobs match and add to those of the stores. The name of George Denyer, cabinet maker, of a Dependant family well documented in Plaistow, is particularly important as his job complements those of the upholsterers. George was a conscientious objector in the Great War, who was allowed to do 'useful work' for an electrical engineer for the duration (see Chapter 2, where in the sad case of Fred Greenfield, George, William Booker and Joseph Lindfield of Warnham travelled to give him support). Reeves and Firman are referred to above, ex-Rowhook shop. Bessie Booker's father was another of the Rusper Bookers. Only Fanny-Jane Durrant as head of the household and Charlotte Spooner were ex-stores, the former ending her days in Loxwood. The use of two children as servants is curious, if still not uncommon then. However, Ethel stayed with the Warnham community for life, dying in 1966 and was buried in Horsham. Hannah may have been orphaned as she was living with relations, aged 4, in 1901.

PLATE 9.3 Examples of Warnham Furniture

Fig 1 - Left, the Coole & Haddock boardroom table, Horsham.

Fig 2 - Top right, a chest of drawers which was sold at auction in 2016, and its proof of origin.

Fig 3 - Above left, Sylvia Standing's antique sideboard, Horsham.

Fig 4 - Right, an antique desk made in 1695, sold at auction in New York by Christies in 2001 for $10,500. The Dependants were confident to restore and sell good antiques as well as their own cabinet work.

Fig 5 - Below, shop front.

One suspects they were well looked after by the residents. Mark may have been sick as he died in Warnham in 1915, having been a Dependant, living in Friday Street, and a trustee. In conclusion, regarding the three census tables, the stability of this tight-knit community is remarkable.

Unique Departments at Warnham Stores

The unique furniture and upholstery department was already making a name for itself before 1911. Yet, as late as 1899, the directory listed the company modestly as "grocers", and in 1907 and 1911, "grocers and drapers", 1913, "grocers". As noted above, Bert Newing (upholsterer and cabinet maker), William Booker (furniture sales), Benjamin Piper (carpenter, and now a director) and Winnie Rose (upholsteress) all played a part in what must have been a recent venture. Perhaps the sisters of the drapery department contributed fabric, and seamstress skills. Someone had to take the initiative to propose this venture into the unknown. Perhaps it was longstanding member of the community, William Booker. From a sales perspective, the proximity of Horsham would have given more sales opportunity than for the more deeply rural stores. Northchapel, however, had a prominently advertised furniture department, retail, not manufacture, and furniture may have been widely available through all stores, for those with the income to buy.

Restoration of antique furniture is confirmed by a walnut cabinet of 1695 which turned up in Christie's New York showroom and sold for $10,500 in 2001! It was labelled with the Warnham company's name. Another piece remained in the Standing family in Horsham. Sylvia Standing allowed it to be photographed. An undated photograph of part of the shop front shows not only furniture, but also bedspreads or quilts, and the sign over the shop stating, "Modern and Antique Furniture". Ron Muggeridge, not himself a Dependant, worked in the joinery shop, so speaks with authority in describing George Denyer as an excellent craftsman capable of fine inlay work. George joined the department sometime before 1911, when he lived in The Cross.

Among its several attributes, at about this time, Warnham Stores gained a strong china department (Plate 9.4), latterly run by Alice Carter and Mary Booker. Some named and specially designed Warnham Staffordshire china is now on display in Horsham Museum, and Marion May has a small collection in her home in Shamley Green, which includes everyday plates, cups and saucers in two patterns, one in blue scrolls, the other with orange tulip-like flowers and blue, possibly loaves of bread.

Warnham Stores in the 20th Century

Like Aylward, Smith, Lindfield, Luff & Co produced calendars and one which has survived from 1912, describes the company in more detail: "Lindfield, Luff & Co., Ltd., wholesale and retail grocers, drapers, ironmongers, house furnishers and upholsterers, antique furniture and curios". Perhaps the most surprising branch is that of house furnisher, as much of the ill-informed commentary on the Dependants in the past has referred to their dislike of anything to adorn their homes. Another calendar of 1914 adds boots and shoes to the mix.

PLATE 9.4 "Cokeler Ware"

Fig 1 – right, the reverse of a saucer with label.

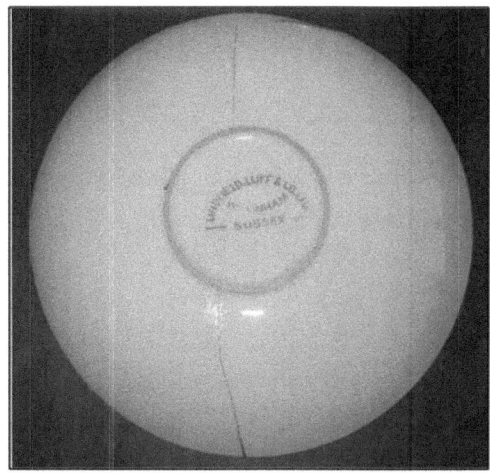

Fig 2 – left, the same saucer with its cup
(a colourful blue and orange pattern),
with a small blue and white saucer.
Fig 1 & 2, courtesy of Marion May

Fig 3 – right, a serving plate in the same pattern.
© worthpoint.com.

Fig 4 – a nearly complete tea and coffee service
in what must have been a common pattern sold by Dependants. © ukauctioneers.com.

Fig 5 – The same china displayed on a sideboard.

Fig 6 – Alice Carter (left) and Mary Booker in the store doorway in front of a china display (the department was upstairs).

Acknowledgement, figs 5 & 6, Ron Muggeridge, Warnham, A History.

Fig 7 – left, calendar for Lindfield, Luff, 1912. As with the Loxwood examples, it is surprising to see this kind of image sold by the Dependants, but they set out to serve the public, and no doubt this is what they wanted.

Fig 8 – below, calendar for Lindfield, Luff 1914. Neither calendar seems to be advertising a product.

In the 1918 Kelly's Directory, Lindfield, Luff & Co Ltd were listed as "grocers, drapers, ironmongers and house furnishers, antique furniture, curios, etc.; hand-painted old-style English ware and china, Warnham Stores". The list remained unchanged in 1930. A second old photograph of unknown date shows the complete frontage, with a sign reading "Drapers, hosiers and outfitters" on the left, over windows displaying a wide assortment of these and other goods, and "Grocery and Provision merchants" on the right, over windows displaying grocery on the right, and china "Cokeler ware" goods to the left, there being four plate glass windows in all, two entrances, and what look like large electric lights to illuminate the displays.

It is said the Dependants owned some land and property behind Friday Street backing onto the Stores, where some of the fresh goods sold in the store were produced. Orchards behind The Cross and along the north side of Friday Street were two plots. Flats were built on this land in recent times. A pair of semi-detached cottages was part of this land, the cottages occupied by Dependant families, in the 1940s, for example, by the Brocks and Wadeys. Several members of the community were farmers, including at Bailing Hill, Stone Farm, Chatfield Mayes, and Old Manor (formerly Street Farm).

Ron Muggeridge is a reliable storyteller, and he makes points which are familiar to anyone who knew the Dependants, for example their thriftiness, and their keenness on making maximum use of halfpennies and farthings in pricing goods (a practice for which other stores were noted, including Loxwood), their refusal to change their dress, not just at funerals – sober dress at all times – and their charity to those in need.

Table 9.5   **1939 Register, Warnham**

Warnham Stores	**William Booker*>**	1864-1949	furniture buyer retd
Lindfield, Luff & Co Ltd	**Ellen Luff*>**	1855-1949	drapery buyer retd
	Benjamin Piper*>	1868-1948	grocer retd
	Amelia Bright*>	1856-1954	draper's assistant retd
	Sally Baker*>	1862-1956	bookkeeper retd
	Charlotte Spooner+>	1863-1944	dressmaker part-time only
	Fanny Carter*>	1864-1947	cook retd
	Herbert (Bert) Newing*	1866-1940	upholsterer part-time
	Mary Booker*	1870-1951	grocer's assistant
	James Lindfield	1880-1949	baker
	Mary Lindfield	1882-1960	cook
	George Denyer+>	1884-1979	cabinet maker, furniture buyer
	Bessie Booker+>	1885-1968	grocer's assistant
	Mary (May) Madgwick>	1891-1984	laundry manageress
	Ellen Lindfield	1891-1960	storeroom manageress, storekeeper
	Ethel Mills+>	1897-1966	bookkeeper
	Eleanor Smith	1903-1941	draper's assistant
	Kate Etherington	1906-1998	grocer's assistant
	Mary (Molly) Farquhar	1912-1999	house and parlour maid
	Phyllis Garman (James)	1921-2002	draper's assistant

*denotes living at Warnham Stores in 1911.   + denotes living at The Cross in 1911.
> denotes living the remainder of their life in the Warnham community. Note, Ethel Mills spent time in Northchapel from 1951 to 1960 as emergency company secretary.

Warnham in 1939

The 1939 register is an additional tool for analysing the period before and during the war. Table 9.5 lists all those living at Warnham Stores, 20 individuals, much the same number as in earlier censuses. However, there are differences. The names are listed roughly in date order, with seven retired Brethren and two part-timers. These are the people one might have expected to have moved to The Cross in old age. Indeed, several had moved out, namely (from 1911 data) Charlotte Spooner, Bessie Booker, George Denyer and Ethel Mills, and were now retired or living above the business for the first time. The other names listed in the table are, predictably, those serving and working in the shop and community. There are no named managers though, so presumably the older retired residents are still active in the company board meetings, such as William Booker and Ellen Luff. Unfortunately, there are no surviving minutes to provide this information. There is evidence that the furniture and upholstery tradition was maintained. The Lindfield name continued to be prominent, as was Booker and Luff, although Joseph Lindfield (Plate 9.2) had died in 1933 and Lucy Luff only in 1938 (see Chapter 4 and Plate 4.2).

Memories of May Madgwick, Mary Etherington and Molly Farquhar

Several of the younger sisters were not yet in Warnham in 1911, viz. May Madgwick, Eleanor Smith, Kate Etherington, Mary Farquhar and Phyllis Garman. Eleanor has proved impossible to trace. May was from Worthing. Her mother, Charlotte Wadey, born in Wisborough Green, and Sarah, her grandmother, born in Kirdford, were also Dependants, as were May's siblings Frederick (Worthing), Harold (Loxwood) and Grace (Loxwood). Warnham History Society interviewed May in 1981. She told them that she was 24 on joining the Dependant community from a time in service and joined the grocery department. After The Cross was sold, she moved to Ellen Lindfield's cottage in Friday Street. On Ellen's death in 1949, May prayed for her future, and was found a retirement flat in Tilletts Close. Kate Etherington was interviewed (extract below) alongside May, as they had lived together since leaving The Cross.

"Miss Etherington is 12 years Miss Madgwick's junior, shares a retirement flat with her, and tends her in her old age. She has been a Dependent (sic) for 56 years, 42 of them in Warnham, and the first l4 in South Norwood. Her parents first lived in Rudgwick, where her father was a grocer, and then moved to Little Lake at Goose Green, Warnham [now Goose Green Farm]. Her Mother was a devout woman, and a believer in the Dependents. Unfortunately, she had T.B. but was frequently visited and cared for by them. Little Kate was taken to the Dependents (sic) Chapel in Byfleets Lane [Warnham] every Sunday for the morning and afternoon services. The Chapel was always packed out. The morning service lasted for three hours, but in spite of this, even as a young child Kate was happy to be there. She was drawn to the Dependents by a feeling of love and joy, which came to her especially in their singing, without music, they 'sang from the heart'."

Phyllis Garman was from Loxwood. She married John James in 1942. Mary Farquhar's story is told below, and she was from as far away as any of the Dependants, perhaps further – North Shields, Co Durham.

Molly Farquhar wrote her story down for Bert Newing. She came to Warnham in 1931, and only moved to Loxwood Combination Stores in about 1955. By 1980, she was one of a small group in The Retreat, Spy Lane. From there she moved to a bungalow, Alma, in 1986, finally to a nursing home (Table 9.6). In Loxwood she was a good friend of Irene Drewett.

Surprisingly, she hailed from the North East, born in North Shields, where she was abandoned by her mother, becoming a slave of her mother's former landlady, who was very cruel to her. She was placed in a home which was just as horrible, moving to another eight homes as she grew up, eventually adopted by a family in Southport, still only nine years old. Sent from there at 14 to a Christian "training home" [for girls in service], she made friends with Irene Drewett. Irene was placed at Loxwood after two more years. Mary was told not to write to her. However, soon, early in 1931, she was found a place in service at Esher with a Mrs Carr who she liked. When it came to a holiday, she was able to arrange to go to stay with Irene in Loxwood, where they attended chapel. The two girls were taken to Warnham Stores one day, and Lucy Luff asked if she would like to stay as a maid, which she agreed to. As Mollie tells it this was a move planned by God for her. Henry Aylward wrote her a letter of welcome and of her presentation to the Lord, which she writes out in full. She quotes the verse from Psalm 27, "when my father and my mother forsake me, that the Lord will take me up". She was 19 years old.

The Cross, 58 Church Street

The Cross was the home at death, after the second World War, for at least half a dozen Warnham men and women who were buried in Loxwood. The total number could be higher. There must have been a retired community there, even if in 1911 and up to the second world war the mix was of a wider and younger age profile. The only death recorded before the war was of Mary-Jane Firman in 1914. So why were the older ones not there in September 1939? Instead, there were six distinct households, separately numbered, each with a married female head of household, the oldest only 37 years old. Many of the occupants, eight in total, are 'redacted', a black line making it impossible to read their details. There are two children listed. One was Doris Hooton, married name Kneller, who died in Bromley, Kent in 1962. The other was Raymond Darling who died in Colchester, Essex in 2006. His mother, Lilian, may have married George Darling from Wandsworth, in Battersea. Assuming all the other eight are children (under 100 years old, and not yet deceased, which is why they are redacted), these families must be private evacuees (not the children of a whole school). Government-led evacuation preceded the start of the war, as did the evacuation of a considerable number of women and children of families which had the means to do so. Might it be that the Dependants' social and conscientious objection views led them to make room for as many as sixteen strangers, the usual residents moving to Warnham Stores?

The Cross, further along Church Street at No 58, is on the same side of Church Street as the stores, opposite the newer Farm Close, near the junction with Friday Street. The ground floor was converted to a shop, Warnham Interiors, recently closed and still vacant. The name continues in the much older attached Cross Cottage, explained above. The Cross was built on to the cottage in about 1875 (shown on the 1876 OS map) by Catherine Churchman. Her husband, William, a landowner in Rudgwick, and occupier of Loxwood Place Farm,

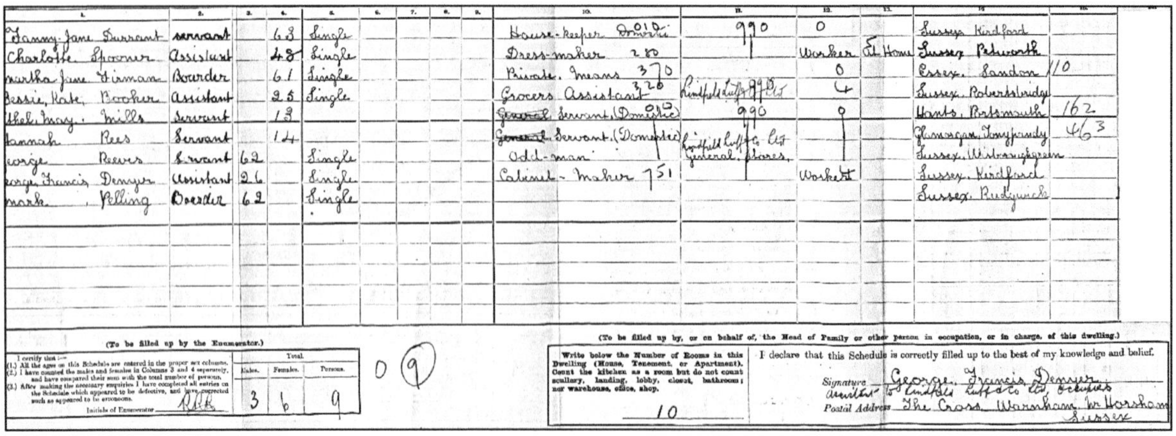

1.		2.	3.	4.	5.	6.	7.	8.	9.	10.	11.	12.	13.	14.	15.
Fanny Jane Durrant	servant	63	Single						House-keeper Domestic	990	0		Sussex Kirdford	
Charlotte Spooner	Assistant	48	Single						Dress-maker 280		Worker At Home	Sussex Petworth	
Martha Jane Tirman	Boarder	61	Single						Private means 370		0	Sussex Sandon	10
Bessie Kate Booker	Assistant	25	Single						Grocers Assistant 320	Linfold Lott & Co	L	Sussex Robertsbridge	
Ethel May Mills	servant	19							General Servant (Domestic) 215	990	0	Hants Portsmouth	162
Hannah Rees	Servant	14							General Servant (Domestic)	Linfold Lott & Co General Stores		Glamorgan Tonypandy	463
George Reeves	Servant	62	Single						Odd-man			Sussex Wisborough Green	
George Francis Denyer	Assistant	26	Single								Worker	Sussex Kirdford	
Mark Pelling	Boarder	62	Single						Cabinet-maker 751			Sussex Rudgwick	

(Enumerator's summary, left:) 0 9 — Total: Males 3, Females 6, Persons 9. Initials of Enumerator: AWK

(Head of family declaration, right:) Rooms in this Dwelling: 10. Signature — George Francis Denyer, assistant to Linfold Lott & Co, Orchids. Postal Address — The Cross, Warnham, nr Horsham, Sussex.

Plate 9.5 The Cross

Fig 1 – above, The Cross, residents in 1911 Census, entries by George Denyer.

Fig 2 – right, photo 2013, soon after the closure of the business which occupied the ground floor of this Dependant house.

Fig 3 - left, also 2013, the rear of the house, with the rear of Cross Cottage, right.

Fig 4 - The Cross in 2020, attached to the timber-framed frontage of the much older Cross Cottage.

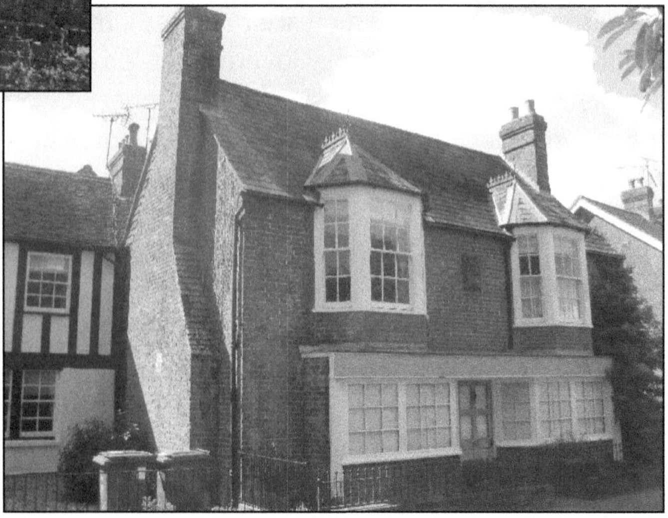

which they had rented from the Onslow family, had died that year, necessitating her departure (her son occupying Mill Farm in Rudgwick). This coincidence with the later farming activities of the Dependants in Loxwood at the same farm, described in Chapter 7, is extraordinary, but of no significance here. She died aged 90 in 1887. The house was bought by Mary Prichard, another wealthy widow (1891 census) and then by Mrs M E Whitfield, whose entry in the 1901 census says most improperly "home by April 1st, so not personally present on census night"! There seems no doubt that the Dependants acquired The Cross in the early 1900s.

There are six deaths, specifically at The Cross, recorded in the registers. The first was Martha Firman, aged 65, in 1914, housemaid, the second Charlotte Spooner, aged 81, in 1944 (no evacuees in the later years of the war), dressmaker. The others were all post-war, and significantly all post-closure of the community at the stores in 1948, which gives an idea of how long this home was maintained by the Dependants: George Denyer, cabinet maker, aged 63, 1948; Ellen Luff, aged 93, 1949, company secretary, drapery and china departments; William Booker, aged 85, also 1949, furniture buyer; Amelia Bright, aged 97, 1954, draper's assistant. All of these were stalwarts of the community, with jobs in Warnham Stores for most of their working life. The Cross would later become something of a 'Retreat', as had the home of that name in Lordshill and later still The Retreat in Loxwood. Martha, Charlotte, and George had lived there since before 1911, except during the war. Ellen and William had transferred at some time from the Stores, possibly when it closed.

In 1939, the Lindfields were still at Cross Cottage, as they were in 1911, having lived in Warnham since the 1890s. Jesse died in 1943. He had early associations with Dependant farming, working for Henry Piper as a young man, as did his older siblings James and Mary-Jane. Lily Lindfield lived at Cross Cottage (60 Church Street), until she died in 1973. This had been the Lindfield family home for many years. The family had all worked for the Dependants in various capacities. Jesse's parents were Dependants, William, a gardener, and Emily. Nellie died in 1979, having been a 19-year-old in Warnham Stores in 1911. Three of the next generation lived at Warnham Stores in 1939. This Horsham family, if related to Joseph, the stores founder, were only distantly so.

Warnham's Relationship with Loxwood – United in Death?

Far more Warnham brethren and sisters were buried in Loxwood than was the case for Lordshill (an equal distance from Loxwood), or Northchapel (only a mile further), and notably more in both earlier and later years. Those who had lived out their lives, or their last years, at Warnham Stores, numbered eleven. There are another 100 plus whose death is recorded in Warnham. It is interesting to see who they were, their relationships and their occupations (includes a few who were hospitalised, but their residence stated).

Table 9.6   Warnham Dependants' Burials at Loxwood

Francis Nightingale	55	1869	Betchetts Farm, (farm labourer)
Mary Garman	55	1870	Friday Street (wife of George Garman, farm labourer)
James Nightingale	30	1872	Cyder Mill Farm (farm labourer)
Elizabeth Wood	23	1875	Warnham Street, (dau of George Wood, farm labourer)
Benjamin Hayler	81	1877	ex Wellers Farm Wisboro Green (farm labourer)

Georgina Horsey	22	1879	not found
William Carter	49	1885	ex Spy Lane, Loxwood (carter, Tom Overington's son-in-law)
William Cock	84	1887	Little London (farm labourer)
Maria Cock	77	1888	Little London (William's wife)
Walter Killner	14	1889	Little London (son of Walter, farm labourer & Harriett)
Susan Garman	62	1891	Ockley (carter's wife)
Joseph Wells	62	1891	Lower Chickens Farm (farm labourer)
Mary Garman	1y 8m	1892	not found
Mary Ann Spooner	25	1894	Warnham Stores (ex-Alfold Bars, dressmaker)
Michael Killner	78	1895	Church St (ex-Chaffields Farm, farm labourer)
Alice Garman	24	1896	Horsham (domestic servant)
Frances "Granny" Luff	87	1901	Warnham Stores (ex-Gunshot Common, Wisborough Green, domestic servant)
William Kitchener	84	1905	Warnham Stores (ex Thakeham Workhouse, farm labourer, uncle to the Luff sisters)
Mary Wells	83	1906	Lower Chickens Farm (widow of Joseph)
Sarah Haylor	82	1907	(Bailing Hill, living on own means)
Sarah Cherriman	60	1907	Lower Chickens Farm (jobbing gardener's wife)
Jane Piper	69	1909	(Bailing Hill, farmer's wife, Henry Piper Sr)
Ellen Luff	31	1910	Warnham Stores (stockroom maid; see Plate 9.2)
George Piper	41	1911	Bailing Hill (farmer's son)
Martha Firman	65	1914	The Cross (private means, housemaid, ex-Rowhook shop)
Clara Cuckow	45	1917	Warnham Stores ("after 16 years of suffering")
Winnie Rose	67	1917	Warnham Stores (upholstress)
Henry Piper Jr	53	1920	Southlea, Church St (farmer's son, Bailing Hill)
Henry Piper Sr	76	1921	Church St (farmer, Bailing Hill)
Fanny Gifford	76	1923	Warnham Stores (seamstress)
Lucy Luff	83	1937	Warnham Stores (managing director)
Mary Wells	81	1939	Warnham Stores (draper's assistant)
Charlotte Spooner	81	1944	The Cross (dressmaker)
George Denyer	63	1948	The Cross (cabinet maker)
Benjamin Piper	80	1949	Warnham Stores (director)
William Booker	85	1949	The Cross (Stores director, furniture buyer)
Ellen Luff	93	1949	The Cross (Stores director and company secretary)
Amelia Mary Bright	97	1954	The Cross (Stores draper's assistant)
Sally Baker	93	1956	Church St (Stores baker)
Lucy Miles	93	1961	Friday Street (carpenter's wife, ex-Stroud Common, Shamley Green, Sy)
May Madgwick	92	1984	Clemsfold Rest Home (Laundry manageress, Warnham Stores)
Mary (Molly) Farquhar	86	1999	Chartwell Nursing Home, Midhurst (house and parlour maid Warnham Stores)

"My little May Madgwick so peacefully at Clemsfold Rest Home Mar 23 in her 93rd year laid to rest at Loxwood Mar 28 at 3.30". quoted in the death register, officiating elder Alf Goodwin.
Ben Piper's funeral was reported in the local newspaper. He was described as reserved, but of kindly disposition, highly respected in the village, and a member of the Horsham Rural Food Committee.
This list is only as accurate as the burial register from which it is extracted. Some Warnham Brethren may well have moved to other places in old age.
Residents of The Cross were mostly those who had worked and lived in the Stores.
Occupations in brackets are those in the 1911 or earlier census.

Memories of 1940s Warnham

Some interesting memories of Warnham just before the stores closed after the Second World War have been kindly provided by email. Below is an edited version of what Roy Taylor sent:

"Before my mother died our house was in Friday Street, two houses down from the Greets Inn. In those days it was 2, Cherry Tree Cottages. It is now 51 Friday Street.

My involvement with the Cokelers came when I was fostered with Ethel and Harry Brock. The Brocks lived at the end of a pathway that ran beside The Cross. Mrs Brock worked at one time in Warnham Stores. I was fostered there as a 9-year-old in 1946 to approximately February 1947, a period of roughly one year. This means that much of what I will be writing are the memories of a 9-year-old, supplemented by a bit of Ancestry research. My mother died from TB in February 1945 and is buried in Warnham churchyard. The Brocks gave me my second of two foster homes, made necessary by the fact that my father was still in the Royal Air Force. Oddly enough, the first was with a Mrs Burgess, whose house was next door to The Cross, on the other side of the roadway which later became a fairly wide concreted path leading down to the Brock's house. The neighbours on the other side of Mrs. Burgess in Church St. were Mr & Mrs Redford, and their children, Roswyn and Roy. Roy is 5 years older than me.

On the other side of The Cross was Cross Cottage, the Lindfield's house. The children William (Willy) and I think Jesse, were a bit older than me as Willy was already at Collyers School in Horsham, while I was still at the village school opposite the green. The Lindfield family were Cokelers. I was taken to the chapel regularly on Sundays by Mrs Brock, but do not remember Mr Brock attending. We were taken in a large London-style black cab driven by Mr Redford. I am fairly certain that the cab was kept at the garage opposite Lindfield and Luff's stores. This was owned by the Cokelers and run by another Mr Lindfield. I seem to recall reading somewhere (possibly in Ron Muggeridge's book) that he lived in School Hill. I believe there were three services at the chapel each Sunday. I think that we probably only attended two as I can remember retiring to a room at the top end of the chapel for refreshments between services. The room was a long thin room behind the long table at which the elders sat facing the congregation. Memories of the service are pretty distant, but I do remember a succession of congregation members standing up and saying their piece. Between services also, the younger ones walked out along Byfleets Lane in the Broadbridge Heath direction. In 1962 while driving along Byfleets Lane, I spotted Mr Redford outside the chapel and stopped for a chat.

I have generally good memories of the Cokeler ladies at the shop and at The Cross but can only recall the name May Madgwick. I would recognise a picture of her, but unfortunately no others. I can remember going to services at Loxwood, probably at Easter or similar, where members from other chapels were present. I have no recollection of farmland owned by the Cokelers, but Ron Muggeridge mentions land and an orchard behind The Cross owned by the Cokelers. The orchard was on the right-hand side of the path leading down to the Brock's house and their neighbours the Wadeys. These are the houses mentioned by Ron Muggeridge on page 36 of his book. My uncle was Francis James (Jim) Munday. Although employed as a baker by the Cokelers, I have no knowledge of him or my aunt attending the chapel. They are buried in St. Margaret's churchyard close to my mother. In 1901 when my uncle was living at the stores, his parents and brother lived next to the Chapel, which was possibly Chapel Cottage. They may also have lived there in 1891 and 1911, but the census entries are not clear My uncle's brother Alfred Munday married Grace Madgwick who was May Madgwick's sister.

My mother, before her marriage in 1936 was housekeeper to Mr Frederick Freeman and also worked in the Post Office in one of his shops. Mr Freeman was a "fairly big noise" in the village. He was also my godfather!"

Note: Ethel Brock died in 1975. The Brocks had previously been part of the Norwood community, living in Sandown Road, where Harry worked as a coalman. Their daughter, Winnie, had joined the Northchapel community. Hubert Redford died in 1975. May Madgwick was one of the last Warnham Dependants. She died aged 92 in 1984. The last surviving member of the Warnham community was a Miss Hills (source: Mick Reed).

The Early Closure of Warnham Stores

Muggeridge gives the date of the closure of Warnham Stores as 1948, surprisingly early. The last time the company appeared in a telephone directory as a shop confirms 1948, "grocers, furnishers". The West Sussex County Times advertised the Clearance Sale held on 11 October 1948. The company had a listed number until 1952 at its changed registered address, 58 Church Street, which was The Cross, The London Gazette reported the winding up of the company, by then a securities and property company, chairman Mr E Lindfield of 55, Friday Street, in 1969-71, so finally ending this enterprise a few years before Aylward, Smith in Loxwood, where the shop continued until 1973. Warnham Chapel remained open until 1976.

Sale particulars, in West Sussex Record Office, confirm and add detail to the stores closure date. In 1959, the building came up for auction with Messrs Churchman as two Lots, together with some properties in Horsham. By this time the stores had been divided into two premises under the ownership of Warnham Properties Ltd, the successor company to Lindfield, Luff & Co, Ltd. Lot 1 was the northern unit, at first run by WJ Owers, grocers and bakers, but which had been in the tenancy of Mr Frederick Cherriman on a 21-year lease from 1951 as a grocer's. Lot 2, the southern unit, was in the tenancy of Lt Col Albert Charles Cooper, on a similar lease dating from 1948, as a draper's, so it would seem, continuing the former use, with no break. Might the company have had some interim arrangement, for Lot 1, such as is described in the next chapter, for the stepped closure of Northchapel Stores? AC Cooper appears in the Loxwood death register when he died in 1969, but it is doubtful he was a Dependant with his military past. The telephone number for his business as a draper ends on the sale of Lot 2 in 1959. Part was also Warnham Furnishers, from a 1949 advert specifically mentioning its location at the former stores and (in another advert in 1949 confirming) a continuation of the business by employees of the furniture and upholstery department, as these skills are specifically mentioned in the advert. This business is likely to have operated out of the buildings behind the stores.

The schedule of title, as given by the agents, dates from 1912, when a further conveyance took place (following the Deed of Trust 1903), just seven months before Keziah Etherington's death, in which the parties were named as follows: Henry Aylward of the 1st part; Keziah Etherington of the 2nd part; Henry Piper, Joseph Lindfield, George Reeves and Mark Pelling of the 3rd part; Joseph Lindfield and Lucy Luff of the 4th part; Lindfield, Luff & Co Ltd of the 5th part. The property was sold, as in the deed nine years earlier, subject to a yearly rent charge (effectively an annuity) of £60 to Mrs Etherington and her assigns, etc. In theory, therefore, the company was liable to pay £60 in perpetuity to Mrs Etherington's descendants. As she had no children, there were no direct heirs and no money changed hands after 24 March 1913, the quarter date before her death. But legally, a Deed of Indemnity was a wise precautionary measure for the company, and one was signed in 1948. The parties to this were: Lindfield, Luff & Co of the one part; Warnham Properties Ltd of the other part.

The Stores therefore continued to serve as commercial premises but has had periods of vacancy. The workshops and other buildings behind are also still there. In the 1950s they were used by Horsham Depositories Ltd, still the address of units in the yard known as Depository Buildings, or The Old Depository. In 1959, the shop let to Mr Cherriman had a double fronted façade, 2 storerooms, washroom on the ground floor, a basement, 3 rooms and a storeroom on the 1st floor, 3 stores on the 2nd floor; the shop let to Col Cooper had a double front, an office, lobby and WC on the ground floor, a basement, 2 storerooms on the 1st floor, 2 storerooms on the third floor, and in addition, in the old house (Cocks) behind, living accommodation consisting of kitchen/dining area, lounge, slip room and bedroom on the ground floor and 1 bedroom above. Today, the shop is now part private house, part premises of Steve Gubbins photography studio at No 24, formerly Frederick Cherriman's shop.

The Bakehouse, once The Depository, became a health club, Warnham Health and Fitness, which recently ceased trading, now replaced by Bodywise Gym and Studios. What might the Warnham Cokelers have made of this? The layout remains almost as the Dependants left it, with an internal yard off a narrow street entrance, and high mainly 3-storey buildings. The arched roof garage has been removed. The building to the north of the shop had been substantially enlarged sometime around 1900. It is divided into several light commercial units. There are now a mix of office spaces. These include a building design company. The rear overlooks a paddock owned, somewhat incongruously in the circumstances, as church diocesan glebe land, beyond which is the recreation ground. The glebe field used to extend behind the vicarage. The cricket ground was already on its site by the end of the nineteenth century. The Dependants were embedded in the community, not apart from it. Opposite, where now there are housing estates, was the large model farm of Warnham Court, and just along the street was the then village hall. On both sides of the site are old timber-framed cottages, one of which was Cocks, the old Post Office cum grocers and drapers of William Tanner until 1879.

Chapter 10

Northchapel

PLATE 10.1 The Northchapel Neighbourhood, late 19th Century and Edwardian Period

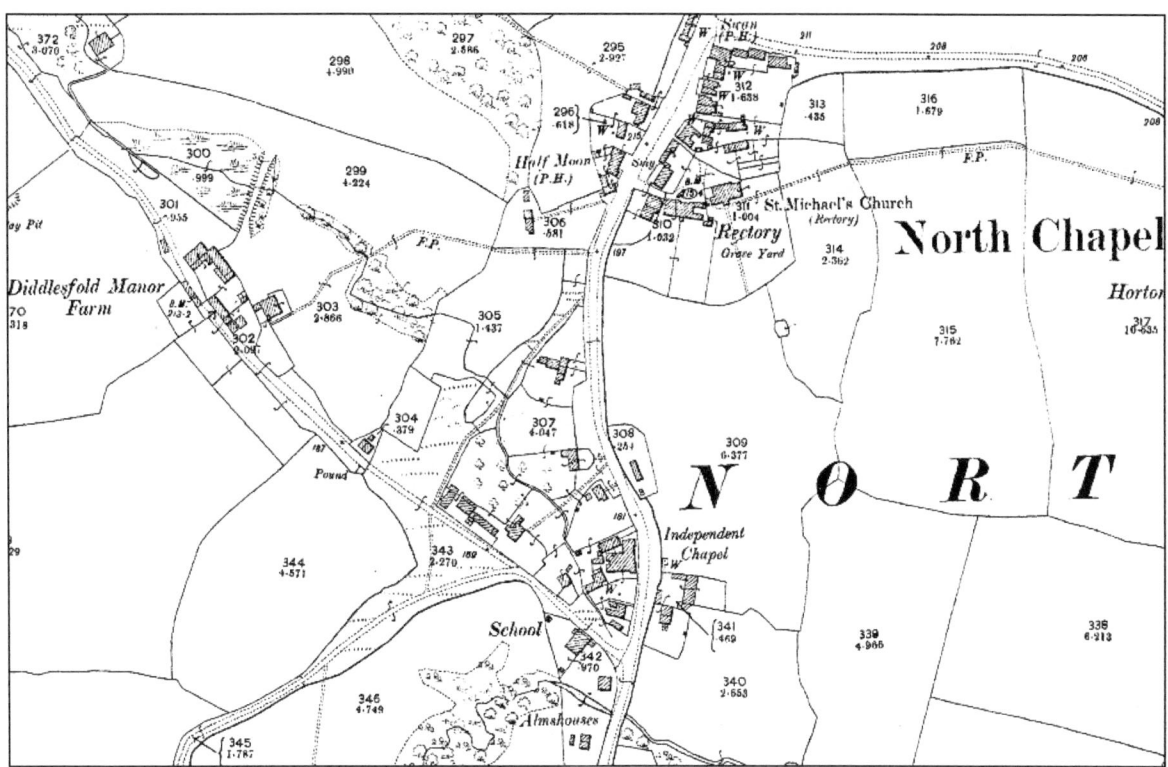

Fig 1 – OS map 1897. The stores and ancillary buildings cluster around the 'Independent' Chapel, on the west side of the street on a triangular plot incorporating Laurel Cottage and the chapel. Diddlesfold Manor is up the lane alongside, and before it (Pound) was Lower Diddlesfold (Table 10.5), and Greenland Farm to the north. The lane off to the south west is to Hillgrove. Goff's Farm was on the main road further south. Note the location of the stores and chapel well to the south of the village centre, and the Almshouses, later to be in the hands of the Dependants, where future houses would be built.

Fig 2 – left, Laurel Cottage as it is today, adjacent to Northchapel Stores.

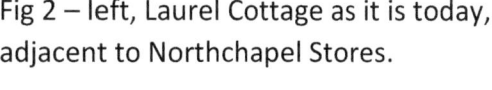

Fig 3 – right, Lilac Cottages, on the north side of the stores, as extended today, purchased from Mr Luff in 1916.

Figs 4 & 5 – Lower Diddlesfold Farm, left a Brown, Durrant postcard, 1918 *(Acknowledgement Pamela Bruce)*, right, a recent photo of the farmhouse.

Figs 6 & 7 – Goff's Farm, below left, old postcard, right, a recent photograph.

Figs 8 & 9 – views of Hillgrove Lane and Hillgrove Common , set in beautiful scenery SW of Northchapel.

Fig 10 – Northchapel Stores, a postcard, looking south, 1905-1910 series, by Inge of Haslemere. Note the gable end of the draper's shop with accommodation above, and the absence at the far end of the high wing built later.

Northchapel is about nine miles west from Loxwood, via Plaistow, so easily walked by the first Dependants, including John Sirgood himself. The Dependants came to dominate the southern approach to the rather linear village on the turnpike to Petworth, now the A283. The sphere of influence of the chapel here (Plate 3.4) extended into Lurgashall, Lodsworth, Ebernoe, Balls Cross, Fernhurst, and even to Haslemere. As elsewhere, early intolerance led to trouble, for example a near riot on the green reported in the West Sussex Gazette in 1865. Sarah Spooner was knocked to the ground, and rotten eggs were thrown.

Northchapel Stores – Genesis

Fortunately, West Sussex Record Office has records and minutes of Northchapel Dependants from 1875 to 1969. The story of Dependant trade here began it is said with baking and selling lardy rolls, eggs, sewing cotton and coal, sometimes door to door. As Jerrome points out, the survival of such stories in later testimony was a living part of worship, and not to be underestimated as oral and handwritten history. Coal is attested to have been Minnie Caplin's speciality.

Harriett Spooner (Plate 10.2), daughter of Northchapel grocer James Spooner and his wife Ann, is credited as the first known local Dependant trader. Her family's shop was at first in Ebernoe, near Kirdford, where her father had farmed 40 acres at Highbuildings, near the common. They moved to Northchapel in the 1860s, to Laurel Cottage, next to where the Dependant premises would soon be built. By 1881, this shop was home not only to James and Ann Spooner (who were an elderly couple by this time), their daughters Mary and Harriett, both in their thirties, but also to lodgers, Jesse Puttock and William Wadey; at the time of the census there was also a visitor, Caroline Pullen. Jesse, previously at Plaistow Place, later became a Dependant elder in Loxwood. 'Kitty' Pullen was at Loxwood's Combination Stores by 1891 for the rest of her life. William Wadey, however, married Harriett Spooner in 1884, ending any prospect of her running Northchapel Stores. They moved away to a home near the village and had several children whilst remaining Dependants. Mary Spooner moved into the new community at Northchapel Stores. The two women had, with their parents, played a crucial part in setting up the Dependant business prior to it moving into new premises. In this way the Spooners had a parallel rôle to the Fosters in Loxwood (Chapter 5). Both Spooner parents died in the next few years and were buried at Loxwood. James's death was announced in the Sussex Agricultural Express, in 1890, aged 80, living at Northchapel Stores, the earliest published reference to the new venture. A 1954 news report (below) claimed the business began about 1874 or 1875.

There was no Northchapel Stores, or at least no community living above one, until after 1881, and none listed in 1882. The Ordnance Survey map of 1875 shows Laurel Cottage on the site, and further back from the road, another longer building parallel to the road, which may have been Steps Cottages, and to the north, the chapel, already erected. This juxtaposition of chapel and stores is similar to Lordshill in Surrey. The land on which the chapel was built had been conveyed to the Dependants by William Spooner of Common Cottage, one of its builders. He was not from the family of James and Ann, but both families were from Ebernoe, so they may have been related. The plot was big enough. Indeed, in 1861, Laurel Cottage had 11 acres of land. The 1880s store seems to have replaced, or incorporated, Steps Cottages, expanded first to the roadside, and outbuildings behind.

By 1891, Laurel Cottage was no longer a shop, and the Dependant community had built its premises. The new stores are also thought to be the work of local builders, William Spooner, the builder of the chapel, and Thomas John Street, Northchapel born. Spooner was a trustee and elder of the chapel, noted as elder in the Loxwood death register. He took on the coal merchant's side of the Dependant business in the 1880s. He later "retired" to the life of a farmer at Hill Grove, a hamlet between Northchapel and Lurgashall.

Tom Street may also have been an elder. His parents, Stephen and Anne had lived at the post office/grocer's shop, where Ann may have helped out. By 1882 Stephen is listed as a grocer in a directory. Tom's wife Susan ended her days in the Norwood community. She was a good hymn writer, creating some that had a strong memorable meter. Other members of the Street family may also have been shopkeepers in the village, at Potlands Cottages.

Hannah Osborne, born in 1853, is reputed to have been one of the founder members of the Northchapel stores, having come it is said from London where she had been in service. In searching for evidence of her, she proved elusive in the usual census sources, but browsing the 1881 census for another person, her name stood out, in the centre of Loxwood, in one of the pair of cottages in the plot which soon would have the Combination Stores, next door to James Overington. She was staying with Mary Foster, a draper. From this, we learn Hannah was also a draper. She is also important as a letter writer for John Sirgood, from at least 1878. There is no evidence for her in Northchapel before 1883, when she addressed one of these letters from there. In January 1881 she was with Sirgood in Warnham, then in Loxwood for the census. John Sirgood wrote to her in 1883 addressing it to "My very dear and precious sister". In 1884, she and many others from Northchapel set out on foot for the Big Meeting at Loxwood. To borrow a much-used Dependant sentence, Sirgood had good hope of her.

Hannah Osborne and Mary Foster were at the forefront of a revolution in 'combination', which was progressing simultaneously in all centres. Mary, the older of the two at 30, was a local Loxwood woman. Hannah was the daughter of a bricklayer from Sturmer in Essex, brought up in Girton, just outside Cambridge. She had a blind elder sister, and a brother who was a tailor, which might explain her interest in drapery. Yet, by Christmas 1887 she was dead, aged only 35, a promising and literate disciple of Sirgood, in the mould of Ann Overington, Sirgood dying only two years before. William Spooner went to Loxwood with the other Northchapel Brethren and led the funeral meeting himself, which no doubt was as always, a joyous occasion. The register records: "Our dear Sister, Northchapel Stores". In her short life, she and Harriett Spooner had begun combination in Northchapel under the name of Osborne & Spooner.

Becoming Brown, Durant & Co, Northchapel Stores had Caroline Brown and Elizabeth Sarah Ann Durant as managers of the drapery and grocery sections respectively, certainly by 1890. In 1891, Caroline, with Ellen Luff from Warnham, was visiting South Norwood, where she was assisting in the drapers, lending her skills, leaving young Mary Cross in charge in Northchapel. They stayed with founder trustee of the Norwood chapel, Charles Taylor. Caroline may have had a connection to the Dependants as far back as 1861 when she was a 10-year-old visitor to Wonersh. Jerrome says she was a good friend of Harriet Sirgood and may have met her in the Surrey community. She was subsequently in service in London, before arriving in Northchapel before 1881 as a draper, lodging with the Huntingfords, a Dependant family. Charles Huntingford, an agricultural labourer aged 77, living with his wife Ann at Hunts Row, had a Northchapel drapery business, according to an 1882 directory, run by 'Carrie' Brown (born in Streatham), and possibly also Hannah Osborne, who was visiting Loxwood at the time of the 1881 census. The Huntingfords had also been early Dependants who, especially Ann, had supported Sirgood in the earliest days. Charles died in 1885, the same year as Sirgood. The latter walked from Northchapel to Loxwood to arrange the funeral just ten months before his own demise, such was the energy and stamina of this man. Ann Huntingford lived until 1907, when she was 93, living with William and Sarah Spooner. Elizabeth Foster, baker, was no relation of the Loxwood Fosters.

Lizzie Durant was previously in domestic service in London. She was named employer and manager of the grocery in 1891. She may have arrived at any time after Harriett Spooner was married in 1884. The censuses tell us she and Carrie were established as managing directors by 1911, with William Luff director and company chairman from 1910 or earlier He was also a chapel trustee back in 1883, when only a labourer. William was not related (or at least not closely) to the Luffs of Warnham and Loxwood.

Table 10.1   1891 Census, Northchapel Stores (Brown, Durant & Co)

Northchapel Street, "Stores"			Place of birth
Elizabeth Durant	35	grocer	Shebbear Devon
Mary Cross	27	draper	Battersea London
Hannah Birch	24	grocer's assistant	Lambeth London
Mary Spooner	43	general servant	Kirdford Sx
Fanny Caplin	42	dressmaker	Lurgashall Sx
Elizabeth Foster	23	general servant	Bramley Sy
Clara Batchelor	59	housekeeper (widow)	Waterlooville Hants
Ann Batchelor	22	bakeress	Portsmouth Hants
Charles Lintott	45	baker (widower)	Chiddingfold Sy
Jane Lintott	26	grocer's assistant	Chiddingfold Sy
Fanny Lintott	24	grocer's assistant	Chiddingfold Sy
William Luff	44	grocer's assistant	Plaistow Sx
Charles Wadey	40	carman	Petworth Sx
[Caroline Brown	49	draper's assistant	Streatham Sy (visiting S Norwood)]

The 14 residing above the stores in 1891 have an eclectic mixture of origins, with more from west of Sussex and London than in other communities. One of the latter is Hannah Birch (Plate 10.2) who had been a pauper and at school in the workhouse in Kensington ten years previously. The community was also different in having families, the Lintotts and the Batchelors. The latter had been living locally in Petworth ten years earlier, Clara eking out a living as a laundress, the Lintotts in Northchapel itself, Charlie a labourer, Jane keeping house, but Fanny in service in Bramley. Charles Wadey had moved to Northchapel from Warnham Stores where he had been a lodger ten years earlier. He therefore had unique experience. He was an older brother of William (see above), who was now married to Harriet Spooner with a family. Fanny Caplin was from a Dependant family in Lurgashall. Her widowed father George, and her siblings John, Jim, Betsey, and Mary Ann were all Dependants in Northchapel. The originators of the business, apart from Elizabeth Durant and Caroline Brown had included Mary Spooner and the late Hannah Osborne.

The 1901 and 1911 Census Years

By the 1890s, the village was noticing the effect of the Dependants on the "miserably poor" attendance at Sunday School, so was said in an 1897 letter from the schoolmaster to the vicar quoted in Pamela Bruce's Parish History. Earl Winterton's suggested that one third of the population of Loxwood and Northchapel belonging to the Dependants, Bruce says, that this figure may have been higher.

Table 10.2   1901 Census, Northchapel Stores, *(Brown, Durant & Co)*

Northchapel Street General Stores			Place of birth
Caroline Brown*	59	manageress drapery dept	Streatham Sy
Elizabeth Durant*	44	manageress grocery dept	Shebbear Devon
Clara Batchelor*	69	cook	Waterlooville Hants
Charles Lintott*	58	baker breadmaker	Chiddingfold Sy
Mary Cross*	37	grocer's assistant	Battersea London
William Luff*	54	foreman of stores	Plaistow Sx
Jane Lintott*	36	grocer's assistant	Chiddingfold Sy
Ann Batchelor*	33	nurse (to sick woman)	Portsmouth Hants
Fanny Caplin*	51	nurse (to sick woman)	Lurgashall Sx
Hannah Birch*	34	general servant	Lambeth London
Elizabeth Foster*	33	bakeress	Bramley Sy
Albert Maple	42	grocer's assistant	Sellindge Kt
Mary Hunt	35	general servant	Northchapel Sx
George Luff	18	baker's assistant	Wisborough Green Sx
Louisa Killner	25	kitchen maid	Warnham Sx
Esther Cumber	30	draper's assistant	Guildford Sy
Caroline Luff	15	draper's assistant	Wisborough Green Sx
Charles Wadey*	50	hire carter (own account)	Petworth Sx

denotes living in Northchapel Stores in 1891.

Ten years on, the stores had an extra four members of the community, which included ten who were there previously. The census makes clear that Brown and Durant are joint employers and partners. Esther Cumber (Plate 10.2) arrived from a service role in Loxwood to the drapery department; she was a future company secretary. An indication of financial independence is provided for Charlie Wadey's little empire in the garage. William Luff has been promoted to a role not observed in other stores. The new members are all young and female, except for Albert Maple, a Kent Dependant. He may have been the first from Kent to join the Dependants, at first in Norwood before 1881. He was a carman at Loxwood ten years later and stayed in Northchapel Stores until his death in 1919. Mary (Polly) Hunt was the youngest and only child of a local family to become a Dependant. The Luffs, George and Caroline, were both younger siblings of Lucy and Ellen Luff, senior members of the Warnham Stores (Lindfield, Luff & Co), and George, Plaistow, later Loxwood, so dividing the family between the three communities. Louisa Killner, it will be noted, was also from Warnham, member of a large family of 15 children. Her parents Walter and Harriett having raised the family as Dependants. Five were still in the community at death, including Louisa, and the youngest, Fred, who set up his eponymous bus business in Loxwood. Just who the carers are caring for is a mystery, probably because they are out in the community.

Laurel Cottage, where it all began, is still there today, and was lived in for many years by Dependants, such as, in 1911 (see Table 10.4), members of the Caplin, Lintott and Denyer households. To the north of the chapel, on ground within the original curtilage, three cottages were built, which were named Lilac Cottages (to match Laurel?). These too were lived in by Dependant households such as the Pannells. In 1911 (see Table 10.4), widow Mary Ann Brooker lived at No 1, and stated proudly she was caretaker of the chapel. At No 2 was Ellen Pannell, and at No 3 were George and Martha Pannell. By 1912, probably in 1906, but said by some to have been earlier, in the 1890s) the Stores grew again southwards, down the hilly street, over an arched carriage entrance still there today, adding a new wing with tunnel entrance through to the rear yard.

Table 10.3   1911 Census, Northchapel Stores *(Brown, Durant & Co)*

The Stores Northchapel			Place of birth
Caroline Brown**	69	managing director	Streatham Sy
Elizabeth Durant**	53	managing director	Shebbear Devon
William Luff**	64	director	Plaistow Sx
Albert Maple*	52	grocer's assistant	Sellindge Kt
Mary Cross**	47	grocer's assistant	Battersea London
Alice Hounslow	47	draper's assistant	Maidstone Kt
Jane Lintott**	46	grocer's assistant	Chiddingfold Sy
Clara Batchelor**	79	pensioner	Waterlooville Hants
Elizabeth Foster**	43	baker's assistant	Bramley Sy
Hannah Birch**	43	domestic servant	Lambeth London
Ann Batchelor**	43	cook	Portsmouth Hants
Mary Hunt*	45	housemaid	Northchapel Sx
Esther Cumber*	40	[company] secretary	Guildford Sy
Caroline Luff*	25	draper's assistant	Plaistow Sx
May Kennard	28	dressmaker	Glynde E Sx
Winifred Brock	22	general assistant	Lower Heyford, Oxon
Elizabeth Denyer	29	grocer's assistant	Plaistow Sx
Samuel Rugman	30	baker	Plaistow Sx
Ethel Puttock	25	grocer's assistant	Brighton Sx
Sarah Kennard	30	housemaid	Glynde E Sx
Alice Spooner	20	kitchenmaid	Clapham London
[Joseph Lindfield	59	visitor (*from Warnham*)	Shipley Sx]

*denotes living in Northchapel Stores in 1901.
**denotes living there since 1891.

Again, there is an increase of four in number, using space gained in 1906. Northchapel Stores (22) had not expanded as much as Warnham (29) or South Norwood (30) at this time, but it now had as many rooms, 16 each. However, stability at the top is evident, as the ages of the long-standing resident workers increases. Just one admits to being a pensioner. There is no increase in male residents.

PLATE 10.2   **Northchapel people**

Fig 1 – top left, unknown sister in front of the stores. Probably pre- Great War, earliest depiction of a Dependant sister's dress at Northchapel.

Fig 2 – centre, Jim Stevens, born 1846, farm stockman, company secretary Richard Hammond & Co Ltd.

Fig 3 – top right, standing l to r, Caroline Luff (b. 1885), unknown, Hannah Birch (b. 1870); seated, Esther Cumber (b. 1872).

Fig 4 – left centre, Esther Cumber, company secretary Brown, Durant & Co, in later years.

Fig 5 – right, Carrie Luff, director Brown, Durant & Co, in later years.

Fig 7 – below left, Ben Talbot, born 1896, coal merchant.

Fig 8 – left centre, includes Daisy King (b. 1908) and Fred W Smith (b. 1901). Chicken sheds at Holly View.

57 Photograph of the Spooner family taken at Bushey Croft in 1923 on the occasion of Shadrach and Harriet Spooner's Golden Wedding. A member of the Dependants, Harriet is wearing the traditional black bonnet and dress. Shadrach was a younger brother of William Spooner, a founder member of the sect in Northchapel, who built the chapel in 1872. The little girl sitting second from the right in the picture is Rose Carter (née Spooner). Her father, Herbert Spooner, standing second from the right, and her uncle, Bill Spooner, far left, both played a prominent part in parish affairs and built the Working Men's Club in 1924

Fig 9 – Harriett Spooner, born 1854, was one of the first to sell goods in Northchapel.
Acknowledgement Pamela Bruce, Northchapel: A Parish History, pub 2000.

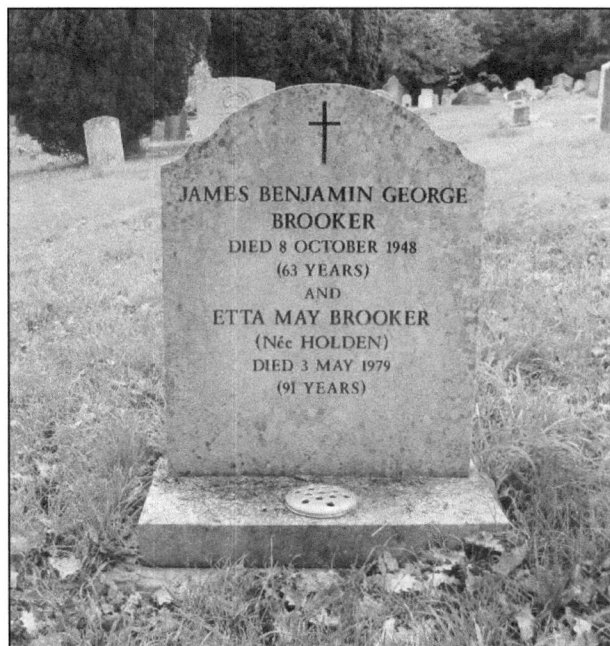

Fig 10 & 11 – churchyard graves at St Michael's Northchapel for the Dependant Holden and Brooker families. Charles and James farmed together at Goff's Farm in 1911.

The aim of the combination movement was always to provide succour and communal living for single women, an aim achieved in all the stores. This meant renewal with new blood, seven newcomers between 1901 and 1911. Alice Hounslow is another from Kent. Sarah and May Kennard were born in East Sussex, but their mother was Sarah Lindfield from Shipley, the place of birth of the Lindfield clan in Warnham (as is demonstrated by Joseph's visit at the time of this census). She too was a Dependant who eventually moved to South Norwood. Other members of the Kennard family came to Loxwood. Moreover, Sarah and May's sister Edith married James Goodwin from the Norwood community. They were parents of Alfred, one of the last elders in Loxwood. Sarah herself went to Hove. Winnie Brock's family moved to South Norwood, and later moved to Warnham, where Winnie died at the relatively young age of 47 in 1936. Elizabeth Denyer was a sister of Annie and several other Dependant siblings and parents. See Chapter 2 for her personal story. Samuel Rugman, however, was not related to other Rugmans in Loxwood. Alice Spooner was a daughter of Seth, a furniture salesman from Northchapel and Alice from Bermondsey. He had moved around a lot in his work (Horsham and Southampton to name two places), hence his marriage to a dockland girl and Alice junior's birth in London. However, her parents lived apart by 1911. Ethel Puttock's past has proved elusive.

Table 10.4   1911 Census, Some Other Dependant Households in Northchapel

Property owned by the Dependants (or soon to be)

1 Lilac Cottages	George Durrant*	58	carpenter
	Sarah Durrant	59	
1 Lilac Cottages	Mary Brooker	56	caretaker at chapel
2 Lilac Cottages	Ellen Pannell	56	private means
	Emily Newman	40	widow
	Margery Newman	12	at school
3 Lilac Cottages	George Pannell	78	old age pensioner
	Martha Pannell	74	old age pensioner
Laurel Cottages	James Caplin*	65	farm labourer
	Mary Caplin	62	
	James Lintott	93	old age pensioner
Laurel Cottages	Leah Denyer*	73	old age pensioner
Myrtle Cottage	George Luff	28	baker at stores
	Amy Luff	25	
	John Tier	24	baker at stores
Almshouses, N'chapel	James Stevens *	88	no occupation
	Jane Stevens *	52	dressmaker
The Alley, N'chapel	Jesse Dalman	38	farm labourer
	Maria Dalman	44	
	Alice Dalman	5	
	Alfred Humphrey	18	farm labourer

Other houses and farms

Northchapel Street	Fanny Luff	61	nurse
Northchapel Street	Eli Pannell*	53	bricklayer
	Harriett Pannell	55	
Northchapel Street	Thomas Wadey	42	coal merchant
	Edith Wadey	44	
	Thomas Wadey	20	carman for father
	Charles Wadey	19	carman for father

Bushy Croft	**Shradrach Spooner**	61	bricklayer
	Harriett Spooner	57	
Fisher Street	**George Pullen**	75	
	Caroline Pullen	71	
	William Pullen*	36	farm labourer
Hillgrove	**William Spooner***	77	farmer
	Sarah (Sallie) Spooner	72	
Greenland Farm	**John Caplin**	64	farmer
	Elizabeth Caplin	59	
	Mary Ann Caplin	55	

For Lower Diddlesfold Farm (Hammond et al) and Goffs Farm (Holden et al), see Dependant Farms in and around Northchapel, below.

denotes attendance at the first AGM of Brown, Durant & Co Ltd in 1910 (see below).

Dependant Farms near Northchapel

The Dependant's farm at Lower Diddlesfold (Plate 10.1) was an integral part of the provisioning of the Stores, providing milk for the confectionery side of the bakery business, wheat (milled at Gwillims Mill) also for the bakery, butter and eggs for sale, all carried on a handcart to the stores. One account of life in Northchapel states that flour was also milled at Coultishaw Mill near Petworth, and that wholesale suppliers were Eversheds of Shoreham for soap, Coxes Lock Mill at Weybridge for bread flour, and Pellett's of Petworth for confectionery. The communal living at Diddlesfold was comparable to Plaistow Place at the turn of the 20th century. Richard "Dickie" Hammond was the farmer, unmarried, and acknowledged leader of his little outlier in 1911 to the 1930s. Assorted Dependants including James Stevens (Plate 10.2) and James Spooner, along with Fanny Stevens (wife of James), Ellen Holden and Ellen Spooner on the domestic front, lived together as a farming and housekeeping community in 1911 (by which date the establishment was grandly called Richard Hammond & Co Ltd). Hammond had once been a stockman on Charles Holden's farm when he had lived at Palfrey House at Balls Cross. Lower Diddlesfold was rented from George Baker, whose estate centred on Stilland Farm.

Charles Enticknap who had been there in 1901, was the father of Catherine, the first manager of Loxwood Stores. Charlie and Sarah Enticknap went to live, by 1911, with their other daughter, Alice, who had married Charlie Holden's brother, Noah, who farmed Redlands Farm in Chiddingfold. Richard Hammond created a genuine community and was also an elder of the chapel. He died in 1938. A year later in the 1939 register, there is no evidence that the farm was still in the hands of the Dependants.

At Goffs Farm, Charles Holden, it is said, did likewise, assisted by his son-in-law James Benjamin Brooker and his wife Etta (aka Hetty), Charlie's daughter, but evidence of a community may be stretching a point, at least in 1911, when his household was just family, including aged in-laws. Charlie Holden died during a chapel meeting in 1930, confirmed even in his declaration of probate. Charles's wife Harriett's parents, Thomas and Harriett Heighes, had been among those whose cottage, in this case at Ramsnest, near Chiddingfold, had been used for early Dependant meetings, which were stopped by their landlord, Lord Leconfield, "being feared".

Table 10.5 **Lower Diddlesfold Farm and Goffs Farm**

1881 **Richard Hammond** ag lab lodging with Moses & Sarah Denyer, Chiddingfold.
From a Surrey farming family in Frensham and Witley. He was already a chapel trustee by 1883, and in the indenture of that year curiously described as a "scavenger".

1881 **Charles Holden** labourer, living with parents, Charles & Mary, grocer's shop, Colhook Commmon, Northchapel (near Ebernoe). There were four other Holden households at Colhook.

1891 _Palfrey Farm, Balls Cross, Kirdford_   place of birth

Charles Holden	farmer	35	Northchapel Sx
Harriett Holden	wife	33	Northchapel Sx
Etta Holden	daughter	3	Kirdford Sx
Richard Hammond	farm servant	34	Frensham Sy
Charles Enticknap	farm servant	56	Chiddingfold Sy
Sarah Enticknap	wife, domestic servant	54	Northchapel Sx

1901 _Lower Diddlesfold Farm, Northchapel_

Richard Hammond	farmer	44	Frensham Sy
Charles Enticknap	yard man	67	Chiddingfold Sy
Sarah Enticknap	wife, housekeeper	65	Northchapel Sx
Ellen Holden	general servant	41	Northchapel Sx
James Stevens	stockman	55	Northchapel Sx
Fanny Stevens	wife, domestic servant	54	Northchapel Sx

1901 _Goffs Farm, Northchapel_

Charles Holden	farmer	46	Northchapel Sx
Harriett Holden	wife	43	Northchapel Sx
Etta Holden		14	Kirdford Sx
Thomas Heighes	father-in-law	74	Empshott, Hants
Harriett Heighes	mother-in-law	63	Northchapel Sx _(later Pullen)_
Annie Clark	assist school mistress	25	Bow, London

1911 _Lower Diddlesfold Farm, Northchapel_

Richard Hammond	farmer	54	Frensham Sy
	Director of Richard Hammond & Co Ltd		
James Stevens	stockman	65	Northchapel Sx
	[company] secretary		
Fanny Stevens	wife, dairymaid	64	Petworth Sx
Ellen Holden	housekeeper	51	Northchapel Sx
	Director of Richard Hammond & Co Ltd		
Edith Mary Spooner	general servant	32	Northchapel Sx

1911 _Diddlesfold Cottages_

James Spooner	carter on farm	69	Northchapel Sx
Bertha Spooner		63	Ebernoe Sx

1911 _Goffs Farm, Northchapel_

Charles Holden	farmer	56	Northchapel Sx
Harriett Holden	wife	53	Northchapel Sx
Thomas Heighes	bedridden 14 years	84	Empshott, Hants
Harriett Heighes	paralysed 7 years	73	Northchapel Sx (married 56y)
Benjamin Brooker	farming	26	Northchapel Sx
Etta Brooker	assists, all farm work	23	Kirdford Sx
Stanley Brooker		9m	Northchapel Sx

There were other Dependant farmers in the wider area, John Caplin and his sisters farmed at Greenland Farm. John had been a trustee of the chapel in 1883, when he was a wood dealer. Noah Holden and William Spooner have already been mentioned. Table 10.5 shows how these communities evolved.

Richard Hamilton retired to Laurel Cottage where he was living at his death in 1938. Bill Hall has recorded his memories in the Petworth Society Magazine, 1991, and some of this section is based on this article. Other information has been gleaned from Northchapel, A Parish History by Pamela Bruce. Other members of the Northchapel community came, for example, from the Cumber, Luff and Talbot families. Frank Talbot, born in 1896, walked to chapel from River, a hamlet in Lodsworth, from the age of six. Not all locals were so well disposed to the Dependants. Arthur Waterlow King of Brookside, near Diddlesfold tried to stop chapel meetings in the early 20th century because they were too noisy!

Fernhurst

Fernhurst is a village six miles west of Northchapel, four miles south of the small town of Haslemere. From the early 1900s at least up to the 1930s, there was a shop (plate 10.3) at Chapel Street, Fernhurst run by Ezra and Emily Varns and family, and a small one on Colhook Common, near Ebernoe, run by Alfred & Blanche Lunn. The Varns family were well known in Fernhurst for going off to Northchapel Chapel (another source suggests they attended a chapel in Haslemere) in their sober Dependant dress, always on foot. The Misses Varns later took on the draper's at Northchapel. The words below are taken from the Fernhurst Society website. Note how the range of goods was similar to that in bigger Dependant communities.

"The main shop along Chapel Street was Varnses, where the pharmacy is now. The shop was staffed by Ezra Varns, his wife and the family of four girls and one boy – Florrie, Nellie, Bertha, Edith and Ernie. Ernie baked the bread and delivered the groceries. The family were Cokelers, a nonconformist religious sect and the women always wore long black skirts and black blouses. They used to go off in their black bonnets on a Sunday morning and go to Northchapel to attend services. They were particularly known for their kindness and courtesy. They also baked particularly good lardy rolls! A bill from 1939 describes their business as Grocer and Draper, Household Furnisher, China, Earthenware, Boot & Shoe Stores. At one time there was an entire bedroom suite in the window."

Table 10.6   1939 Register – The Shop, Chapel Street, Fernhurst

Ezra Varns	1877-1956	bread baker	died Northchapel
Emily Varns	1875-1946	invalid	died Fernhurst
Florence Varns	1903-1987	shop assistant, delivering goods	died Northchapel
Bertha Varns	1905-1958	grocer's assistant	died Northchapel
Edith Varns	1908-1966	domestic duties	died Northchapel
Nellie Varns	1911-1998	draper's assistant	died Eastbourne

All the daughters remained spinsters in the way of Dependants. All except Nellie, who lived into the late 1990s, were living in Hillgrove Lane Northchapel after their mother died, and the business closed. In the extended family Rachel Varns, 60, died 1943, was daughter of Ezra's brother Peter, her funeral at Ebenezer Chapel, Fernhurst. She had been a Dependant.

<u>PLATE 10.3</u>   Fernhurst and Lodsworth

Fig 1 – the former Varns shop in Chapel Street, Fernhurst.

Fig 2 – right, Jim Randall's shop, Lodsworth c1900.

Fig 3 – below, Randall's shop, c1905, Randall's delivery cart.

Fig 4 – below right, Mrs Charlotte Randall (in chair, 1824-1909) with her daughter Jemima Stevens.

LODSWORTH, PETWORTH.

Lodsworth

There was a similar story in Lodsworth (Plate 10.3), five miles to the south, but earlier. Jim (James) and Charlotte Randall kept the village grocer's shop. Jim also had land he farmed. He had married Charlotte Ayling of Wisborough Green – her father William was one of the oldest Dependants. Jim was from Lurgashall. At first, they lived in a cottage near Gospel Green in Northchapel, Jim a labourer, and presumably where they worshipped. After the birth of two children, they moved to Lodsworth to take the shop about 1879, a time when all the energy of the Dependants was turning to retail combination. Their children Jemima, and John, worked in the shop when of age. The stores in Lodsworth became a minor centre, and several of those who lived there (Mary Bridger) or visited there (Emily Hughes 1911) over the years were Dependants. Jemima married Walter Stevens who died in 1908. Jemima had a large family hence two went to live with their grandparents. She became housekeeper to the Smith family at Cobdens Farm at Lickfold in Lodsworth. Living with her was Nellie Bridger, who later joined the community in Northchapel Stores. One of the children, Wallace Smith, went on to become a baker at the Lordshill Stores. His elder brother Henry, who had already left home, became the partner in Smith & Croucher at Lordshill Stores. John Randall married but continued to live in Lodsworth and work as an assistant at the shop where he was newsagent and cycle agent, the only reference to newspapers in this story, as Dependants had little or no interest in the wider world defined as "news". Indeed, after his father's death in 1916, he took over the shop and was still there in 1939. However, he was not recorded in the Dependant death or burial register.

Table 10.7   1911 Census, Lodsworth Stores

			Place of birth
James Randall	65	general shopkeeper and farmer	Lurgashall Sx
Charlotte Randall	62		Wisborough Green Sx
Ella Stevens	15	shop assistant (granddaughter)	Lodsworth Sx
Harold Stevens	13	scholar (grandson)	Lodsworth Sx
Emma Ayling	35	shop assistant (niece)	Slinfold Sx
Mary Bridger	58	domestic servant	Northchapel Sx
William Hammond	32	baker	Northchapel Sx
John Pannell	18	baker	Petworth Sx
Emily Hughes	70	visitor	Siddlesham Sx

Northchapel Stores – the Company Minute Book, 1910-1950

Although it is clear from the timeline in the censuses that Brown and Durant were in charge from the late 1880s, the surviving Brown, Durant & Co, Ltd Minute Book in its original handwriting but without covers, begins with the company's first meeting at Northchapel Stores on 5 October 1910. This seems to be different from Aylward, Smith in Loxwood where the coincidentally similar date for the start of their minute book in 1911 gave no indication it was a novel business arrangement. The Northchapel meeting appointed Carrie Brown and Lizzie Durant to be Directors, William Luff to be Chairman, Esther Cumber to be Company Secretary at a stipend of £20 per annum, with board and lodging, and Walter Parr of Loxwood to be auditor (as he was for Aylward, Smith & Co, and possibly Lindfield, Luff too as he was an ex-Warnham man). Their bankers would be London County and Westminster

Bank, Haslemere. 46 shares were issued, and a dividend agreed of 5%. There would be a dividend of similar size almost every year of the company's life.

Table 10.8   Attendees at the First AGM in 1910 of Brown, Durant & Co Ltd

Mary Cross*	James Caplin	Annie Batcheller*
Hannah Birch*	John Caplin	Winnie Brock*
Albert Maple*	Elizabeth Denyer*	Caroline Luff*
Mary Brooks*	Mary Hunt*	Jane Lintott*
Jane Stevens	Richard Hammond	William Spooner
Ellen Holden	Leah Denyer	James Stevens
George Durrant	Ethel Puttock*	Eli Pannell
William Pullen	Charles Carter	Charles Holden
Alice Hounslow*	May Kennard*	Samuel Rugman*
Elizabeth Foster*	Edith Spooner	

Living at Northchapel Stores 1911

There were four from Little Diddlesfold. Others came from nearby – Laurel Cottages, Lilac Cottages, Highcroft, Almshouses, and one from Goffs Farm. From further away, came brethren from Fisher Street, Hill Grove, Greenland Farm, and Barfold near Haslemere (Charles Carter, estate gardener).

The company got off to a bit of a rocky start, with a deficit in 1913, which led to the sacking of Mrs Adsett, a secretary, and two younger officials, unnamed, because of "discrepancies in stock". However, this was the only example of possible malpractice in 58 years. Brown, Durant never dabbled in property in the way Aylward, Smith did, but in 1916, with healthy balances, 3, East Terrace (formerly Alley Cottages?) in the village was bought, and the three Lilac Cottages next to the Stores were purchased, all from William Luff, for £1,179. The next move was to set up an Emergency Fund to render aid to those in need. Then in 1920, 4 cottages and a garden of 1¼ acres belonging to Misses Annie and Mary Ann Caplin were given to the company. There is no mention of where they were, but the sisters lived with their brother John at Greenland Farm. In return the sisters were given an annuity for life – both died in 1942. The plot may have been 1.4 acres to the south of the village, where Holly View (later Holly House)was built, and where the sisters lived in 1939. New Cottages (later Dell Cottage), The Narr and Myrtle Cottages were built (see Plate 10.6) there. Myrtle had been completed before 1911 as Table 10.4 has shown. Holly House has the date 1912 and initials JC on the gable end, perhaps John Caplin's; he is known to have lived there in 1916. It seems likely all these were built by the Dependants in the 20th century, none of them of much architectural merit.

By 1920, William Luff's health was failing, and Sam Rugman stepped in as chairman. William died in November, aged 74. He was the eldest son of a farmer who moved around from farm to farm, first in Plaistow, then in Burton, then in Lurgashall. William moved away from home, instead of continuing his father's business. Why? In 1881 he and his sister Eliza Jane were in Fisher Street, Plaistow where they and James Caplin were neighbours and highway labourers, so maybe they had heard and followed one of the Dependant preachers there, which led him to join the new community in Northchapel as a grocer's assistant. His sister, who also joined the brethren, died in 1885, though she had been fit to walk to a Big Meeting

PLATE 10.4   Northchapel Stores, Then and Now

Then…

Fig 1 – left, said to be from an 1897 calendar. The simplicity of the building and frontage suggest this. Note the height of the road relative to the shop, which may have been a flood risk on the slope, and the railings.

Fig 2 – right, another early photo, probably pre-Great War, but later than Fig 1. The road seems to be lower, with steps and a new frontage to the gable ended part. This department is drapers and outfitters and has a third storey. A low wall replaces the railings, with evidence of a drainage ditch. A horse & cart heads south in the distance, possibly some sheep. There are

three bicycles parked outside the shop, and four children are artfully posed.

Fig 3 – left, a new inelegantly roofed extension has been added to the south, adding

frontage and accommodation, and further changes to the window frames in the foreground. The signage states "North Chapel Stores. Brown, Durant & Co Ltd. Bakers, family grocers, ironmongers, and general furnishers, drapers and outfitters". A tunnel entrance has been made near the blinds.

Fig 4 – above, shop frontage in c1930. The fixed canopy is still in place. The advert reads "APIS unstainable knives are the best. All guaranteed". APIS knives were made in Sheffield by Joseph Rodgers & Sons.

Now...

Fig 5 – Northchapel Stores and Post Office, a few years ago before the present ownership. The windows above have been altered. The shop does not include the gable end, or the building added to the left of the tunnel entrance. Part of the old front wall still stands. The drapers, sold in 1959, a separate shop (Drapers Cottage). The blinds were blue.

Fig 6 – now a Londis store, with Post Office, photographed by the author in 2013. The dominant colour is now green, and less cluttered.

Figs 7 & 8 – the southern newer end of the building, now a private house called Seria, with new flats built behind.

Fig 9 – the sign painted in the tunnel entrance, seen on Fig 8, for the Cycle Depot.

Fig 10 – below aerial view of the complex. Note the two former accommodation wings at the rear. The chapel is the detached roof just north of these wings (now a house).in the southern corner is Shere 4x4, a motor vehicle company. The site is now densely occupied, with parking at the rear. *Ack: Google Maps.*

in Loxwood the year before with others from the Stores. Like Walter Nash, Richard Nightingale and Richard Hammond, to name but three, a farmer's son may have had the necessary leadership and educational qualities to be an elder or Chairman.

Under Rugman's leadership, in 1923, three cottages called Alley Cottages were sold for £200, two with sitting tenants, Jesse Dalmon and Mrs E Trussler, both Dependant families. These were previously Stillwells Rents, but the name has disappeared, located somewhere between the church and the Swan Inn, perhaps East Terrace, which is in an alley off the street.

A workroom and two bedrooms were added to Northchapel Stores and the stables converted to an engine room for the first electric lighting, installed by Lister & Co, purchased from Damson & Co; a car for Wallace Smith's delivery round (Plate 10.5), which gave him more time to do odd jobs around the stores and garden, was purchased through Aylward, Smith. All this in 1923. The stores everywhere had a series of delivery rounds for each day or half day using vans to take out the grocery orders, bread and cakes, etc. Not all the delivery men and women were necessarily Dependants. In a newspaper report applying for an off-licence (see below), it was claimed that Northchapel Stores had 500 customers, most in outlying cottages over a 4-mile radius, for whom a delivery service was provided by two vans three times a week. This would have given the stores a very dispersed sphere of influence taking in (clockwise) Ebernoe, Balls Cross, farms near Petworth, Lodsworth, Lickfold, Dial Green, Lurgashall, Hillgrove, Fernhurst, farms near Haslemere, Roundhurst, Ramsnest, farms near Chiddingfold, Fisher Street and Shillinglee.

PLATE 10.5   Delivery van

Wallace Smith delivering bread for Northchapel Stores about sixty years ago.
This was the first van owned by Brown, Durant and Co.
The walking stick was used to fish out loaves from the back of the van.

Moreover, the next year petrol tanks and pumps were installed, water laid on to the washhouse and new washdown lavatories added to the chapel property, the last costing £160. In a further year of change, 1925 saw the creation of a road for cars to cross the old garden next to the furniture shop to get to a new garage behind the bakehouse, and new sanitary arrangements for Laurel Cottages. As with many things Dependant, this is an embrace of modernity, not for its own sake but out of practical necessity or expedience.

The Stores were doing well. Wages totalled £150 that year. A one-off donation of £200 was affordable to reimburse Aylward Smith for accommodating the directors at Big Meetings. In 1927, the practice of awarding directors a bonus began, set at £100, and continued for many years afterwards at varying rates.

Lizzie Durant retired on grounds of ill health in 1929 after 40 or more years' service and died in Northchapel in 1932. Her funeral in the village was reported in the West Sussex Gazette, one of the largest ever seen there, with over 200 attending, including some from Warnham, Bramley, Norwood and Brighton. The service (probably in the chapel, not the parish church) was led by Harry Aylward from Loxwood, assisted by Ben Booker and Ben Piper from Warnham Stores. She was laid to rest in a section of St Michael's churchyard reserved for Dependants. No evidence has come forward for any similar burial area, say at Shalford. Carrie, who had died a year earlier in 1931 had also retired in 1930 through age and infirmity (she was 89). Harry Aylward led her funeral meeting too. She had chosen to be buried in Loxwood. They had given their life's work to the stores. Alice Hounslow then became a director. Mary Cross also died in 1936, aged 73.

Spotlight on the 1939 Community

In table 10.9 below, Florence Franks later married, demonstrating the official use of the 1939 register right through to the 1950s, and the beginnings of the NHS. Births are given accurately. The entire list was of single (S) women and two men. Alice Hounslow was the oldest, Kathleen Edwards the youngest (and destined to be the last Dependant alive anywhere, so it is believed; see below).

The following had been in the Stores in 1911 – Samuel Rugman, Esther Cumber*, Alice Hounslow, Ann Batchelor** (died 1944, aged 77), Hannah Birch** (died 1962, aged 95), Ethel Puttock, May Kennard, Caroline Luff*, Elizabeth Denyer.

*Denotes also there in 1901; **denotes also there in 1891, a time span of about 50 years.*

New members were Phoebe Halfacre (what a lovely name!), Nellie Bridger, Edith Wright, Florence Franks, Esther Cole (known by her second name, Lizzie), Kathleen Edwards, Daisy King and Frederick W Smith (Daisy & Fred Table 10.2), who between them injected much needed youth. There would be few additional names at any later date. How Phoebe became involved Is hard to say. Born in Middlesex to a family from Berkshire, father an upholsterer, she became cook to a clergyman in a parish near Basingstoke for many years. Nellie (Ellen) Bridger was from a large extended family of Bridgers in the Lodsworth area. Born in Wisborough Green she lived with her grandmother in Tillington for many years before moving as servant to Jemima Stevens (see above, Lodsworth) at Cobdens Farm, Lodsworth, hence her induction to the Dependant community, and transfer to Northchapel. Edith Wright is another mystery, as she was born in Liverpool, was a servant in Manchester in 1911. How did she, one of only two or three Dependants from the north, come south? Florence Franks was a granddaughter of William Franks of Rudgwick, an early convert. Her uncle Stephen was a miller in Wonersh and a leader of the Lordshill community. Other members of her extended family were part of the Loxwood community. Lizzie Cole came from Sevenoaks, one of the numerous converts in Kent, many of whom migrated to the South Norwood community. Lizzie was in service in North Croydon in 1911. Finally, Daisy King was a daughter of Agnes, housekeeper to the Caplin sisters at Holly View (Table 10.9B). Agnes was originally from Wisborough Green, widowed at a young age with several children. Her late husband Richard was from Norwood Park, in which area (and in Penge) they had lived since their marriage, so again one may hazard a guess of a history of involvement in South Norwood and/or in Loxwood. For Kath Edwards, see below.

Table 10.9   1939 Register, Northchapel
A.   The Stores, Northchapel

The Stores, Northchapel	119	1	Ringman, Samuel D.	-	M	24 Jan. 1881	S	Stores Manager.
		2	Smith, Frederick W.	-	M	19 Aug. 1900	S	Bread Baker & Roundsman.
		3	Cumber, Esther	-	F	31 July 1870	S	Secretary, The Stores.
		4	Hounslow, Alice	-	F	1 April 1864	S	Old Age Pensioner.
		5	Batchelor, Ann E.	-	F	12 Aug. 1867	S	Old Age Pensioner.
		6	Birch, Hannah	-	F	15 April 1867	S	Old Age Pensioner.
		7	Halfacre, Phebe E.	-	F	19 Sept. 1875	S	Cook.
		8	Bridger, Nellie M.	-	F	29 June 1887	S	Domestic.
		9	Wright, Edith G.	-	F	29 April 1885	S	General.
		10	Puttock, Ethel M.	-	F	6 Mar. 1886	S	Housemaid.
		11	Kennard, May	-	F	27 Aug. 1882	S	Dress Maker.
		12	Luff, Caroline	-	F	29 Aug. 1885	S	Drapery Buyer.
23-6-50L AKA M		13	Denyer, Elizabeth PIERCE	-	F	28 Jan. 1882	S	Grocers Assistant.
		14	Franks Florence L.	-	F	12 Jan. 1903	S	Grocers Assistant.
		15	Cole, Esther E.	-	F	19 May 1897	S	Drapery Assistant.
		16	Edwards, Kathleen J.	-	F	10 Jan. 1919	S	Drapery Assistant.
		17	King, Daisy P.	-	F	17 April 1909	S	Grocers Assistant.

The neat handwriting in the above example, and the unique presentation of the 1939 Register, both lent themselves to pasting it, as published, as a table. Acknowledgement: findmypast.com.

B.   Other Northchapel properties occupied by Dependants in 1939
Dependant properties

Lilac Cottage	**Frederick Jones**	1890-1974	general labourer
	Rhoda Jones (Pannell)	1894-1961	domestic duties
	and 1 other		
2 Lilac Cottages	**Elizabeth Pullen**	1876-1969	incapacitated
	William Pullen	1875-1948	general estate labourer
	and 1 other		
4 Lilac Cottages	**George Pullen**	1866-1940	retired
	Madeline Pullen	1869-1952	domestic duties
Laurel Cottage	**Edith Spooner**	1879-1964	private means
Laurel Cottage	**William Pannell**	1857-1940	incapacitated
	Lucy Pannell	1891-1982	housekeeper
	Eliza Pannell	1887-1969	domestic duties
Holly View	**Elizabeth Caplin**	1852-1942	retired
	Mary Anne Caplin	1855-1942	retired
	Agnes King	1875-1960	housekeeper
1 Myrtle Cottages	**George Cooper**	1888-1956	forester

	Philadelphia Cooper	1872-1947	domestic duties
2 Myrtle Cottages	Frederick T Smith	1868-1951	general labourer
	May Winter	1893-1950	housekeeper
Village street			
4 East Terrace N'chl St	Jesse Dalman	1873-1959	council labourer
Elm Cottages	Horace Gander	1882-1966	painter
Northchapel Street	Lilian Gander	1891-1962	domestic duties
Oaklands	James Brooker	1885-1948	general labourer
	Etta Brooker	1887-1979	domestic duties
	and 3 others		
	Harriett Holden	1857-1949	retired
Four Tree House	George Howick	1858-1945	police pensioner
	and 4 others		
Northchapel Street	Thomas Wadey	1868-1948	farm labourer
	Edith Wadey	1866-1948	domestic duties
	Fanny Wadey	1889-1959	incapacitated
	Thomas Wadey	1891-1955	haulage contractor
	and 1 other		
Hillbrow N'chapel St	Elizabeth Talbot	1874-1959	domestic duties
	Benjamin Talbot	1896-1947	coal and coke merchant *(Plate 10.2)*
	and 3 others		
Oaklands N'chapel St	Alfred Lunn	1890-1973	painter
	Mary Blanche Lunn	1887-1973	domestic duties
	Agnes Holden	1859-1941	old age pensioner
Outlying properties			
Hillgrove Lane	Jane Stevens	1858-1942	old age pensioner
	and 4 others		
Little Lunnon	Joseph Bicknell	1877-1950	copse cutter
Colhook Common	Mary Bicknell	1879-1970	domestic duties
21 Pitfold Rd	George Tribe	1873-1950	jobbing gardener
Shottermill Haslemere	and 2 others		

For the Varns family in Fernhurst see above, Table 10.6.
Two Dependant homes do not feature, so had not yet been built: The Narr and Dell Cottage.

There are some 50 named individuals in the death/burial registers who were alive in 1939, both in the stores and in the wider community. Only about a dozen were in paid employment, many of the rest of pensionable age. Surnames listed above resonate through the past century – Pullen, Spooner, Pannell, Caplin, Brooker, Holden, Wadey, Lunn and Stevens, for example. However, these were the last generation, and few survived beyond the 1950s and 60s.

Brown, Durant & Co Ltd, 1930s to 1950

Sam Rugman, meanwhile, had become a notable elder and business leader of the Northchapel community. He presided over the bicycle shop at the southern end of the Stores. He kept the ship afloat until 1948, through the depression and war, years that were much more "trying", to use an oft-repeated word in the minutes, than in his early years. However, the good balances and bonuses came year on year. Behind the bicycle shop the garage became another part of Sam Rugman's little empire. At the other older end were the grocery, ironmongery, furniture, drapery and clothes, much as in all the Dependant stores. The steam bakery was modern, as in all the stores, run on coke, not faggots, in one of the buildings at the rear.

In 1935, Walter Parr retired from being auditor. Henceforth, the auditor would be an outsider, Mr Hunt of Horsham, who also served as auditor to Aylward, Smith. The services and maintenance were clearly precarious in the trying conditions of the 1930s as firstly, in 1937, the well fell in, and had to be repaired urgently by Petworth Engineering Co as the water was undrinkable. At the same time, ten rooms needed redecoration by Horace Gander, followed by painting of the exterior paintwork in 1939 by Stemp Bros, and replacement of roller shutters for the ironmongery, grocery and china department windows by Dean of Putney. The landing, staircase and passage were also redecorated. Then the electricity engine gave out, so for the first time, part of the premises was connected to the mains. There are no details to match these from Loxwood.

A truly labour-saving device was bought in 1940, an electric kneeder for the bakery from Messrs Gilbert and Hunt for £105, probably, as in Loxwood, because of a shortage of workers due to local men being called up. In 1942, the freehold of Holly View (now Holly House) was transferred from Sam Rugman to the company, following the deaths of the Misses Caplin. Sam now received an annuity of £26 for life. The war years were quiet years at Northchapel.

Alice Hounslow was the next resignation through old age in 1947. Alice came from Maidstone. She had been at Northchapel Stores since the 1880s. She was 85 when she died. The post-war years of rationing and shortages continued to make for a trying time. In 1949, Sam Rugman died, and with him, the cycle shop which was sold as a going concern to Allen & Sons in 1950. Sam was only 68 and had also been the elder at the chapel for 20 years, attending a service and writing to the vicar with a donation the night before his death. He was well liked and respected by the whole village. Elizabeth Denyer and Esther Cumber, who had all this time served loyally as company secretary, were made directors. Mains water was laid on to Laurel Cottage and the cycle shop. Sam's place as chairman was taken by Esther Cumber who was by then 79 years old. Young blood was now in serious short supply – even Elizabeth Denyer was 68. At this point, it is useful to note who was still active in the company. Most years, much the same names occur in attendance at meetings.

As with Aylward, Smith in Loxwood, Brown, Durant published their own local postcard series. The business adopted the telephone as soon as a service was available in 1925 and was in the directory until 1960 (registered office Holly View). The premises are still trading today as Northchapel Stores, the only former Dependant store so to do.

Table 10.10   Attendees at the 1950 AGM of Brown, Durant & Co Ltd

Esther Cumber* 80 director	Ethel Puttock* 60	B Pullen (n/k)
Caroline Luff* 65 director	Frederick William Smith 49	Edith Spooner* 71
Elizabeth Denyer* 68 dir'or	Frederick Smith 82	Alfred Lunn 59
Esther (Lizzie) Cole 51	May Winter 58	Blanche Lunn 62
Hannah Birch* 80	Edith Wright 65	Daisy King 42
May Kennard* 67	Phoebe Halfacre 74	Kath Edwards 35
Nellie Bridger 63	Elizabeth Talbot 76	*also attended 1910

Northchapel Stores – The Company Minute Book – 1950-68

A statement in the minutes in 1950 refers to the difficulty of carrying on the business, the ages of staff and the possibility of selling the business. Holly View would be enlarged as a home for those in the Stores when the business was sold, Hodgson, Lunn & Co to be the architect, Mr A Lunn to be the builder. The stores were also to be connected to the main sewer by Mr Lunn. The premises were valued: the freehold £1200, fittings and fixtures £1562. It was agreed to offer the business for sale for £20,000, including goodwill, etc. However, the end was to come by degrees and in 1953 was declared "urgent".

In 1951 Ethel Mills was brought over from Warnham as company secretary, replacing Esther Cumber, who hitherto was both chairman and secretary at the age of 80. There was a lack of expertise among the remaining brethren and sisters. Mr Norris Jones was appointed a Director in 1953, having bought a nominal £1 share, intended to be the solution as a sale was just not going to happen as desired. He ran a shop in Warnham and agreed to give Northchapel two days a week as manager of the Stores, remunerated with 75% commission on profits, and his expenses paid, from 2nd November 1953. As a result, the shop account was to be separated from the investment account.

He re-opened the bakery in 1954. Staff were now mainly outsiders, notably the Moller family also from Warnham. Blanche Lunn continued to work in the grocery department, and Lizzie Cole and Carrie Luff in the drapery department. The directors discussed a decision to let the drapery business on a 21-year repairing lease, rental £228 per annum for shop, storeroom and flat to Lizzie Cole, but as she wished to retire in three years' time, plan B was adopted: sell the business for £2,500, or less if stock could be reduced. This did not prove possible either. The premises had a wholesale reorganisation. The furniture department moved from the shop to a building at the back, leaving antique pieces on window display. Mr Brock, not a Dependant, was expected to make the department pay his wages and general expenses. The furniture sales area became a café selling items from the bakery and grocers. A van had to be replaced too – there were still one full-time and a part-time roundsmen.

Norris also attempted to get an off-licence in 1954 but was turned down by the licensing authority. In 1955 he was successful. It is no surprise there had never been sales of alcohol, but now the survival of the business was at stake, and Dependants had little influence. It was also revealed that £2000 had been spent on renovating the stores, "where there had been a grocer's business since 1885" *(West Sussex Gazette, 18 March 1954)*. This date is attuned with the facts discussed at the beginning of the chapter.

In 1955, Esther Cumber finally relinquished the chair at the age of 84, to be replaced by Caroline Luff (Plate 10.2). A new secretary was not appointed until 1960, when Lizzie Cole took it on. As a result of all the changes Caroline's term started with a loss, but this was only for one year. In 1957, the whole of the premises known as Northchapel Stores, together with the existing garage buildings at the rear, then let to Messrs Allen Bros, were to be reconstructed in accordance with the plans prepared by Mr FJ Hodgson, of Hodgson, Lunn in Guildford. To enable this to be carried out, Norris Jones was authorised to terminate the tenancy of Allen Bros. It was also necessary to meet in Holly View, and from 1957 onwards this was the case.

Esther Cumber was from a Dependant family. Her parents, William and Carrie, spent much of their lives at South Norwood, working in the Stores there, and living nearby. Her aunt Carrie was at Lordshill where she was an elder. After Esther's mother died, her father moved to Northchapel, where he died in 1931, aged 83. The family originated in the Lordshill area. Esther herself was born whilst the family lived for a while in Guildford.

As for the drapery business, it's fate was finally decided in 1959, when sold to the Misses Varns for £3,500, with a leasehold rent on the premises of £175 per annum. From the death register it seems likely they were Florence and Edith. Their sister Bertha had died in 1958. The Misses Varns lived on the lane to Hill Grove; see Table 10.6 above.

In 1958, Jones was authorised to sign a contract for the sale of the grocery, provisions, hardware and off-license business to Mrs J.B. Baldwin of 34, Boltra Gardens, London SW15. The off-licence was transferred in May. The deal was sealed at the AGM on 2 September. In 1960 Norris Jones was asked to resign and paid off with £2000 compensation for loss of office.

Some Newspaper Reports

Individual Dependant communities were seldom newsworthy except for the bigger funerals, and those in more recent decades Those discovered online include:
- 1932, Lizzie Durant, director. One of the largest in living memory, with large parties of members from Loxwood, Bramley [Lordshill], Norwood, Chichester and Brighton, 300 present. The service was conducted by Henry Aylward (Loxwood), Ben Piper and William Booker (Warnham). "The district mourns the loss of one whose unassuming kindness was widely known and valued." The burial was at Northchapel church.
- 1940, Noah Holden, farmer, latterly bricklayer, born at Colhook Common, had lived in Chiddingfold and then King's Road Haslemere (where a Dependant chapel was located). He was a "devoted member" of the community, who had once worshipped in Northchapel, married for 56 years with one son, funeral conducted by Sam Rugman (Northchapel) and William Booker (Warnham).
- 1940, William Pannell, died aged 83, a real character, a "Lurgashall type" (where he used to live). Uneducated, he had many stories, was quick and humorous. He started work minding sheep for 2d a day at Shillinglee, working on farms for Lord Leconfield all his working life. The funeral was conducted at Lurgashall by Sam Rugman and Jim Stevens (Northchapel), with 2 sons and 2 daughters present.
- 1941, Miss Emma Ayling, a niece of Jim Randall at Lodsworth, where she worked in the shop in 1911. She had spent many years in hospitals and a nursing home but was remembered for good humour "amid concealed suffering" in the stores. A hymn of her own writing was sung at the funeral in Northchapel conducted by Sam Rugman, Jim Stevens and William Booker. She was buried at Northchapel church.
- 1946, Louisa Cobby, Upper Diddlesfold, Hillgrove Lane, aged 68, widow of farmer William Cobby, who latterly had moved to The Narr, and Beggar's Corner. Funeral

taken by Sam Rugman. Relatives included Brooker, Bicknell and Stevens families. The name Cobby does not appear in the registers.

- 1949, Sam Rugman, 68, leader of the Northchapel Dependants died suddenly, having attended chapel the night before. He came to Northchapel 40 years previously. He had "great integrity of character and gifts of leadership". For 20 years he had been spiritual leader and business manager. His funeral was at Loxwood where he was interred at the Dependant's graveyard, the service conducted by Jim Stevens. The Northchapel community will "face the future…strong in the faith that he has made 'a safe landing'".
- 1950, Miss Alice Hounslow, known, apparently, as 'Dovey', 85, had lived and worked at Northchapel Stores for 50 years – "we miss that sweetness pervading the house". Her funeral and interment were at Loxwood, conducted by Walter Nash.

The End of a Community

In 1962 the remaining tenants of the community were requested to pay a rent for their accommodation in Holly View, their home since 1960. The little group were now elderly. Carrie Luff herself, the last chairman, died in 1966. Her will (Plate 10.7) is of interest as it names some of the then residents of Holly View: Esther (Lizzie) Cole (died 2002, in Chichester) having lived at Dell Cottage, Elizabeth (Bess) Denyer (died 1975 at The Narr), Fred Smith (died 1986 at Dell Cottage), Daisy King (died 2002 in Chichester), and Kath Edwards (also at Dell Cottage, but died 2008 in Bognor Regis – see below). Her beneficiaries were her companions. At some point after 1966 Holly View must have been too large for the remaining elderly Dependants; it was sold, and subsequently renamed Holly House as shown on the OS map 1975. The Narr and Dell Cottage are neighbouring properties. Caroline's executrices were Lizzie Cole, and Bessie Hempstead of Loxwood. Her signature was witnessed by Alf Goodwin and Kate Rugman, both of Loxwood.

Fred Smith wrote a note on an undated scrap of paper, naming residents of Holly View, of whom, additional to the above were May Kennard (died 1966), Hannah Birch (died 1962) and Agnes King (died 1960). Amelia Kennard, a widow, is in the burial register as a Holly View resident at her death in 1962, though she and her husband formerly lived in Croydon, and he was no relation of May. Also still living there in 1962 were Nellie Bridger (died 1967), Edith Wright (died 1972). Esther Cumber (died 1956). Phoebe Halfacre (in 1958) and Ethel Puttock (in 1961) had already died.

Who survived longest of the Dependants in Northchapel? Esther Elizabeth Cole died in hospital in Chichester in 2002, age 92. Daisy Primrose King, 1908-2002, also died in Chichester. However, she was not the last Dependant, as she died about three months before even Elsie Piper in Loxwood. Northchapel has the rather sad distinction of having had the last Dependant alive, having had eight at the time of the (modern) Domesday Survey of 1986. It had also been the largest community by some measures. Pamela Bruce refers to Kath Edwards, who did not join the community until Sam Rugman's time, when she was only 15, as the last surviving member, but initially I failed to track her down (the Dependant register finishes in 2002). Ancestry.com and government probate records give a date of death as 11 December 2008 for Miss Kathleen Maisie Edith Edwards who died at Bognor Regis. She was born in 1915 (most likely in Kings Norton, Birmingham), so was aged about

93. Rugman had been leader from 1920 to 1949, so her arrival at age 15 in about 1930 would make sense (see Table 10.9). Her unmarried status strengthens the case. Numerous aged Dependants were admitted to hospitals or care homes in those last years, where they were to die some distance from their former community.

In 1969, company liquidation was proposed. The last page or pages of the minute book have unfortunately not survived, but the attendees at this last recorded meeting were Daisy King, B.N. Pullen, Edith Wright, Alfred Lunn, Elizabeth Denyer, Fred Smith, Kath Edwards, Lizzie Cole, and Mr DP Clack for the auditors.

The properties the Dependants owned have long since been sold. The Stores however continued to trade without a break and is now not only the village shop but also the post office. To the rear and south side are flats, Amblefield Court, and a property called West View is to the rear. Included to the north is one named Drapers Cottage (the former draper's shop). The chapel is now The Old Chapel, the deeds of which show the surviving Trustees of the Dependants sold it to Donald and Lena Callingham as late as 1990. Next to Laurel Cottage along the side road is Shere 4 x 4, a car sales business, on the site of the former store's garage and petrol pumps. Lilac Cottages are still divided into three cottages.

The Northchapel minutes show the decline of the community and business in considerable detail. It seems likely that similar events and trauma may have happened elsewhere in their "Retreat" from the world.

PLATE 10.6   Retirement Homes

Fig 1 – Holly House (was Holly View), believed to have been built in 1912 (as the wall plate suggests) by John Caplin (furthest south in Fig 4).

Fig 2 – below, in a brick finish, Myrtle Cottages occupied before 1911 (second from the south, Fig 4).

Fig 3 – right, Dell Cottage (rebuilt?). Porch discernible in Fig 4.

Fig 4 – aerial view of the 1¼ acre plot sold by the Misses Caplin to Brown, Durant & Co in 1920, containing then four cottages, Myrtle, Holly View, Dell (was New Cottages) and The Narr.

The only one not pictured is The Narr, which lies hidden behind tall vegetation, dead centre in this view, and is now two dwellings, East and West. *Ack: Google Maps.*

Plate 10.7   Carrie Luff's Will, 1965

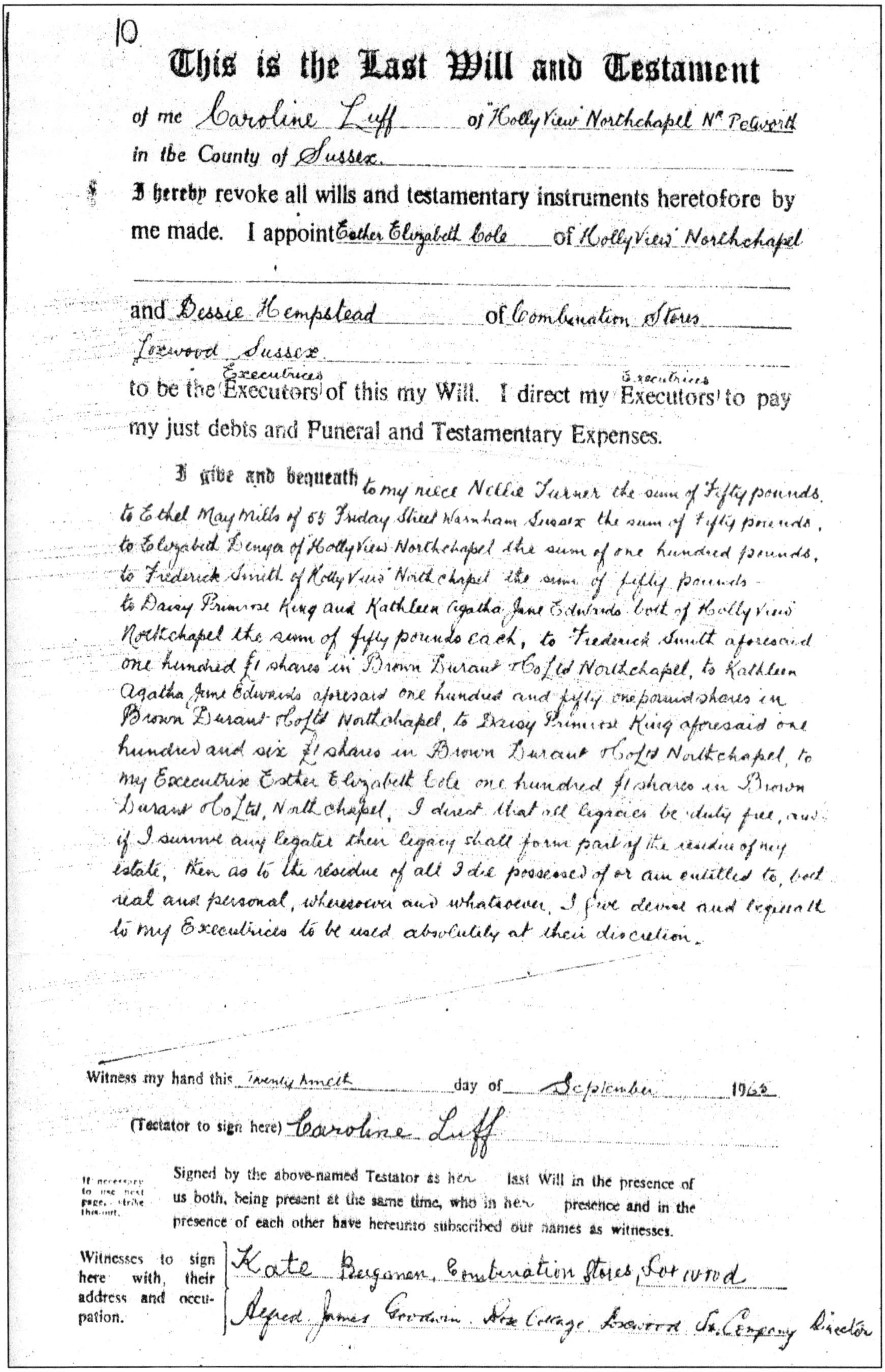

This is the Last Will and Testament

of me *Caroline Luff* of "Holly View" Northchapel N^r Petworth
in the County of *Sussex.*

I hereby revoke all wills and testamentary instruments heretofore by me made. I appoint *Esther Elizabeth Cole* of *Holly View Northchapel*

and *Bessie Hempstead* of *Combination Stores*
Loxwood Sussex.
to be the Executors of this my Will. I direct my Executors to pay my just debts and Funeral and Testamentary Expenses.

I give and bequeath *to my niece Nellie Turner the sum of Fifty pounds. to Ethel May Mills of 55 Friday Street Warnham Sussex the sum of fifty pounds. to Elizabeth Denyer of Holly View Northchapel the sum of one hundred pounds, to Frederick Smith of Holly View Northchapel the sum of fifty pounds to Daisy Primrose King and Kathleen Agatha Jane Edwards both of Holly View Northchapel the sum of fifty pounds each, to Frederick Smith aforesaid one hundred £1 shares in Brown Durant & Co Ltd Northchapel, to Kathleen Agatha Jane Edwards aforesaid one hundred and fifty one pound shares in Brown Durant & Co Ltd Northchapel, to Daisy Primrose King aforesaid one hundred and six £1 shares in Brown Durant & Co Ltd Northchapel, to my Executrix Esther Elizabeth Cole one hundred £1 shares in Brown Durant & Co Ltd, Northchapel, I direct that all legacies be duty free, and if I survive any legatee then legacy shall form part of the residue of my estate, then as to the residue of all I die possessed of or am entitled to, both real and personal, wheresoever and whatsoever, I give devise and bequeath to my Executrices to be used absolutely at their discretion.*

Witness my hand this *Twenty Amith* day of *September* 19*65*

(Testator to sign here) *Caroline Luff*

Signed by the above-named Testator as her last Will in the presence of us both, being present at the same time, who in her presence and in the presence of each other have hereunto subscribed our names as witnesses.

If necessary to use next page, strike this out.

Witnesses to sign here with their address and occupation.
Kate Bergonen, Combination Stores, Loxwood
Alfred James Goodwin, Rose Cottage, Loxwood Sx. Company Director

224

Chapter 11

South Norwood

Where is South Norwood?

South Norwood is in the Borough of Croydon, about eight miles from central London and two miles north east of the centre of Croydon in the SE25 postcode. The spine road through the area is Portland Road, now the A215, leading to the area known as Woodside (Plate 11.1), which had a station, now reinvented as a tram stop to Croydon. One mile north-west is Norwood Junction station, with useful community links to London Bridge, to Southwark, to Clapham Junction. Both offered links to Horsham, near the Warnham community in the 19th century. One imagines the rail link loomed large in the thinking of John Sirgood and others when the community first emerged, with the building of the chapel in about 1878, rather later than the other six. As explained in Chapter 3 the likely date of a move from Southwark was in 1875.

The Norwood Dependant community was set up at the junction with Cobden Road. In pursuit of information on this community it transpired that local historians had lost sight of its origins. Some even thought it was a Quaker community. Seen from the Surrey-Sussex borders, this is an outlier, but seen from the perspective of John Sirgood's beginnings in South London, it is less so. Indeed, it became, as befits its urban location, a large community with large premises. Their original premises, 226 Portland Road, was a corner grocer's shop between Woodside Road (now Avenue) and Cobden Road, an area developed within a once rural estate called Enmore Park. The area was part of Croydon County Borough in Surrey until 1965 when it was transferred along with Croydon into Greater London. Charles Taylor was said to be the first elder here, and Charlie Circus a significant hymn writer.

Who Were the Original Members?

Charles William Taylor was a literate man, writing many letters and hymns, and, like Mann, Brightman and Haynes, a chapel trustee (Chapter 3). He was a little older than the other three. Born in Louth, Lincolnshire, the son of a miller, he was married to Louie and was a hairdresser at 26 South Norwood High Street, through to at least 1911 (photo Plate 11.2). It is certain that he lived in Norwood before the building of the chapel. Taylor is said (by Jerrome) to have asked Sirgood if it would be appropriate to have a chapel there, to which he replied, *"Well, Charles, you may never need the money, but you'll be sure to need the grace"*. The Taylors largely funded the chapel. In 1876, a death announcement recorded the demise, at 26 High Street, of their four months old son Samuel. Charles died in 1935 and was buried in Loxwood, when his address was given as 26 Park Lane, in central Croydon. Jerrome devotes much space to Charlie and his wife, Louie; it is his interviews with Alf Goodwin (see below, *passim*) which provide the reported statement above.

Jerrome's research has shown the strong possibility of a break between Sirgood and the Southwark-group of Peculiars in the early 1870s at the time of his mentor William Bridge's death in 1874 (when as I have indicated in Chapter 1, Sirgood was in his London period, based mainly in Clapham). There is, Jerrome quotes, in a Warnham book of letters, one annotated "about the strife in London". Taylor, a good friend to Sirgood, was originally an Anglican. Is Taylor a link to Sirgood's journeys to Lincolnshire? An undated letter throws a faint light on the origins of Norwood as a community. *"… so we are not going to meet there anymore but till we get a place [in Southwark?] some will meet at Norwood and those that cannot we propose to meet at Brother Killner's but I expect we shall soon get a place."*

Plate 11.1   Location in South Norwood

Fig 1 – OS map 1:2500, the stores, chapel (named Chap) and surrounding streets in 1913. The stores front Portland Road, south of the pub (PH) between Cobden Rd and Woodside Ave (No 126), the grocers, and south of the latter junction (Nos 128-134), the bakers (with outbuildings behind) and drapers built since 1896. See Plate 3.6 for earlier maps.

Ack: all maps, old-maps.co.uk.

Fig 2 – OS map 1953/54 1:2500, enlarged. Subtle changes were made over the intervening years to both 226 and 228-224 premises. Nos 1, 3 and 5 (upside down) can be seen on Cobden Rd. No 5 (Beulah Cottage) was substantially enlarged at the rear of the chapel. Likewise, 228, south side of Cobden Road, is now very large, wrapped around the rear of 230-34. Outbuildings are more substantial, leaving little room for vehicles in the yard.

Fig 3 – OS map 1966-70 1:1250 (larger scale than Fig 1 & 2), captures the end of the life of Randall, Slade. The map may indicate a sell-off of the rear of 228-23 for manufacturing, or that the shops were closed (thought to have been in 1969) before the map was made. Only at the end of its useful life did the chapel have its correct name.

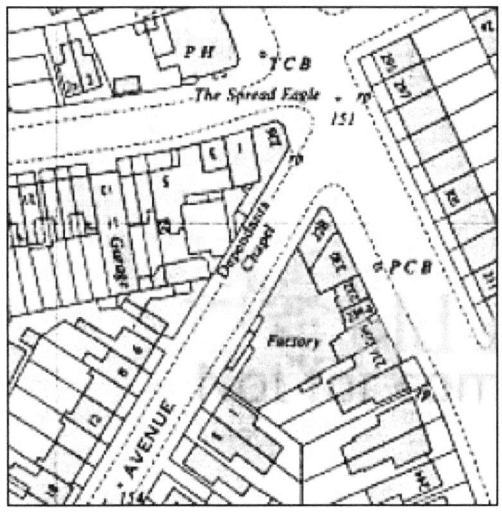

As for Killner, he could be one of the Horsham Killners who feature so much as Dependants. James Killner from Horsham was resident with his family in Crescent Road, Croydon, in 1881, not so very far from South Norwood. It suggests that there was already a small following in and near Norwood in the 1870s.

Louie Taylor was very much a leader too, and wrote letters on her own account, in which we learn of her travels to the communities of Northchapel and Plaistow, and of her commercial expertise, all in the shadow of Sirgood's last years. Like Ann Overington in Loxwood, she worked closely with his 'leading ladies'. Jerrome considers Louie put over Sirgood's charisma better than anyone and used accessible language to do so. Louie was in contact with among others Lizzie Durant, Carrie Foster and Hannah Osborne at Northchapel, and Ellen Luff at Warnham. She also assisted at Loxwood, and other communities, remembered Alf Goodwin. She had married Charlie when she was only 17. Charlie was youngest of 17 children, according to Alf, but in fact he was the eldest child. Oral history must be taken with caution. In the case of the Dependants it often made good testimony in chapel.

Charles Circus was living in Denmark Road, just behind the stores and chapel in 1891 with his wife and young family. He died in 1913. Little is known about him.

Another trustee and elder, James Brightman, (put "on the platform" by Sirgood himself) was born a farmer's son in Hitchin, Herts, but can be traced to Chiddingfold, Surrey, near Northchapel, where his sister, Sarah (later a member of the Hove community), was born in 1873. In Chiddingfold, the family must have been attracted as newcomers to the Brethren. By 1881, James was in Penge Road, South Norwood, a contractor. He later became a stalwart member of the Stores, first as a baker, then as butcher, and by 1911, in charge of the meat store. See Tables 11.1 and 11.2. He died in 1925 and was buried locally.

George Haynes, a chapel trustee is also said to have been the first elder at Norwood. He was a painter and decorator, first in Birchanger Road, then Carmichael Road, then Holmesdale Road, finally Apsley Road, all in reach of the Dependant chapel and stores. Born in Hornsea, Essex, he died in 1913, and was buried locally.

Premises and Personalities, 1882-1895

See Plate 11.4, pages 244-5 for recent photographs of these buildings to help you find your way around a complex geography. The car servicing business (Total Car Care) at No 228 occupies the original Randall, Slade bakery and bakehouse. It is the deepest of the four premises here and therefore also fronts the re-named Woodside Avenue on the 1912 OS map (Plate 11.1). A now separate building behind, facing Woodside Avenue still has the date "Est.1882" embossed on it (Plate 11.3). Also embossed on an adjacent wall was the name of Randall, Slade & Co Ltd (now removed). This points to an early beginning of the company, second only to Warnham's. Ford, Randall & Co was the name given in the early days, first listed in a directory in 1887, though earlier directories are believed lost. The date 1882 could very well be the foundation of the partnership between Ford and Randall. Just six Ford, Randall Dependants lived communally in 1891.

However, the bakery and other buildings here at 228-234 Portland Road were not built until later. The company began at smaller premises, 226 Portland Road, at the junction of Cobden Road and Woodside Avenue with Portland Road. The 1891 census indicates there were no occupied premises or house from 230 to 238 Portland Road inclusive, with two unoccupied unnumbered buildings (Table 11.1). When the bakehouse was constructed, the company's name had changed, and they wished to be considered an established business. Besides, the original premises at 226 were designated a grocery shop (1891). Drapery was sold at 1, Cobden Road in 1890-5 (A Slade & Co). This was the first and larger of two buildings at the rear of 226 Portland Road, attached to it, but as they lay back were given a Cobden Road address. Surprisingly, perhaps, the new location for chapel and stores was next to a pub, The Spread Eagle! It now trades as The Gold Coast Bar and Restaurant. The Dependants were known for absolute temperance.

In 1895, on an OS 1:11056 scale detailed plan of that date, the buildings at 228-234 Portland Road were still not built, although the houses further south were. Handley's five-acre brickfield was on the site until about 1890 but was no longer in production and had been restored for housing on Woodside Avenue and Portland Road frontages. This was to provide a growing market for sales at Randall, Slade.

Table 11.1   1891 Census, South Norwood *(Ford, Randall & Co, and A Slade & Co)*

226 Portland Road (Ford, Randall & Co)   Place of birth

Julia Ford	54	grocer	Cheltenham Glos
Maggie Bate	29	grocer's assistant	Newport Salop
George Randall	34	grocer's assistant	Hammersmith Mdsex
James Brightman	38	baker	Hitchin Herts
Ruth Jamnell	37	grocer's assistant	Langford Beds
Julia Hawkins	28	grocer's assistant	Sutton Mandeville Wilts

1 Cobden Road (A Slade & Co)

Alice Slade	32	draper	Dorchester Dt
Mary Hanks	39	draper's assistant	Malmesbury, Wilts

With no surviving company records, no tradition in local history circles of any understanding of the Dependants (although some help was gratefully received when prompted), and most references to South Norwood an afterthought in the literature, it is fascinating to try to understand how the dynamics of the community evolved.

Julia Ford was a grocer, born in Cheltenham. In service since before she was 14, she became a cook in wealthy households first in Cheltenham, later in Beckenham, Kent. By 1891 (possibly as early as 1882) she was with the Norwood community as head of the grocers at 226 Portland Road, aged 54. Unfortunately for the community, she died only three years later, her age registered as 58 in 1894. She is in neither the Dependant death register nor burial register, so perhaps her relationship was more business than religious. She was soon dropped from the company trading name. The 1891 Kelly's Directory records "Ford Julia (Mrs) & Randell George, grocers, 226 Portland Road". Recorded as married contradicts the censuses where she is single, no doubt a mistake, for which this publication is notorious.

George Randall, whose name is in that of the company from the start, was nevertheless described as a grocer's assistant in 1891, but was soon to be in charge of the bakery for many years. He was described as employer, therefore a director, in 1901 and manager in 1911, until his early death in 1915 aged only 58. Coincidentally, he was the same age as Julia at her death 21 years earlier. His origins were in Hammersmith where his father was a sawyer. He had been named in the 1880 indenture (Chapter 3), living at 69 Penge Road, Penge, a mile or so away to the north-east. There, he was working as a bootmaker, in a house shared by other young Dependants, siblings Olive and Phillip Mann, whose bootmaker's shop it was. Also living there were Annie Powell (of the Loxwood community) and James Brightman, a bricklayer, thus a household of close disciples of John Sirgood, another bootmaker by trade. Phillip Mann, born in Northchapel, was a trustee of the South Norwood Chapel. He was buried in Loxwood in 1923.

Two clues point to the origins of Dependant activity leading up to the above-mentioned date of 1882 carved on a building. Firstly, Annie Powell was living in nearby Penge in 1881. She later became manager of grocery at Loxwood. See Chapter 5.

Secondly, James and Emily Foster, together with brother Harry, all from Loxwood, Sussex, were also then living at 1 Church Cottages in Cobden Road. James was a carpenter, 30-years old. Their parents were among the oldest Dependants in Loxwood. Another older brother, Felix, began the grocery business in Loxwood that became the Combination Stores. The Foster household highlights the fluidity and linkages between communities and families at an early date. Opportunities were provided in the Dependant network, and there were strong connections with Loxwood which would last as long as there were Dependants alive.

By 1896 the chapel ("non-conformist, seats for 100") had been added to the OS map (Chapter3). it was located behind both the grocer's and draper's shops filling the available land, and so accessed off Woodside Avenue. This may have been the replacement for an earlier building, as there is strong evidence for a chapel from the early 1880s. Where it was is not entirely a mystery as an 1880 directory lists a mission house on Cobden Road.

Company Expansion from 1896

According to local directories, the company name changed to Randall, Slade & Co Ltd about 1896 (A Slade drapers continuing). By 1901 the stores, now wholly Randall, Slade included newly built N° 228, across Woodside Road (now Avenue), as a baker's shop (with its "hygienic steam" bakehouse, with its chimney visible on photos, and probably stables and space for delivery vans at the rear, either built then or later). No 228 mainly housed the men, whilst N° 226 remained the grocer's, in which all the residents were female. The new 228-234 business premises, with accommodation above, were built on brownfield land (undeveloped in 1891): the area to the south having been, as stated above, a brickfield. Houses were built fronting South Portland Road, except the corner site, which one suspects was already owned by the Dependants. This was at the time, the very edge of the London built-up area. From observation of the buildings, it seems likely the expansion was in two phases. 228 is of simple construction, and not as grand (or as high) as 230-234.

By 1891, Alice Slade had a draper's shop with Mary Hanks as a Dependant assistant at 1, Cobden Road, located there from 1890 to 1899. The drapers continued to trade under her

Plate 11.2   People of South Norwood

Fig 1 – top left, Charles Taylor (hairdresser, 1848-1935) and Louisa (Louie) Taylor (1852-1939), two of the first elders in S Norwood.

Fig 2 – top right, William Cumber (1848-1931) from Lordshill; Norwood greengrocer; later of Northchapel).

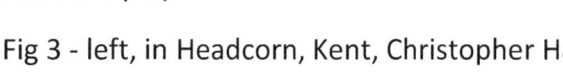

Fig 3 - left, in Headcorn, Kent, Christopher Hale (1885-1986) and his father Alfred.

Fig 4 – below left, Chris came to Norwood as a teenager, as did his sister Miriam. He worked as the baker's roundsman (photo in Spring Lane). On his marriage he settled back in Headcorn. He moved to Loxwood in 1960. He died aged 101.

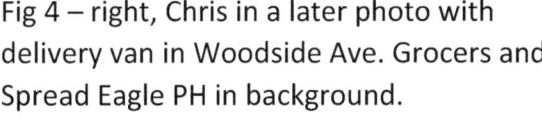

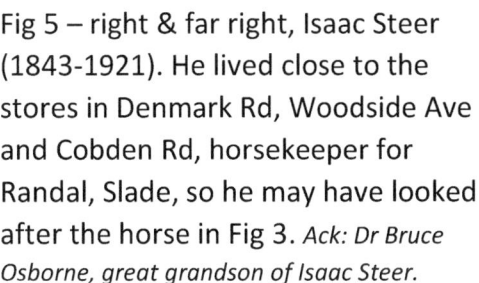

Fig 4 – right, Chris in a later photo with delivery van in Woodside Ave. Grocers and Spread Eagle PH in background.

Fig 5 – right & far right, Isaac Steer (1843-1921). He lived close to the stores in Denmark Rd, Woodside Ave and Cobden Rd, horsekeeper for Randal, Slade, so he may have looked after the horse in Fig 3. *Ack: Dr Bruce Osborne, great grandson of Isaac Steer.*

Isaac Steer

Plate 11.3   Some Images of Buildings

Fig 1 –Part of the surviving bakery complex, rear of 228 Portland Rd, facing Woodvale Avenue. Like similar buildings in other community stores, it would have had a hoist into which sacks of flour could be raised to the door now at the top of stairs. The date, "EST. 1882", is likely to have been added later as the date the stores were established, when this set of buildings (including the rear of Portland Road buildings, left) were built after 1896. The yard and building have now been a garage, Total Auto Care, for many years. *Ack: Google maps.*

Fig 2 - An older image of unknown date (before or after closure), which shows the same date 1882, but also the name Randall, Slade & Co Ltd carved in the stonework. *Ack: Dr Bruce Osborne, great grandson of Isaac Steer.*

Fig 3 – The Spread Eagle Public House stood next to the grocers, all the time the temperate Dependants were there, door facing the store. It is now The Gold Coast, a bar with Ghanaian restaurant. *Ack: John Windell*

Fig 4 – The Gold Coast today, with part of 226 Portland Road visible across Cobden Rd. *Ack: fluidlondon.co.uk.*

name at No 1 after she moved to Randal, Slade next door. At 3 Cobden Road there had been a short-lived Ford, Randall butchers, but may have been entirely residential by 1901. A directory lists 1 Cobden Road as the greengrocers (Ada Gifford, greengrocer lived at No 3). The Dependant businesses became consolidated at 226 and 228 Portland Road, including the Cobden Road premises to their rear. There were still no Nos 230-234. Building work may have been under way to extend southwards.

Interestingly, the next building in the street, 236 Portland Road, was a private house in 1901, the home of an undoubted Dependant family household: Alfred and Eliza Hunt, together with two of their children (Clara and Minnie), a son-in-law, a sister-in-law and two Dependant boarders. Alfred was a "white meter and gas fitter". His Loxwood burial records that he died in a fire accident in 1909, aged 69. This family may also have been among those converted in Kent as they came from Canterbury and Maidstone. Hunt's widowed sister-in-law, Fanny Gifford, moved to Warnham. A young Charlie Carter from Newpound Common near Loxwood, was a boarder. He was Loxwood elders' Tom and Anne Overington's grandson. This house became part of the stores later on.

Table 11.2   1901 Census, South Norwood *(Randall, Slade & Co)*

226 Portland Road, grocer's shop — Place of birth

Alice Slade*	44	grocer shopkeeper	Dorchester Dt (employer)
Clara Millbourn	36	housemaid	Maidstone Kt
Margaret Bate*	39	grocer's assistant	Newport Salop
Harriet Drewett	28	commercial clerk	Kentish Town London
Mary Hanks*	49	draper's assistant	Malmesbury Wilts
Ettie Goodwin	17	housemaid	Headcorn Kt
Edith Rugman	21	draper's assistant	Bramley Sy
Mary Walsham	28	draper's assistant	Woodnesborough Kt

228 Portland Road, baker's shop

George Randall *	45	baker shopkeeper	Hammersmith Mdsx (employer)
James Brightman*	48	baker's assistant	Hitchin Herts
Sydney Croucher	25	coal porter	Headcorn Kt
William Furguson	32	baker's assistant	Fulham Mdsx
Ernest Goodwin	20	grocer's assistant	Headcorn Kt
Alfred Edwards	19	baker's assistant	Ewhurst Sy
Edwin Ellliott	30	grocer's assistant	Peckham London
Christopher Hale	15	baker's assistant	Headcorn Kt
Ruth Samuel	46	needlewoman	Stanford Beds
Elizabeth Talbot	40	housekeeper	Felpham Sx
Harriett Burrows	73	needlewoman	Marylebone Mdsx (widow, visitor)

3 Cobden Road

Ada Gifford	33	greengrocer	Canterbury Kt
Kate Pannell	28	confectioner	Plaistow Sx
Emma Fry	28	assistant grocer	Twickenham Mdsx
Mary Munday	24	assistant grocer	Wotton Sy
Julia Hawkins*	38	assistant grocer (visitor)	Sutton Mandevile Wilts
Cecily Hawkins	37	domestic servant (vis)	Sutton Mandeville Wilts

*indicates those living in the stores in 1891.

In 1901 (Table 11.2 above), living over the main stores, there were nineteen Randall, Slade Brethren, in the two single sex households referred to above, although the men's number included two females to look after them. An analysis of where these men and women were born is instructive. One might expect a migratory population in a growing outer London suburbanised village, but this group include some who come from Dependant hotspots, viz, six from Kent, one each from Bramley and Ewhurst in south Surrey, one from the south coast of Sussex. Two more come from the Home Counties north of London, three from western England, and just six from London (none from Croydon or Lambeth, but one from Peckham).

Who Were the Live-in Dependants of 1901?

Alice Slade was assistant to her mother's furniture business in Dorchester before moving to Norwood. In 1901 and 1911, Alice was manager of the grocery business, probably for many years after, too. She died in Norwood in 1932, aged 78, presumably buried locally. Little else is known of this important founder of the business.

Maggie Bate and Ruth Samuel had both come to Kensington, Julia Hawkins had come to Wimbledon, all as servants, and Mary Hanks to Croydon as a cook before coming to South Norwood. Mary was joined by her young niece Nellie by 1911. Nellie was the daughter of Mary's younger brother Walter who lived in Malmesbury. Beatrice (Beatie), who arrived in Norwood sometime after 1911, was another niece, a daughter of Thomas Hawkins. Beatrice died in Norwood in 1964 aged 86.

Harriett Burrows, a widow much older than the others, had been in service in Peckham, where she may have first come across Dependants. There are few pointers to this ephemeral Peckham Dependant community.

Kent origins were common. Clara Millbourn was one of the Kent Dependants. She did not come to South Norwood much before 1901, staying until her death in 1926. Ettie Goodwin, only 17, was from Headcorn, Kent. She lived with the Dependants in 1901, but in 1911 she and her mother Mary Anne lived in nearby Addiscombe, where she died aged only 30 in 1913. Mary Ann, also a Dependant was a widow who ran a butcher's shop, where Ettie was clerk. This family were not related to the Thornton Heath Goodwins, so prominent later in Loxwood. Mary Anne died in Addiscombe in 1941.

Sydney Croucher originally also from Headcorn was employed as a coal porter, suggesting that like some other communities this was a staple product. He and his brother Ray (who had arrived in Norwood by 1911) were significant players. Ray went on to run the Lordshill shop as Smith, Croucher. Sydney died in 1938, but Ray, the younger of the two died in 1977. Another brother Harry was in Norwood living with the Brock family, Harry and Annie Ellen, who later moved to Warnham (see chapter 9), or in daughter Winnie's case, Northchapel. In 1901 Harry Croucher had moved to Battersea.

Mary Walsham, born in Woodnesborough Kent, was living with her mother and siblings in the large Isle of Thanet workhouse in 1901 before somehow finding her way to South Norwood. Having been given a leg up by the Dependants, she moved back to Kent to live with her brother's family as their cook. William Furguson, although born in Fulham, was living in Maidstone with his stepfather and mother before coming to Norwood.

The Giffords were from Margate where Ada's parents were fruiterers. It is no surprise to find her a greengrocer in the Norwood stores in 1901, and manager by 1911. Her mother, Fanny, now widowed, had also moved to Sandown Road in Norwood, living almost next door to the Brocks and Sydney Croucher. Fanny is mentioned below. Ada died in 1916, only 49. Her sisters, Florence Ethel (known by her second name), who became manageress of the greengrocers; Helen (Nellie), also a Dependant was also involved with the retail business. Florence Ethel died in 1950; Nellie lived to 95 (1975) and had moved to Loxwood, where she lived at The Retreat. She was also buried there.

Harriet Drewett, known as Harlie, born in Kentish Town, was I think sent to live with her grandmother at first, aged eight, in Hampshire, then in Northchapel, in Laurel Cottage next to the stores, coming then to Norwood, where she stayed through the 1901 and 1911 census. After which, she moved to Hall House, Loxwood, working in the Combination Stores as a bootshop assistant. She died in The Retreat in 1964. Was she a sister of Sarah Drewett also in Loxwood? Sarah's parents moved to Cobden Road, where her father John was a carman, probably for Randall, Slade.

Others were from the Surrey-Sussex border villages. Edith Rugman and her brother William were born in Grafham near Bramley, Surrey. Edith was a draper, later housekeeper, William a baker. Their parents, George and Pollie were members of the nearby Lordshill community. George's brother John had shared a house with John Sirgood and William Hampshire in Lordshill before Sirgood's death. The Rugmans were a loyal Dependant family. William died in South Norwood in 1954; Edith died in 1965 at The Retreat, Loxwood.

Alfred Edwards was born in Ellens Green, Ewhurst, a baker in 1901, as was his sister Ellen who had joined the Dependants by 1911. By 1911, Alfred had re-joined his family working on a farm in Warnham, but there is no evidence that they were Dependants there. By 1939, Ellen (Nellie) was also in Warnham looking after her mother. She may have returned to Norwood. She died somewhere in SE Surrey 1960 aged 82, Alfred likewise in 1974.

Emma Fry (grocer) had a sister Clara (a draper) in Loxwood at the same time, 1891. They and their siblings and father had been living in Cobden Road with an uncle working with the London City Mission. Altogether his household had eleven children! Emma died in South Norwood in 1932. Clara married Eli Etherington and died in Warnham in 1935.

Mary Munday was named 'Ada' in 1901 but she spent all her adult years as a Norwood Dependant first in the grocery, then as a cook. Born within a few miles of Warnham in Wotton, Surrey, to Warnham Dependants Jim and Mary Munday, she moved to South Norwood after 1891.

Elizabeth Talbot had been a servant in Chichester for over 20 years before coming to Norwood. Had she been attending the Dependant chapel there? In 1911, still at the South Norwood Stores, her sister-in-law was visiting. Amy Talbot (Howick) had married Elizabeth's brother John. They lived in Petworth Sussex with two children.

Randall, Slade & Co in 1911

As shown above, after 1896, and the naming of the business Randall, Slade, the shop premises first expanded further to embrace 226 Portland Road but by 1911 included all of 226-234 Portland Road, purpose-built by or for the Dependants. Norwood Stores became the largest of the Dependant combination stores. Its speciality, not available in the village stores was tailoring – Harry Aylward at Loxwood, a portly man with a 54" waist, had his suits made here. A 1911 directory confirms that the grocers was still at 226, in a stand-alone building between Cobden Road and Woodside Avenue which extended back into 3 Cobden Road. This is confirmed by a photograph of Christopher Hale, the baker, with his delivery van taken a few years later (Plate 11.2). At 228 was the baker's and confectioner's (where also there may have been a café as one of the residents was a waitress, not seen in any other community), with the bakehouse at the rear, a building which in part still stands, with what was loft storage above. At 230-234 was the spacious draper's in its new building, a dominant handsome 3-storey building with a stone balcony on the first floor. These premises from 226-234 were a significant split-site presence on this double corner site. No 236, not part of the main building, built as a house (see above), became an addition to the retail premises later. A photograph showing the writing on a delivery van makes it clear it was part of the business. Apparently, you could see Crystal Palace from the front windows.

Alf Goodwin, who was brought up in Norwood, has said that the departments were run quite separately: greengrocer, butcher, grocer, baker and confectioner, draper, shoes, men's tailoring and furniture. This seems to be confirmed by the way the 1901 and 1911 census data was collected for discrete households. The number of non-retail rooms as given in the census was 16 in the stores (comparable with other communities), and six in Beulah Cottage. The 1911 Kelly's Directory entry was: "Randall, Slade & Co Ltd. Grocers 226, confectioners 228, & drapers 230, 232 & 234, Portland rd. & grocers 12 Holland rd", the last named, a small satellite shop nearer the centre of South Norwood. In 1913, the entry is somehow shortened and confused by the printers and 3 Cobden Road appears either to have become a butcher again, or it never closed. In 1918, order was restored to the 1911 quote above. Also, in 1918, the home of Julia Hawkins (one of the early shop girls of 1891) and her friend Alice Carpenter at Cross Road, South Croydon, was listed as Randall, Slade, as was the home of Mary Ann Goodwin (of the Kent Dependants) and her daughter Ettie in Warren Road in East Croydon, so expanding the geographical range and providing modest employment for women. Incidentally, there were also within the boundaries of South Norwood a surprising number of farms remaining in 1911.

In 1911, nine of the women, working in the Stores were at Beulah Cottage, an intriguing Hebrew name, also the name of an area of Thornton Heath. In 1890, a newspaper advertised the house, already with the name, so it was not an idea of the Dependants. At this date it already had two w.c.s and four bedrooms, so was a useful asset to the community. The house was 5, Cobden Road (the odd numbers were behind the grocery store). 1 and 3 Cobden Road were already annexed. The latter have been demolished and replaced by two modern retail units, but Beulah House still stands proud, gable end to the street, on three floors, and the oldest house in Cobden Road.

Table 11.3   1911 Census, South Norwood (Randall, Slade & Co)

<u>226 Portland Road</u>   <u>Place of birth</u>

Alice Slade**	58	grocery manager	Dorchester Dt
Elizabeth Talbot*	51	grocery assistant	Felpham Sx
Clara Millbourn*	45	laundress	Maidstone Kt
Edith Rugman*	31	none	Bramley Sy
Amy Talbot	38	(visitor, married)	Felpham Sx
Mary Hawkins	40	bookkeeper	Ashford Kt
Annie Simmans	24	confectioner	Thornton Heath Sy
Ellen Edwards	33	draper	Ewhurst Sy
Margaret Taylor	59	waitress	Preston Lancs
Ruth Samuel*	56	housekeeper	Stanford Beds
Harriet Drewett*	38	none, invalid	Kentish Town London
Florence Ethel Gifford	23	fruiterer	Margate Kt
Helen Gifford	26	confectioner	Canterbury Kt
Maud Stoneman	29	furniture	Canning Town, London

<u>228 Portland Road</u>

Alice Kennard	25	draper's assistant	Falmer Brighton
Miriam Hale	20	draper's assistant	Headcorn Kt
Nellie Hanks	16	draper's assistant	Swindon Wilts
Sydney Croucher*	33	butcher's assistant	Headcorn Kt
Raymond Croucher	25	baker's assistant	Headcorn Kt
Albert Marshall	30	grocer's carman	Whyteleafe Sy
George Randall**	54	manager bakery dept	Hammersmith London
Mary Hanks**	59	manager drapery dept	Malmesbury Wilts
Margaret Bate**	50	outfitter's assistant	Newport Salop

<u>230 Portland Road</u>

Edwin Elliott*	40	company secretary	Peckham London
George Piper	25	baker's assistant	Sandhurst Kt
Christopher Hale*	25	baker & confectioner	Headcorn Kt
Harry Smith	23	grocer's assistant	Sutton Valence Kt
William Rugman	29	baker's assistant	Bramley Sy
Ernest Goodwin*	30	baker's assistant	Headcorn Kt
James Brightman**	58	manager meat stores	Hitchin Herts

<u>5 Cobden Road 'Beulah Cottage'</u>

Kate Pannell	38	confectioner's clerk	Plaistow, Sx
Ada Gifford	43	manager greengrocers	Canterbury Kt
Annie Smith	24	butcher's cashier	Sydney NSW
Mary Munday	32	grocer's assistant	Wootton Sy
Eliza Pannell*	24	grocer's assistant	Lurgashall Sx
Fanny Maple	56	housemaid	Sundridge Kt
Ellen (Nellie) Reeves	22	general servant	Cowfold Sx
Emma Fry*	38	grocer's assistant	Twickenham Sy
Emma Warnes	38	outfitter's assistant	Swainsthorpe Nfk

*denotes living in the stores in 1901; **denotes living in the stores 1891 and 1901.

Five of the nine in Beulah Cottage (Plate 11.4) were from the Surrey-Sussex border villages. There would have been one more if Ann Overington had lived a few more months. That there were 39 in residence in 1911 well exceeds all other communities. There are no locally born people involved. This strongly supports the idea that this is a planted community. Even Londoners are not very numerous. The dominance of Kent converts is even more marked than in 1901, with 13 altogether. Sirgood must have had a lot of success in gaining new Brethren in Kent years earlier. Perhaps the location was too remote from the core in the Sussex-Surrey borders to be a sustainable community, hence in-migration was encouraged. A photograph has survived of Christopher Hale with his father Alfred, a carpenter, outside their Headcorn weather-boarded Kent cottage (Plate 11.2). Christopher died in 1986 aged 100, having lived his last years at The Retreat in Loxwood. He was pre-deceased by his sister Miriam in 1971. She moved into the stores before 1911 and by 1939 had become a director. She moved to Loxwood, and died in hospital in Chichester in 1971, aged 80. The Hales had been next-door neighbours of Mary Ann and Ettie Goodwin in Headcorn. Ernest Goodwin was another of this family.

Who Were New Live-in Dependants in 1911?

There were 39 of them (Table 11.3 above), compared to 25 in 1901 and eight in 1891 (contrasting with only 16 in 1939). The 'high point' may well have been before the Great War. Amy Talbot, Ellen Edwards, Ethel and Helen Gifford, Nellie Hanks, Miriam Hale, Ray Croucher, Ernest Goodwin, and William Rugman have been written about above, in connection with relatives.

Some are elusive! Mary Hawkins was brought up in Ashford, Kent, but is not a relative of Julia and Cecily from Wiltshire. Mary stayed in South Norwood to at least 1939, but died back in Ashford in 1963, aged 92. Maud Stoneman was born in a pub, The Road, in Carshalton, Surrey. She went into service locally. No evidence of her future after 1911 has come to light.

Kate Pannell was born Sarah Kate in Plaistow, Sussex in 1873. Her father James was one of trustees of the chapel at Loxwood. He was widowed soon after Kate's birth. Kate came to Enmore Park, almost on the doorstep of the future stores, before 1891, in which year she was servant to Fred Collingwood's household. He was a merchant's manager. Ten years later she was confectioner for Randall, Slade living at 3 Cobden Road. She worked in this department for many years, moving to Portland Road by 1911. In 1939, she had become a director, company secretary, and buyer. This nurturing of talent was not untypical. She died in 1953. She was in a group photo, visiting Loxwood, Plate 7.1.

Harry Smith, born in Sutton Valence, a neighbouring village to Headcorn, Kent, was brought up by an uncle in Headcorn. Annie Smith was no relation, and indeed is unique in Dependant circles, born in Australia. In 1901 she had arrived in Croydon and aged just 14, where she was placed in service with a family of woollen merchants at 112 Portland Road, just a few doors away from the stores. Her full name was Harriet Sarah Annie. She later moved to Loxwood, where in 1939 she was working selling boots, living in Hall House. She died in 1965, aged 75, by which time she lived in the Combination Stores.

George Piper was yet another Kent man, from Sandhurst. He remained in Norwood until his death in 1960. In 1933 he and Elsie Randall were married, in the Croydon area, possibly in

South Norwood church. They lived at 7 Cobden Road in 1939, George still a baker's roundsman, probably very well known in South Norwood. She was originally from Plaistow Sussex. Her parents were George and Ellen who moved to Loxwood before 1911. Did Elsie move to Norwood? It must be presumed so. After George's death in 1960, Elsie returned to Loxwood. Astonishingly, she lived there until she was over 100. She died in a Worthing nursing home aged 104 in 2002 (Plate 4.3), the second oldest Dependant at death over their entire existence, and the last entry in the death register. Her funeral was taken by a non-Dependant, Mr Barbour of Emmanual Fellowship, Loxwood (there were none left alive). She has left us a moving description of a Lordshill funeral in 1917 (Chapter 10). George's niece, Doreen Piper, wrote, in about 1991, *"Mr George Piper and my father Arthur worked at Randall, Slades. My uncle was a deliveryman in the bakers and as far as I know worked there for most of his working life. He got my father a position in the grocery store after he left the army in 1918. He left about 1926 to better himself at Tonbridge in the International Stores. My uncle married Miss Elsie Randall from Loxwood, after permission from the Brethren, and they had one daughter, and lived at Cobden Road, near the stores and the chapel. My aunt Elsie now lives with her daughter. They have recently moved to Findon Valley near Worthing. My aunt is in her 90s and extremely deaf, but still manages to knit and write letters to the family."*

By contrast, Annie Simmans from nearby Thornton Heath was brought up by her father after the death of her mother, but as a teenager she found herself in the Cottage Home Schools of the Kensington & Chelsea Union in Ewell, Surrey. From here she was fortunate to find her feet in South Norwood in her early 20s, where she stayed for life, becoming confectionary manageress. Her funeral was in Loxwood in 1968, after spending her last years in The Retreat there.

Albert Marshall was also from not far away. He had been working on the railway in South Croydon in 1901 and had previously lived in Whyteleafe on the fringe of Croydon with his widowed mother. He and Annie were the only 'locals' in the stores community in 1911 – there were none in 1891 and 1901, a remarkable fact about this community.

Alice Kennard's family was discussed in Chapter, 10, Northchapel. One of her sisters, Edith, married James Goodwin (see below). Alice was still working in the stores in 1939. She died aged 72 in 1958 in hospital at Cuckfield, Sussex and was buried in Loxwood.

Margaret Taylor widens the net for new recruits to Lancashire, where she was still a married woman in 1901. How she came south the join the Dependants is not known, but at the age of 59 she was a widow and a waitress, whether for customers or staff is not known. She stayed. Her Norwood death is recorded in the register in 1935, aged 84.

Ellen (Nellie) Reeves was one of numerous Reeves converts in Sussex. Born in Cowfold Sussex, the family soon moved to Warnham. In 1901, still only 12, she lived with her uncle Eli Etherington in Warnham, another Dependant family. After many years in South Norwood, she ended her days in The Retreat, Loxwood, dying in hospital aged 88.

At 21, Cobden Road, lived a trio of ladies, Rose Holland, Harriett Burrows and teenager Mildred Simmons. Harriett had been in the stores for ten or more years and was 83 in 1911.

She died in 1929 aged 99. Her grandfather was William Bridges, the preacher who had converted John Sirgood. Alf Goodwin, the last elder of Loxwood, and therefore of the Dependants as a body, remembers her from when he was a small boy in Norwood, giving a direct link to the very germination of the Dependant idea.

Table 11.4   Birthplaces of South Norwood Communal Residents

	1891	1901	1911 (Stores)	1911 (Beulah Cottage)
Kent	6	6	11	2
London area	1	5	5	
W England	3	3	4	
S Surrey	2	2	3	1
Other Home Counties	1	2	3	1
Sussex coast	1	1	3	
N Sussex				3
E Anglia	1			1
Northern England			1	
Australia				1
TOTAL	15	19	30	9

Telephone lines were becoming available locally, and in 1913, the company had a telephone line, but it would be 10 more years before they could phone Loxwood or other rural communities!

Other Families in Norwood in 1911

There were independently run Dependant grocer's shops at 12, Holland Road and 21, Cobden Road, South Norwood, also at 27, Cross Road, and 12, Warren Road in Croydon itself. Dependant Mary Ann Goodwin managed the grocer's at Warren Road. The others were non-residential.

Isaac Steer (Plate 11.2) and family lived at 2 Cobden Road, directly behind the grocery store. He was born in Kirdford, his wife Eliza in Wisborough Green. Both were from early Dependant families. Eliza was a Pacy (see Chapter 2). Formerly, Isaac had lived in Reigate, and his family say he then used to walk to Norwood to preach, using a map drawn for him by John Sirgood. He was described as a short active man. He became a bricklayer by trade. He was horse keeper for the Dependants by 1911, looking after the horses for the delivery carts. The 1912 map clearly shows a yard and outbuildings, some of which would have been stables, behind the bakehouse on Woodfield Avenue. By 1924 the stables had become a motor garage for the company, and in turn today is Total Auto Care (3 Cobden Road).

In Denmark Road, off Cobden Road, lived William and Carrie Cumber, a family from the Lordshill community. William worked in the greengrocery department in South Norwood. After Carrie's death, he returned to Sussex. His sister, also Carrie, remained in Lordshill, where she was an elder. This family was one of the most widely spread in its presence and influence.

Table 11.5   1939 Register, South Norwood *(Randall, Slade & Co)*

A – Company Premises

<u>226 Portland Road</u>
Nellie Anfield	1899-?	baker's dispatch hand
Edith Rugman**	1880-1965	housekeeper

<u>228-234 Portland Road</u>
Kate Pannell*	1875-1955	director, hon. sec. & buyer
Florence Ethel Gifford	1887-1950	manageress fruit dept
Helen (Nellie) Gifford*	1884-1975	shop assistant
Emma Warnes*	1874-1956	domestic duties
Mildred Mann	1896-1964	booking clerk
Miriam Hale*	1890-1971	director & drapery buyer
Annie Simmans*	1886-1968	confectionary manageress
Mary Munday*	1878-1957	cook
William Rugman*	1881-1954	bread baker

<u>5 Cobden Road (Beulah Cottage)</u>
Gertrude Killner	1899-1987	draper's shop assistant
Ellen (Nellie) Reeves*	1888-1976	housemaid
Mary Hawkins*	1870-1963	pensioner
Ruth Ray	1897-1969	baker's shop assistant
Alice Kennard*	1886-1958	shop assistant

B – Nearby Community

<u>7 Cobden Road</u>
George Piper*	1885-1960	baker's roundsman
Elsie Piper	1898-2002	domestic duties
Person redacted		

<u>9 Cobden Road</u>
James Wall	1878-1978	general labourer
Mary Anne Wall	1878-1967	domestic duties
Person redacted		

<u>6 Woodside Avenue</u>
Amelia Pyke	1869-1957	domestic duties
Memilo Pyke	1875-1992	saleswoman baker & confectioner

<u>148 Portland Road</u>
William Holland	1900-1948	boot repairer
and 1 other		

<u>380 Woodside Avenue</u>
Florence Butchers	1880-1958	domestic duties
Constance Greenfield	1908-?	butcher's cashier
Maurice Batten	1905-1986	baker's roundsman
Edna Batten	1911-1976	domestic duties

<u>34 Ashburton Road</u>
Edwin Elliott*	1870-1954	company secretary retired (Randall, Slade)

<u>8 Bywood Avenue</u>

Edith Goodwin	1876-1963	domestic duties
Edith (Bessie) Goodwin	1901-1986	domestic duties
Dorothy Goodwin	1903-1985	baker's shop assistant
Alfred Goodwin	1906-1996	gent's outfitters manager & buyer
and 1 other		

<u>135 Bingham Road</u>

Ernest Goodwin*	1880-1969	baker's roundsman
Alice Goodwin	1887-1995	domestic duties
Mary Goodwin	1854-1941	old age pensioner
and 1 other		

<u>105 Birchanger Road</u>

Beatrice Hawkins	1879-1964	incapacitated

<u>21 Brocklesbury Road</u>

Joseph Lomne	1886-1956	motor mechanic
and 1 other		

<u>69 Penge Road</u>

Isabel Hunt	1876-1967	boot shop mistress
Clara Hunt	1874-1960	boot shop mistress
John Stilton	1873-1943	general labourer

*denotes living at the stores in 1911; ** denotes living at the stores in 1901 and 1911.

Across Portland Road, was Oakley Road. Here the Goodwin family lived. James (Jim) Goodwin, from Thornton Heath, was working, presumably at the stores, as a butcher's assistant. His wife Edith (née Kennard) was a sister of Alice who was at the stores (above). Their family included Alfred, born in 1906, who many years later was destined to be the last elder at Loxwood. Walter Nash is said to have intervened in Alf's conscientious objection to the War to get him moved down from Norwood to Loxwood. Jim died in Norwood in 1938. Edith (Plates 4.1 and 7.1) moved to Loxwood to live with Alf in Walcot, then Rose Cottage, next to the Combination Stores until her death in 1963, when Cyril Killner took her funeral to spare Alf from doing so.

George Tate was the fifth trustee, and first named, of the chapel trustees in 1883, and named in both leases. He lived in Darnley Cottage on Portland Road, further north on this long thoroughfare, where he is described as a "writer and [en]graver" in 1881, and an employer, and explained in the 1883 indenture as a glass gilder. He too was a married man. Both he and his wife were Londoners.

Jesse Edwards, named in the indenture, was from a family which lived in Dorking workhouse when he was a boy. In 1871 he was starting out as a decorator in central Croydon. By 1881, he lived at 2 Church Cottages, Cobden Road with his wife Mary, at the opposite end of the road from the Dependants' buildings, next to a United Reformed Church. Jesse was born in Wotton, Surrey, and worked as a decorator all his life. After Mary's death in 1888 he moved to Loxwood. Jesse was not related to Alfred or Ellen, although they were born near each other.

One who ended her days (possibly just on a visit) at Beulah House, where she died in 1910, was widowed Ann Overington, an elder from Loxwood, "the mother of Loxwood Church", where she had been very influential from Sirgood's first days there (Chapter 4, Plate 4.3). The Loxwood registers contain an astonishing number of individuals from Norwood, some buried there, others just listed in the death register. The rural Brethren felt a strong affinity to their urban counterparts, whose lives were in some way the same, but in other ways so different in context. One wonders how accepted they were in this suburban area.

It is possible after 1939 (table 11.5A above) to attempt a history of department and company management. In 1891 the small start-up company Randall, Ford on Portland Road was in the hands of Julia Ford and George Randall, whose store was a grocers and bakers. Alice Slade had the drapery next door in Cobden Road.

Ten years later, Alice Slade had moved across to the grocery department, George Randall likewise to the bakery department. There is no clear leadership of the drapery department, possibly Mary Hanks. Harriet Drewett was clerk.

In 1911, the management structure was more formal. Alice Slade was still grocery manager, George Randall bakery manager. Mary Hanks was now confirmed as drapery manager. James Brightman was manager of the meat store, hence butchery. Ada Gifford was manager of the greengrocers. Kate Pannell had oversight of confectionary as clerk. There is now a company secretary, Edwin Elliott. This will have been in line with company law from 1908. Other stores also had someone in this position from that time onwards. Mary Hawkins served as bookkeeper. No individual is named director, but we may assume the department heads were directors of Randall, Slade & Co Ltd.

In the most recent available data for 1939, the dispersal of personnel creates a little confusion. With both Randall and Slade now deceased, and Elliott identified as retired there is no named company secretary. Kate Pannell however is described as honorary secretary, director and buyer (for grocery perhaps as there is no manager). Miriam Hale is also a director and drapery buyer. Ethel Gifford is manageress of the fruiterers; Annie Simmans has moved into the rôle of manager of confectionary. William Rugman is billed as baker, possibly manager. Alf Goodwin, although living in 8 Bywood Avenue, a 15-minute walk away, is manager and buyer for the gent's outfitters. There is no reference to sales of shoes or furniture in these sources, but Alf Goodwin is on record as saying they were sold.

There are some doubtful names in the list above who are not living 'over the shop'. For example, living in Woodside Avenue with widow Florence Butchers (a known Dependant local to South Norwood, as were other members of her husband's family), were Constance Greenfield, from Yorkshire, butcher's cashier, and Maurice Batten, a local lad. Maurice's father was a 'stores cellarman', who had lived in Woodside Avenue in 1911. Neither Maurice, a baker's roundsman in 1939, nor Constance were known Dependants, suggesting they might have been outsider employees of Randall, Slade.

Plate 11.4   Recent Images of the Stores

Fig 1 & 2, right 226 Portland Rd (grocers), left, 228-234 (bakers and drapers). Woodside Ave, with Beulah House left. is in between.

Ack: all images, except Fig 5, Google Streetview, Figs 1 & 2, 2011 and Fig 3, 2019.

Fig 3 – above, panorama of both groups of buildings: 226 Portland Road (former grocers, and original 1880s premises) centre; 228 (painted cream) left , former bakers/confectioners with bakehouse & outbuildings behind); 230-234/236 (with boarding 2019 for conversion from offices to warehouse & shop(see Fig 4 below) far left, former drapers with accommodation above. Spread Eagle (Gold Coast) far right. Cobden Road (20mph limit) also right. Woodside Avenue (no entry) left.

Fig 4 – left, Beulah Cottage, 5 Cobden Road, the gable end, centre. To its left are two newbuild shops at Nos 1 & 2, once part of 226.

Fig 5, new entrance to Cash for Clothes warehouse/shop, 236 Portland Rd. *Ack: Facebook.*

Fig 6 – Satellite image of the environs of Randall Slade & Co Ltd (north to top).

- Portland Road is the wide main road.
- Cobden Road is west to east.
- Woodvale Avenue is SW to NE.
- Spread Eagle PH (now Gold Coast) is north of Cobden Road, wine glass symbol.
- 226 Portland Road is at the apex between Cobden Rd and Woodvale Avenue (2 new shops behind (2 & 3 Cobden Rd), Beulah Cottage, 5 Cobden Rd, next, is set back.
- Chapel site is the light coloured flat roofed building, the part with skylights, angled to the Woodvale Avenue, immediately south of the 2 new shops.
- South of Woodvale Ave, the sharp-angled corner building is 228, the bakery.
- Roofs behind it facing Woodvale Ave were the bakehouse and other outbuildings.
- The wide range of roofs with the pale coloured balcony on the frontage were 230-234, and the next building is 236 both facing Portland Road.

Ack: Google Maps, 2019

Others such as Gertrude Killner from Loxwood, Amelia Pyke, who was born in Ewhurst on the Surrey border, and her daughter Memilo *(sic)* born in South Norwood, each ended their days in Loxwood. Mary Anne Wall died in Loxwood; her sons William and Frank also moved to Loxwood, where Frank became manager of Hilltop Stores, purchased by Aylward Smith in 1944.

Those who seem certain to have jobs with Randall, Slade, even though they do not live 'over the shop' or in Beulah Cottage, were George Piper, Memilo Pyke, Constance Greenfield, Maurice Batten, Dorothy and Alfred Goodwin, and Ernest Goodwin. There may well be others.

Only five names are identified as new members of the stores' community since 1911 (not to say there were not others who came and went in this 28-year period). One imagines that there being fewer new and old hands, that the rate of conversion as well as the need for such a sheltered life was much reduced in the post-Great War period. Interestingly, though, the ages of those at work was not exceptionally high. The oldest in Beulah Cottage was May Hawkins, aged 69, and a pensioner. Only three others were over 60. Of the newcomers, the oldest was Ethel Gifford, whose family relationships are explained above. Millie Mann was born at 13 Cobden Road, where she grew up! Both her parents were Dependants. William, born in Northchapel, Sussex, was for a time a carman, most likely to have been working for Randall, Slade (1901). Ruth Way was an adopted child, born in Teddington, Middlesex, living there with the Carter family, shopkeepers. Ruth is typical of so many girls who found refuge, a welcome, work, and a faith in Dependant stores, and stayed for life; she died in The Retreat, Loxwood, in 1969, yet another Norwood resident of this Dependant home.

One issue which was not significant to rural Dependants was the incessant bombing and V1 flying bomb (aka doodlebug, buzz bomb) attacks over south London during the war. High explosive bombs and incendiaries were common between 1940 and 1941, as many as 42 in South Norwood alone. The closest bomb to fall was in Belmont Road on the other side of Portland Road. Incendiaries fell in two locations in Cobden Road, mercifully not immediately behind the stores. In 1944, 16 flying bombs fell in South Norwood, many destroying at least two houses, and their occupants. On 29 June at 7.00am, one fell on Denmark Road between Cobden Road and Enmore Road which killed six and *"wiped out a good bit of Denmark Road* (reports John Windell whose father was landlord of the Spread Eagle for many years), *rocking the foundations of the Spread Eagle pub, so much that it sent an upright piano across the saloon bar coming to rest against the cellar door trapping those that were sheltering there. Wall ties now hold the building together."* The Spread Eagle was next to Randall, Slade Stores. Five houses were destroyed, and 20 more damaged. Croydon had the greatest density anywhere of flying bomb hits in 1944.

The Final Years

A surprising number of Norwood residents died in Loxwood or lived there in their later years, some making an early move to work in Loxwood (itself short of shopworkers) for a while. There was no suitable retirement address locally in Norwood, with even then high prices for property, and no land on which to erect any purpose-built home as was done in Loxwood, Warnham, Northchapel and Lordshill. The Retreat, the retirement home in Loxwood, belonged to a South Norwood trust, and by the 1980s was handed over to a

Loxwood trust, which still manages it for the village to this day. This added to a sudden decline, and the quick forgetting of the community's existence.

The death registers at Loxwood, which record just deaths, no matter where, show the last recorded death in South Norwood itself was of Alfred Butchers in 1982. His father had been a local postman. He, his wife Sarah, and other members of the family were Dependants. Alfred was born in South Norwood in 1906 and was 76 years old. However, his was an exception as the previous last were Beatie Hawkins in 1964, a late arrival to join relatives, Ernest Goodwin and Ruth Way in 1969. Unfortunately, not all Norwood deaths were recorded, especially early on and in the last years. The last former Norwood Dependants recorded living in Loxwood at the date of death were probably William Wall who died in 1978, Nellie Reeves in 1974, Nellie Gifford in 1973, and Eliza Pannell in 1969. In the early years, no 19th century deaths were recorded in Loxwood. The first in the 20th century, ironically, was the unfortunate death of Loxwood elder Ann Overington on a visit to Norwood in 1910. She was brought back to Loxwood for burial. That seems to have started a snowball effect of burials in Loxwood. The next being Olive Mann in 1911.

The death dates for the 1939 listing give a clue to the end of the community. There were three deaths in the 1940s, ten in the 1950s, twelve in the 1960s, four in the 1970s, three in the 1980s, three in the 1990s and one in the 2000s. Peaking in the 1960s, only three occupants of the stores' addresses survived into the 1970s, much the same as in other communities. For example, Miriam Hale died in 1971, Nellie Reeves in 1976, Edna Batten in 1976, and Maurice Batten and Edith Goodwin in 1986, Gertrude Killner in 1987, Memilo Pyke in 1992, Alice Goodwin in 1995, Alf Goodwin in 1996, not forgetting centenarian Elsie Piper in 2002.

Randall, Slade was still trading in 1969, the last year for which there was an entry in the telephone book. On Portland Road, 226 (the grocery shop) was a solicitor's a few years ago but is now vacant; at the rear (the bakery and bakehouse) is a car repair business, with three flats above, in part of the main building, and extending into another entrance on Woodside Avenue; 230-236 (the drapery shop) was until 2018 an insurance consultant /property agent occupying most of the main building. In 2019 228-238 became a large clothing store called Cash for Clothes, a national second-hand clothing dealer, part of East Anglian Simply Textiles Ltd, who have recycling, decluttering, diversion from landfill and payment for usable clothing as their objectives. The main customer entrance is at 238 which was next door to Randall, Slade; this has preserved the façade of the building previously the financial services company. Perhaps the Randall, Slade drapers would approve?

Croydon Oral History Society put together many memories of 'the old days' in the 1990s, publishing the accounts in several volumes. In *Talking Of Croydon No.3: South Norwood 1892 – 1992* (Plate 11.5), under the heading of Shops, across two pages, are the memories of Bill who worked for Randall, Slade. He described such details as the bacon slicer, the ham cooker, the bagging of loose groceries, and the insight to regard them as the 'first supermarket'. but he was not a Dependant, also of Margaret, who knew of them but had the common erroneous notions of who they were – Quaker, Puritan for example. She remembered the women's dress precisely.

Richard Treadwell, formerly of Woodside Avenue, wrote to me, *"I would go shopping with my mother who would go to different shops for different things – Home & Colonial in Portland Road for luncheon meat, corned beef and sausages, Mr Lee's in Woodside village for cheese, bacon, tins and bottled stuff, and Randall, Slade for rice (for rice pudding), raisins and sultanas. These products were sold loose. After being weighed and bagged, a note was shot across the shop on a wire above our heads by the man behind the counter to a cashier in a booth who would take payment. I remember the shop being rather gloomy, as were the people who ran it – no cheeky banter."*

In the early days, in 1897, surprisingly, George Randall and Alice Slade were summoned for selling 'short bread'. A Mrs Mansfield bought a half-quartern loaf. When sold, it was 2½ oz short of 2 lbs. Having been twice warned, the defendants were fined 40s with 5s 6d costs. The fine was paid.

Usually, the boot was on the other foot. In 1909, Randall, Slade sued a local tailor for non-payment of a bill for £4 5s 10d. In 1917, when supplies were difficult to get, and some people were on hard times due to the War, a servant Mildred Peters, 23, was charged with obtaining under false pretences from 230 Portland Road, a nightdress, 2 chemies, 2 camisoles, 2 pairs of stockings, knickers, 2 blouses, 3 pinafores, a pique coat, 2 chemises, a petticoat, a frock, knickers, 3 sleeping suits (the last six all children's), 3 vests, etc. to the value of £7 10s 9¾d. The same year a 14-year-old boy, Charles Wilson, a repeat offender, was similarly charge with taking biscuits, sugar, and brawn to the value of 3s 3d on the fictitious account of another person. His distressed father intervened privately, and the bench sent the boy to a reformatory until the age of 19. Such cases reveal much of the wide range of goods served in the stores.

South Norwood remains an anomalous location of uncertain roots. Yet it became rooted deeply into its stores and chapel site, if not as much into the wider community as some others. The main ways in which these South London Dependants integrated was through their retail business and their delivery vehicles, both a common sight on the streets and a lifeline to many. Also, it must be remembered there was the usual dispersed community of households both in nearby streets and further afield, some of them trading or offering a service either as part of Randall, Slade or not. The chapel had negligible impact as they seem to have been a closed community, as elsewhere, except for local people being very aware of their sober and old-fashioned dress. Local newspapers did not even carry stories of funerals as they did for the Surrey-Sussex border communities. How much easier it was to be lost in the urban jungle. That they arrived before the jungle closed in is significant, both in terms of the initial choice of site, and in the opportunity, it offered for growth. The lack of any opportunity for retirement locally in the mid-20th century hastened the eclipse of the community more than elsewhere. It is a missed opportunity to find that there are no records of them of any substance, and no testimonies or stories, just a few letters which tell almost nothing of the community beyond their faith. There was little mission activity, and almost all the Brethren came from elsewhere, to put down roots. Last, but not least, this community was not as old as the main centres further south. There is little evidence of it before 1880, 30 years after John Sirgood travelled south, and only 5 years before his death.

There is a useful account of the Dependants of Loxwood and surrounding villages in a small book written by one time employee of the Loxwood Stores, Connie Bayley, subtitled "Forgotten Villages…", but seen from the Dependant heartland, Norwood is the real forgotten community. It is hoped it will be less of a closed book after reading this chapter.

Plate 11.5   Oral History

Some shops in Portland Road

Randall Slades 1910   *& Bakers*   Margaret

One shop was run by Quakers under the name of Randall Slades. They had a terrace of shops in Portland Road which ran from just opposite Belmont Road and round the corner of Woodside Avenue. The shops comprised a butchers, a drapery, a shoe shop and some furniture. The bakery was in Woodside Avenue and they did a nice selection of cakes. There was also a greengrocery shop which just went round the corner to Cobden Road. In Woodside Avenue, opposite the bakehouse, there was their chapel and every evening and weekend one could hear them singing.

The women all wore very long dresses, but mostly blouses and skirts - dresses were not worn very much then. They had their hair drawn back quite straight with not a wrinkle in it nor a curl. It would be done in a plait, curled up at the back of the head. The womenfolk, even the girls, all wore little black bonnets with ribbons tied under the chin. They wore short jackets over these skirts, all in a dark colour. They wore that kind of attire all the way through that I knew them. They were Quakers, some called them Puritans. There was a son and a daughter at the butchers. The boy was at school with my brother and the girl was at school with me. So far as I can recall they were the only children in all that collection of grown-ups. There were two storeys above the shops and they all seemed to live up there on Portland Road and in various houses just around there. The shops are still there today but in a vastly different guise.

Randall Slades 1916   Bill

When I left Birchanger School in 1916 I went as an errand boy to Randall Slades in Portland Road. I used to deliver groceries on an errand bike - a big tradesman's bike. I also worked in the grocery shop. Bacon, sugar and everything all had to be cut and weighed up - it wasn't pre-wrapped and prepared like it is today. Bacon had to go on the machine, sugar had to be taken from a large sack and weighed up and put in a funnel bag. Butter came in half hundredweight boxes. We used to take a big lump off and put it in trays so people could see it. They would say 'I'll have half a pound of fresh (or salted) butter'. Then you would get the pats, take off a piece near enough the right weight and put it on the scales and take a bit off or put a bit on until it was right; then bang it in shape and wrap it up, in greaseproof paper.

We had a man that cooked the ham on the premises in iron pots. No water touched them. There was a big copper and these iron containers took one ham each. It was like a big metal tank with the gas underneath and about as big as a sofa would be - you could walk round it. It would take about half a dozen whole hams and it was just the heat cooking them. They were all screwed down so no water could get at them and then he would take all the skins off, crumb them and put them in the fridge to freeze. He was a specialist man - that was all he did. When it came out of the freezer it was like iron. Then it had to be cut up. We had a bacon machine - they had only just come out. It was belt driven and the belt went down in the cellar and then it came up and drove the machine in the shop. The bacon was all sliced up on a tray and people would come in and say 'I'll have half a pound of ham', or 'a quarter' and with a fork you would put it on the scales - whatever they wanted. It was

beautiful ham, it melted in the mouth.

When tea came in we did have some packets, like Brooke Bond, but we used to have a lot of loose tea as well, but it, - and sugar, rice, you name it - it all had to be weighed and bagged up. They had two people upstairs and they did all the weighing, tying and packing. It would be put in stiff paper bags and if it was a small quantity it would be a paper funnel.

There also used to be biscuits which came in 7lb tins, not all wrapped in packets like today. McVities, Huntleys, Crawfords, MacFarlanes and many other well-known names. You served from the tins. Each tin had a separate kind of biscuit - whatever they wanted you weighed up. There was one shilling back on the tin and they all had to go back to the manufacturers.

Deliveries

A horse and cart was used for the deliveries and they had a stable at the back of the shop for this. We would be out to 8 and 9 o'clock at night doing the deliveries. They were very busy people. There was no shop like them for miles around. They had a shop for every sort of thing. They were the first supermarket!

Learning to drive a T-type Ford 1920s

When they gave up the horse they got a van, a T-type Ford, and I learned to drive on that. There was no starter button; you had to turn a handle on the front of the engine, outside the van. There were no gear boxes. You had to press the lever to the floor, put the pedal on the floor, there were three pedals - the left hand one you pressed to the floor as far as you could get it, that was bottom gear. Then you let it come back up and that was top gear. The hand brake pulled them together into neutral. When you let go, the hand brake went straight into high gear and the middle pedal - you had to press on that - that was in reverse. The right hand pedal was your foot brake. It was hard going - it could kick back on you. In the winter it was terrible, keep on wind, wind and wind. Even big lorries had nothing but the starter handle.

They asked me if I would like to go to their service and I sang with them but I just went once because I said I would come. I never went again.

James Smith 1890s   Fred R

In South Norwood there was a famous builders known in the trade as 'Jiggerme' Smith. My grandfather worked for them as a plasterer. Their premises were in Carmichael Road and at eight o'clock on workdays a bell was rung and the men who worked in the stonemason's yard there went in. They did work all over London. Mullen, who was then the estimating clerk for James Smith for some years, eventually left and set up his own firm of Mullen and Lumsdens at the foot of Pembury Road. *(You can see the bell on the left of the building in the photograph on page 14.)*

12   13

Fig 1 – Croydon Oral History Society, *Talking Of Croydon No.3: South Norwood 1892 - 1992* (annotation not by the author).

Chapter 12

Chichester, Felpham and Hove/Portslade

Dependant Communities of the Sussex Coast

In the 1883 chapel indenture, in Chichester, Michael Woolgar conveyed part of a field (100ft x 50ft) called Joyes Croft on St Pancras Street; it was "already built". Chichester was the first community on the south coast. Felpham, near Bognor, was only in the planning stage. Hove, as far as can be ascertained, was far into the future. Portslade is often cited as its predecessor meeting place. Walter Hart from Chichester became the first Hove elder.

Less is known of these communities, and there were never any combination stores. However, in Chichester, the first elder, Michael Woolgar, was also to make his own shop a centre of Dependant activity. Chichester was the centre for those in villages around such as East Dean. Before 1898, there was no chapel at Felpham. Jim Hale, the Dependant carrier, regularly brought the Felpham Brethren to Chichester chapel. After 1939, when there was no longer a chapel at Felpham, remaining Dependants were brought to Chichester by hired bus.

Chichester

Michael Woolgar was an imposing bearded individual (Plate 12.1), born in Steyning in 1845 into an agricultural labourer's family. His parents indeed were paupers in 1871, when their grandson George Michael (son of Michael's sister Susan) was staying with them in Steyning. On Michael's marriage, he was a blacksmith in Liss, Hampshire, but his wife Emily died after giving birth to three children, the last, another Michael, born in Chichester, so the family must have moved there by 1873 *(source: obituary).* Michael Sr set up the Chichester Coal Company, only later did he obtain premises as a master grocer at 10a, The Hornet. Living with him was Fanny Pannell as his housekeeper, a daughter of Dependants Henry and Emily of Chiddingfold, and soon to be wife of Fred Hughes (see below). Somehow, Michael had become a Dependant either in Liss or in Chichester. Coincidentally, his next-door neighbour for many years was a Bible Christian Chapel. On the other side were two adjacent pubs The Half Moon and The Prince Albert, a similar juxtaposition of God and the devil's drink to South Norwood. The Dependant's chapel was built a short distance away on land that would then have been the edge of the built-up area. Adelaide Road is north off St Pancras (road), to the east and outside of the city walls. The chapel, no more left than a fragment of wall, is now incorporated in 1 and 2 Chapel Cottages; it was on the corner of Adelaide Rd and Joys Croft, less than 10 minutes' walk from The Hornet.

In October 1874, Woolgar (still a blacksmith) was arranging a service for Bible Christians in the Oddfellows Hall in Crane Street in the centre of the city. Accusations of interruptions and the throwing of missiles were made of a group of men, one of whom was James Biles, who were then warned off going there by the magistrates. Other members of the congregation were named, William Sadler of Funtington (later, a trustee of the chapel, born in 1827) and Mrs Catherine Budd. The news report went nationwide. Michael Woolgar's obituary states that this building (now on modern Orchard Street, part of the inner ring road) was used as a chapel in 1873, almost as soon as he moved to Chichester. The chapel in Adelaide Road was still in use at his death in 1927.

In 1883, the Dependants took a man named William Welcome to court for disturbing the services by for example asserting the elders, Michael Woolgar and Walter Hart, were false teachers, "You red hot hypocrite". He was told by the bench to keep away. This issue dragged on; in 1889, Welcome was again in court for disturbing services, declaring his wife had become a member of the congregation, and asserting that Woolgar had encouraged her in drunkenness (very unlikely!). The bench decided she had joined of her own desire, and that despite some provocation on Woolgar's part, Welcome should be fined £40, a considerable amount. By 1881, Woolgar had moved on from blacksmithing, retaining the coal business (1901, Table 12.1 below) to be a grocer, later also a draper and dairyman.

Table 12.1   The Woolgar Household in Chichester Censuses

1881   10a The Hornet, St Pancras, Chichester   Place of birth

Michael Woolgar	35	master grocer	Steyning Sx
Louisa Woolgar	11	scholar	Liss Hants
Jane Woolgar	8	scholar	Liss Hants
Michael Woolgar	6	scholar	Chichester Sx
Fanny Pannell	28	housekeeper	Chiddingfold Sy

1891   M Woolgar & Sons, The Hornet, St Pancras, Chichester

Michael Woolgar	45	grocer & draper	Steyning Sx
Michael Woolgar	16	grocer's assistant	Chichester Sx
Ellen Charlotte Boiling	28	grocer's & draper's assistant	Felpham, Sx
Ellen Goff	15	grocer's & draper's assistant	Chichester Sx
Fanny Hughes	27	cook	Chichester Sx
Mabel Kitchill	15	housemaid	Binsted Sx

1901   M Woolgar & Sons, 40-42 The Hornet, St Pancras, Chichester

Michael Woolgar	56	coal merchant grocer etc	Steyning Sx
Ellen Charlotte Woolgar	36		Felpham Sx
Louisa Woolgar	30	grocer's clerk	Liss Hants
Jesse Woolgar	9		Chichester Sx
Ernest Woolgar	6		Chichester Sx
Percy Woolgar	4		Chichester Sx
Harold Woolgar	2		Chichester Sx
Lily Woolgar	2m		Chichester Sx
Fanny Hughes	36	general servant	Chichester Sx
Eleanor Edwards	16	general servant	Chichester Sx

1911   M Woolgar & Sons, 40-42 The Hornet, St Pancras, Chichester

Michael Woolgar	65	grocer & dairyman	Steyning Sx
Ellen Charlotte Woolgar	47	assisting in the business	Felpham Sx
Louisa Woolgar	40	shop assistant	Liss Hants
Jesse Woolgar	19	dairyman assistant	Chichester Sx
Ernest Woolgar	16	dairyman assistant	Chichester Sx
Percy Woolgar	14	shop assistant	Chichester Sx
Harold Woolgar	12	school	Chichester Sx
Lily Woolgar	10	school	Chichester Sx
Cecil Woolgar	9		Chichester Sx
Fanny Hughes	48	general servant	Chichester Sx

1939   M Woolgar & Sons, 24-28 The Hornet, St Pancras, Chichester

Charlotte Woolgar	1863	grocer, own account
Ernest Woolgar	1894	dairyman & farmer
Fanny Hughes	1862	incapacitated

Plate 12.1   Chichester

Fig 1 - Michael Woolgar, 1845-1927, and his second wife Charlotte Ellen (aka Ellen Charlotte) Woolgar, 1864-1954. She was disabled from before her husband's death.

Fig 2 – below left, M Woolgar & Sons, grocer's shop in the 1960s.

Fig 3 – below right, the premises today, in The Hornet, now 3 shop units, otherwise little changed.

Fig 4 – inset, initials (MAAM?) and date of construction of shop – 1871.

Fig 5 – Harry Hart, 1858-1937, & Fanny, 1860-1937, outside their Selsey home. Fanny is wearing typical Cokeler dress, as is Charlotte Ellen above, without the bonnet

Michael Woolgar Jr became his father's assistant on leaving school, but after his marriage he and his wife left the district, moving to work in Hampshire. He stayed long enough for the business to take the name M Woolgar & Sons. Ellen Charlotte Boiling from Felpham joined them, selling drapery as well as groceries. Her parents, George and Jane were Chichester Dependants who had named her Charlotte Ellen, which she reversed for most of her life, reverting to Charlotte as a widow. Michael Sr and much younger Ellen (Plate 12.1) – she was younger than Michael's eldest daughter Louise - were married soon after this (in 1891) and went on to have six more children. Ellen Goff, another Dependant, also worked in the shop, but died a few years later. Ellen's parents, Edmund (Ted) Goff and Ellen Goff were also Dependants. Ted was a butcher in Southgate. Born in Bepton, Sussex, he died in 1910. his wife Ellen, nee Fisher, born in Steep, Hants, pre-deceased him in 1907. Fanny Hughes was cook and remained a lifelong Dependant. She died in Loxwood in 1943. Mabel Ketchell, housemaid, may have also been a Dependant.

By 1901, the premises had been renumbered and enlarged as 40-42, The Hornet. With their growing family, Fanny Hughes remained as general servant. Michael and Ellen ran the business together, also the coal merchants (Chichester Coal Company in Caledonian Road), Louisa assisting in the clerical side of the business.

In 1911, the same enlarged living accommodation consisted of eleven rooms, the household little changed, but now three of the children were working in the shop, specialising in a dairy from their own farm (a healthier generation now drank more milk). Knitting wool, appropriately, became one of the later specialities. Michael died in 1927, aged 80, and is buried in Portfield Cemetery, Chichester. His son, Ernest, took on much of the business. Ernest's younger brother, Harold, became a farmer near Sidlesham. When Michael Woolgar Sr died, he left the bulk of his estate to Ernest and Harold. In the will, Michael stated that he had a one third interest in Florence Farm, Birdham, held on lease; also, he held the lease of the Westhampnett Dairy Farm and owned the freehold of his home and shop at 40-42 The Hornet. The estate was valued at £2,818 4s 3d, which was a lot of money for 1927.

In 1936, the street (Plate 12.1) was again renumbered, the business becoming Nos 24-6. In 1939, Ellen (now calling herself by her registered first name Charlotte) was in sole charge despite being disabled, probably using assistants who lived elsewhere, whilst Ernest, although living at home, was running the farming side of the business. The loyal Fanny was now unable to work. Charlotte Ellen died in 1954.

Marion May (Shamley Green) was told that a Mrs Earwicker who worked at the shop up to the 1960s wore the Victorian dress of the Dependants, which would suggest she, and maybe her husband, Frank, may still have been Dependants. If she was Gwendoline Earwicker, née Curtis, as seems likely, she was possibly the last Dependant in the Chichester community, dying in 2003, much later than might have been assumed. Gwendoline Curtis, born 1917, was already a shop assistant in 1939. The photo (Plate 12.1) shows the shop in the 1960s, with little change since in the building itself, now three shop units.

Table 12.2 lists most of those from Chichester who are recorded in the Loxwood registers (undoubtedly an underestimate). The family with the most recorded deaths is the Hughes

Table 12.2   1911 census, Chichester and Nearby

Chichester				Place of birth	
40-42 The Hornet	**Fanny Hughes**	48	general servant	Chichester	d 1943

Woolgar's Stores – see Table 12.1

2-3 Oving Road	**Frederick Hughes**	46	furniture dealer	Funtington Sx	d 1928
	Fanny Hughes	58		Chiddingfold Sy	d 1938

Fanny, née Pannell, married Frederick in 1889

	Frederick Hughes	19	upholsterer	Chichester	d 1948
54 Adelaide Road	**Kitty Boiling**	50	(invalid/cripple)	Felpham Sx	d 1929
54 Adelaide Road	**Jane Staker**	73	(widow)	East Dean Sx	d 1931

(Separate single-person households at same address)

56 Adelaide Road	**William Hughes**	69	farm labourer	Chichester	d 1914
	Eliza Hughes	71	(deaf)	Chichester	d 1933
18 Russell Street	**Edward Newman**	65	blacksmith	Chichester	d 1932
62 High Street	**Thomas Rogers**	83	farm labourer	Lavant Sx	d 1911
154 St Pancras	**Caroline Shepherd**	65	carman's wife	Selsey Sx	d 1921
136 St Pancras	**George Edwards**	53	labourer	Heyshott Sx	d 1933
	Eleanor Edwards	53		Flansham Sx	d 1933
37 St Pancras	**George Baker**	58	hot drinks barrow	Oving Sx	d 1915
19 Florence Road	**George Boiling**	68	farm labourer	Felpham Sx	d 1928
	Jane Boiling	62		Clymping Sx	d 1930
18 Green Lane	**Harry Green**	60	upholsterer	Wiltshire	d 1936
	Jane Green	58		Wiltshire	d 1932
Tangmere	**John Duke**	64	farm labourer	Bosham Sx	d 1923
Birdham	**Alfred Powell**	54	carpenter	Apuldram Sx	d 1925
Hunston	**John Slade**	64	poultry keeper	Dorset	d 1941
Fishbourne, Clay Lane	**William Upfield**	45	gardener	Harting Sx	d 1946
	Clara Upfield	40		Felpham Sx	d 1955
Felpham					
3 Vicarage Cottages	**Doris Rice (Cowell)**	4	school	Felpham Sx	d 1973

Doris married James Cowell in 1926

Flansham lane	**Fanny Burnand (Talbot)**	44	housekeeper	West Dean Sx	d 1942

Fanny married Richard Talbot in 1924

Selsey, High Street	**Harry Hart**	53	house decorator	Selsey Sx	d 1937
	Fanny Hart	49	assist in b'ness	Eastbourne Sx	d 1937
	Rose Hart	25	assist in b'ness	Eastbourne Sx	d 1950

Rose married Leonard Homer in 1925.

East Road	**Leonard Homer**	22	fisherman	Selsey Sx	d 1958
Lodsworth Sx					
Randall's Stores	**Emily Hughes**	70	(widow)	Siddlesham Sx	d 1918
Chichester (1901)					
18 Southgate	**Edmund Goff**	b1848	butcher	Bepton Sx	d 1910
	Eleanor Goff	b1847		Steep Hants	d 1907
Funtington (1901)					
	William Sadler	b 1827	farm labourer	West Dean Sx	d 1910
Royal Navy (1901)	**Richard Talbot**	b 1872	seaman	Felpham Sx	d 1941

Richard may have been at sea in 1911

family. Widow Emily Hughes was living with the Randalls in Lodsworth in 1911 (Chapter 10). Fanny, as has been shown above, lived with the Woolgars, but she moved to Loxwood before her death in 1943, where she was buried in the chapel graveyard. The youngest Hughes was Fred who in 1939 had a furniture business in The Hornet. His father, also Frederick, from Funtington, had traded in furniture in Oving Road, and had married Fanny Pannell who used to live with the Woolgars (Table 12.1, 1881 census). She was a daughter of Harry and Emily Pannell, Dependants, born in Kirdford, Sussex.

John Duke, born in Bosham in 1850, and William Sadler, born 1827, both agricultural labourers from the village of Funtington, joined Michael Woolgar as chapel trustees in 1883, as did Walter Hart, born 1853, a furniture dealer in Chichester. Walter had a brother Harry. Harry and his wife Fanny (Plate 12.1) lived in Selsey as had Walter. Walter advertised furniture auctions and valuations, removals, warehousing, upholstering and undertaking in the late 1890s and his shop in Southgate offered "complete house furniture and undertaking in all its branches", using an image of a railway wagon in 1902-1903. Walter left to be elder of the new Hove meetings in about 1904/5. In 1901, members of the Hughes and Ellen Boiling's family lived on Adelaide Road. George and Jane Boiling from Felpham/ Flansham area moved to Chichester, even though he was farm labourer.

Table 12.3   1939 Register, Chichester and Nearby

Chichester

24-28 The Hornet	**Fanny Hughes**	1862-1943	incapacitated
Woolgar's Stores, see Table 12.1			
119 The Hornet	**Frederick Hughes**	1891-1948	house furnisher
	Lilian Hughes	1884-1966	domestic duties
54 Adelaide Street	**Richard Talbot**	1871-1941	gardener
	Fanny Talbot	1865-1942	domestic duties
Jays Croft	**John Slade**	1845-1941	retired (blind)
	Naomi Slade	1866-1954	domestic duties
19 Florence Road	**William Upfield**	1866-1946	farm labourer
	Clara Upfield	1870-1955	domestic duties
5 St James Square	**Gwendoline Curtis**	1917-2003	shop assistant
	Gwendoline married Frank Earwicker in 1940.		

Selsey

Kelowna Beach Road	**Leonard Homer** 1878-1958	fisherman	
	Rose Homer	1886-1950	domestic duties

Bognor Regis

Felpham Road	**James Cowell**	1904-?	coach station cleaner
	Doris Cowell	1906-1973	domestic duties

Although living in a smarter city, the brethren dressed as conservatively as those in the inland villages and must have been noted by locals for their strange ways, though it has been reported that the Woolgar shop was well liked and considered the best on price and service in the locality. Woolgar Sr himself was nicknamed The Bishop, on account of his long beard. Chichester has a long history of non-conformism, into which Woolgar's chapel may have fitted well, other than having to put up with disturbances as recounted above. There were also numerous examples of non-conformist splits and schisms in the mid-nineteenth century. Dependant worship would have fitted this model. There are also strong links to

Funtington (NW of Chichester in the Downs), Selsey, and Felpham. Did John Sirgood or another early preacher visit and hold meetings in these places and perhaps in Chichester itself in the 1870s or early 1880s?

By 1939, the Dependant community in Chichester had shrunk to a small number of families. It is not possible to say if Charlotte Woolgar was in any sense the leader, but it seems likely the shop continued to provide an informal meeting place. She died in 1954, her son Ernest in 1957. Ernest's brother, Harold, who had farmed the family holdings near Chichester, died in 1976. The chapel remained in use beyond 1949. Probably barely in use, it was still named as Dependant Chapel on a map of 1974. An entry in Wikipedia cites its final closure and conversion to residential use in 1975. Fanny Talbot, Doris Cowell, and Gwendoline Earwicker, and possibly Harold Woolgar, were among the last to attend.

Felpham

Just seven of the Felpham community make it into the Loxwood registers. All seven died before the Second World War, which ties in with the end of the chapel's life, c1939. Perhaps the name best known is that of Jim and Eliza Hale. Jim was from the New Forest, moving to Felpham in the 1870s, where he got a job as a carrier, later also a coalman on Flansham Lane, almost next door to where the chapel was built in 1898. Catherine Boiling, who was crippled, lived with them. Dependants Richard and Harriett Cole lived next door. Charlotte Ellen Woolgar, née Boiling, daughter of William Boiling of Felpham, had lived here as a girl.

The Hales moved to Sycamore House next to Felpham School. Their daughter Florence was a dressmaker, and took Keziah Franks, daughter of the miller and elder of the Lordshill, Surrey, community as her apprentice. Jim Hale's neighbours here were George and Esther Boiling. George was a milkman. Other near neighbours were William and Martha Longman. Although there does not seem to have been a shop in Felpham, there were Dependants in business, serving their community, which was always the Dependant way.

Hove

Hove chapel was built much later, the only one in the 20th century (1905).

Table 12.4   The Hove Community
From an anonymous handwritten list, created between 1979 and 1985. It lists those who at some time lived in the Hove/Portslade/Brighton area. All names reliably found in the 1911 census have been removed and are listed in Table 12.5 below, similarly for the 1939 Register in Table 12.6. In the latter, it was sometimes difficult to marry up names and dates, so there are a few discrepancies. This short list is of those remaining who have not been accurately identified.

Mr Ingram d	Mr Mills d	Mr Rusbridge d
Mr Hutchings d	Joseph Randall d	Mr Rusbridge
Mrs Pannell d	Mrs Hoodray d	Miss Burton d
Mrs Steer	Jack Taylor	*Annie Holden d 1925*
Edith Howe d	Mary Lindfield (Rogers)	*Albert Butchers d 1955*
Mrs Brookfield d	Edith Wright d	*Gracie? Fowler d 1937*
Mrs King d	Mrs Hook d	
Mrs Wadey d	Melita ? d	

d - deceased at the time of writing the list. italics – additional unidentified names from the registers.

When the chapel was built, the gridiron streets around it were recently constructed, and it seems likely the chapel was built at the same time. Although the building is clearly not a house on the 1911 OS map, it is not labelled as a chapel either, then or in the 1930s, but finally in 1952 it is labelled "chapel". Curiously, directories refer to it first as a Mission Hall, then as Christian Meeting Room, and finally, catching up again, in 1951 as Dependants Chapel. On balance, it seems certain to have been a Dependant meeting room from 1905.

A list of 65 members of the community was made by a hand unknown probably around 1980 (see Table 12.4). Unfortunately, many of those listed were not given Christian names. Checking them all against the Loxwood registers yielded only a proportion of "hits". This list is nevertheless a remarkable survival of the Hove community, the more so because a collection of Hove letters in West Sussex Record office only survive as torn shreds.

Far from being isolated on the south coast, there were families from Surrey/Sussex border villages who moved there. Henry Greenfield, who became a market gardener, was born in Wisborough Green, Mary in Shalford, Surrey. William Woodford, who became a brewer's van man, and Millie came from Kirdford. James Herrington, a wood dealer, was born in Plaistow, in Kirdford parish, and Phoebe, an Overington, was born in Loxwood, where they had lived. The Luff family came from Northchapel, where George was a baker in Northhapel Stores. Others born in the north of Sussex were Lucy Killner (Warnham), Tom Overington (Rudgwick), Olive and Winifred Pannell (Northchapel), and Annie Candy (Wisborough Green).

Fred Greenfield's travails as a prisoner following his conscientious objection to the call-up in the First World War are discussed in Chapter 2. His working life was a success, owning his own company, which grew from a greengrocer on Boundary Road (the boundary between Hove and Portslade), first listed in a directory in 1934. By 1940, this turned into Greenfield & Sons, removal contractors and storage. It is thought the company vans were still seen around Hove in 1957. See Plate 4.3. Fred died in 1959. He was a family man, married to Edith (Bessie) Russell, daughter of William and Susan Russell, also Dependants in Hove.

Despite many Dependants who were conscientious objectors in the two world wars, research shows some young men were not, either because they rejected their parents' faith, or because of peer and lawful pressure, or a mix of both, or they had joined up before the war (not, however, what one might expect from a Dependant family). Some inevitably died. I am indebted to Judy Middleton, Hove historian, for pointing out to me some possible ones. Frank and Martha Attree, parents of Olive Garman, a lifelong Dependant, lost their son Ernest at the extraordinarily young age of 16. He was a boy sailor in HMS *Hawke*, torpedoed in the North Sea on 15 October 1914. This must have troubled the Dependant community greatly, but in his case, he had joined the Navy, soon after leaving school, in September 1913, well before war became inevitable. It is hard to believe Frank and Martha agreed to this. Three other Attrees from Portslade were killed but it is not thought they were from Dependant families.

Another, much older, was Frederick Candy, son of Albert and Annie Candy. He was born in 1882, so was among the older servicemen. His Royal Field Artillery records show he enlisted as early as 1904 as a territorial in the Home Counties Brigade, RFA, giving his age as 21. He had already been working at the Brighton and Hove gasworks, where his father and at least one brother worked. In the 1901 census he was one of over 60 gas workers in company dormitory accommodation, so he had already left home, and its possible stifling religious atmosphere. A married man, he was killed in France, aged 36, on 20 September 1918, remembered on both the Portslade and the gas company war memorials (see below for more information on the Candy family, and on William Overington, another death in service during the Great War). Henry Nunne's nephew (Ernest, Royal Sussex), like Henry of German ancestry, was also killed on 30 June 1916, but there is no known Dependant connection.

Table 12.5   1911 Census, Hove, Portslade, Brighton, and Southwick and Elsewhere

Hove   Place of birth

3 Worcester Villas	**Walter Hart**	59	coal merchant	Selsey Sx
	Fanny Hart	34		Chichester Sx
	Walter Hart died 1945, funeral & interment at Loxwood, Fanny in 1952.			
2 Marine View,	**Beatrice Browne**	50	private means	London
Kingsway	**Eliza Ingram**	60	private means	Croydon Sy
	Beatrice and Eliza were sisters; Beatrice died in 1938.			
43 Walsingham Road	**Olive Attree**	19	general servant	Portslade Sx
	Frank and Martha's daughter, married Harry Garman, 1919.			
54 Westbourne Villas	**Charlotte Russell**	42	dom servant	Bath Som
	Lucy Killner	16	dom servant	Warnham Sx
92 Sackville Road	**William Russell**	38	coal merchant	Portslade Sx
	Susan Russell	36		Portslade Sx
	William Russell died 1937; Susan in 1946.			
10 Goldstone Road	**Ida Brookfield**	32	tea agent (blind & deaf)	Midhurst Sx
78 Goldstone Villas	**Ruby Taylor**	20	grocer's daughter	Ventnor IoW
13 Ellen Street	**Alfred Woodford**	49	brewer's vanman	Kirdford Sx
	Millie Woodford	48		Kirdford Sx
	Millie Woodford died in 1920.			
20 E St Leonard's Ave	**Thomas Overington**	55	horse feeder for	Rudgwick, Sx
			furniture removals & coal merchant	
	Frances Overington	26		Hassocks Sx
	William Overington	12	school	Hassocks Sx
	Thomas Overington died 1938 at Upper Shoreham Road, funeral & interment in Loxwood.			
9 Livingstone Road	**Frederick Edwards**	41	house painter	Brighton
	Martha Edwards	39		Brighton
17 Grange Road	**Louisa Holder**	22	general servant	Hove
38 Carlisle Road	**Florence Martin**	20	parlour maid	Uckfield Sx
6 St Andrew's Road	**Frank Walker**	29	market gardener	St Leonard's Sx
	Catherine Walker	38		St Leonard's Sx
	[Benjamin Piper	42	company director	Warnham Sx]
	Ben Piper was visiting from Warnham Stores. Frank's two sisters, like him, single, were also part of this household (not known Dependants). Frank Walker died in 1961. Catherine died in 1953.			
7 Westbourne Place	*Thomas Attree*	*74*	*old age pensioner*	*Northiam Sx*
	Jane Attree	*74*	*(blind)*	*Wiltshire*
	Thomas died 1920, Jane died 1911.			
17 Pembroke Avenue	*Olive Pannell*	*22*	*general servant*	*Northchapel Sx*
	Olive Pannell married Charles Taylor in 1912.			
41 Rutland Gardens	*Winifred Pannell*	*20*	*cook*	*Northchapel Sx*
	Sisters, Olive and Winifred, were daughters of Dependants Eli & Harriett.			

Portslade

2 Bampfield Street	**Frank Attree**	43	general labourer	Wiltshire
	Martha Attree	42		Peckham Midsx
14 Norway Street	**Albert Candy**	48	foreman fitter	Wiltshire
	Annie Candy	41		Wisborough Grn Sx
	Kate Candy	12	school	Portslade Sx
	Albert Candy died 1928.			
59 Norway Street	**John Page**	39	carter wood merchant	Burpham Sx
	John Page died 1929.			
59 Norway Street	**Henry (Jim) Clevett**	58	carman for contractor	Clapham Sx
	Sarah Clevett	73		Offham Sx
	Sarah Clevett died 1923, Henry in 1938.			
125 Trafalgar Road	**Henry Greenfield**	52	market gardener	Wisborough Grn Sx
	Mary Greenfield	51		Shalford Sy
	Frederick Greenfield	21	packer	Portslade Sx
	See Plate 2.3. Mary Greenfield died 1930.			
14 Station Road	**James Page**	56	manager coal merchant	Burpham Sx
	Annie Page	51		Watersfield Sx
	Annie Page died 1934.			
17 Franklyn Road	**Henry Nunne**	60	chicken farmer	Germany
	Henry died 1929.			

Brighton

151 Lewes Road	**Elizabeth Parkin**	66	(deaf for 10 years)	Yorkshire
	Elizabeth Parkin died 1913.			
9 Park Crescent	**Annie Hiles**	48	general servant	Lincolnshire
	Annie Hiles died 1929.			
7 Shanklin Road	**Richard Whitehead**	47	telephone wireman	Newport Mon
	Richard Whitehead died 1936			
16 Cromwell Street	**Frederick Kennard**	22	labourer	Brighton

Southwick

2 Butts Road	**Edward Young**	41	tea agent (blind)	Southwick Sx
	Fanny Young	40		Portslade Sx
	Edward Young died 1929.			

Other locations
Northchapel Sx

Northchapel Stores	**Sarah Kennard**	30	housemaid	Glynde Sx
Myrtle Cottage	***George Luff***	*28*	*baker at stores*	*Wisborough Grn Sx*
	Amy Luff	*25*		*Loxwood Sx*
	Amy died in 1937.			
Loxwood Sx village	**James Herrington**	40	wood dealer	Kirdford Sx
	Phoebe Herrington	42	dressmaker	Loxwood Sx

East Chiltington Sx

Chapel Cottage	**Joseph Hunt**	5	school	East Chiltington Sx

Luton Beds

	Sarah Brightman	37	milliner, straw hats	Chiddingfold Sy

Families in italics are those found and added from the Loxwood registers. The table includes some families who had moved away from, or had yet to come to, the coastal conurbation. Where known, the date of death is given for those who did not live until 1939 (see Table 12.6 below).

A web which links all the Dependant communities by blood and marriage can be traced between Hove and South Norwood through the Brightman family. Sarah came to Hove having worked as a milliner in the Luton hat industry. She was a younger sister of James Brightman (see Chapters 4 and 11), one of the founders of the Norwood community, who was a friend of John Sirgood. The family were farmers from Bedfordshire; she was the only child born in Chiddingfold Surrey, perhaps when her father had obtained farm employment there for a brief period, close enough to Dependant communities to have been influenced by them, but Sarah is more likely to have gained her faith from her brother's influence. Some legitimacy could be claimed, as with the Overingtons (below), for this late flowering community from its links with earlier elders.

Bert Candy was another Portslade family man in Norway Street. How did Albert Candy from Wiltshire become the only member of his family in the Loxwood registers? He worked as a gas engine fitter for the Brighton and Hove Gas Company. The explanation lies with his wife Annie who was born in Wisborough Green, probably in Loxwood. In the 1871 census she (a baby) and her mother (Mary Holloway, née Powell) were living with the Powell family on a farm in Chiddingfold, Surrey. Ten years later, she was living with her Holloway grandparents in Rowhook (Warnham). The Powells were also the parents of Ann Powell, one of the founders of the Loxwood Combination Stores (see Chapter 6). This was not the only relationship link between Powells and Holloways: in 1871, Ann Powell was living with her brother-in-law, Mark Holloway, also a Dependant. With this background, Annie had most likely become interested in the Dependant ways. Yet, she moved to Portslade before 1891, as a housekeeper to the man she would marry in 1892, and who already had a family from his first wife. Probably coincidentally, the creation of a Dependant community in Portslade and Hove came about in the next few years, suggesting she was one of the first attenders, maybe even hosting meetings at their house in Clarendon Place, or later in Clarence Street and then Norway Street.

Joseph (Joe) Hunt was one who went in the opposite direction. Unusually for a Dependant, he was married three times. He first married Winifred Herrington from Loxwood in 1933. The couple were married in Hove. She died, I think, in 1946 in Kingston-upon-Thames to where they had moved from Hove before 1939. Did he then return to Hove? He married Mrs Winnie Parsons of Loxwood but not until 1983, finally Kate Pullen in 1991, both marriages in the Chichester Registration District. Had he links with the Chichester community, perhaps? He left Hove (or Chichester) for Loxwood in 1992 (plate12.2), ending his days with Kate at The Retreat, Loxwood. Born in the year the Hove chapel opened, he died in 1994, one of the last Dependants. A compositor by trade, he was proud to have set the print of the Dependants' Hymn Book in 1958.

The elder or leader of the Hove community was Walter Hart, a coal merchant and employer in 1911, who had moved there from Selsey, where he had been a stalwart of the Chichester community, along with his brother, who remained there. It is interesting to discover that several other Hove Dependants worked in the same trade. James Page was a manager of a coal business, William Russell also a coal merchant on his own account. Might Page have worked in Russell's Sackville Street business, or for Hart? Of the three, only Russell was a local man.

Walter Hart was perhaps asked, persuaded, we do not know, to go to Hove when the chapel opened, and soon married Fanny Edwards, his housekeeper, much younger than him. They

Plate 12.2 Hove People and Businesses

26th April, 1954

Dr. to

Terms: Cash on Delivery

Phone: Hove 48221
Hove 47295

Greenfield & Sons (Hove) Ltd.

Orders by Post or Telephone will receive Prompt Attention

Directors: F. C. Greenfield E. E. Greenfield

REMOVAL & STORAGE CONTRACTORS

89/101 BOUNDARY ROAD, WEST HOVE

Any Distance Any Load

Expert attention Low charges

Our service covers Britain

Part loads also wanted

For Removal from Hove to Olive Road Hove.	£	3 0 0
Paid deposit.		1 0 0
Balance.	£	2 0 0

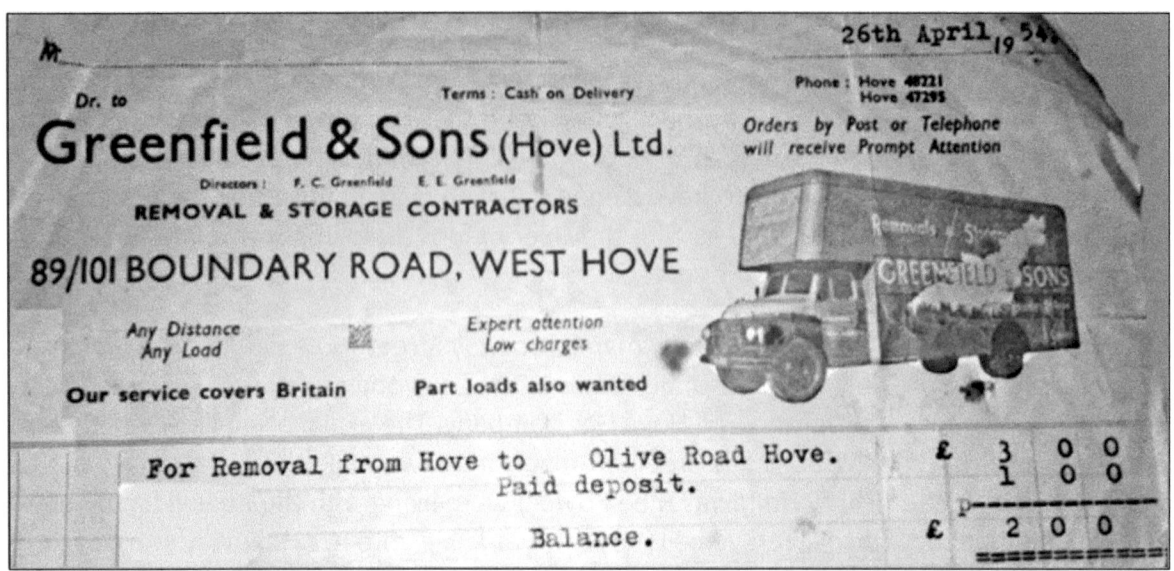

Fig 1 – Fred Greenfield, 1898-1959, became a successful businessman. This invoice is dated 1954. How times have changed – removals for £2! See also Plate2.3.
Ack: Judy Middleton, © H Bardsley.

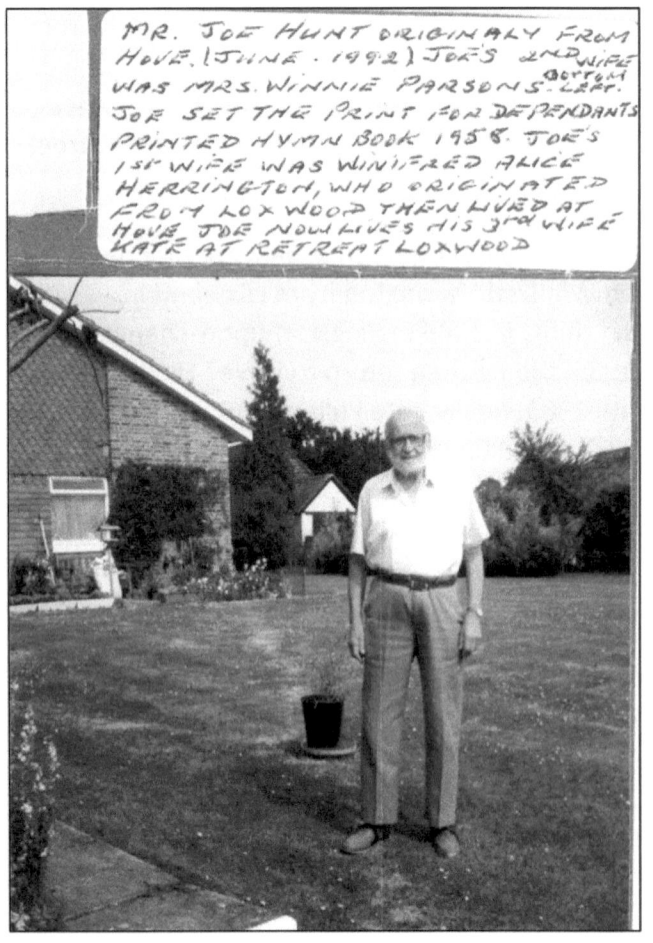

Fig 2 – Joe Hunt, 1905-1994, was the last of those associated with the Hove community to die, but he had only spent a small part of his life there, during his first marriage. Here, in 1992, he is pictured at The Retreat, Loxwood. His wife is not in the photo, despite the annotation suggesting she is! He is an important part of Dependant history as the typesetter for the 1958 hymn book.

Fig 3 – right, Joe Hunt's second wife, Winnie Parsons. He married her after the death of Ron Parsons, a Loxwood Dependant.

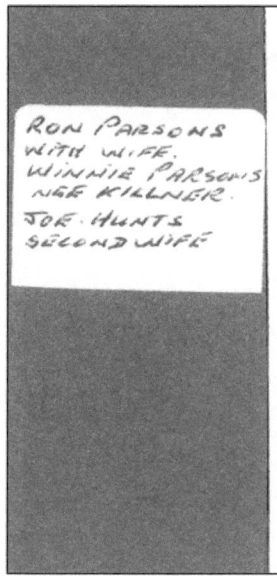

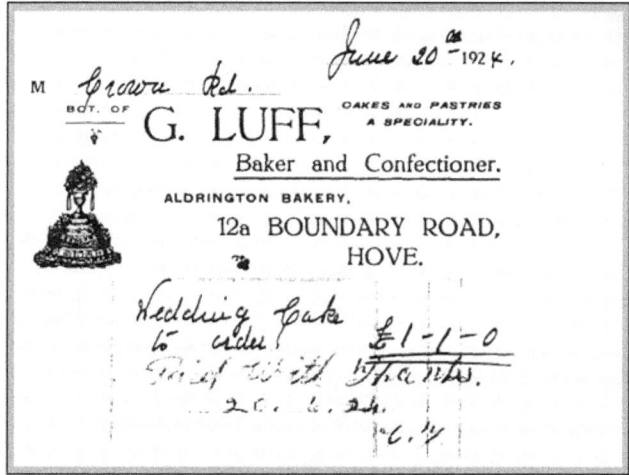

Fig 4 – left, George Luff, 1882-1948, was a baker with experience of working at Northchapel. He was not related to the Warnham Luffs. This invoice is dated 1924. *Ack: Judy Middleton.*

Fig 5 - above, an unnamed 'bath chair man' in Queen's Gardens, Hove; both Henry Nunne and James Page were 'bath chair men'. *Ack: Judy Middleton.*

Fig 6 – left, Olive Garman (née Attree) from Hove, born in Portslade, with her older husband, Harry, in Loxwood.

set up home in Worcester Villas, Portslade, the next-door suburban village where many of the Hove community seem to have lived. On the date of the 1911 census, they were able to include their second child, a boy, unnamed, 4 days old (soon given his father's name of Walter). There is no evidence of the Hart children remaining in the community as adults. The chapel was one railway stop to the east, and certainly in walking distance (1 mile). He became an undertaker later, previously a furniture dealer when in Chichester. Did this bring him into contact with the Warnham Dependants' furniture specialists? A recorded connection with Warnham was the visit being made by Lindfield, Luff director, Benjamin Piper, to Frank Walker and his sisters, Catherine, and Eleanor, at St Andrew's Road, also in Portslade. Walter died in 1945, aged 92, and was buried in Loxwood. What role, if any, the Walkers played in the community is not known. They have not been found in the area in 1939.

It seems appropriate to follow Walter Hart with one of the most significant members of the Hove community, Thomas Henry Overington, born in Rudgwick in 1855 to Thomas and Ann Overington of Loxwood. As a small boy he lived with his parents next door to John Sirgood in Spy Lane, Loxwood. Tom and Ann were described in Chapter 4, where it was shown that they were both elders of the community, Tom conducting many funerals in the Loxwood chapel, Ann teaching children and writing letters. Thomas Henry seems to have moved on as a teenager, first to a local farm worked by another Dependant, then to Keymer (Hassocks), Sussex where he spent many years working on the railway. He had married Mary Pullen, a local Wisborough Green girl from a Dependant family, in 1881. He first appears in Hove aged 55 in the 1911 census as a widower with a daughter in her twenties and a son of 12 at school. His occupation was horse feeder for a furniture remover and coal merchant, which immediately suggests employment by his fellow Dependants. Tom Junior lived in Hove until his death in 1938, aged 83. Evidence points to him still being committed to the community after his years away. He was given a funeral and burial in Loxwood, one of the few Walter Hart conducted. His was one of thirteen Overington burials in Loxwood, from 1868 to 1954.

Tom's son, William, who was born in 1899, turning 18 in 1918, was just of an age to be conscripted into the army to serve in the Great War. Despite his family history, he was not a conscientious objector. Sadly, his short period of service ended with his death on 24 August 1918 during the final push into Germany. Private 36360 Overington, serving with 8th East Surreys, gave his address on joining as Shamley Green, Surrey, the parish of the Lordshill community. So, had he given up the faith of his grandfather's family or not? We shall never know. His name is recorded on the Loxwood War Memorial in St John the Baptist church. His remains lie in the CWGC plot in Berlin Southwestern Cemetery at Stahnsdorf. Bodies of servicemen who died all over Germany were brought here in the 1920s, or if no remains, their death is commemorated here. That he is commemorated in Loxwood, rather than in Hassocks, Shamley Green or Hove is telling – but telling of what? After the war, his father lived with James Page (possibly his employer in his coal business) at 43 Payne Avenue, close to the chapel. School records reveal Tom and the two eldest boys, Ernest and Leonard, were in Loxwood from late 1891 to 1902. The boys joined the village school there from a school in Hassocks. To investigate this further, the war service, if any, of older siblings were investigated. The eldest boy, Horace, served in the Duke of Cornwall's Light Infantry, but records are scanty. Before the war, Horace Overington had returned to his family roots, working as a baker, possibly at the Combination Stores, Loxwood, where he lodged with

Table 12.6   **1939 Register, Hove, Portslade, Brighton and Elsewhere**

<u>Hove</u>

3 Grange Road	**Alfred Woodford**	1861-1951	lorry driver (retired)
	Sarah Kennard	1880-1951	housekeeper

Sarah Kennard moved to Loxwood; died in hospital Midhurst; funeral and interment at Loxwood.

10 Goldstone Road	**Ida Brookfield**	1878-1959	(deaf, dumb and blind)
68 The Drive	**Louisa Holder**	1887-1967	house maid
84 Boundary Road	**Henry Greenfield**	1859-1946	greengrocer (retired)
55 Boundary Road	**Frederick Greenfield**	1898-1959	managing director, Greenfield &
	See Plate 2.3		Sons Hove Ltd, removals & storage
	Edith Bessie Greenfield	1900-1983	housekpr, coy director, office work
15 Boundary Road	***George Luff***	*1882-1948*	*baker (widowed, retired)*
66 Byron Street	**James Page**	1856-1947	bath chair man (widowed, retired)

James moved to Loxwood and was buried & interred there.

40 Glebe Villas	**James Herrington**	1870-1940	wood merchant (retired)
	Phoebe Herrington	1867-1953	domestic duties
191 Elm Drive	**Sarah Brightman**	1873-1961	milliner (retired)
	Annie Goldsmith	1866-?	independent (widowed)

<u>Portslade</u>

1 High Street	**Walter Hart**	1852-1945	undertaker (retired)
	Fanny Hart	1877-1952	domestic duties

Walter, funeral & interment at Loxwood

14 Norway Street	**Annie Candy**	1870-1952	domestic duties (widowed)
	Kate Candy	1899-1985	daily domestic

<u>Brighton</u>

24 Hampden Road	**Frederick Kennard**	1889-1974	permanent way (railway) worker
121 Down Terrace S	**Emily South**	1913-1979	domestic duties

<u>Southwick</u>

79 St Aubyn's Road	**Olive Taylor**	1888-1976	domestic duties (widowed)
151 Albion Street	**George Remnant**	1890-1955	milk roundsman
	Winifred Remnant	1890-1975	domestic duties

<u>Shoreham-by-Sea</u>

16 West Street	**Fanny Young**	1871-1944	domestic duties (widowed)

<u>Other Locations</u>
<u>Bosham, Chichester</u>

Rosemary Salthill Rd	**Frank Attree**	1867-1959	furniture remover (retired)
	Martha Attree	1868-1955	domestic duties

Frank died in Loxwood; funeral & interment in Loxwood

<u>Loxwood Sx</u>

Hillcrest Vicarage Hill	**Harry Garman**	1875-1966	head gardener

<u>Plaistow Sx</u>

The Orchard Ifold	**Florence Martin**	1892-1980	unpaid domestic

Florence Martin died at New Church Road Hove in 1980; funeral & interment in Loxwood

<u>Hassocks Sx</u>

Sunkist Brighton Rd	**Frederick Edwards**	1875-1950	house painter (retired)
	Martha Edwards	1873-1956	domestic duties
	Olive Garman	1891-1979	domestic duties

Olive Garman, funeral & interment at Loxwood

<u>Kingston-upon-Thames Sy</u>

10 Fassett Avenue	**Joseph Hunt**	1905-1994	compositor
	Winifred Hunt	1903-1946	

David Thayre, another Loxwood Dependant. Of the other two sons, Ernest may have died in the Loxwood area in 1909. Leonard appears not to have served, but in 1911 he too was boarding in Loxwood and working as a grocer's assistant, again, possibly at the Combination Stores, perhaps since leaving school.

Another connection with the Overington family was made when Phoebe Herrington (see above) moved, with husband James, from Loxwood to Hove. She was born an Overington. When Obed Overington's probate was declared in 1906, James Herrington was one of his executors, Phoebe being his daughter. Obed was brother to Tom Sr. There were several Herringtons in Loxwood and the Plaistow district of Kirdford, who were early converts.

Henry Nunne is of interest as a German national who lived in Portslade in 1911, a chicken farmer on his own account. Ten years previously he had lived in Aldrington, working as a bath chair man, also on his own account, living with his brother August, who was a window cleaner, and his wife and family. Henry died in 1929. The Dependants' connections with Germany, detailed in Chapter 4, occurred later, in the 1930s.

Sarah Kennard, born near Lewes, may be unique to Hove in that as a younger woman (1911 census) she was a housemaid in the Northchapel Stores community, alongside her elder sister, May. Their father, Jim, was a Dependant who was living in South Norwood at his death in 1936, but who had earlier moved to Falmer, near Brighton. Their mother was Sarah Lindfield, possibly related to the Lindfield family of Lindfield, Luff & Co, Warnham Stores. By 1939, Sarah was housekeeper to a Hove Dependant and widow, George Woodford. However, like other Kennards, she moved to Loxwood, ending her life in Jubilee Villas, Dependant-owned properties next to the Combination Stores. She was buried in Loxwood on her death in 1951. Of her large family, William and Alice, younger siblings, were also Dependants; William lived in Cromwell Street Brighton in 1911 and 1939. Alice had joined the South Norwood community at Norwood Stores by 1911. She was still working there in 1939.

Emily South, living in Brighton as a widowed housekeeper to Fred Kennard in 1939, was married twice, (1) Arthur South, a painter, 1907-30, and (2) in 1951, to Robert Mitchell, a labourer, 1913-97 (revealed as an amendment in the register which was used for official purposes into the early 1950s).

In 1911, there were 16 identified households in Hove, seven in Portslade, four in Brighton and one in Southwick. In addition, there were three in the north of Sussex who lived in the coastal conurbation at some time. In 1939, from a smaller sample, the numbers were Hove nine, Portslade seven, Brighton four and Southwick two. Norway Street in Portslade (three households in 1911, one in 1939) stands out as a locale of note, as does Boundary Road, three in 1939. Overall, this is a huge urban area, so it is unlikely there would be a strong pattern emerging from this small sample. There was no store around which to cluster. Walking to chapel would have been possible from a wide area. One other observation: the ageing of the community is apparent from the number of retired people, which, including spouses, is about 16, roughly half the sample. In 1911, no more than five would have come into this category. In 1911, fewer than a dozen were born in the coastal towns. There were few new names by 1939.

Chapter 13

Review and Commentary:

Musings from Newspapers, Magazines

and Other Publications

The earliest references must be the two tracts that John Sirgood himself wrote in answer to his critics in the 1860s, discussed in Chapter 1. There was at least one newspaper that picked up on the story. Unsurprisingly it was a non-conformist journal.

The Non-Conformist, 26 June 1861
Under the headline, *Attempt to Prevent Lay Preaching in Sussex*, it went straight to the notice handed to John Sirgood in March of that year. Much of its content, including Rev Rogers reply was reprinted in full. Undoubtedly, this brought the matter to a wider audience.

Empire (Sydney, NSW), 1 November 1861
In an article entitled Religious Intolerance, *"we bespeak our reader's attention to the story of the Shoemaker of Loxwood"*. The story was indeed told in a riveting way, all culled from Sirgood's *Intolerance in the Rural Districts of West Sussex* and ended with the exhortation to contribute a brick to the chapel about to be built. *"It was bruited* abroad, an interest has been excited in the little cause at Loxwood, which has resulted in the determination to build a chapel there. A piece of ground has been obtained …."* Unsurprisingly, at this distance, there was a tone of incredulity that the English could be so bigoted. It must be supposed that the comments quoted were based on an English newspaper that had been circulated, otherwise how could the writer have known there was a chapel being constructed in Loxwood?
*Bruit – to spread a rumour.

West Sussex Gazette, 5 January 1864
See also Chapter 3. Under the headline *Brawling at Loxwood Chapel*, Frederick Standen, on the information of James Hampshire, was charged with riotous, violent and indecent behaviour at a service led by John Sirgood. As with other such articles, and events, the accused had been causing problems for a couple of years. On this occasion, he and friends including Henry Bridger were laughing, giggling, talking and using his handkerchief to wipe his and their noses and fling the dirty item on the floor, apparently very funny. They stayed for the whole service, nearly 3 hours, and then Edward Fuller blocked the exit, was pushed out and then struck Hampshire. James Reeves was a second witness, Charles Kitchener a third. PC William Tribe stated he had never been inside, and therefore had seen nothing untoward, but that there had been complaints over the last two years. Standen was fined £2 plus costs, or prison, and Fuller £1 plus costs. Both paid. This is an example of newspaper accounts of one of the earliest trials for bad behaviour towards the Dependants at worship.

West Sussex Gazette, unknown date, 1864
In 1864, in the same article as the one cited for Cocklers (below), the alternative of 'Cuckolders' was used. This potentially opens a contentious area of discussion around relationships. Jerrome, in *John Sirgood's Way*, picks up on this. He writes that accusations were commonly made of free love. This usage, however, pre-dates the Combination Stores where such accusations might have made some sense, even if wrongly placed. Admittedly, the sect was already known for its disinterest in marriage.

However, the author's research has found evidence from successive census addresses for cottages at Cuckolds Corner. Moreover, the 1875-6 Ordnance Survey map names the corner cottages on the later site of New Songhurst Farm. Furthermore, one was home up to the 1870s to Obadiah and Ruth, parents of Tom, John, Jane, and Obed Overington, the first two named Loxwood elders, and was but a field or two away from the location of the chapel in Spy Lane. By 1881, with both elderly couples who had lived there for many years now deceased, the cottages were noted 'unoccupied', but one appeared occupied for the last time in 1891.

There were cottages in this area, close to both New Songhurst and to Merry Hills, as shown on old maps such as Yeakell, Gardner and Gream's map of 1795 (this showed the roads as they were before the turnpike to Alfold Crossways was built in 1757). A caveat should be made: this map's accuracy cannot be guaranteed. On it, the old 'king's highway' followed the western and northern edges of Loxwood (Spy) Common, swinging up Merry Hills Lane (now a private road) and, significantly, turning sharp left, as it still does today, in the far northern corner of the common – a corner in two senses. By the time the more accurately surveyed 1st Edition Ordnance Survey map was made, soon after 1800, as well as the turnpike there was a track to Cuckolds Corner crossing the eastern side of the common direct from the future site of the Dependants' chapel. The Cuckolds Corner cottages were clearly marked, but not named.

The cottages stood on the edge of the common, as is frequently observed in many manorial commons. Those who lived there would have been among the poorest 'squatters', perhaps with rights of common, up to its enclosure in 1830. Their houses would only have survived by good fortune, and certainly not if the landowner (Loxwood House estate) wished to replace them with a new farm, as at New Songhurst, or sell land for a new mansion house, Merry Hills, built in the 1870s for Robinson Smallpiece.

It is therefore entirely possible that local people made a strong association between the Dependant meetings and the Overington home. Perhaps meetings took place there in the 1850s. Perhaps John Sirgood stayed there. However, this is not as strong a case as it seems. Firstly, neither of the Overington parents were known to be Dependants. Secondly, both Tom and John were living away from home by the 1850s. Tom was in Tisman's Common, Rudgwick in 1851. He married Ann Reeves soon after. They set up home in Spy Lane. John joined his brother in Tisman's Common and was there into the 1860s, before returning to live at Hall House. The Cuckolders name remains an oddity, but an intriguing alternative to Cokeler.

Jerrome may have been confused about the Overington home as he suggests Four Houses, a little nearer Alfold on the turnpike, one of a group of cottages, where Dependants Stephen and Charlotte Overington lived. Stephen may have been Obadiah's brother.

Hastings and St Leonard's Observer, 1 March 1873
The searchable National Newspaper Archive, an archive of mainly regional papers (also available at findmypast.com), has turned up several articles not previously noted, which are dealt with in date order. The earliest is from the Hastings and St Leonard's Observer, 1 March 1873 and has several unexpected and useful references. Unsurprisingly at this early

date it was about persecution, but it used the popular name of Cokelers in its modern spelling, and most interestingly it reported an event at Southwater, near Horsham, in a cottage which was a registered place of worship.

The author has known for a long time that some of his distant relatives from Southwater and Nuthurst became Cokelers, or Dependants, but had, until this discovery, no proof of any worship in that locality. The only name mentioned in the article is that of Mark Covey, who is stated to have expounded the reading from the Bible, the usual Dependant testimony. Covey was born in Wisborough Green in 1837 and died in Chichester, probably living at Roundstreet Common south of Loxwood in 1915. He was buried in the Loxwood chapel graveyard. He spent his entire life working on farms in that area, so must have been asked to go to Southwater to lead this service, a typical request in the early history of the sect.

It is possible that the meeting, which was described as "very small", about 10-12 worshippers, included Michael Killner, an agricultural labourer living in Southwater Street at this time, with his wife and a younger son, Thomas, a carpenter. Michael had moved to Warnham by the time of the next census in 1881. Michael was father of several known Dependants who had left Southwater before 1873: Henry, who had already moved to work with Richard Nightingale at Stone Farm, Warnham; Michael, also in Warnham at Malt Mayes Farm; Sally, in service in Brighton, later to join her brother Henry; Walter, who had moved to Betchetts Farm, Warnham with relatives, the Sayers family, also Dependants. Another son, Stephen died in Southwater in 1870, but was buried at Loxwood. Descendants of Michael Killner were among the last Dependants alive in Loxwood.

Was this meeting in the Killner's cottage, perhaps? Did they move to Warnham, where the chapel was being built in 1873 to open the next year, to escape this harassment? The persecution in Southwater was by two boys who entered the house, giggled during the testimony, and released three birds during the meeting. They were accused of "the sin of interruption" by Covey. The boys when summoned to the bench were let off with a caution.

North Britain, 3 October 1875
This could have been culled from any number of newspapers across the land; the story went viral. *Disturbing a Congregation of Bible Christians* offered a glimpse into the beginnings of a Dependant group in Chichester which had apparently not yet taken the name. The leader Michael Woolgar had arranged a meeting in the Oddfellows Hall before there was a chapel in the town. The usual disturbances created by a man called (appropriately) Biles, involving missiles, cayenne pepper, talking through the service, and insults hurled at Woolgar, were however not enough for a successful prosecution.

Sussex Agricultural Express, 6 November 1883, and 6 July 1889
On the first date there was no prosecution, just a warning. A similar event and accusations with cries of *"You red hot hypocrite"*, this time in the new chapel on Adelaide Road, was decided on with a fine of £40. The man's name was Welcome, even if he wasn't.

West Surrey Times and County Express, 24 October 1885
An obituary for John Sirgood appeared in the West Surrey Times and County Express, 24 October 1885, which confirms that he died at the Combination Stores, Loxwood, *"a branch grocery establishment"*, and suggests the number of adherents to be about 1000. It also

referred to the sect as 'Cocoalers' but says little about either Sirgood or the Dependants. *The Brighton Gazette, 26 October 1885*, is quoted at the end of Chapter 1.

West Sussex Gazette, 10 June 1897
A letter in reply to a short note in the previous issue about whether there were any Coglers left alive in Kirdford was sent by someone who clearly knew Dependants, who tried to explain why they were Cokelers and not Coglers, using the most common reason relating to cocoa consumption, and poopooing the notion of Antimonianism* being central to their faith. The writer knew of the two pamphlets published by Sirgood to refute criticism, and praised the Dependants for their character as upright, honourable, and industrious people. The editor added to this a paragraph from the Daily Mail in which the origin of the Book of Cople story seems to have emerged, and which was spreading, as the next item explains.

(Greek anti, "against"; nomos, "law"), doctrine according to which Christians are freed by grace from the necessity of obeying the Law of Moses. The antinomians rejected the very notion of obedience as legalistic; to them the good life flowed from the inner working of the Holy Spirit. In this circumstance they appealed not only to Martin Luther but also to Paul and Augustine. [Encyclopaedia Britannica]. It has been said the Dependants, did not accept the concept of the Holy Trinity, therefore not that of the Holy Spirit. However, in Plate 12.1, fig 2, the 1958 Hymn Book contradicts this, perhaps a change in thinking over time.

Hampshire Telegraph and Sussex Chronicle, 13 November 1897
One of the odder explanations of Dependant nickname, Cokeler, in its various spellings, was the one quoted in the Hampshire Telegraph and Sussex Chronicle on 13 November 1897. It asserted that they were called Cogelors because of their veneration of the Book of Cople *"which lays down certain rules for life and worship"*. It went on to say Cokeler is a corruption of Copler (the names given to the Dependants are explained in the Introduction to this book – The Book of Cople did not exist). According to this source, Sirgood came from Walworth, where it states there were still meetings in 1897. Walworth lies just east of Kennington (where the Sirgoods lived at their marriage), so this is of interest. The supposed existence of meetings in this part of London is worthy of note, true or false. Interestingly, in view of the importance of farming, notably in Loxwood, the article also referred to a Dependant farm at Loxwood as early as 1897, where is unknown, in addition to a "co-operative" shop.

National Review, September 1904
1904 was a vintage year for unwanted attention in the press. Irish peer, Viscount Turnour, soon to become Earl Winterton, contributed an article to the National Review. In that year, he was also elected to the House of Commons, where he would make a name for himself as a politician and government minister, serving as Conservative MP for Horsham (with varying boundaries) from 1904 to 1951, a very long innings.

In *The Cokelers: A Sussex Sect*, Turnour includes Lurgashall in his list of parishes, which is accurate as the Enticknap, Pullen and Spooner families, to name but three, came from here. He included Lodsworth in one corner of a western Low Weald triangle of remote woods, commons, and fields with Plaistow and Northchapel, and as such was prime Sirgood territory. Lurgashall lies in the west of this area, and Roundhurst, a tiny hamlet, is referred to in one of Sirgood's hymns. Turnour's best effort at numbers is 900 and shrinking (he agrees with the figure given at the time of Sirgood's death, 2000), though claiming one third of the total population [of adults?] in Wisborough Green and Northchapel.

PLATE 13.1 Miscellaneous Media

Fig 1 – The article quoted by numerous other writers by Earl Winterton MP of Shillinglee Park, Plaistow in Sussex County Magazine, November 1931.

Foreword

THE compilers of this Hymn Book wish to give thanks to Almighty God, Father, Son and Holy Spirit, for the wonderful way that the writers of the hymns have been led to express their praises, prayers, thanksgivings and the histories of the people of God throughout the ages.

They commend them to all men and women of goodwill and pray that God's richest blessing may be on all who read or sing these hymns.

They believe that most of these hymns have never been published previously and wish to express their thanks for being now allowed to use them in this way. Should they have infringed any copyright they ask forgiveness and will in any subsequent edition make acknowledgment of same.

This compilation has been undertaken with the authority of "The Dependents" Loxwood, Sussex, and published in the year of our Blessed Saviour, one thousand, nine hundred and fifty-eight.

ENTERED AT STATIONERS HALL

Fig 2 – the Foreword to the Dependant Hymn Book, 1958.

Fig 3 – two ladies in The Retreat, Loxwood, provided information for an article headed The Gentle Folk published sometime between 1984 and 1992 in an unknown publication.

Two of the few remaining Cokelers Miss Memilo Pyke and Miss Molly Farquhar at home at The Retreat, Loxwood.

Fig 4 – above right, 1885 a report of a Big Meeting, weeks before the death of John Sirgood.

LOXWOOD.

THAT PECULIAR SECT, known as "Cokelers," held a regular field day, on Bank Holiday, at the Chapel in Spy Lane. There was a large number of Brethren from various other stations: and public meetings were held morning, afternoon, and evening. These were presided over by the Rev. J. Sirgood, supported by Rev. J. Overington and others. The meetings were carried on in a similar way to the Salvation Army. There were upwards of 300 persons present.

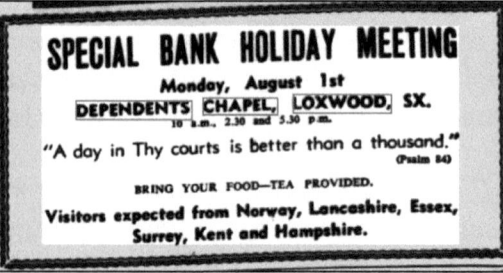

SPECIAL BANK HOLIDAY MEETING
Monday, August 1st
DEPENDENTS CHAPEL, LOXWOOD, SX.
10 a.m., 2.30 and 5.30 p.m.
"A day in Thy courts is better than a thousand." (Psalm 84)
BRING YOUR FOOD—TEA PROVIDED.
Visitors expected from Norway, Lancashire, Essex, Surrey, Kent and Hampshire.

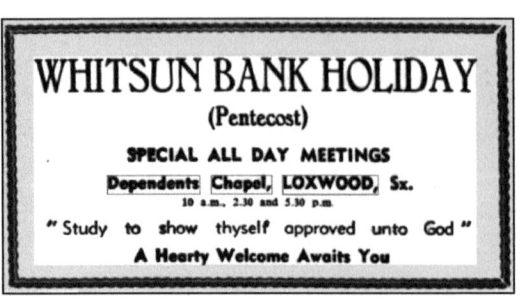

WHITSUN BANK HOLIDAY
(Pentecost)
SPECIAL ALL DAY MEETINGS
Dependents Chapel, LOXWOOD, Sx.
10 a.m., 2.30 and 5.30 p.m.
" Study to show thyself approved unto God "
A Hearty Welcome Awaits You

Fig 5 – left, 1920s, an advert, the Big Meeting at the Whit Bank Holiday.

Fig 6 – right, a similar advert from 1955 for the August Bank Holiday. The three show how Big Meetings have been a longstanding tradition.

Fig 7 – in 2003 Marion May organised a successful exhibition of Cokeler artefacts, photographs, etc.

Ack: findmypast.com (figs 3-6).

Religion and way of life now lost

Lord Hill Stores, in the late 1920s. It was run by members of The Dependants, known locally as The Cokelers.

An exhibition on the life of a small religious group called The Dependants, once based on the Surrey/Sussex border, opens at Salters Gallery in Castle Street, Guildford, on Saturday, August 6. It will be staged by Marion May. Here she outlines the life of the society that was also known as The Cokelers.

FEW people today will have heard of The Dependants (Dependant on Christ) whose religion and way of life is now lost forever. Founded in the 1850s by a shoemaker, John Sirgood, the Society of Dependants established small religious communities on the

The founder of The Society of Dependants, John Sirgood

At Northchapel Stores Turnour found 13 employees behind the counters, not counting other workers, and at Warnham a total number of 31. Turnour begins a trend among writers in discussing their honesty, industry, and clean-living rather than adopting the patronising tone of earlier writers, and of those who had opposed the Dependants orally and in writing in the early days. But he it is who gives credence to rules such as 'no flowers' – picked up immediately.

In 1914, *Sussex Archaeological Collections Vol 56, pp161-191*, John C Buckwell wrote an exhaustive and superbly researched history of Loxwood in which he discusses seven properties still in the hands of Loxwood church (the parish church). Among these was "a croft formerly named Cokkes, near the Manor Pond at Loxwood, but now known as Pond Field, numbered 224 on the map". He traced these fields back to a conveyance of 1531, and several others over the following century.

In appointing trustees in 1615, the field is referred to as tenements and a garden, suggesting houses built thereon. The spelling Cokkes is consistent throughout. Plot 224 on the 1879 Ordnance Survey map, which Buckwell must have been using, is the field immediately behind the Combination Stores. The site of the Combination Stores was in Plot 225, the irregular shape of which strongly suggests it might have been carved out of a larger field, which with 223 to the south of the pond, would locate the original Cokkes croft as <u>all</u> the land around the pond in the corner of the roads to Alfold and Rudgwick.

However, a map in Buckwell's essay on which he has helpfully named Plot 224, also shows that Plot 224 was part of a pre-19th century enclosure of Loxwood Common being nearly all of the land in the triangle made by Guildford Road, Station Road and Spy Lane, which must have been allotted to, among others, the church trustees, at an earlier date than 1615. Now, the plot on which the Combination Stores were built (225), and Plot 223 were to remain part of the common until the Loxwood Parliamentary Inclosure Award of 1830. It looks very much as though Rose Cottage, still on the site (225) today, was a squatter's cottage on the edge of the common, hence its irregular shaped garden, regularised as an allotment in 1830. The pair of cottages now on plot 223, and several others down the hill, are Victorian, so must have been built on other allotments made in 1830 when Chapel Green was enclosed. None of this would detract from the observation above that Cokkes included, historically, and in oral tradition, the land on which the Combination Stores were built. Of course, the name Cokelers goes back further than the foundation of the Combination Stores, but what if the cottage now called Rose Cottage was an early meeting house? What if Cokkes Field itself was used for meetings? Old maps show it to be secluded, with an entrance off Chapel Green (Station Road). Either theory might describe the folks who met at Cokkes, the 'Cocklers' *(West Sussex Gazette, 1864),* the Cokelers. One other fact needs to be remembered from early on in this history. Opposite the Stores is Hall House which itself gained a strip of land in the front garden as an allotment in 1830, when the owner was John Hemming, an auctioneer. It is not known if the term Cokeler originated in Loxwood. The Leconfield Estate papers consistently refer to 'Coglers', yet another spelling, perhaps recognising the speech of local folk, maybe simply a rendering of Cocklers in the vernacular. The 1874/5 OS map refers to "chapel (Coglers)". As Tourner rightly says, "It is a most remarkable thing that no one can satisfactorily explain the origin of a name only 50 years old [in1904]".

Turnour was in no doubt that the combination of farming with the stores was already part and parcel of the latter's success. He writes, *"The Cokeler farmers sell their butter, milk, bacon, eggs, etc., at their local stores, a state of affairs which one may call 'Free Trade within the Empire', since not only do the Cokelers themselves supply the stores with provisions to sell, but they obtain nearly all their necessities of life from the same source".* He goes on (bearing in mind he was a candidate for Parliamentary election at the time) to discuss how much better the "farming interest" would be improved in this country if they adopted this system of stores, especially near the towns. He regarded Cokeler tenants as sought after for their collective and mutual help, industriousness and lack of distraction.

The Evening News, 31 August 1904
A short piece entitled *"Strange Sect of Sussex Puritons",* based on Turnour's article.

Portsmouth Evening News, 31 August 1904
Inevitably, the provincial press also quickly picked up on the National Review article. In this newspaper, the article was brief, but highlighted several of the more unusual aspects of the Dependants – Cokelers who drink cocoa, no flowers, no marriage. *"In all their villages, they run stores, which even let a motor car out on hire."*

The Times, 21 October 1904
The Times picked up the National Review article too, in the context of the General Election, reporting from Horsham about the likelihood of the votes of the 400-500 Dependants (men only, of course) going to the Liberals or the Conservatives, or abstention. The reporter opted for the last, as he probably rightly considered the Dependants a lost cause politically speaking, not for apathy, but for lack of interest in controversy. The Times questioned whether the Dependants' interest in combination for trade in their stores (and the tendency of all non-conformists to vote (Liberal), might make them lean towards the politics of

Chamberlain who was fighting for "free trade within the Empire". Implicit in the report is that Lord Turnour had written his article just before an election with votes in mind, or perhaps it was part of his homework in getting to know his potential constituency better. Whatever the reason, he was already resident at Shillinglee in Plaistow, in the heart of Dependant country, and must have known some of them as estate workers and tenants.

Western Times, 26 June 1907
In the way of provincial newspapers of the time, obscure and frankly uninteresting news, to our eyes, was passed around the country, so that a columnist in the west country might discuss the strange Christian sects and religions to be found in London, in a column headed *'London by Day and by Night'*, as also had the papers in New South Wales (above). On this day, following lengthy matters under discussion in government and Parliament, the correspondent turned to the International Conference of the Evangelical Alliance, which in turn became musings on the 300 Christian sects in London, alongside such sentences as *"The Parsees worship the sun in Bloomsbury"*. Referring to the Cokelers, it described *"the disciples of William [sic] Sirgood, the Walworth shoemaker"*. From other examples given, Dependants were not the only sect to get this patronising treatment.

Worthing Gazette, 22 March 1916
In *Sussex by the Sea*, a regular and thoughtful column, the writer discussed conscientious objection at some length. Central to his theme (and with a bias towards the national cause) were the various Dependants who had come before the Horsham or Petworth tribunals determining military service exemption. He showed there was concern in Dependant circles that the document provided for each Dependant CO was not being seen by the members of the board at hearings. This was a copy of the 'memorial' sent to the Prime Minister before conscription was introduced. The Petworth board responded it had indeed seen it, and that several men had been allowed non-combatant rôles. Two had appealed on the grounds that they might have to serve in hospitals near the front in army control. This did not impress the columnist.

Lancashire Evening Post, 3 July 1920
In a column called *Men and Matters*, headlined *The Ways of the Dependants*, this paper lets on that it followed up on an article by FE Green in a journal called *The Nineteenth Century*. This may have stimulated the next two articles as well. In this paper the story of Sirgood and the establishment of numerous chapels is rehearsed, and it goes on to discuss the economics of running shops for the common good, Sirgood's socialist tendencies based on the Sermon on the Mount. Far from worshipping money these are people who close the shops for prayer and sing psalms on the way to chapel. A reduction by half, to 1000, on the alleged 2000 who mourned at Sirgood's funeral was partly attributed to holding the unmarried woman *"in higher esteem than those who have suffered the martyrdom of marriage"*.

Birmingham Daily Gazette, 3 August 1920
"Monday, Loxwood Sussex. The Holiest People in the World, Strange Vigil of Prayer in a Sussex Village". This described an August Bank Holiday 3-day Big Meeting (Plate 13.1) with the chapel overfull and visitors from other communities. The writer rehearsed all the usual content, partly from talking to Mr Bernard Hempstead, who had been in Loxwood for 10

PLATE 13.2   Newspaper Illustrations

Fig 1 – the earliest photographic illustration found was from 1926, when the now defunct Daily Chronicle used this photo of three Loxwood women in traditional dress, above the caption "members of an anti-marriage sect".

Fig 2 – in 1931, the Sunday Express sent a photographer to Loxwood chapel to capture arrivals for a service. They could not spell 'Cokeler'. "No cars" was patently untrue, as the Loxwood community had a thriving garage.

Fig 3 – in 1982, the end was indeed nigh (just 32 alive, if Mr Miller can be believed). Yet again the article features Loxwood. The muddle in referring to the Dependants as Peculiar People will have come about because Rowland Leswell (Chapter 7) was a former member of the Essex church.

Dying days of a secret sect

by Ray Miller

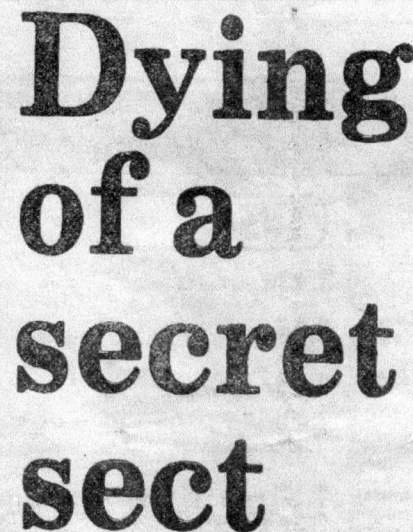

GOD, they say, moves in mysterious ways. And in the whole wide world there can be few stranger moves than those of a religious sect hidden away in the sleepy Sussex village of Loxwood, west of Billingshurst.

Once they were called the Peculiar People, a title they were proud of. To them the phrase is taken from the Bible and means beautiful. Those of us who live in the ordinary world might be tempted to take its meaning literally.

For a start, the brethren of this tiny Christian sect are nearly all celibate — and thus on the verge of extinction.

They don't smoke, don't drink, don't go to the cinema, theatre or football matches, and don't watch television or buy newspapers. They are also conscientious objectors.

Once their community at Loxwood was almost cut off from the world. The 200 members had eight shops of their own, four delivery vans, 35 people on the payroll, made their own bikes, ran the first taxi service and owned the first car in the village.

But the Peculiar People say it's God's will

Peaceful

Now there are 32 left. And they accept their pending demise as God's will and with smiling, humble and peaceful faces they await an end that they themselves have brought about.

Says one of their two current ministers, 76-year-old Rowland John Leswell: "We know our own belief is the cause of our own extinction and we are happy to accept God's will."

The group was also known as the Dependents — because they are dependent on God. They first came to Loxwood in 1850.

They were founded by a man called John Sirgood who had been a member of a similar sect called the Peculiar People in Essex and who came to Sussex with his wife and belongings on a handcart to start his own version of the sect here.

what to do. They are free to choose themselves and be individuals. But we are happy to stay within our beliefs."

Because they now realise the sect's days are numbered, its members have recently renewed contact with the Peculiar People in Essex, whose numbers have also diminished but not as much as their Loxwood brothers.

When the last of the Peculiar People has died in Sussex all property and possessions will pass to Essex. With 20 of their remaining members over 80 and the other 12 in their seventies, that won't be too long.

Graves

Mr Leswell joined the sect in 1939 and soon afterwards was exempted from military service because he thought that aiding and abetting the crime of war was worse than committing the crime in the first place.

He gave up a job as a carpenter with his father's firm in Essex to come to Loxwood, where he worked as everything from butcher, chimney

lives we have the ability to live above the power of sin.

"We are looking to take part in the first resurrection. We believe there will be a call to all those who love and fear God. A trumpet will sound and the dead will arise and we will be with Him for ever."

Such is the quietly held creed that has sustained the Dependents for more than 100 years — and which is also about to end their existence.

Once they had friends in a similar sect in Germany and believers paid visits to each other. But now no one is young enough to travel.

Tough

Added Mr Leswell: "I don't know that you can say it's a shame we will die out — it's just an effect of circumstances. But we were wonderfully happy people about here.

women particularly were mostly in service and only got half a day off a month. Working for ourselves meant we could attend chapel. No one today understands how tough it was in those days.

"We took small wages and ploughed it all back. Now all the shops have been sold and the people have shared the profits. But always we have tried to live our lives without interfering with anybody."

Tolerance

The Dependents do not mourn at funerals because they say their dear ones have gained "great victory and eternal life." They still read their own hymns, they sing in meetings, occasional readings of the 600 or so letters written by their founder.

Mr Leswell, who is also secretary of the sect, said he first married because, like other young chaps, young

But he was the last male to join the Dependents at Loxwood.

The sect's closely guarded existence in Loxwood drew this comment from Mr Chris Ashton, editor of Quicksilver Messenger, a Brighton-based magazine dealing in old Sussex facts and myths. "Hard work, tolerance, prosperity and contentment in old age — not a bad combination. Perhaps there is something we could learn from them."

But when the Dependents have gone they won't be forgotten.

They own a bungalow in Spy Lane, Loxwood, called The Retreat, which can accommodate 11 people. When the last dependent has died it will be handed over to the village to be used for old people, irrespective of whether they are religious or not, together with funds to run and expand it.

Thus the memory of the Peculiar People of Sussex will

● Rowland John Leswell, one of the last of a once-thriving Sussex religious sect, outside the chapel. Inset, the sect's founder, John Sirgood.

years, including dress, the length of the services, the plain way of life and worship, the lack of tombstones, music, flowers, ornaments, and so on, discouragement of marriage, and especially the lack of interest in holiday, of charabancs. He found them to be calm, strong, erect in their simple faith, *"hidden in the Sussex hills and dells. Do not disturb them."*

Free Lance, Vol 21, 15 September 1920
A short but appallingly written piece in a diary section called 'Entre Nous' - it should have been kept 'entre eux'. Take this sentence: *"You will notice on the faces of the Loxwooders an aspect of deep, profound and appalling gloom."* Enough said.

Daily Chronicle, 28 September 1926
This was a report by a female reporter, and the first to contain a photograph, of a young woman in a bonnet, *"with a peach-like complexion, turquoise blue eyes, and nut-brown hair twisted round her head in innumerable small plaits"*. Another photo showed three young girls going to chapel, including the one in the close-up, under the caption "Members of an anti-marriage sect" (Plate 13.2). Interviewed, she answered (in bold font) *"I am not interested in theatres, picture houses, fashions, games or men"*. It is interesting to hear the woman's view on children, *"I am fond of children. We think it better not to incur the grave responsibility of bringing souls into this world"*. The reporter learnt about the joy of funerals, and the woman she interviewed made clear it would be a happy thing to die. She also interviewed the postmaster whose considered view was that *"We have nothing but good to say about them"*.

In the wildly varying numbers game, this reporter estimated only 100 would attend the Big Meeting taking place at the time of her visit. She mentioned that a small oak tree marked the spot where John Sirgood is buried. She also spoke to Henry Aylward.
Note, The Daily Chronicle was a national newspaper published up to 1930.

The Essex Newsman, 2 October 1926
This newspaper had a columnist who spread his 'news' light-heartedly across the better part of a page, and meandered therein from one story to another, alighting on the Dependants, by way of marriage in New York, *"The members of which believe in neither fashions nor men, nor the pleasures of life"*! The occasion for this outburst was the Big Meeting in Loxwood that always took place around this time. *"Husbands and wives are allowed to join, but I cannot imagine why."* Before launching himself into another topic on fashion, he finished with, *"Perhaps the modern scanty dress of young women has something to do with the recruiting power of the new [sic] denomination"*. He was totally unaware of the Dependants' links with the Peculiar People in Essex. He may have culled from the Daily Chronicle article above, although it bears no comparison.

The West Australian, 6 November 1926
Australia relayed in its entirety a story from The London Daily News written after a visit from a reporter to a Big Meeting. Somewhat oversimplified, it re-played the usual titbits of information dressed up as though the whole of Loxwood belonged to the Dependants (rather as did Entre Nous, above, this time headlined *"A Puritan Village"*). Its novelty was in impressing on readers that the village was deserted because the shops were closed (it was a

Bank Holiday). The writer was able to report on Henry Aylward leading in a hymn of great length.

Derby Telegraph, and others, 12 December 1927
This lengthy article, under the headline *"Queer Sect",* was syndicated by the Press Association, who had clearly sent a reporter to speak with at least one Dependant, described as a deacon. Henry Aylward is named as leader and head of the firm, Aylward, Smith & Co Ltd. Among a number of accurate comments about their origin in the [Plumstead] Peculiars, conduct of meetings, hymns, the importance of testimony, here called 'experiences', attitudes to marriage and other sacraments, the Big Meetings, "the departmental store", its provision for women otherwise unable to get to meetings, etc., are some curious revelations, which may or may not be entirely true. On dress, the reporter described women wearing *"tightly fitting bodices buttoned high in the neck, their skirts reaching almost to their ankles, and their invariable headdress is a small bonnet. The men have no uniform, but like the women they choose clothes of a sombre hue."* It was pointed out that women in the drapery department sold cloth for gaudy clothes even though they would not wear it themselves.

It was estimated up to 200 might attend meetings. Among the less well-substantiated claims were that Sirgood was a potman before becoming an itinerant shoemaker. This is not the only source to imply Sirgood having turned away from youthful use of alcohol, but no earlier source suggested he worked in an inn. It is clearly apocryphal that Sirgood's first convert was a woman who was tending her pigs, but it fits the narrative of working-class conversion, and female conversion in particular. There is similarly no proof that Sirgood was more than once thrown in a ditch for his pains, but it chimes with the known accounts of persecution. Admiration for the business had moved on from expressing surprise at the hire of motor cars in 1904 to surprise that they sold motor bikes in 1927. One of the latest converts, a man aged 85, was said to come to the Big Meeting from Hastings on his tricycle, taking two days to get to Loxwood.

Sunday Express, 24 May 1931
Next to a good photo showing two women, one youngish in bonnet and dark clothing carrying a shawl, the other older and wearing her shawl close around her head, and a man, clearly elderly with a trilby and stick, and with a white full round-the-chin beard, this article was in a fairly modern layout with an eye catching four headlines in various font sizes, some bold, some not. These begin *"Strange Old-World Colony".* As with several of these articles, the news was related to a Big Meeting, this one at Whitsun. Among the familiar litany of facts quoted it referred to the shunning of wireless, but otherwise was unremarkable (Plate 13.1).

Launceston Examiner, 14 July 1931
This Australian paper enjoyed turning the tables on England by calling Loxwood an *"Old World Colony – Strange People".* After several months had elapsed, this article appears to have been sourced on the Sunday Express, above, even stealing the headline. The content offered nothing new (to us, that is).

Sussex County Magazine, Vol 5, November/December 1931
The 1904 article by Lord Turnour was re-printed in 1931, under his later title of Earl

Winterton (Plate 13.1). It generated some comment in the next issue. At this time, two daughters of the preacher (and contemporary of Sirgood), Peter Pacy of Plaistow, were still alive, living at Hogwood, near Ifold, where Pacy had at one time been Head Gardener. Pacy was held to have told the writer (Henry Styles of Lewes) that the origin of Cokeler was that Sirgood after preaching outside a pub, on being offered a beer, would say he wanted cocoa. Styles remembered Pacy preaching at the Hove chapel, but questionable as Pacy died about the time the Hove Chapel opened in 1905. He also thought the Pacys were of Huguenot descent.

Another contributor, RJ Sharp of Chichester, claimed the Chichester Cokelers were known locally as Ranters (a term which dates from the time of the Commonwealth after the English Civil War). Michael Woolgar, who had the store in The Hornet (see Chapter 12), was thought of as a much-respected tradesman. Woolgar had a long white beard, which gave him the nickname of the Bishop. He remembers the Felpham contingent coming into Chichester on the carrier's cart, latterly by chartered bus on Sundays. Those at East Dean walked in.

Surrey Advertiser, 3 September 1932
An article headed *Who's heard of the Cokelers?* was inspired by a letter to The Times the previous week by Earl Winterton MP (who was Lord Turnour when writing in 1904) when he mentioned them as an aside. The writer calls their religion joyful with a strong Puritan element. He also subscribes to the Cokkes Field school of thought on their name.

Western Daily Press, 4 February 1933
This account, bizarrely, appeared under the heading of *Notes of a Bristol Naturalist,* and followed on from a piece about alder and hazel trees. This is perhaps because it is based on an article in The Countryman magazine, then relatively new, by Earl Winterton. It had nothing to say that had not been said before. The Tewkesbury Register, 31 December 1932, had also referenced The Countryman article, a source which the author has not seen.

Daily Express, date unknown
A number of articles from national newspapers or torn from magazines have circulated, mostly without date. Some can be guessed within a decade by their content and style. Most were inter-war. This one was long and ranged widely. It was clearly written when a reporter attended a Big Meeting. It misspelt "Cocolers" and made a non sequitur in linking this to cocoa manufacturing Quakers. However, more accurate was its description of the women's dress, adding to the quotation above from the Press Association in 1927 the use of shawls, black boots, and a black straw hat as an alternative to the velvet bonnet. Uniquely, it noted the men often had a fringe of hair around their face and chin, something easily verified in numerous photographs. It noted the fresh complexions of the women. However, it rather belittled the complexity of their worship, highlighting single sentences such as *"My pig has had a litter"*, followed by *"Praise be to the Lord. Halleluia!"* from the meeting. Tom Rugman was referred to as a leader and asked for his views on marriage. It then stated, more controversially, *"They do not like children. When a child is born, the community goes into mourning, and is subdued."* It continued by describing more accurately (corroborated by the story of her father's life by Elizabeth Denyer, quoted at length in Chapter 2), that children were brought up as far from real life as was practicable, and given the choice of whether to stay or go; clearly, some did leave.

Daily Mail, date unknown
This article was also the result of sending a reporter down to Loxwood, one who was astonished at how rural it was. He spoke at length with Henry Aylward about marriage, (yet again), about the nature of the meetings, one of which he had attended, the lack of music, art or other decoration in the chapel, the lack of tombstones, and emphasised the work of visiting the sick and elderly folk which many younger members used to do every week in the evenings, an aspect of their lives easily forgotten. This writer suggested that numbers at the Big Meetings could reach 1000.

Rockhampton Morning Bulletin, 24 May 1937
This Queensland paper treated its readers to a serious discourse on dissenting sects, under the headline *Only Death Provides an Excuse for Jubilation*. It called the Dependants one of 400 different faiths in England. The writer liked Loxwood and liked the outlook of the Dependants. He compared them correctly with the Peculiar People, before going on to discuss other faiths.

West Sussex Gazette, 26 January 1939
The funeral of Miss Ethel Mary Smith, one of the first to be in a newspaper, perhaps as she had been both a manager (Company secretary) and a "Sister-Minister" (elder) of the chapel. The latter term was probably the reporter's. She was 76, and had spent 7 years in Warnham, 45 in Loxwood, so had been in the sect since she was 24, and in Loxwood since 1894, at the birth of Aylward, Smith. The article attests to her kindliness above all else. The reporter was amazed so many came from other communities, as well as from Loxwood, including William Booker and Benjamin Piper from Warnham who conducted the service. Henry Aylward led prayers. A hymn was sung composed by Sarah Woods, a deaconess. Only two relatives were mentioned, a sister and husband.

Later that year, on Henry Aylward's death there was no article, but Aylward, Smith themselves placed an announcement of thanks for sympathy, etc.

Sussex County Magazine, December 1942
Donald MacAndrew of Pallinghurst, Rudgwick wrote about the Dependants in an article called *The Sussex Cokelers: A Curious Sect*. It is not clear why he wrote it or what authority he might have had. He was a son of Ernest MacAndrew, JP, owner of Pallinghurst, and a well-known horseman, hunter and landowner. Mr MacAndrew must have known Earl Winterton from his activities in the Chiddingfold Hunt, and Lord Leconfield's Hunt, and Point to Point races held at Tismans Common on his estate. Little is known about Donald. He was in his mid-30s when he wrote this article. He married in 1943, and then spent most of his life in Rhodesia.

MacAndrew began rather unfortunately by casting an aspersion that *"these people resemble us little more than do, say, the natives of Bali"*. Decline was well set in by the 1940s, and he claimed that the two communities in Chichester and Hove had barely a score of members between them, and the whole movement had around 200, probably an underestimate. His description of the religious origins of the Dependants was as accurate as anyone's, and he dealt with many matters sympathetically. One revelation not seen elsewhere was that the

Northchapel Dependants kept the nearly dead Sussex cider industry alive, despite their eschewing alcohol themselves.

However, he followed his insult quoted above with an even more contentious statement regarding "trial marriage". His exact words were, *"A system was therefore introduced whereby any Brother wishing to wed could, having obtained the sanction of the Elders, enter into a trial marriage with the lady of his choice* [note, not the other way round], *to be allowed some two years later perhaps, should both parties be yet willing, by lawful matrimony, and this is still practiced in the villages where, however, strict Cokelers even now discountenance marriage entirely. As may be guessed, the system has been in the hands of their persecutors, who could always say that the Cokelers encouraged immorality."*

This was red rag to the bull! The following is taken verbatim from the January 1943 issue. It may be the only time the Dependants refuted comment in public since Sirgood in the 1860s; clearly touched a nerve.

Sussex County Magazine, January 1943
"The Cokelers - from the Religious Body of Dependents (sic)"
At a meeting of the Trustees, it was agreed to bring to your notice the false statement in your issue of December 1942, especially on page 148, the paragraph stating that we have introduced a system of "A trial marriage etc." This should have been proved to be true before being published world-wide. We hereby ask in the name of reason that in your next issue you should rectify this error without fail. Such a system has never been practised among us as a people. In fact, has never ever been suggested, or thought of. The publishing of it as you have is nothing less than defamation. There are several other things mentioned that are not correct but the one mentioned is the one that really matters to us, as it may be very injurious to our cause.
Signed on behalf of the Body of Dependents *(sic)*:-   WILLIAM BOOKER (Chairman)
                                                                              WALLIS *[sic - Walter]* JOHN NASH (Secretary)"

This was also a rare insight into the governing body of the Dependants. The author knows of no other document that refers to the "Body". At the time, its chairman was the leader of Warnham Dependants, to whom Walter Nash clearly deferred, as Booker was the older man. Walter may have had cause to be embarrassed by MacAndrew, as he was himself party to an embarrassing event. See Chapter 2. The editor and the writer of the article pointedly refused to apologise, referring the reader to the 1904 Turnour article in which Dependant attitudes to marriage were *"a direct incentive to immorality"*. The Dependants probably had not liked reading that either, just four years after the birth of Nash's illegitimate son by Annie Denyer (see Chapter 2).

To return to MacAndrew's article, he commented on their wealth accrued through their trade, but rightly said that members recycled their earnings within the company, describing them as *"stauncher communists than many who follow Marx and Engels."* But he went on rather judgmentally to suggest extreme *"preciosity of speech"* – talking in the idiom of the Bible – and dress – a woman will *"choose to array herself"* in century old servant's dress – and worship – copying hymns in longhand. He refers to the chapels as *"ivory chapels"* (cf ivory towers) and, to cap his already flowery language, he invokes Isaiah in considering the Lord's sparkling jewels to be of polished chrysoprase (a fine gem), which seems *de trop* when writing of such an abstemious people, almost insulting, certainly patronising. The chapel is now turned into an *"ugly bare little chapel"* (ivory?), with a tink, tink bell (that much is true), but his description of a meeting was accurate, as he clearly sat through one, but tinged, in more detail than the newspapers above had space for, by the outsider's incredulity at the intensity of proceedings in a way that I suspect would not be written today, after so many variations of faith have been presented to us on our screens at home. He is trying to be respectful, but it does not quite work. One might have imagined he would have read the re-printed article by Winterton in this very journal, but he makes no reference to it. Yet, for many years this remained the most up to date article on the Dependants.

West Sussex County Times, 27 February 1953
This was an example of one of many funeral reports in the 1930s to 1960s, on this occasion for Elizabeth Holden, aged 84, interred at Loxwood chapel, who had typically moved as young girl from Warnham to the Loxwood community, where she spent 64 years, latterly a director in Loxwood of Aylward, Smith & Co. Even in the newspapers the language of the Dependants comes through, *"She was one of God's faithful stewards, truly loved for the work well done. It was asked, what was she worth?... this will be revealed when the books are opened by the one who will give the reward."* Her main interests were in helping others. Tribute was paid to *"the great work she has done in our midst".*

West Sussex Gazette, 14 March 1957, and passim
The delightful *Mrs Paddick's Diary* ran for many years in this newspaper, written in Sussex dialect. On this date the piece was about the Dependants, *The Cokelers by a Sussex Woman*, and gently describing them poking a little fun with lines such as, *"An they sang I dunnamany hymns, but here's a queer thing, mum. They hadn't got no hymnbooks …. But after the service we went into a back room an' had a cup of tea, an' so did everyone, free, gracious, an' for nothing …. They don't believe in folk gittin' married. That was I dunnamany years agoo, so if they still goo on that way, there can't be many Cokelers left, can there, mum?"* Quite.

This generated quite a correspondence over the next three weeks, all very positive, and with some references to earlier sources. Little new information was forthcoming, except from two correspondents. Stanley Godman of Lewes wrote of the quality of carol singing from the Hove members visiting local hospitals; John Corp of Twineham (previously a farmer in Warnham and Rudgwick) wrote of Henry Piper, an elder and trustee of Warnham chapel, *"a farmer, and a good one too"* at Bailing Hill Farm in Warnham. Jesse Lindfield and Henry Killner were other Dependants working on the farm, rented from the Lucas estate (1901 census).

West Sussex Gazette, 2 May 1957
In response to yet another Winterton intervention, this time regarding persecution of Dependants, a well-informed "Well-wisher" wrote in to give chapter and verse on
- Henry Piper of Warnham, whose story is told by his son Benjamin in Chapter 2. The writer confirms (or has read) the same source used in Chapter 2, dating the removal of the family from Chaffields Farm to a barn at Cidermill in 1870-2.
- Tom Rugman of Loxwood was dismissed from employment by Mrs Smallpiece at Merry Hills Loxwood, also evicted to a barn, also with a family, maybe about the same time as the above, or a few years later (photo Plate 4.1).

- Hannah Birch, Northchapel, and Lucy Sherlock, Lordshill and Warnham, two housemaids aged 19 dismissed. Both were still alive in 1957.
- G Howick dismissed from Pickhurst in Chiddingfold in 1867, a place where he had worked for 50 years.

Whether these are true is not possible to say, except for Piper. Earl Winterton replied with his thanks and commented that there had been much religious hostility in Victorian times, which still regrettably continued into the 20th century. A flurry of letters followed from various sources, none of which added anything new. It is the case that the stories of the Cokelers stayed in circulation and were constantly recycled, no more so than in 1957.

The Dependent's Hymn Book, 1958

The one publication the Dependants themselves published was their hymn book. Having sung hymns for getting on for 100 years, and with the decline of the sect, all the many hymn lyrics (if that is an appropriate word) had been passed down by oral tradition. This little book represents a significant addition to the literature. It was a small format volume, as befits something to go in a lady's bag, a man's pocket, or sit on a pew. Oddly, this item is called Dependents, not Dependants. The terms were often interchangeable, but the 'e' is strictly wrong (Plate 13.1).

The People, 8 Dec 1963

The Sad End of a Simple Faith by Martin Dale told the story, complete with a photograph (rare inside any chapel) of widower Alfred Kelsey, aged 81, reading from the Bible to Nellie Franks, aged 89, between them the last surviving members of Lordshill congregation. Nellie was his housekeeper, so they were together every day anyway. *"By holding two services each Sunday, Nellie and I are maintaining our faith."* Nevertheless, the reporter was told there were still a hundred left alive. Kelsey died in 1970, Nellie (Eleanor) in 1967. She was known as the Angel of Shamley Green for her visits to the sick and her laying out of the dead.

Daily Mirror, c1968

The author has a transcript of this brief article, *Sex and the Smallest Sect*. It reported an interview with 68-year-old Alfred Goodwin. It suggested there were about 70 members still alive. Hove, Northchapel, and Warnham were still functioning. Alf is reported as saying (and the voice is authentic Goodwin), *"People come to us and join in at our testimony meetings, if they feel they want to be converted. Fortunately, we do have a few new followers, but for the most part our members are very old. While we feel that members should not be married our outlook for survival is not encouraging."* Words like "self-effacing" and "tranquillity, a quality not to be dismissed" are used.

Sussex Life, The Warnham Brethren, by Vida Herbison, c1970

Warnham Stores had already closed and been turned into an antique shop by the time this article was written. The author interviewed Miss Ellen Lindfield, aged 80, daughter of the stores founder. She was born in 1890, so the date given for this article must be 1970-71. Ellen died in 1979.

Evening Argus, 29 June 1982
Dying Days of a Secret Sect, but the Peculiar People say it's God's Will, by reporter Ray Miller – the title says it all. With 30-40 members left in Loxwood (20 over 80, another 12 over 70), the article harks back to a time when "200 members had eight shops of their own, four delivery vans, 35 people on the payroll, made their own bikes, ran the first taxi service and owned the first car in the village". Eight shops? This may refer to the departments in the Combination Stores, together with the Post Office and Hilltop Stores. "God's will" was quoted from Rowland Leswell, then aged 76, and twice married himself. Leswell had come to Loxwood from the Peculiar People of Essex in 1939 – thought to be the last male to join the Loxwood Dependants - and he told the Argus that contacts had been resumed because the Loxwood days were numbered. He revealed that once the Combination Stores had closed for good, the profits were shared among the remaining members. He reckoned that John Sirgood had written as many as 600 letters. Other comments by Leswell have been added to the section on this interesting man, in Chapter 7.

"The Gentle Folk", anon, unknown publication, c1984-92
This article, using the date of 1984 as closure for the Dependant community, was, over three pages, authoritative, accurate, and as its title suggests, unprovocative and gently persuasive of their qualities. It ranged over well-worn historical developments, but near the end threw in a few useful snippets. Some of the information came from interviews with two elderly ladies, by then living in The Retreat, Spy Lane, an 11-room rest home which had by this time been handed over, by a South Norwood trust, to new village trustees – *"the last generous act of the Cokelers of Loxwood".* Other generous acts referred to (though with self-interest too) were the asphalting of a Loxwood road, and the extension of electricity to a road where it had not been laid on. Such acts showed they were not just living in the past, the writer pointed out. The two ladies were Memilo Pyke (died 1992) and Mary Farquar (died 1999). They were at pains to say that towards the end, it was only the older Dependants who held on to the traditional ways of dress, a fair point, not applying to their generation as much as the previous one, at least in their later years. Above all, the article preferred the story of quiet contribution to the community over that of concentrating on oddities as so many previous ones had done (Plate 13.1).

Surrey Advertiser, 1 August 2003
In the summer of 2003, Mrs Marion May of Shamley Green, who has helped the author, providing many copies of documents and photos, and has also written a booklet, *The Story of the Dependants,* for Shamley Green History Society, almost single-handedly arranged a large exhibition at Guildford Museum Salters Gallery from 6 August to 6 September 2003. In the lead up to this, a phone-in session on local radio had provided Marion with much friendly reminiscence from so many places around the two counties. A little information was provided as a taster of the exhibition, and a talk by author Peter Jerrome, which was a huge success on a hot day, there being so many in the Sussex/Surrey borders who remembered, worked for, were neighbours of, or are related to Dependants (Plate 13.1).

Storrington Museum Newsletter, 24 August 2006
This anonymous article was written by a member who used to live in Loxwood, next door to a house with three unmarried Dependant siblings. The article dealt accurately with the facts and made comparisons to St Cuthman and the Mormons in choosing a place to make roots

and conversions. It spoke of one of the first converts being one of 17 in the family, not seen written elsewhere, and imagined the suspicion that might have been felt in the villages for anyone from London. Other well-made points included the continuity after Sirgood's death, and that there was never any split as in so many Christian denominations.

The story of St Cuthman (born 681) is one which also occurred to the author in a recent visit to Steyning. He was an Anglo-Saxon hermit. The story as told below has so many parallels with John Sirgood's story that one wonders if either Sirgood or someone close to him knew enough of the Cuthman story to borrow from it, the wheelbarrowing (especially this), the derision, the church building, the help of the community and evangelisation.

Approaching the end of this chapter with the full story of Cuthman, it is hoped it does not offend non-conformist readers in this more ecumenical age with its analogy derived from Roman Catholicism.

Some time ago I stayed at my aunt and uncle's house in Steyning, a sleepy little town in West Sussex. Though now about five miles from the coast, this was once a prosperous port with a market and a mint. This thriving centre for trade was known as the Portus Cuthmanni (Cuthman's Port), named after the local saint, whose picture appears on the town sign.

He has a rather bizarre iconographic symbol: St Cuthman is normally shown pushing his mother around in a wooden wheelbarrow. More recently he achieved further fame by becoming the subject of a play by Christopher Fry, The Boy With a Cart (1939). This was performed at the Lyric Theatre, Hammersmith, in 1950, directed by John Gielgud and with Richard Burton playing the part of St Cuthman. Who, then, was this Anglo-Saxon saint, who managed to attract the attention of one of our finest modern playwrights and two of our greatest theatrical knights?

The earliest surviving written record of Cuthman's life is a volume of the Acta Sanctorum, published by the Bollandists at Antwerp in 1658. According to the story, Cuthman was a shepherd who grew up either in the West Country or at Chidham, near Chichester. He was probably born in the late seventh century and may have been baptised by St Wilfrid himself, the 'Apostle of Sussex.'

Even as a young boy, Cuthman showed signs of his closeness to God. One day, while tending his sheep, he drew a line around them with his staff so that he could get away to collect food. On his return, he found that the flock had not left the invisible boundary. This miracle may have taken place in a field near Chidham, which for centuries was known as 'St Cuthman's Field' or 'St Cuthman's Dell.' It was said that a large stone in the field, 'on which the holy shepherd was in the habit of sitting,' held miraculous properties.

A turning point in Cuthman's life was the death of his father, which left both him and his mother destitute. They decided to leave their home and journey eastwards – in the direction of the rising sun. By this time, Cuthman's mother was an invalid and so he had to push her in a wheeled wooden cart. A rope that stretched from the handles to the saint's shoulders helped carry the burden. When the rope snapped, he made a new one out of withies. The local haymakers laughed at Cuthman's rather pathetic efforts, but Providence soon responded to their merriment by sending a sudden rainstorm, destroying their harvest. Later versions of the story say that, from that moment onwards, it always rained in that field during the haymaking season. Cuthman decided that once this replacement rope made of withies broke, it would be a sign from God to settle at that place and build a church. This happened at Steyning, which, according to the Acta Sanctorum, was 'a place lying at the base of a lofty hill, then woody, overgrown with brambles and bushes, but now rendered by agriculture fertile and fruitful, enclosed between two streams springing from the hill above.' The Bollandist monks have also provided us with Cuthman's prayer as he reached this blessed spot:

Father Almighty, you have brought my wanderings to an end; now enable me to begin this work. For who am I, Lord, that I should build a house to your Name? If I rely on myself, it will be of no avail, but it is you who will assist me. You have given me the desire to be a builder; make up for my lack of skill and bring the work of building this holy house to its completion.

And so, this unlikely builder began constructing a worthy sanctuary in honour of the One who had guided him safely along his journey ad orientem. Many of the local inhabitants helped him in this great task and on one occasion, according to the legend, he even received Divine assistance. The builders were having trouble with a roof-beam, when a stranger appeared and provided them with a solution. When asked his name, the newcomer replied: 'I am He in whose name you are building the church.'

And so he built a wooden chapel in Steyning, probably on the site of the present church of St Andrew's. This building was certainly well established by 857, when King Ethelwulf (father of Alfred the Great) was buried there.

It seems that pilgrims visited the tomb of St Cuthman and that his intercession led to many cures. During the reign of St Edward the Confessor, the church at Steyning was given to the Abbey of the Holy Trinity at Fécamp, Normandy. This Benedictine house, founded in the seventh century, is famous for its 'Benedictine' liqueur, which today is commercially produced in the grounds of the old abbey. It was to this monastery that the Black Monks took the body of St Cuthman and his feast (8th February) was celebrated at many of the religious houses of Normandy. Thus, St Cuthman became well known on the continent – as can be seen in a mid-fifteenth century German engraving of the saint by Martin Schongauer and in the writings of the seventeenth century Bollandists.

Meanwhile, the church at Steyning was rebuilt and dedicated to St Andrew. However, St Cuthman was not forgotten in his beloved land. A 'Guild of St Cuthman' was in existence at Chidham on the eve of the Reformation and a misericord in Ripon Cathedral supposedly depicts him pushing his mother in a three-wheeled barrow.

The colourful tale of St Cuthman presents us with a charming example of filial piety, prayer, evangelisation and church building in Saxon England. In the words of Christopher Fry:

It is there in the story of Cuthman, the working together
Of man and God like root and sky; the son
Of a Cornish shepherd, Cuthman, the boy with a cart,
The boy we saw trudging the sheep-tracks with his mother
Mile upon mile over five counties; one
Fixed purpose biting his heels and lifting his heart.
We saw him; we saw him with a grass in his mouth, chewing
And travelling. We saw him building at last
A church among whortleberries…

Fr Nicholas Schofield MA, STB, FRHistS, Parish Priest at Our Lady of Lourdes and St Michael, Uxbridge, and Archivist of the Archdiocese of Westminster.

Acknowledgement: Stories from the Steyning Museum Archives, steyningmuseum.org.uk.

Family Historian Magazine, February 2008

The modern hobby of genealogy has permeated this book throughout, enabling detailed research on individuals to build a portrait of whole communities. It is no surprise that Alec Tritton was commissioned to write a series of columns on non-conformist sects. The Peculiar People of Essex in January 2008 were followed in February by the *The Cokelers* (Plate 13.3 below). The piece is well-researched and embellished by plausible stories. It gave the kind of insight into family history which it is hoped the author's book will do too.

Worship, weird and wonderful

The Cokelers

Mid-19th century Sussex sect – the Cokelers – had at its height a few thousand followers, who lived and worked together in a peaceful community, built seven chapels, and hired out the only motor taxi in the district: **Alec Tritton** follows in the footsteps of the faithful

Last month we looked at the Essex faith healers known as the Peculiar People, which were influential in the life of another faith healer John Sirgood, the founder of the Society of Dependants colloquially known as the Cokelers. John Sirgood was born in Gloucester in 1821 and moved to South London in the early 1840s where he plied his trade as a shoemaker and met and married on 17 March 1845 Harriet CoAhead. It was during this period that John met William Bridges of the Peculiar People and underwent a spiritual conversion. Indeed it is claimed that on at least one occasion he 'raised the dead'. Unlike James Banyard of the Peculiar People though, John soon realised that he was better at curing souls rather than bodies!

Initially he went around South London preaching but soon found that the further he journeyed, the more genuine response he found and thus he closed his shop, packed all his belongings in a hand cart and with his wife tramped the dusty road of Surrey into Sussex. Arriving in Loxwood, initially preaching in fields and cottages, this almost exclusive Sussex sect was founded in 1850. Eventually the sect built seven chapels at Loxwood, Plaistow, Warnham, Chichester and Northchapel, all in West Sussex, Hove in East Sussex, Shamley Green in Surrey and Norwood near London, but none of these were ever licensed for marriages.

Learning from early sects, the Cokelers established their own stores at Norwood, Warnham, Shamley Green, Loxwood and Northchapel to provide employment for members and to keep their money within the community by buying from Cokeler producers. These became very successful and provided much needed employment for the younger female members who were often turned out of service because of their beliefs. By 1904 the Warnham store employed 36 men and women and at Loxwood they opened a steam bakery and a motor taxi could be hired – the only one in the district. By the time of his death in 1885 John Sirgood had a following of nearly 2,000 people, mainly simple farm labourers and artisans. John was laid to rest in a simple grave without any headstone in the Dependant tradition. The church he started continued, but their gentle way of life was no match for the 20th century and numbers steadily dwindled such that 50 years ago only 15 people attended the morning service in Payne Avenue, Hove which eventually closed in 1978. In August 1996 the last elder living, Alfred Goodwin, died and was buried in the green plot behind the chapel in Spy Lane, Loxwood. In a world that often seems to have gone mad, the Cokelers were reasonably sane...

Did you know?
They were known locally as the Cokelers and legend has it that this comes from their habit of drinking cocoa and abstaining from alcohol. It was certainly an austere sect; no alcohol or flowers in the house, entertainment and music were frowned upon, and only the Bible was read at home.

Local expertise

Many documents relating to the sect are held by the Petworth Society but not the burial register, which would hold the details of the circa 500 graves in Loxwood. The Petworth Society meets monthly September-May in Leconfield Hall, Petworth, West Sussex.

Family historians can so often benefit from local expertise. Try contacting a local history society; they may be able to offer help with former businesses, inhabitants, and ways of life, all of which can provide clues to your family history. The Local History Directory at www.local-history.co.uk is organised by county, providing contact details for local record offices, archaeological societies and local studies centres.

Chapter 14

In Conclusion

The Dependants were much liked in the 20th century within their own village or town communities and much admired for their selflessness and generosity, both in spirit and in kind. Of course, they looked after their own so well. The development of retirement houses, The Cross in Warnham, Holly View in Northchapel, The Retreat in Lords Hill and, eventually, another Retreat in Loxwood, enabled the communities to continue as remnants after the various stores closed. There were also elderly married couples and widows living outside these enclaves. In most cases the chapels outlasted the stores. The name Retreat is wholly appropriate in the sense of a well-managed retreat to a death welcomed as the end of a journey, *"soon my journey will be ended/and my joy will greater be/I shall live in that fair city/with the King who died for me/who died that I might live forever/in the realms of peace"* [words written by Mary Parsons who died in 1921 at Warnham].

After all, death had been an all-consuming problem as the numbers formerly young enough to work were not succeeded by a new generation in the years after the Second World War. Visiting the sick in hospitals was a readily enjoyed activity, with cakes left over from the store bakeries taken and distributed in the ward. The number who died in hospital rose gradually, as can be observed in the death register.

It was also a time of retreat from the very organisation that had nurtured them for many young people born to Cokeler parents. The stifling religiosity of life was too much for many, and even for some young people who lived in the Stores community. One such is Rita Dumbrell, born Rita Polley, whose first husband John Phillips had been a Director of Aylward, Smith & Co. Rita only spent one year in the Combination Stores. To go out of an evening required much subterfuge. Normally, a chaperone would be required. It is not surprising in the age of television and the first stirrings of youth culture that restraint on dress, particularly for the young women, and particularly on Sundays, also awoke a rebellious spirit in many. Had there been more young people the social mores of the Dependants might have made a better accommodation with modernity. As we might now say, a critical mass was no longer possible.

Perhaps the strangest thing is that once John Sirgood and the other early preachers who went out to the farms and commons in the 1850s, 60s and 70s had died, there was little if any sense of mission to the outside community. Exceptions were of course to be found, and some joined in the last century, such as Irene Druett and Molly Farquhar, both from very difficult backgrounds.

I am very aware that my uncle Walter Nash who was an elder, and chairman of Aylward, Smith, for about 25 years, did little to rectify this situation. He presided over a growing empire of property and farming enterprises, which adapted to modern technologies, yet also had to preside over many funerals – 57 from 1936-1960 – so that his successor Alf Goodwin had little chance of any process of recovery. Instead, Alf led the retreat with good grace, humility and steadfastness in his faith to his last breath.

Nevertheless, it is a proven case that over the last thirty years the Dependants or Cokelers (the name everyone now remembers them by) remain strong in the folk memory of West Sussex and Surrey. It was proved so when an exhibition was mounted for a whole month in August and September 2003 in the Salters Gallery of Guildford Museum, by fellow enthusiast and non-Dependant, Mrs Marion May of Shamley Green (Plate 13.1). With the passing of this time of memory it became important to publish this book, before even the memory itself goes for ever, and in doing so to record some of the individuals and families who were the Body of Dependants.

The built environment of all the communities has an enduring legacy of chapels, stores, and houses. These will exercise the minds of local historians of the future, to whom this book will be a boon. Loxwood, Shamley Green, Warnham, Northchapel and South Norwood are the locations with the greatest legacy. Th cover photograph chosen for this book could as easily have been a recent photograph of the same street view.

The Society of Dependants had arisen from a determination on the part of John Sirgood to make a difference in mid-Victorian working class society, to combat the evils of poverty, drink, large families, servitude and loose morals, in much the same ways as many other reformers, such as Joseph Rowntree, a Quaker, and religious groups, such as the various branches of Methodism (the Wesleyan mantra was, "Make all you can, save all you can, give all you can"). The Dependants had an easy relationship with each other, with commerce, with the outside world and with their Maker, a community of souls. As John Montgomery observed in 1962, in *Abodes of Love*, "in a peculiar world, they seem reasonably sane".

Appendix 1

Some Dependant Probate Records
National Probate Calendar, 1858-1966

Probate records available online, *England & Wales, National Probate Calendar (Index of Wills and Administrations), 1858-1995*, provide a unique insight into final addresses, links between senior Dependants as executors, even between communities, and of course net worth of their estate. It is difficult to interpret the latter, but it gives insight into ordinary people's lives at a variety of dates from late 19th century to the last Dependants alive. The unmarried brethren and sisters usually left little, but in a few cases, usually married couples, property ownership may have inflated the figures. Some died intestate, not as many as one might have expected, more among the early deaths, and in a few later cases surprisingly so.

The list below is only a selection of the brethren and sisters and is far from comprehensive. Where possible those who contributed greatly to their Dependant community are included, as are an eclectic collection of other individuals who seemed worthy of investigation to the author as a sample of Dependants. The names are grouped alphabetically by community, in date order of death. Any details of occupation or marital status are as in the database, including that of the executors. In early probate records, there were more details (but value of estates given as 'under £...'), for more recent deaths executors are not included. In nearly all cases, executors are other Dependants, or close relatives. Some senior brethren are executors numerous times. The community sensibly approved of the process and seems to have actively encouraged it.

As has been stated earlier in this book, the author has worked from a copy of the death and burial registers. Whereas the original death register is still missing, the original calf-bound official burial register is kept in the safe in the rear of the chapel at Loxwood. In fact, it is still a working document as several recent burials have been recorded of members of the Emmanuel Fellowship, now the users of the building. The safe had seven keys, it is said, so that it could only be opened by seven elders being present. Today, it is simpler to open. Plate A1.1 has images from the register.

Plate A1.2 has images of several certificates also kept in the safe. Some are certificates of registry of death, others are certificates for disposal, and a few are coroner's orders for burial, the batch spanning the years 1911 to 2002, with only two surviving from earlier dates. They have the date of death, age at death, and the last address of the deceased, where appropriate a hospital or nursing home. The information matches that in the burial register, so does not offer any new insights beyond confirmation of the data.

Joseph Sirgood, 1877, Windmill Row, Kennington, stationer
To Caroline Sirgood, wife
Under £200   *[John Sirgood's brother, not a Dependant]*
John William Sirgood, 1885, Lordshill Cottage, Shamley Green, Wonersh
To Henry Piper, Byfleets Lane, Warnham, farmer
£575 5s 4d

Chichester

Edmund Goff, 1910, of 44 Broyle Road, Chichester, butcher
To Charles Goff, Post Office clerk and Annie Goff, spinster
£230

Plate A1.1

Register of Burials

Fig 1 – the calf skin cover.

Fig 2 – the first page, showing the first funeral in 1866, taken by Rev. Henry Rogers, the Congregational minister at Petworth, whose help was needed to make the chapel a registered place of worship.

Fig 3 – The last page, with the last Dependant burial, Elsie Piper, aged 104, in 2002. All the previous ones were Dependants; the ones which follow were members of the Emmanuel Fellowship who had taken over the chapel (and includes one more on the next page, that of Pastor Roy Barbour in 2018). All the signatures on this page are those of Emmanuel pastors. The other notable name is that of Alfred Goodwin, the last elder, who died in 1996

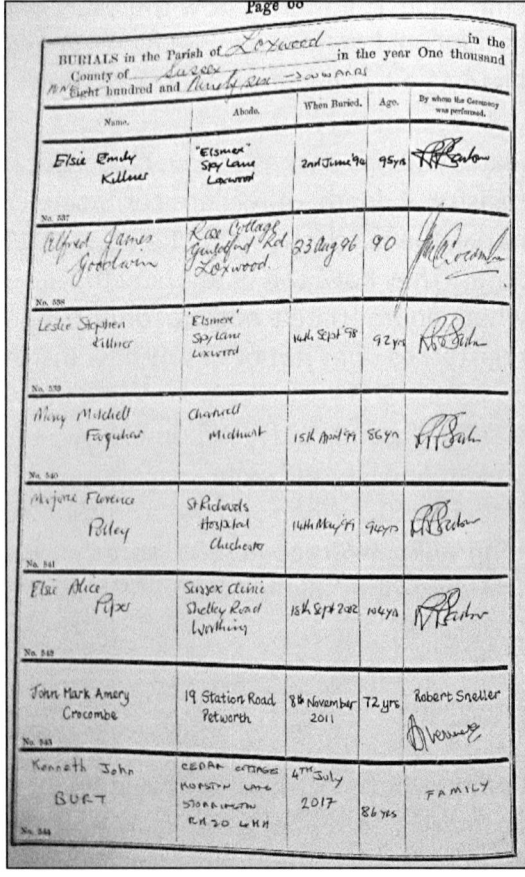

Michael Woolgar, 1927, 40 The Hornet, Chichester
To Ellen Woolgar, widow, Harold Woolgar, dairyman
£2,818 4s 3d
Henry Joseph Hart, 1937, of La Roque, Beach Road, Selsey, and High St, Selsey, at High St
To Fanny Hart, widow
£463 13s 7d
Frederick Hughes, 1948, 10 The Hornet, Chichester
To Lilian Hughes, widow
£14,808 5s
Charlotte Ellen Woolgar, 1954, 24 The Hornet, widow, at Southsea (widow of Michael)
To Jesse Woolgar, cycle & wireless dealer, and Harold Woolgar, farmer
£1,709 18s 3d

Felpham

James Hale, 1936, The Sycamores, Main Road, Felpham, 1936, to Samuel Rugman, stores manager (Northchapel), and George Denyer, cabinet maker (Warnham)
£4,931 19s 10d

Hove

Albert George Candy, 1927, 14 Norway Street, Portslade
To Annie Candy, widow and Frederick Greenfield, contractor
£600 5s 7d
Thomas Overington, 1938, 43 Payne Avenue, Hove
To Louisa Overington, spinster
£506 19s 5d
George Luff, 1948, 12 Boundary Road, Hove
To Nellie Amy Turner, married woman, and William George Luff, master baker
£3,062 16s 9d
Frederick Charles Greenfield, 1959, 101 Boundary Road, Hove (conscientious objector)
To Albert Greenfield, fruiterer
£87,043 6s 10d
Frank Charles Attree, 1959, Dunromin, Loxwood
To Bessie Winton, widow
£1,776 13s 6d
Sarah Marian Brightman, 1961, 63 The Drive, Hove, spinster
To Ernest Dudley King, solicitor
£1,570 18s
Olive Ruth Garman, 1979, Woodberry House, Heath End, Petworth
£2,222

Lordshill

William Hampshire, 1900, Lords Hill Grocery Stores, Lords Hill Common, Shamley Green
To Stephen Franks, miller
£60

John Rugman, 1904, Lordshill Cottage, Shamley Green
To Henry Piper, farmer
£192 10s

Charles Hackman, 1917, Lordshill Common, Shamley Green
To Leslie Street, grocery manager
£62 15s

Mary Foster, 1932, Lordshill, Shamley Green, spinster
To Benjamin Piper, retired grocer
£146 14s 6d

Leslie Street, 1939, Lordshill, Shamley Green
To Edith Alice Bradshaw, spinster
£1,452 3s 11d

Jacob Henry Earle, 1948, Norley Gardens, Norley Common, Shamley Green (Peaceful Place, Shamley Green)
To Alfred Kelsey, baker's roundsman, Eleanor Emma Franks, spinster
£917 16s 5d

Henry Thomas Smith, 1960, Southall, Middlesex
To Henry George Smith, cabinet maker
£2,646 8s 11d

Eleanor Emma Franks, 1967, 2 Pond Close, Shamley Green
To a solicitor
£4,388

Alfred Kelsey, 1970, Cedar Lodge Conv Home, Caterham
£1,278

Raymond Croucher, 1977, Balby, Doncaster
£4,115

Loxwood

Stephen Overington, 1868, Four Houses, Loxwood
To Hannah Overington, spinster, daughter, Camden Town, London
Under £200

Felix Foster, 1880, Loxwood, grocer and farmer
To Sarah Foster, widow of the relict
Under £300

Obed Overington, 1906, Loxwood, no occupation
To Caleb Overington, licensed victualler, and James Herrington, wood contractor
£197

James Etherington, 1908, Loxwood
To Henry Aylward, grocer
£35 10s

Harriett Enticknap, 1908, Plaistow Place, Plaistow
To Richard Nightingale, farmer
£113 4s

John Overington, 1909, Loxwood, retired farm labourer
To Jane Overington, spinster
£243 9s 2d

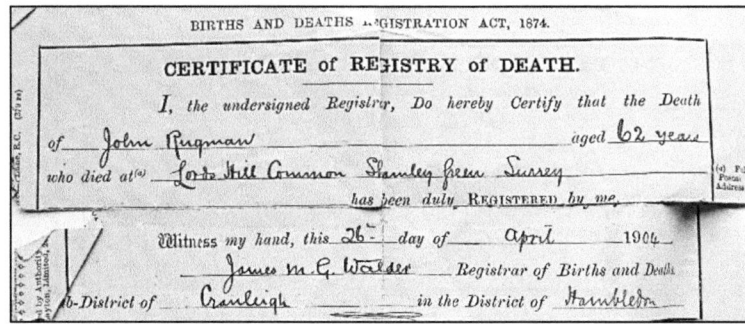

Plate A1.2

A Selection of Certificates at Death

Fig 1 – the oldest to survive: registrar's certificate, John Rugman, 62, Lordshill, 1904.

Fig 2 – a coroner's order, following an inquest, Richard Nightingale, 62, Plaistow, 1916.

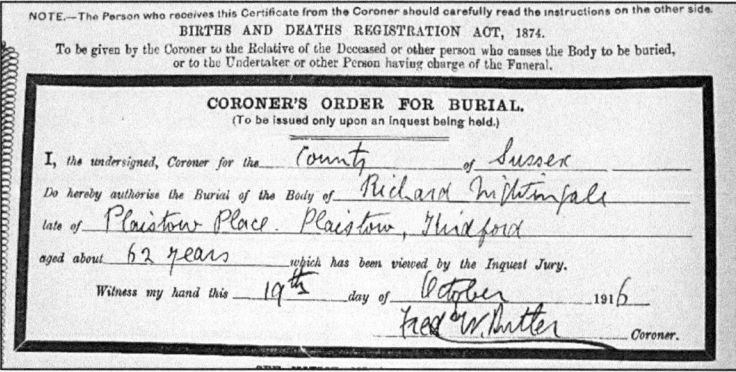

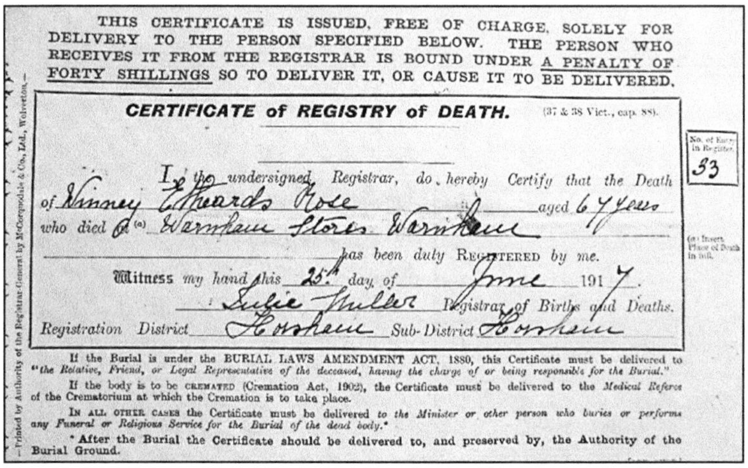

Fig 3 – registrar's certificate, including the small print, Winney Rose, 67, Warnham, 1917.

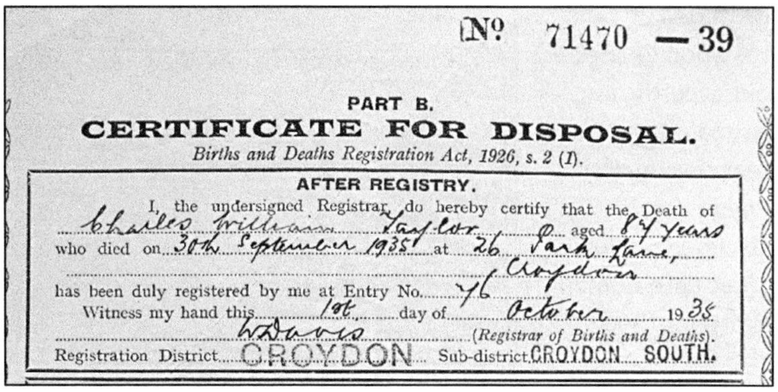

Fig 4 – a disposal certificate, Charles Taylor, 87, of South Norwood, retired to Croydon, 1935.

Fig 5 – a disposal certificate, Caroline Brown, 89, Northchapel, 1931.

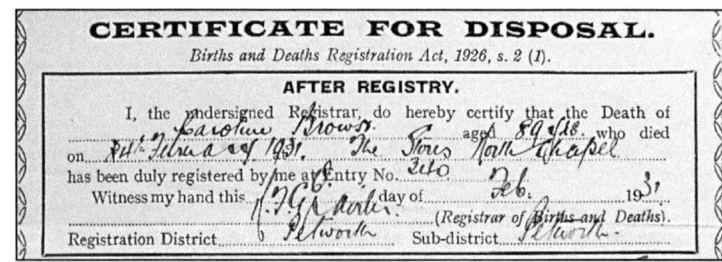

Fig 6 – a registrar's certificate, Owen Puttick, 68, Loxwood 1911.

Fig 7 – a disposal certificate. Walter Hart, 92, Hove, 1945.

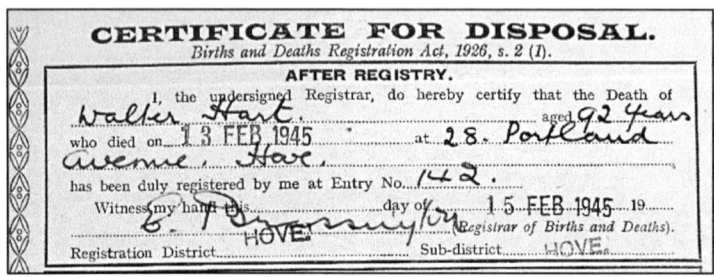

Fig 8 – a burial certificate, issued after registration, Walter Nash, 89, of Loxwood, at Royal Surrey County Hospital, Guildford, 1960.

Fig 9 – the last to be buried at Loxwood Chapel, a burial certificate, issued after registration, Elsie Piper, 104, of Loxwood, at Sussex Clinic Care Home, Worthing, 2002.

Keziah Etherington, 1913, Loxwood
To Henry Aylward, stores manager, and George Baverstock, farmer
£480 7s 3d

Jane Overington, 1916, Hill Grove, Loxwood, spinster
To Walter John Parr, retired draper, Thomas Rugman, retired farmer
£203 17s

Richard Nightingale, 1916, Plaistow Place, Plaistow, farmer
To Henry Aylward, stores manager, and William Booker, furniture buyer
£4,112 10s 8d

Henry Killner, 1917, Orchard Cottage, Loxwood, retired farmer
To W J Parr, retired draper
£591 15s

Henry Killner, 1924, Loxwood Place Farm
To Henry Aylward, Ethel Smith
£762 16s 2d

George Luff, 1930, Loxwood (Royal Surrey County Hospital, Guildford)
To Caroline Luff, spinster
£283 6s 6d

Eliza Bellchamber, 1930, Rose Cottage, Rickmans Lane, Plaistow
To Harry Garman, baker
£75 0s 11d

James Denyer, 1931, Melbourn House, Plaistow
To George Denyer, cabinet maker
£426

John Holden, 1933, Hall House, Loxwood
To Henry Aylward, stores manager
£595 14s 4d

George Baverstock, 1933, The Sycamores, Rickmans Lane, Plaistow
To Arthur Wooldridge, builder
£1,156 3s 6d

Walter John Parr, 1935, Oakgrove, Spy Lane, Loxwood
To Elsie Emily Williams, spinster
£3,328 11s 8d

Ernest Jonathan Standen, 1935, Elm View, Loxwood (husband of Catherine Enticknap)
To Grace Munday, wife of J Alfred Munday
£780 11s 5d

Ethel Mary Smith, 1939, Combination Stores, spinster
To Bessie Hempstead, spinster, and Walter John Nash, farmer
£1,569 16s 7d

Henry Aylward, 1939, Combination Stores, Loxwood
To Bessie Hempstead, spinster
£1,560 13s 2d

Archer John Eames, otherwise Archer John, otherwise John Phillips, 1942, Canal Villa, Loxwood
To Fanny Phillips, spinster, and Arthur Phillips, farm labourer
£2,944 6s 9d

Michael Killner, 1947 Alfold House
To Kate Killner, widow, Cyril Henry Killner, farmer
£9,550 14s 10d
Sarah Woods, 1951, Combination Stores, Loxwood
To Sybella Smithers, and Bessie Hempstead, spinsters
£686 3s 9d
Elizabeth Holden, 1953, Combination Stores, Loxwood
To Bessie Hempstead, spinster, and Walter Nash, farmer
£5,210 5s 3d
Walter John Nash, 1960, Combination Stores, Loxwood (Royal Surrey
 County Hospital, Guildford)
To Bessie Hempstead, spinster
£6,669 12s 4d
Annie Denyer, 1963, Hall House, Loxwood
To Ethel May Mills, spinster
£675 17s
Wesley Bernard Hempstead, 1965, Oak Lodge, Rudgwick
To Charlotte Hempstead, widow
£14,799
Kate Rugman, 1977, Combination Stores, Loxwood
£8,323
Bessie Hempstead, 1980, Combination Stores, Loxwood
£41,373
Rowland William Leswell, 1984, 2 Jubilee Villas, Loxwood
£82,388
Elsie Emily Killner, 1994, Elsmere, Spy Lane, Loxwood
£130,746
Joseph Charles Hunt, 1995, 7 The Retreat, Spy Lane, Loxwood
Not exceeding £125,000

Northchapel

Hannah Osborne, 1887, Northchapel
To William Luff of Northchapel
£87 16s 8d
William Newman, 1915, Valewood Farm, Lurgashall (Haslemere)
To Albert Maple, grocer, and Walter Parr, retired grocer
£1,792 13s 6d
James Randall, 1916, The Stores, Lodsworth, grocer and farmer
To Walter Parr, retired draper
£4,234 17s 2d
John Caplin, 1917, Holly View, Northchapel, retired farmer
To William Luff, business manager
£1,109 5s
William Luff, 1920, Northchapel Stores, grocer's manager
To Walter Parr, retired draper, and Richard Hammond, farmer
£603 8s 7d

Charles Holden, 1930, Goffs Farm, Northchapel, at Dependants Chapel
To Etta May Brooker, wife of Benjamin Brooker
£3,101 4s 5d
Caroline Brown, 1931, Northchapel Stores
To Esther Cumber, spinster
£319 7s
Elizabeth Durant, 1932, The Stores, Northchapel
To Samuel David Rugman, manager, Esther Cumber, spinster
£224 15s 6d
Richard Hammond, 1938, Laurel Cottage, Northchapel
To Samuel Rugman, stores manager
£2,792 8s 10d
Mary Ann Caplin, 1942, Holly View, Northchapel
To Samuel Rugman, stores manager
£857 10s
Samuel David Rugman, 1945, Northchapel Stores
To Ethel May Mills and Caroline Luff
£2,951 15s 5d
Alice Hounslow, 1950, The Stores, Northchapel
To Ethel May Mills, spinster
£438 14s 4d
Ezra Varns, 1956, Hill View, Northchapel (ex Fernhurst)
To Florence Varns, spinster
£7,261 13s 6d
Esther Cumber, 1956, Holly View, Northchapel, spinster
To Ethel May Mills, spinster
£848 7s
Hannah Birch, 1962, Holly View, Northchapel, spinster
To Caroline Luff, spinster
£605 14s
Caroline Luff, 1965, Holly View, Northchapel
To Bessie Hempstead, spinster
£2,918

South Norwood

Julia Ford, 1894, Avenue Stores, Portland Road, South Norwood
To George Randall, baker
£25
Henry George Randall, 1915, 226/8 Portland Road, South Norwood
To James Brightman, butcher, and Mary Slade, spinster
£464 16s
Ada Gifford, 1916, 5 Cobden Road, South Norwood
To Edwin Elliott
£195 3s

Phillip Mann, 1923, 69 Penge Road, South Norwood
To Ethel Smith
£1,115 16s

James Thomas Brightman, 1925, 228 Portland Road, South Norwood
To Alice Slade, Mary Hanks, spinsters
£2,211 7s 9d

Alice Mary Slade, 1932, 226 Portland Road, South Norwood
To Mary Hanks
£2,173 6s 11d

James Frederick Goodwin, 1938, 8 Bywood Avenue, Croydon
To Edith Goodwin, widow
£194 3s 6d

Mary Ann Hawkins Hanks, 1943, 5 Cobden Road, South Norwood
To Edith Rugman and Sarah Pannell, spinsters
£995 16s 8d

Sarah Ann Kate, otherwise Kate, Pannell, 1953, 226 Portland Road, South Norwood
To Miriam Hale and Annie Simmons, spinsters
£6,814 1s 9d

Harriet Ann Drewett, 1964, The Retreat, Spy Lane, Loxwood (ex S Norwood)
To Annie Simmans and Miriam Hale
£681

Annie Simmans, 1968, The Retreat, Spy Lane, Loxwood (ex S Nowood)
£13,885

Ernest George Goodwin, 1969, Walcot, Guildford Road, Loxwood (ex S Norwood)
£7,989

Miriam Hale, 1971, The Retreat, Spy Lane, Loxwood (ex Norwood)
£22,322

Helen (Nellie) Gifford, 1975, Roseacre Nursing Home, Compton, Sy (ex S Norwood, lived at The Retreat, Loxwood)
£1,585

Christopher Hale, 1986, Birchtrees Rest Home, Easebourne, Sx (ex S Norwood, lived at The Retreat, Loxwood)
Not exceeding £40,000

Peckham

Joseph Thomas Elliott, 1909, 17 Waller Road, New Cross
To James Foster, timber merchant, James Light, miller, Elizabeth Thorpe
£1,817 1s 3d

Warnham

Michael Killner, 1895, Chaffields Farm, Warnham, farm labourer
To Sarah Killner, spinster
£41

Henry Piper the younger, 1920, Southlea, Warnham, retired farmer
To Henry Piper, retired farmer
£784 2s 6d

Henry Piper, 1921, Southlea, Warnham, retired farmer
To Benjamin Piper, retired grocer
£2,699 4s 6d
George Reeves, 1925, The Cross, Warnham
To George Denyer, cabinet maker
£592 13s 11d
Joseph Lindfield, 1933, Warnham Stores
To James Lindfield, baker
£257 8s 4d
Lucy Luff, 1937, Warnham Stores
To William Booker, furniture buyer
£366 8s 8d
Herbert Thomas Newing, 1940, Warnham Stores
To William Booker, retired furniture buyer
£130 16s
Jesse Lindfield, 1943, Cross Cottage, Warnham
To James Lindfield, company director
£585 13s 3d
George Francis Denyer, 1948, The Cross, Warnham
To Janes Lindfield, baker, and Ethel May Mills, spinster
£1,715 11s 10d
Benjamin Piper, 1948, Warnham Stores
To Ethel May Mills, spinster, Ellen Lindfield, spinster
£3,417 6s
Ellen Luff, 1949, The Cross, Warnham
To Ethel May Mills, spinster and Bessie Kate Booker, spinster
£1,129 18s 10d
William Booker, 1949, The Cross, Warnham
To Ethel May Mills, spinster
£2,227 6s
Lucy Miles (née Shurlock), previously of Lordshill, 1961, 55 Friday Street, Warnham
To Ethel May Mills and Ellen Lindfield, spinsters
£415 3s 11d
Ethel May Mills, 1966, 55 Friday Street, Warnham
To Ellen Lindfield and Bessie Booker
£4,017

Appendix 2

The Chapel Indenture 1880

This is not the easiest of documents (a hand-written copy) to interpret dates. the document is entitled "Indenture 24 May 1880". By this time all the chapels listed have been constructed and opened for worship. The process has taken nearly 20 years. Perhaps the document is a summing up of the legal position. The Dependants had to work within the law of the land. This is a slightly abbreviated copy of the hand-written document.

It begins with a list of the parties, the trustees, to the indenture, legal agreement, or contract.

Of the 1st part
William Hampshire of Wonersh, labourer
Edward Mitchell of Wonersh, labourer
John Sirgood of Wonersh, bootmaker
Charles Hackman of Godalming, clothier

Lordshill Chapel Trustees

Of the 2nd part
William Spooner of Northchapel, brickmaker

Of the 3rd part
Charles Heather of Graffham Sussex, sawyer

Of the 4th part
Richard Hammond of Chiddingfold, scavenger
William Luff of Northchapel, labourer
John Caplin of Lurgashall, wood dealer
William Batchelor of Petworth, labourer

Northchapel Chapel Trustees

Of the 5th part
Henry Piper of Warnham, farmer

Of the 6th part
Joseph Lindfield of Warnham, labourer
Mark Pelling of Warnham, labourer
George Reeves of Slinfold, labourer

Warnham Chapel Trustees

Of the 7th part
Charles Denyer of Loxwood Wisborough Green, labourer
Peter Pacey of Loxwood Wisborough Green, labourer
Obed Overington of Loxwood Wisborough Green, labourer

Of the 8th part
David Thayre of Loxwood Wisborough Green, brickmaker
James Randall of Loxwood Wisborough Green, carpenter
Owen Puttick of Loxwood Wisborough Green, labourer

Richard Nightingale of Loxwood Wisborough Green, farmer

Of the 9th part
David Thayre
Obed Overington
James Randall
Peter Pacey

Loxwood Chapel Trustees

Of the 10th part
Michael Woolgar of The Hornet Chichester, grocer
William Sadler of Oakwood Funtington Sussex, labourer
Walter Hart of Caledonian Road Chichester, carman
John Duke of Oakwood Funtington Sussex, labourer

Chichester Chapel Trustees

Of the 11th part
James Light of 90 East Lane Bermondsey, cordwainer
William Walter Love of 15 Redford Row Streatham, stationer
Joseph Radwell of 26 Cathin Street Rotherhithe, carman

Of the 12th part
James Light
William Walter Love
Joseph Radwell
Joseph Elliott of 45 Hill Street Peckham, stationer & paper bag man

Radnor Street [Peckham] Chapel Trustees

Of the 13th part
George Tate of Darnley Cottage Portland Road South Norwood glass gilder
George Haynes late of 4 The Pavement Birchanger Road
now of Carmichael Road South Norwood, painter
Charles Taylor of High Street South Norwood, hairdresser
Phillip Mann of Penge Road Surrey, bootmaker

Of the 14th part
James Brightman of Penge Road Surrey, contractor
Jesse Edwards of Church Cottage Cobden Road South Norwood, decorator

Of the 15th part
George Tate
George Haynes
Phillip Mann
James Brightman

Norwood Chapel Trustees

At a Special Church Meeting convened of Members of the Congregations of seven churches or chapels, all trustees were appointed. Others present were exhorted "to execute these presents".
[presumably in 1880, no date for meeting given]

There follows a recitation of the conveyances for each chapel and curtilage, or parcel of land. The headings are added for clarity. Although there are seven chapel trusts, there are eight chapels in the list below. The additional one is at Felpham in Sussex, in the trusteeship of the Northchapel Trust. It was probably not yet complete, as no rent had been paid. The lease on Radnor Street Peckham only commenced in 1882. It is questionable whether Peckham was complete, perhaps by 1883 when the document was signed. Hove was not yet built, nor was the one at Plaistow.

Lordshill, Shamley Green

William Hampshire grants and conveys a messuage cottage or tenement together with a piece or parcel of land adjoining, ¾ acre, in Wonersh adjoining Stanards Lane and Lordshill Common.
The chapel is already built.

Northchapel

William Spooner grants and conveys land cottage garden ground formerly in the occupation of Mary Reid and George Spooner.
The chapel is already erected at Northchapel.
William Spooner was tenant [holding his land by copyhold] on the Rolls of the Manor of Petworth.

Felpham

Charles Heather conveys to Northchapel a piece of land formerly waste, of 6 perches in the Manor and Parish of Felpham on the north side of the highway from Felpham to Middleton bounded on the north by land of Richard Gibbon, on the east by land of Edward Dyer, on a 1000 year lease dated 24 July 1795 and subject to a lease dated 4 July 1795 made between Matthias D Oyley and Richard Harris.
No rent has been paid since 1868.

Warnham

Henry Piper conveys a messuage or tenement with garden and orchard, ¼ acre, in Warnham abutting Farm Oak on the east, land formerly of Dendy Napper on the west formerly demised to Richard Sendall.
Warnham Chapel built thereon.

Loxwood

Charles Denyer, Peter Pacey, Obed Overington, David Thayre, Owen Puttick and Richard Nightingale convey to Loxwood a field or close of land, 1 acre, west of Spye Lane bounded on the south and east by land belonging to General Onslow and on the north by land belonging to Henry Hemming.
The chapel is already built.

Chichester

Michael Woolgar conveys a piece or parcel of ground part of a field of Joyes Croft at the rear of the northwest side of St Pancras Street in the Parish of St Pancras Chichester, in depth southwest to northeast 100 feet, in width northwest to southeast 50 feet, bounded on the northwest and northeast by land belonging to Thomas Reynolds, on the southeast by a strip of land intended for a road, and on the southwest by a road.
The chapel is already built.

Peckham

James Light, William Walter Love and Joseph Radwell convey a piece of ground on the west side of Radnor Street Peckham on a lease dated 2 January 1883 between Joseph Elliott, James Light, William Walter Love and Joseph Radwell. Unexpired lease is 41 years and three quarters from 29 September 1882.

South Norwood

George Tate, George Haynes, Charles Taylor, Phillip Mann and James Brightman and Jesse Edwards convey to the Northchapel Trustees a piece of land and premises at Cobden Road South Norwood.
The chapel is erected.

A lease dated 19 November 1879 between John Enmore Jones, and George Tate and George Haynes on an unexpired lease of 90 years from 25 December 1878 subject to yearly rent of £9. 10s subject to a mortgage of £350 and interest dated 17 March 1880 between George Tate, George Haynes and Jonah Verinder, Joseph Johnson and John Cooper trustees of the Penge Perseverence Permanent Building Society in respect of a sum of £200 and arrears of interest from March last still owing.

The chapels' purpose was then recited.

Chapels " ...to be fit and needed for the purpose or may by erection thereon or otherwise become or for the time being to be fit for the purpose to be used occupied and enjoyed as a place for the Public Worship of God according to the usages of the Protestant Dissenters of Congregational Denomination now registered as and commonly called Dependants... assembling for worship therein and for the instruction of children and adults and for Church meetings and for the promotion of such other religious and philanthropic purposes..."

The words "deacon" and "elder" are used. Seven religious tenets of faith are set out in detail in the second part of the indenture. It is not the intention to give full details of the faith and beliefs here.

Additional witnesses subscribing to the indenture:

Lordshill
Alfred Pannell of Alfold, labourer
William Puttick of Dunsfold, draper.

Northchapel
Thomas John Street of Northchapel, bricklayer
George Pannell of Northchapel, labourer

Warnham
Alfred Pannell of Alfold, labourer
William Puttick of Dunsfold, draper
Loxwood
Felix Foster of Loxwood, carpenter
James Pannell of Alfold, carpenter

Chichester
Mark Green of Chichester, baker
George Howick of Tangmere, labourer

Peckham
George Barratt of Neale Street Camberwell, engraver
John Branch of Westerfield Gardens Peckham, coachbuilder

Norwood
George Randall of Penge Road South Norwood, bootmaker
Frederick Green of Stroud Green Shirley Surrey, gardener

Signed sealed and delivered:

Charles Heather

In the presence of   Thomas H Stubbs Gent of Phoenix Wharf Lambeth SE,
                       Thomas Bonson of Ventnor IoW brickmaker.

2 March 1883

Appendix 3

Additional Maps

Two maps on each page show the wider area around each community. The first is at a scale of 6 inches to one mile, and is made in the 1890s (dates differ); the second is from the late 1940s at a scale of 2.5 inches to 1 mile (dates differ). Many of the outlying farms, commons and nearby villages can be located on one or both of these maps.

Ack: findmypast.co.uk, original mapping copyright Ordnance Survey, except this page, magic.defra.gov.uk/MagicMap and Plate A3.8, google.co.uk/maps.

The maps are on pages as follows:

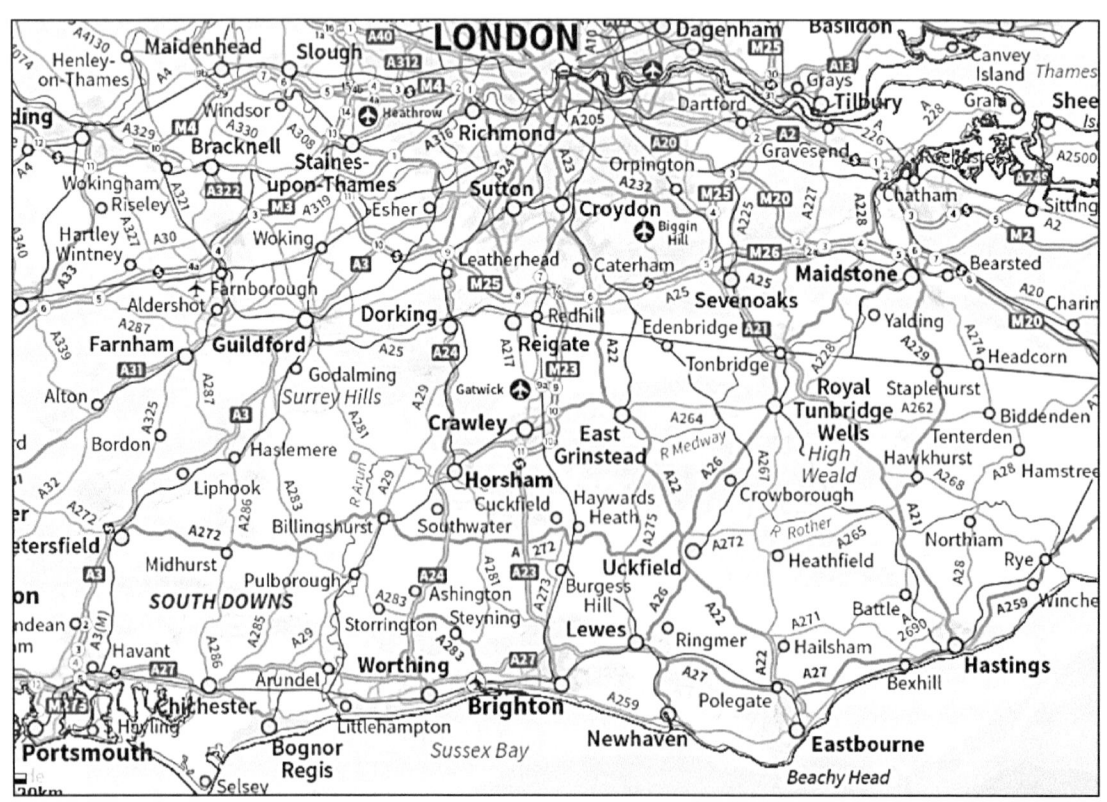

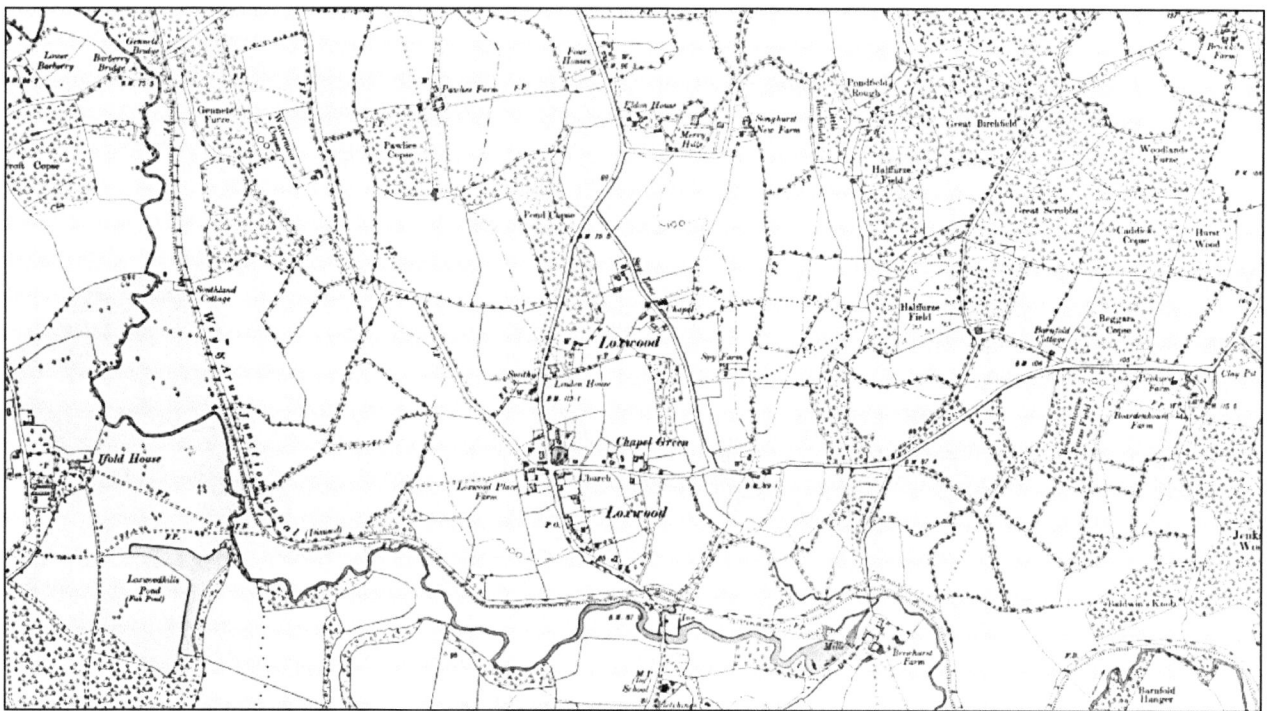

Plate A3.1   Loxwood, West Sussex

Top - the chapel (Spy Lane); the Combination Stores by the pond on the corner opposite Loxwood Place Farm. Other places mentioned in the text include Pawlies Farm, Four Houses, Ifold House estate.

Bottom – Plaistow village, including Plaistow Place, Quennell House, Rickmans Lane (site of earlier chapel).

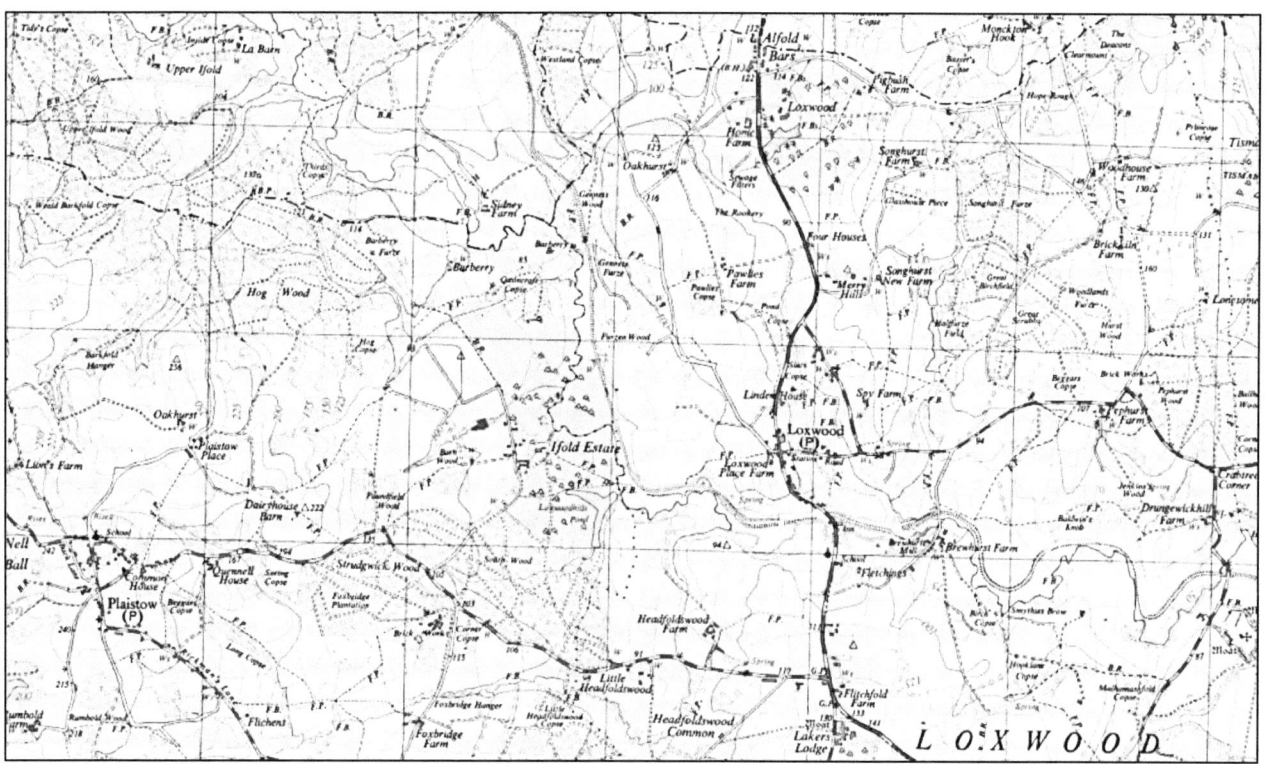

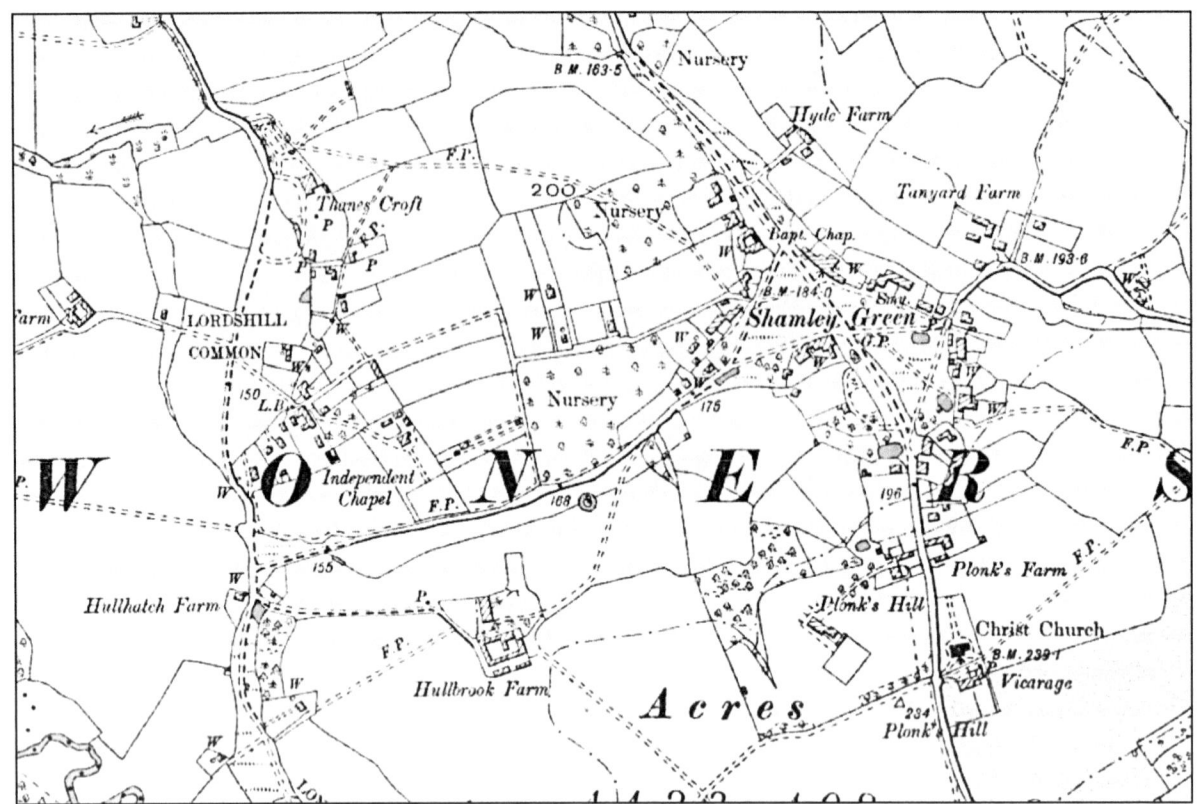

Plate A3.2   Lordshill Common, Shamley Green (Wonersh), Surrey

Top – the chapel, named Independent, is by the common and behind the stores. Other places mentioned in the text include Hullbrook Farm, Plonks Farm, Tanyard Farm.

Bottom – Bramley (village & parish) including Gatestreet Farm (well to the south), Norley Common, including Wonersh Lower Mill (shown disused), Grist Hill Farm, Strood Farm (& green).

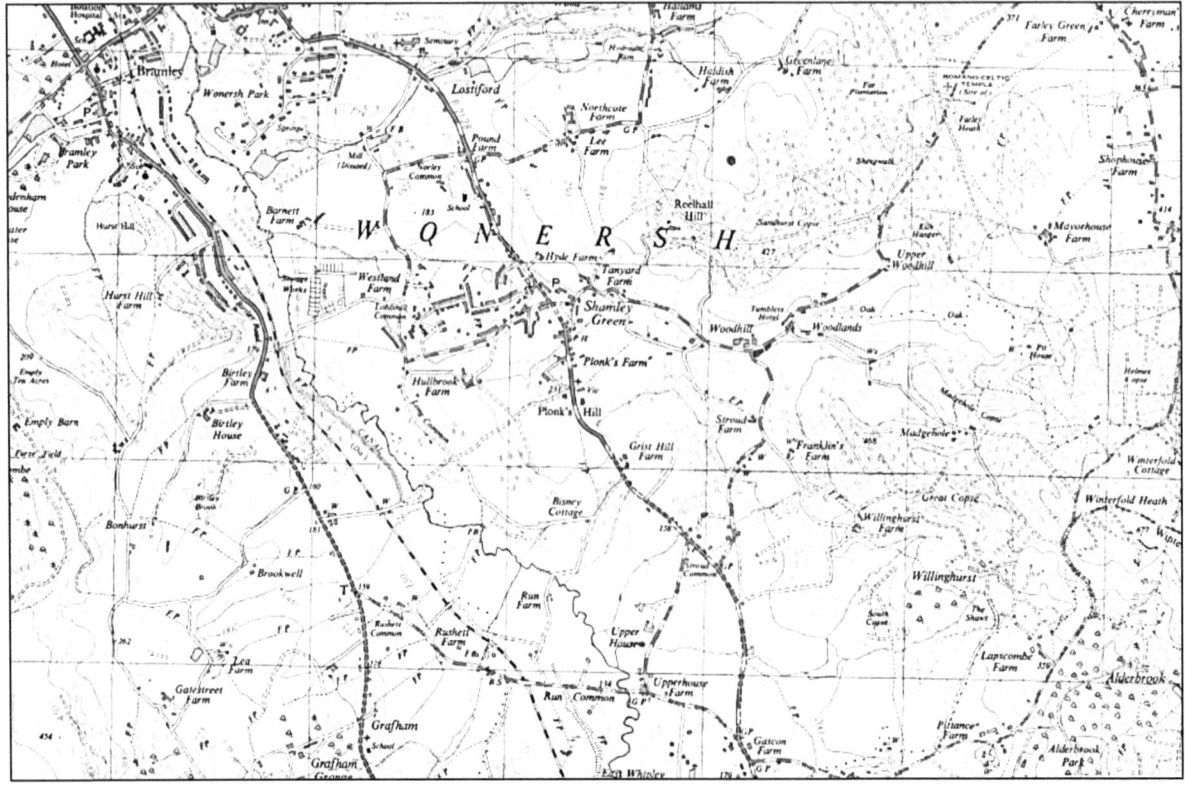

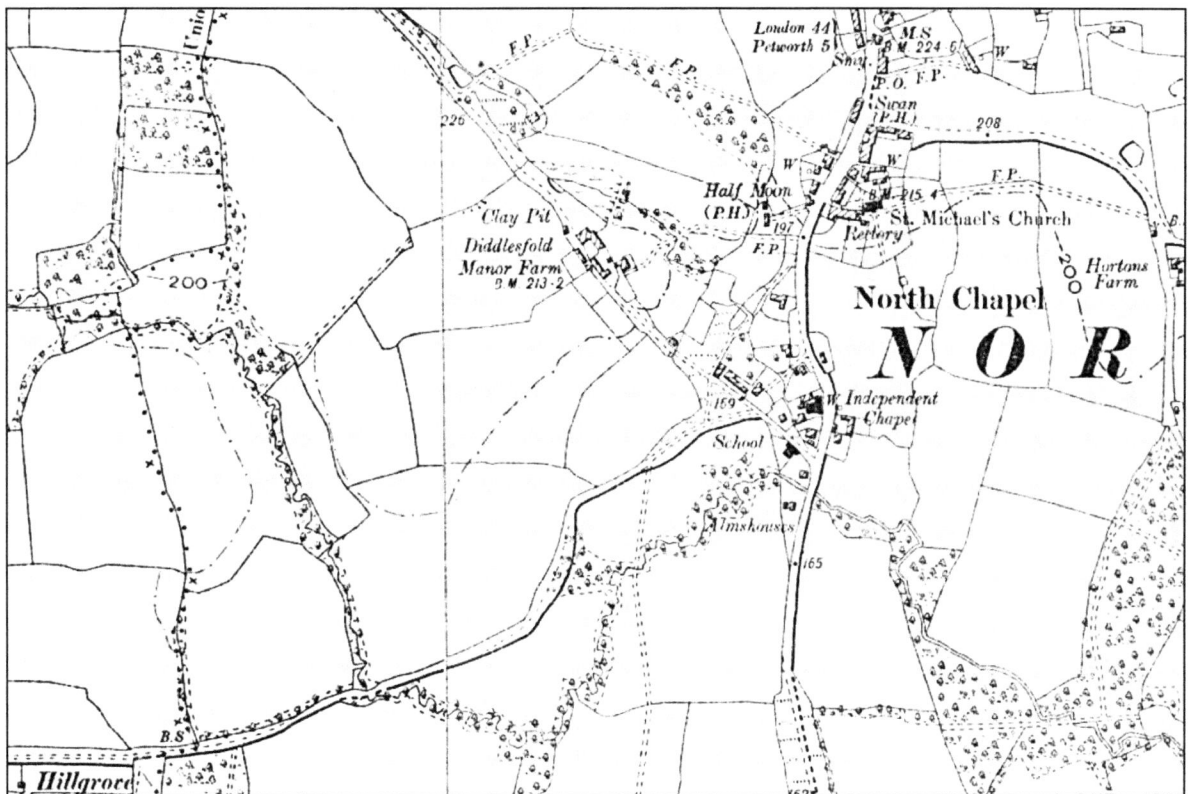

Plate A3.3   Northchapel, West Sussex

Top – the stores and chapel (named Independent) are close together on the west side of the road, opposite the name. Other places mentioned in the text include Diddlesfold Manor Farm and Hillgrove (hamlet).

Bottom – Hamlets named in the text include Hillgrove, Fisher Street, Ebernoe, Roundhurst Common. Shillinglee is north of the lake in the north east. Haslemere is several miles NW, Lodsworth is well to the south, Fernhurst is to the west of Lurgashall and Chiddingfold to the north.

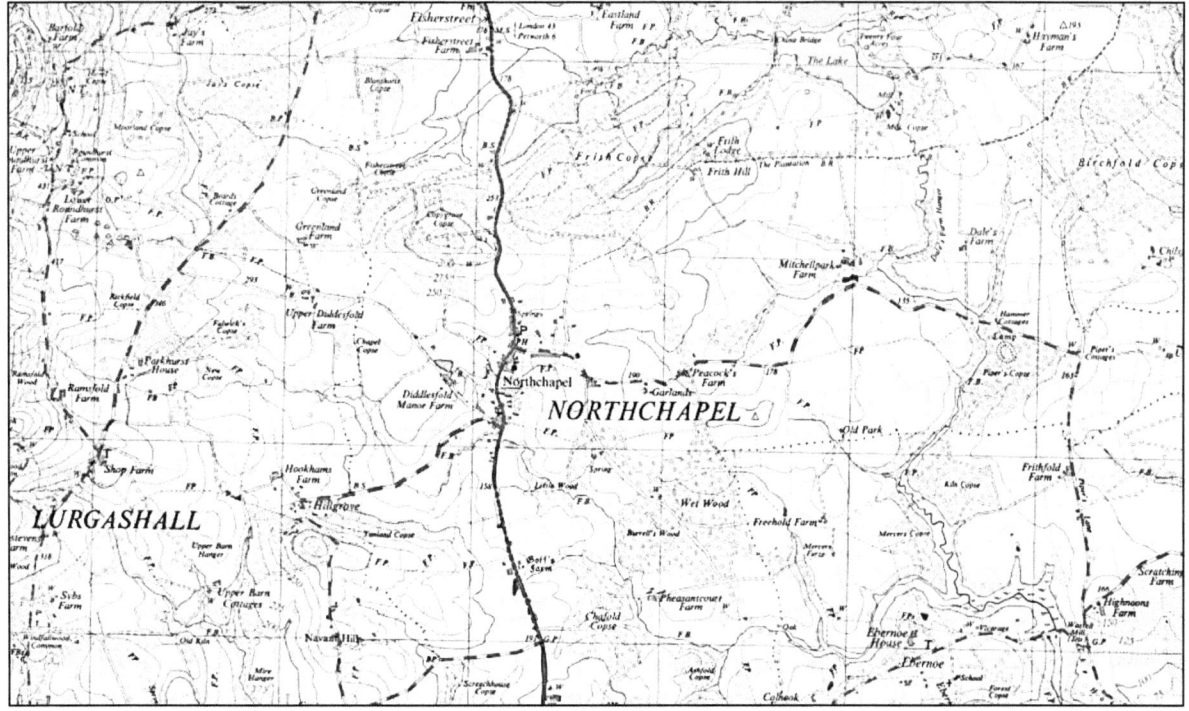

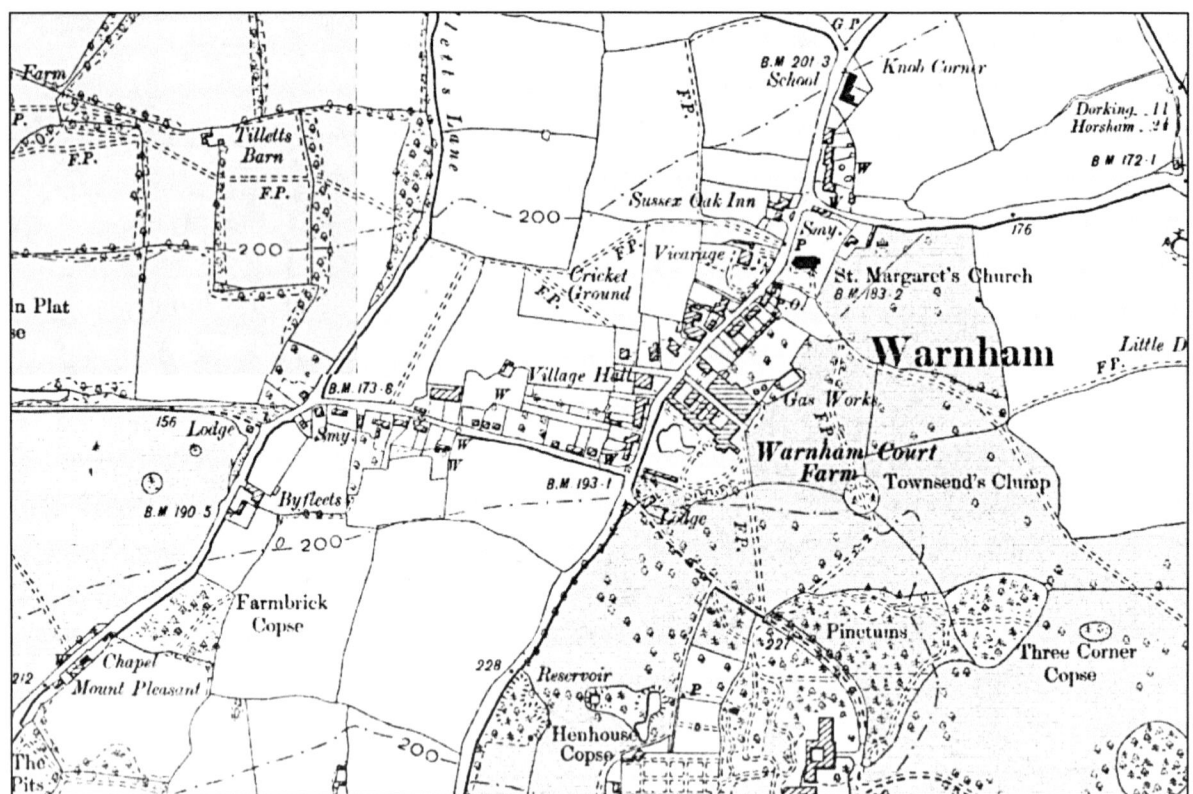

Plate A3.4   Warnham, West Sussex

Top – The chapel is at Mount Pleasant; the large stores are on the village street between the Vicarage and the Village Hall.

Bottom – other places mentioned in the text include Rowhook (hamlet) including Little Millfields (shop), Stone Farm, Bailinghill Farm and Lower Chickens Farm. Horsham is to the south east.

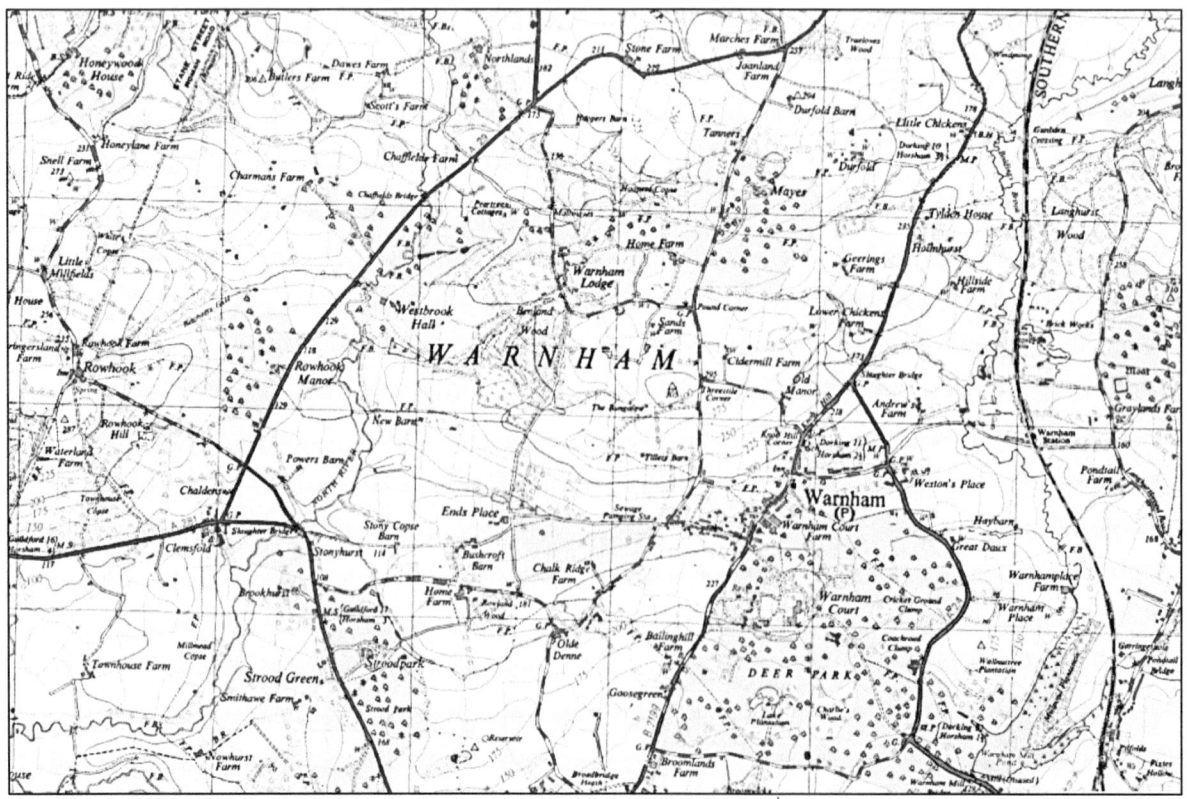

Plate A3.5   South Norwood, London Borough of Croydon

Top – the suburbs of South Norwood and Woodside are new developments. Cobden Road and Woodside Avenue, off Portland Road (then forming the eastern edge of the built-up area), are adjacent, equidistant between a firework 'manufactory', and Portland Road brick works to the east. The chapel (named Chap.) is on Woodside Avenue. The stores are at the Cobden - Woodside apex next door.

Bottom – South Norwood can be seen in its urban setting, NE of Croydon, west of Beckenham.

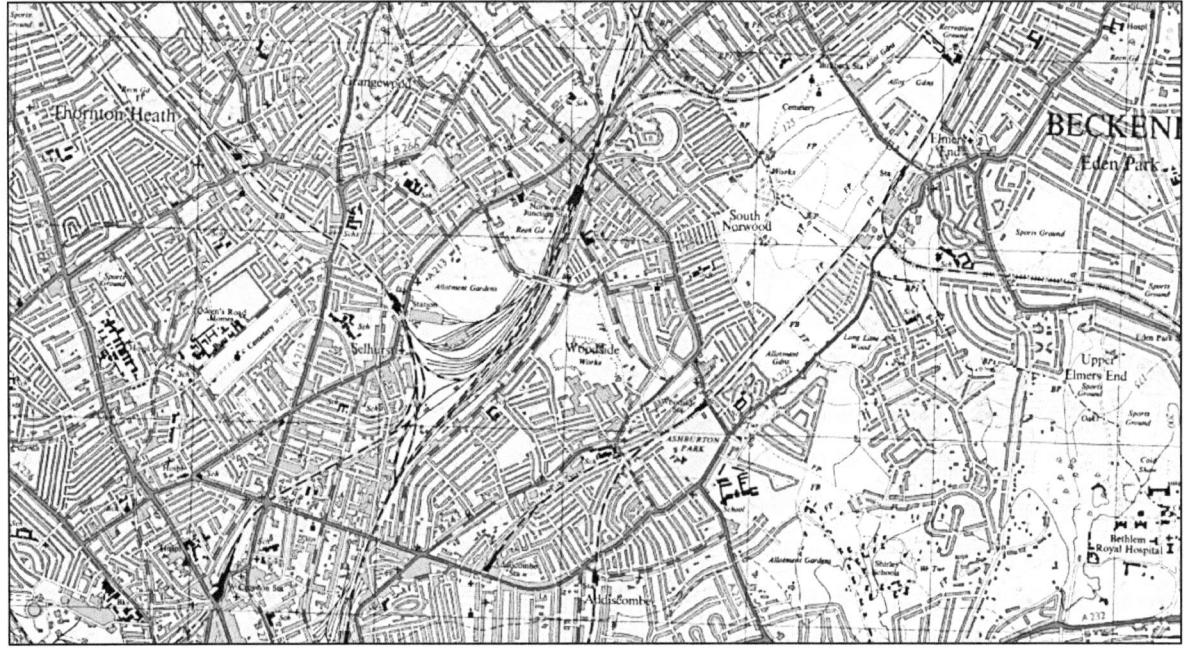

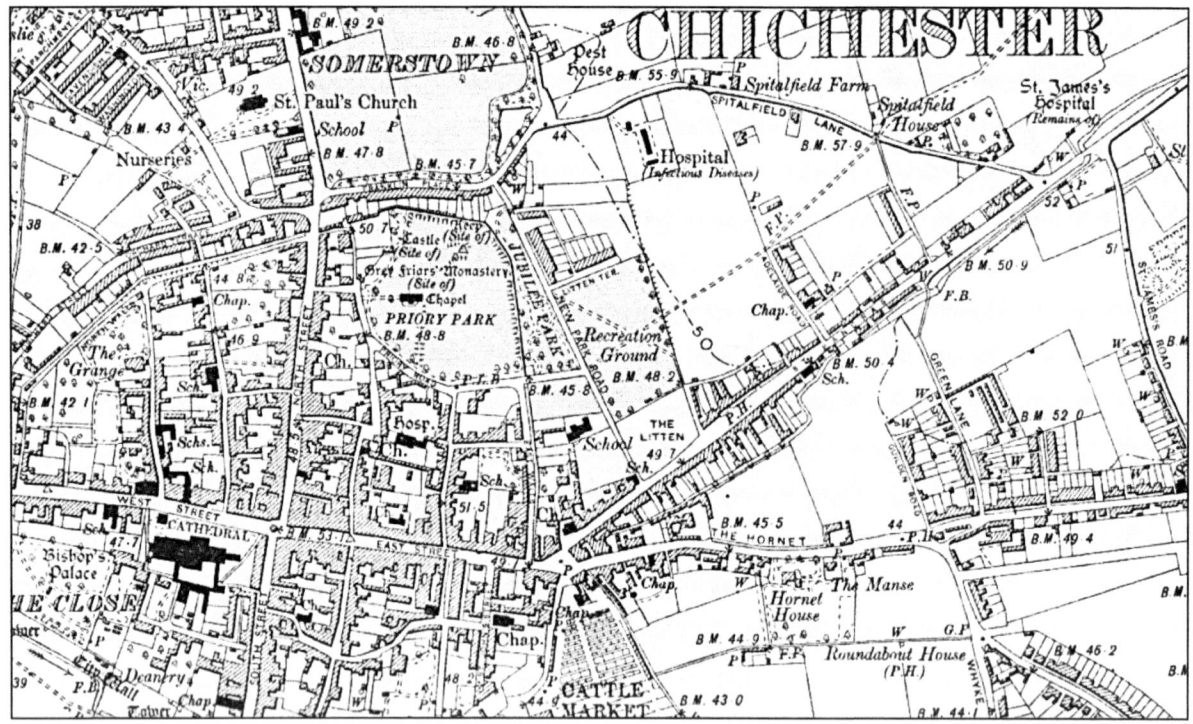

Plate A3.6   Chichester, West Sussex

Top – The Hornet is a street heading east from the city. Michael Woolgar's shop was next to the chapel (Chap.), which was not the Dependant chapel. That is another chapel (Chap.) on Adelaide Road further north, off the main road named St Pancras.

Bottom – another place mentioned in the text is Felpham (a village on the coast east of Bognor), with a Dependant chapel on Flansham Lane, a road heading north east from the village. Other places mentioned include Hunston and Oving near Chichester, and Selsey, which is well south of Chichester on a coastal promontory.

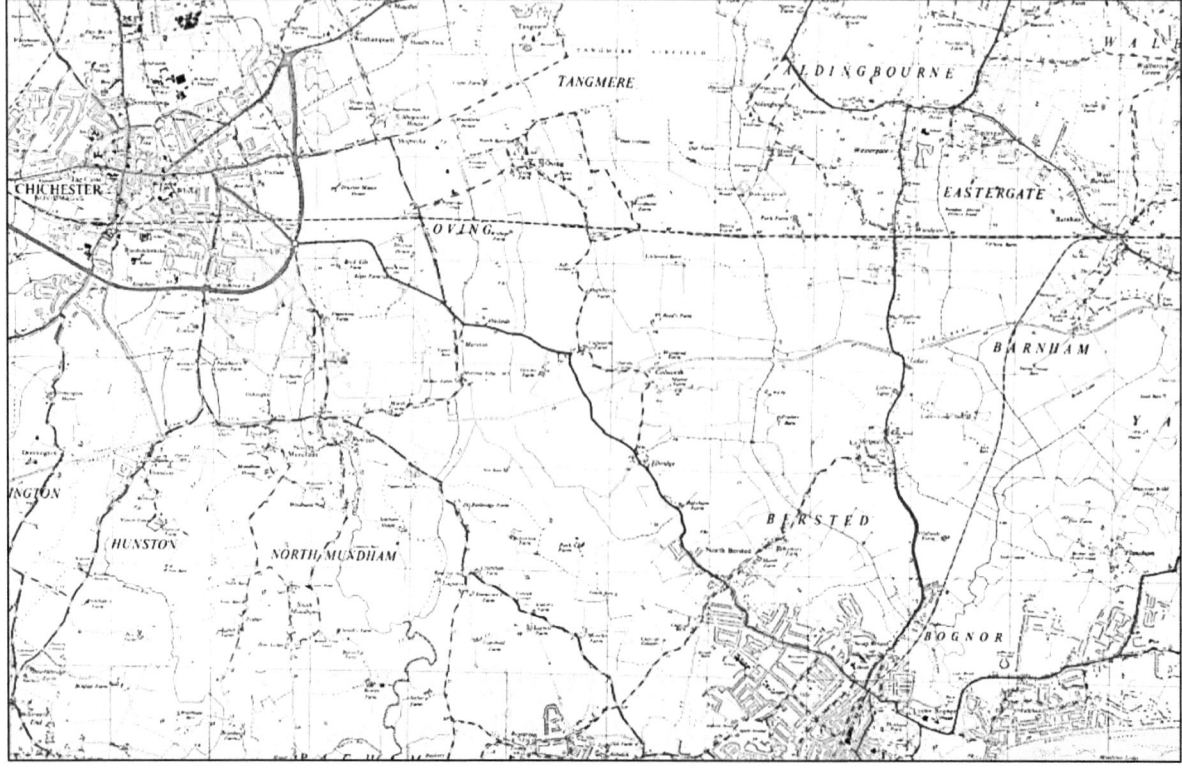

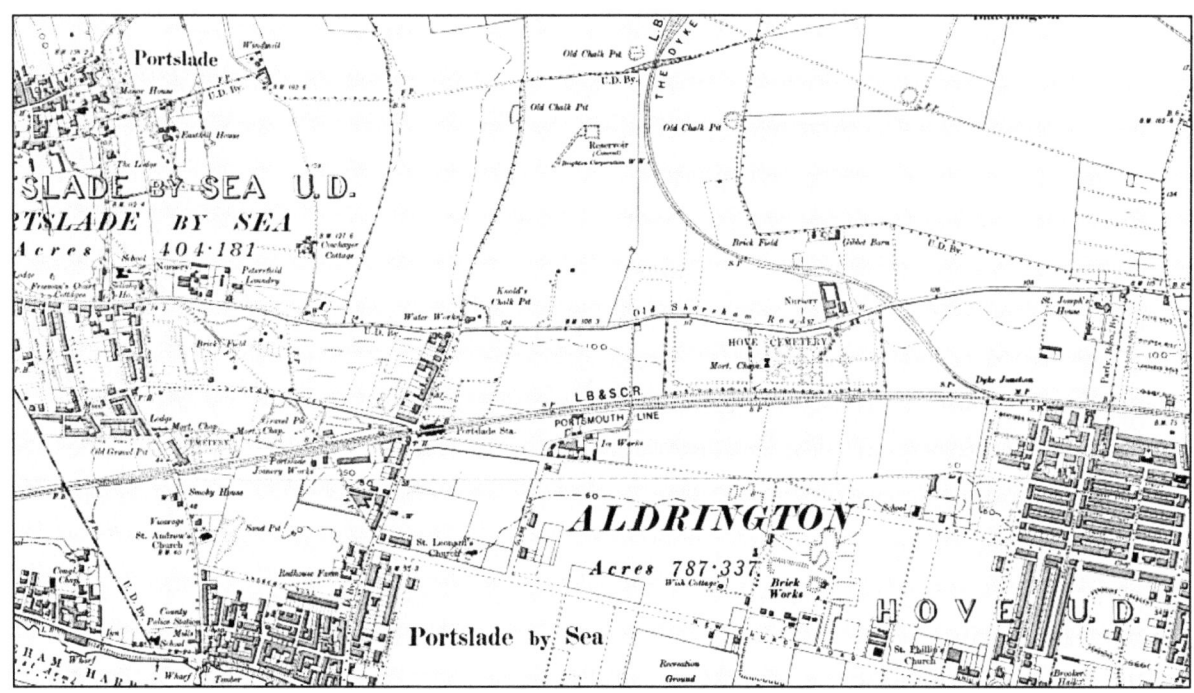

Plate A3.7   Hove, City of Brighton and Hove, Sussex

Top - this map pre-dates the building of the area of Hove known as Aldrington, south of the railway line, where the chapel would be built some 5 years later. Portslade and Portslade-by-Sea are to the west.

Bottom – the area has been built-up for well over 50 years. Careful perusal will show a **+** symbol for the chapel just south of and close to the railway. It is SE of the large cemetery by the A27, Old Shoreham Road. Many of the Hove Dependant community lived in Portslade and Southwick, and others in Brighton to the east.

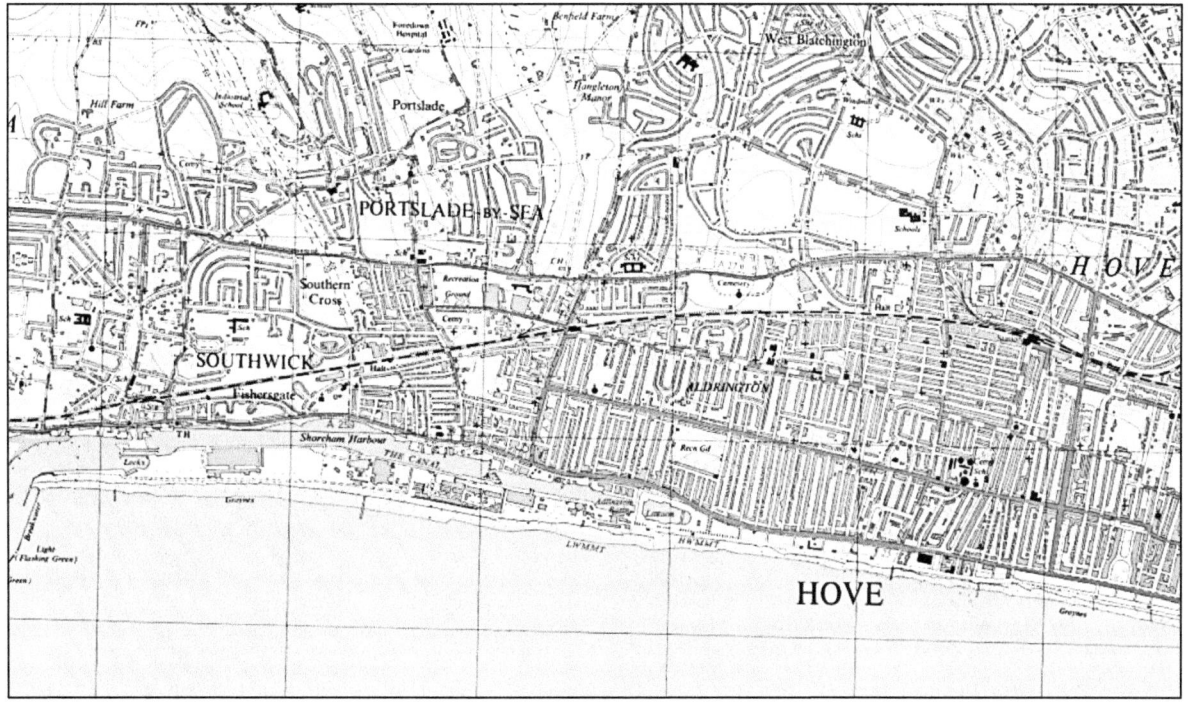

Plate A3.8   Kent

The Kent hinterland centred on the village of Headcorn from where a significant number of Dependants came. Headcorn parish is outlined, next to the village of Smarden. Canterbury to the NE, Sevenoaks to the NW (and Sundridge, a village on the western fringe), Maidstone to the north, and Margate on the NE coast are also shown in Table A2.1 below. The map also shows that the community at South Norwood, near Croydon, was the closest to Kent, particularly to Sevenoaks/Sundridge, and the most common destination.

Table A3.1		Origins of, and Communities Joined by, Kent Brothers and Sisters					
		Birthplace	Location 10 years before first Dependant location	First Dependant location	Census Date 1st Location	Subsequent location(s)	
Henry	Aylward	Sundridge	Sundridge	Loxwood	1891		became leader of the Loxwood Dependants
Abraham	Aylward	Brasted	Sundridge	Loxwood	1891		parents of Henry, James and William Aylward
Charlotte	Aylward	Chiddingstone	Sundridge	Loxwood	1891		parents of Henry, James and William Aylward
James	Aylward	Sundridge	Sundridge	Loxwood	1891		Henry's brother
William	Aylward	Sundridge	Sundridge	Loxwood	1891		Henry's brother
Elizabeth	Cogger	Maidstone	Maidstone	Loxwood	1901		
William	Cole	Sundridge	Sevenoaks	Loxwood	1911		
Emma	Cole	Sundridge	Sevenoaks	Loxwood	1911		William Cole's wife, Henry Aylward's sister
Charlotte	Cole	Sevenoaks	Sevenoaks	Loxwood	1911		daughter of William & Emma Cole
Grace	Cole	Sevenoaks	Sevenoaks (b 1902)	Loxwood	1911		daughter of William & Emma Cole
Edith Anne	Cronk	Leigh	Sevenoaks	Loxwood	aft 1911		widowed before leaving Sevenoaks
May Winifred	Cronk	Sevenoaks	Sevenoaks	Loxwood	1909*		daughter of Edith Annie Cronk
Herbert	Cronk	Sevenoaks	Westerham	Loxwood	aft 1911		stepson of Edith Annie Cronk
Sydney	Croucher	Headcorn	Headcorn	Norwood	1901		
Raymond	Croucher	Headcorn	Headcorn	Norwood	1901	Northchapel and Lordshill	
Clara	Cuckow	Boxley	Maidstone	Warnham	1901		
Fanny	Gifford	Canterbury	Margate	Norwood	1901	Warnham	widowed before leaving Margate
Helen	Gifford	Canterbury	Margate	Norwood	1901	Loxwood	daughter of Fanny Gifford
Ethel	Gifford	Margate	Margate	Norwood			daughter of Fanny Gifford
Ada	Gifford	Canterbury	Margate	Norwood	1901		sister-in-law of Fanny Gifford
Mary Ann	Goodwin	Sutton	Headcorn	Norwood	1901		widowed mother of Ernest & Ettie
Ettie	Goodwin	Headcorn	Headcorn	Norwood	1901		
Ernest	Goodwin	Headcorn	Headcorn	Norwood	1901	Loxwood	
Christopher	Hale	Headcorn	Headcorn	Norwood	1901	Loxwood	Hales lived next door to Goodwins in Headcorn
Miriam	Hale	Headcorn	Headcorn	Norwood	1911	Loxwood	sister of Christopher Hale
Mary	Hawkins	Ashford	Ashford (1891)	Norwood	1911		
Alice	Hounslow	Maidstone	Maidstone	Northchapel	1911	Northchapel	
Mary	Hounslow	Maidstone	Maidstone	Northchapel	1911	Northchapel	grandmother of Alice Hounslow
Afred	Hunt	Canterbury	Maidstone	Norwood	1901		brother-in-law of Fanny Gifford
Eliza	Hunt	Canterbury	Maidstone	Norwood	1901		Alfred Hunt's wife
Clara	Hunt	Maidstone	Maidstone	Norwood	1901		daughter of Alfred & Eliza Hunt
Isabella	Hunt	Maidstone	not known	Norwood	1911		daughter of Alfred & Eliza Hunt
Fanny	Maple	Sundridge	not known	Norwood	1911		
Albert	Maple	Sellindge	Sellindge	Norwood	1881	Loxwood & Northchapel	1881 lived with Dependant Haynes family in Norwood
Clara	Millbourn	Maidstone	Maidstone	Norwood	1901		
Herbert	Newing	Maidstone	Maidstone	Warnham	1901		
George	Piper	Sandhurst	Sandhurst	Norwood	1911		
Winny	Rose	Upchurch	not known	Warnham	1901		
Harry	Smith	Sutton Valence	Headcorn	Norwood	1911		
Mary	Walsham	Woodnesborough	Margate (1881)	Norwood	1901		

*Dates in brackets indicate 20 years before. For several people, locations were impossible to verify - the person may have been in a location where they were not enumerated, or incorrectly enumerated. Column 5 is particularly significant, as it seems possible this area is where most heard the message of John Sirgood's mission. Albert Maple from Sellindge seems to have been the first, before 1881. * May Winifred (Winnie) Cronk attended Loxwood School from 1909 and again from 1911, when in the care of Mrs Charlotte Cole.*

Plate A3.9   Loxwood, 1914, Inland Revenue Plan

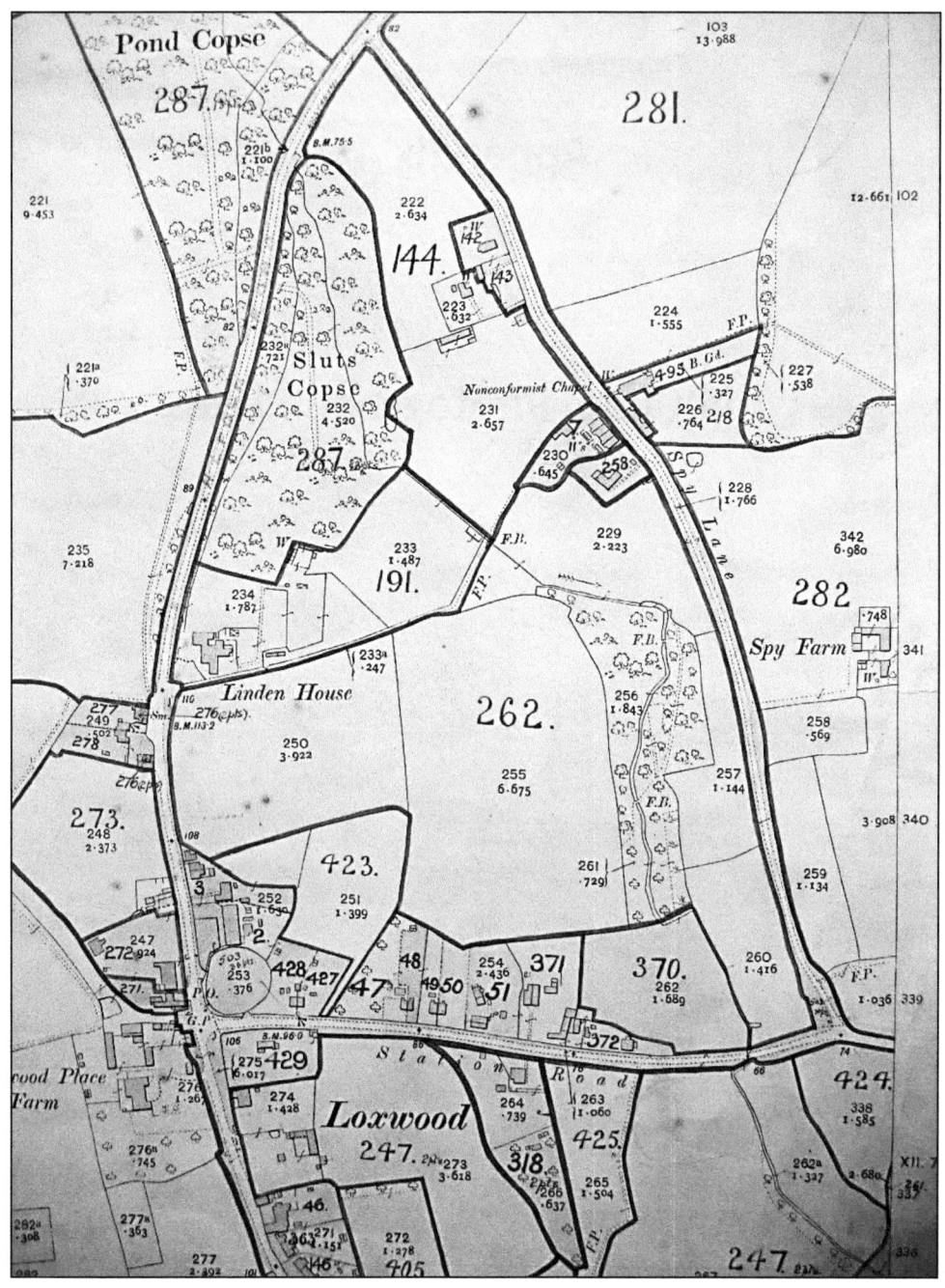

The national so called "domesday maps", or Board of Inland Revenue Valuation Office Field Plans, of 1910-1915, were OS maps overlain by plot numbers - assessment numbers. This is useful as it indicates ownership of Dependant properties at a time when the society was well embedded in Loxwood. Plot 2 was the Combination Stores, 3 was Jubilee Villas, 272 was Hall House (271 being the former Foster's drapers, then the Post Office) and 273 its farmland. Loxwood Place Farm was not then in their ownership. The old chapel-of-ease was formerly on Plot 429; in 1914, only the cottage remained. 278/277 were formerly Foster's then Puttick's grocers, from 1890s including a smithy and a new house. On Spy Lane, Plot 7 had The Old Cottage, where John Sirgood once stayed with the Overingtons, and the recently built cottages for Dependants opposite the chapel, which was 495, and graveyard, 218. Chapel Green had recently been re-named Station Road. Lastly, plot 46 was Mr Elliott's house and shop, recently sold to Mr JA Harris (from whose widow Aylward, Smith & Co purchased the business in 1944). A footpath (FP, and footbridge, FB) can be discerned from opposite the blacksmith, used by the Combination Stores community to chapel.

Appendix 4

Additional Photograph Plates

Plate A4.1   Loxwood Dependants, Group Photos Through Four Decades

Fig 1 – 1932, l to r, back row, Mabel Spooner, Fanny Phillips, Walter Nash, Winnie Cronk.
Middle row, Kate Rugman, Henry Aylward, Lizzie Holden. Front row, Irene Drewett, Bessie Hempstead, Millie Underwood.

This summer garden group is notable for having three important members of the community, Walter Nash, Henry Aylward and Bessie Hempstead. All the women have severe hairstyles.

Fig 2 – 1940s, outside Loxwood Chapel, dressed for chapel, left to right, Bessie Hempstead, May Goodwin, Sarah Drewett, Winnie Cronk, Alfred Goodwin, Kate Rugman, Mabel Spooner, Cyril Killner.

Fig 3 – below, 1950s, at the chapel gate, l to r, Cyril Killner, Mabel Spooner, Winnie & Jack Smart, Gladys Killner, three not known. Fewer now wear formal dress to chapel. Jack is believed to have been blind.

Fig 4 – above, 1950, an unusually good quality image.

Back, l to r, Ron Parsons, Bessie Goodwin, Sybella Smithers, Florence Phillips, Lucy Pannell, Alfred Goodwin, Mable South, Bessie Hempstead, Mabel Spooner; middle, Mrs Edith Goodwin, Sally Drewett, Mrs Cox, Sarah Woods, K Pannell (of Norwood), Kate Rugman; front, Winnie Cronk (holding dog), Irene Drewett, May Goodwin, Edith Holden (seated), John Phillips.

Fig 5 - below, undated, but probably also c1950. Among the many faces are Walter Nash, left, Bessie Hempstead, seated centre. Most of them are also in other photos. Some older readers may see faces they recognise; others can compare with the known faces in this plate.

Fig 6 - 1957, an elderly Walter Nash who died 1960, is seated centre, Alf Goodwin back left. The young men were Arthur and Dennis Killner, sons of Gilbert and Ethel Killner, but offer a startling contemporary contrast to their elders. The group is thought to be of some of those (mainly non-family) who attended the funeral of Gilbert and Ethel's 15-year-old daughter Freda.

See Plate 2.2, the family outside chapel.

Fig 7 - below, 25 December 1960. No decorations but an emphatic 'yes' to Christmas presents, relaxed dress and comfortable surroundings: Mabel Spooner, Bessie Hempstead, Winnie Cronk, Annie Denyer (in the corner, and much the eldest), Irene Drewett.

Fig 8 – below, a 1960s group of Combination Stores staff (not all Dependants) on a day out - to judge by the clothing and background.

Several people appear again and again, having lived above the Combination Stores or in close comradeship, and worshipped together, for most of their adult lives (the Killner siblings, and the married Smarts, for example did not live communally).

Plate A4.2 Loxwood Female Groups, Mainly Residents of Combination Stores and Hall House and Single Women

From top left clockwise:
Fig 1 – unknown date (?1930s).
Fig 2 – (?1950s) Memilo Pike, Kate Rugman, K Higgins, Lucy Pannell, Gwen Bradshaw, Elizabeth Holden, Winnie Cronk, Irene Drewett.
Fig 3 – probably at Felpham. Sybella Smithers, Mabel South, Bessie Goodwin, Gladys Killner, May Goodwin, Mrs Edith Goodwin (seated).
Fig 4 – Lucy Pannell, Winnie Cronk, Sybella Smithers.

Fig 5 – possibly 1940s, with farm background, possible names: Miss Barber, Fanny Phillips, Florence Phillips, Lily Leswell, Mabel South, Anne Stenning, Miss Powell (seated). Child a Muggeridge?

Fig 6 – not a group as above, but a family group, the Phillips family, taken possibly near one of several locations where they lived in Surrey.

Left, Alfred Phillips, 1842-1928; Selina Phillips, 1843-1915, two of their eight children. A remarkably good quality photograph.

Alfred was a brickmaker, briefly living in Loxwood in the 1890s, having spent his life, before and after, moving frequently between brickworks in the general area of Dependant communities. At his death, he was described as "Haslemere brother Phillips".

Alfred and Selina were the grandparents of the Phillips siblings of Loxwood, including John, who became leader.

Plate A4.3

First to last in Loxwood

Fig 1 – one of the oldest photos. This is Owen Puttick, 1843-1911, and his wife, Mary, 1851-1922.

Owen was a trustee of Loxwood Chapel in 1883, listed as one who conveyed the land for the chapel. He was, then, a labourer, who lodged with the Foster family at Black Hall, itself a cradle of combination retailing. He and Mary Foster were married soon afterwards, Owen to run the grocers, Mary the drapers. See Chapter 5.

They ended their days at Jubilee Villas.

Alfred Goodwin, 1906-1996, the last elder of the Dependants at Loxwood (or anywhere else) and the last managing director and company secretary of Aylward, Smith & Co Ltd, is seen here (location uncertain) when he was a very elderly survivor. He died at the age of 90, very deaf, but cheerful and optimistic to the end at his home, Rose Cottage.

Plate A4.4 **Northchapel**

Fig 1 - A group at Northchapel Stores, undated, many in their shop aprons. *Ack & ©Martin Snow*

Family group of Dependents at Northchapel
Martin Snow © 2003

Fig 2 – George Luff, 1882-1948, Northchapel baker. As a young man, he lived at Northchapel Stores. After his marriage to Amy Puttick, they lived at Myrtle Cottage. Amy was daughter of Owen and Mary Puttick (Plate A4.3), pioneers of the Combination Stores in Loxwood. Later they moved to Hove where George had a bakery in Boundary Road (Plate 12.2). George was a son of George and Mary Anne Luff (née Greenfield) who worked for Richard Nightingale in Plaistow for many years, and nephew of Ellen and Lucy, stalwarts of the Warnham community. If the caption above is correct, the lady seated is Mary Ann Luff, his mother, 1847-1925. The location of the photo is not known, but the significance of marriage for some within the Dependant communities is undisputed, contrary to the oft-quoted disapproval of marriage by many writers.

Plate A4.5   Loxwood: Church and Chapel, Then and Now

Then...

Fig 1 – Loxwood's old Church of England chapel-of-ease, the village then part of the parish of Wisborough Green. Photo 1874, just a few years after the building of its rival chapel in Spy Lane.

Located by the pond where the Combination Stores were built. The road alongside, now Station Road, was known as Chapel Green.

Fig 2 – the rival Dependant chapel in Spy Lane, opened 1861, following years of harrassment from the gentry of the established church.

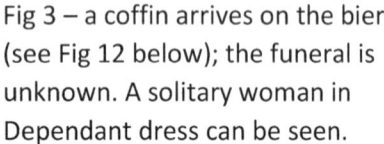

Fig 3 – a coffin arrives on the bier (see Fig 12 below); the funeral is unknown. A solitary woman in Dependant dress can be seen.

Fig 4 – this view from the stores bakery frontage across the pond and island, which Dependant residents cared for, is of "Old Church Cottage", the curate's house once attached to the chapel-of-ease, which stood to its right. An Aylward, Smith & Co postcard.

Fig 5 – this is a painting, by an unknown artist, of one of the four dwellings at Four Houses, located opposite the private road to Pawlies Farm, north of the village. Dependants who lived in one or other of these small cottages included Obed and Caroline Overington, and Stephen and Charlotte Overington.

This was one of the first locations, possibly the first, according to one source, for John Sirgood's outdoor preaching. This would have been in the early 1850s. The Overingtons were among the first and most faithful converts. Other sons of Obed and Caroline, Thomas (also his wife Anne) and John became elders.

Now…

Fig 6 – St John the Baptist Church, Loxwood, replaced the old chapel-of ease in 1902, on a new site opposite the then school buildings. Since the 1970s it has been a united benefice/parish with Alfold

and moved into the diocese of Guildford. *Ack: parish website.*

Fig 7 – Loxwood Chapel has never ceased to be a place of worship, unique among Dependant chapels. Until restrictions because of Covid-19 (2020-2021), the Emmanuel Fellowship allowed a community not-for-profit café operated by volunteers in its spacious back room and kitchen. Emmanuel Fellowship is a worthy successor to the Dependants. Inevitably there have been interior alterations, with some features remaining from the past, as illustrated on the next page. The chapel is now licensed for weddings; there have been one or two a year of members of the congregation. There have also been a handful of funerals and burials of Emmanuel Fellowship pastors. There are still no baptisms. *Ack: Fig 7, Fellowship website. Figs 8-11, by kind permission of Emmanuel Fellowship, 2020.*

Figs 8 & 9 – the interior of the chapel in 2020; one of the two original oil lamps retained to this day. The pews have been removed, some of them still stored in an outbuilding, and one or two remaining in the meeting room, an echo of the row of old pews from the chapel-of-ease in the parish church.

For photographs of the chapel in its Dependant heyday, see Plate 3.2.

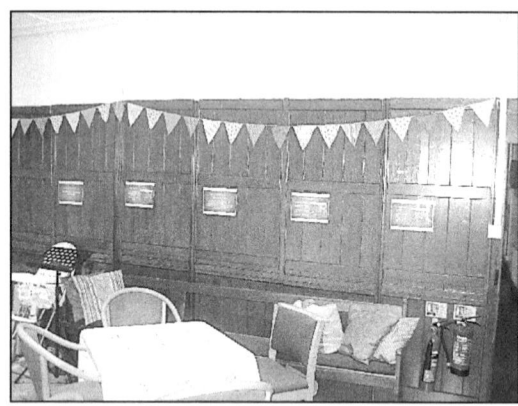

Figs 10 & 11 – the meeting room, of which no photograph survives from its days in use by the Dependants. The kitchen door is open in Fig 10. Fig 11 illustrates something unknown to the author until he was shown around in 2020. The wooden panels can be raised for a large chapel congregation, such as those on bank holidays, with many gathering in the meeting room behind the "desk", as the Dependants termed their altar. Moreover, the floor of the meeting room is slightly raked, so giving those at the back a better view of proceedings. A clever idea, possibly unique.

Fig 12 – the funeral bier is also stored in an outbuilding. It was on display for a meeting in Loxwood's

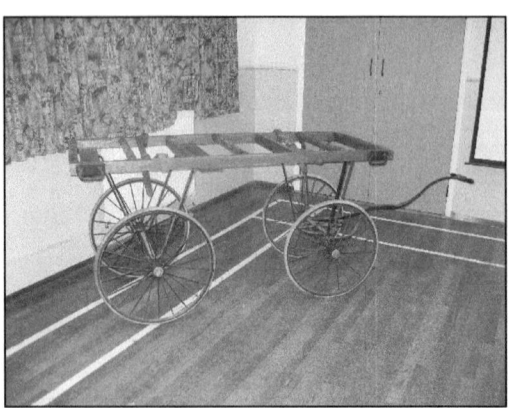

North Hall when the author gave a talk on the Dependants in 2012.

Fig 13 – and finally, **then...** the only known photo of a chapel service, which chapel unknown.

Cokelers in their Chapel

Plate A4.6   Some Portraits

Clockwise from top left,

Fig 1 – The Bradshaw siblings in order of birth, Edith (1873-1977), Florrie (1875-1958), Jack (1888-1973), Gwen (1898-1989). The Bradshaws have the distinction of coming from Gloucestershire, as did John Sirgood (though the youngest, Gwen, was born in East Sussex).

Fig 2 – Phoebe Parsons, 1876-1948, and Kate Rugman, 1878-1977, sisters.

Fig 3 – Tom Rugman, 1852-1935 (father of Phoebe and Kate) with Kate, at his home, The Myrtles, Loxwood.

Fig 4 – Kate Rugman, in old age, still living at The Myrtles

Fig 5 – this photo is labelled Mr & Mrs Spooner, probably William (1862-1948) and Anne (1866-1926) living at Hall House in 1911 with children Mabel, Grace and Alfred.

Fig 2 – right, George Baverstock (1843-1933), a farmer, and Sarah (née Wells, 1844-1929) of Barkfold Farm, Plaistow. Sarah had the distinction of being the last sister to be 'put behind the desk' (an elder) by John Sirgood.

Fig 3 – left, Ellen Randall of Plaistow, 1855-1943. She would have been 44 at Elsie's birth (her husband, George, 42) - clearly correct in the 1901 census enumeration, which listed four children.

Fig 4, left, her daughter, Elsie, front left, at Plaistow School, who later married George Piper, a baker from Kent. They lived in South Norwood. Born in 1898, Elsie lived until 2002. She left a vivid description of a funeral written when only 17. At her death, she became the last Dependant to be buried in Loxwood Chapel's graveyard.

References and Acknowledgements

Further Reading (some difficult to find)

Jerrome, Peter, *John Sirgood's Way, The Story of the Loxwood Dependants*, The Window Press, 1998.

Reed, Mick, *'The Lord Does Combination Love': Religion and Co-operation Amongst a Peculiar People*, in Yeo, Stephen (Ed.), *New Views of Co-operation*, Routledge, 1988.
Reed, Mick, *'The Lord Does Combination Love...',* internet publication.

Bayley, C. H., *Ifold, Loxwood & Plaistow, Forgotten Border Villages*, Ifold & District Local History Society, 1988.

Muggeridge, Ron, *Warnham, A History*, The Field Place Press, 1985.

Austin, Janet, *Kirdford, The Old Parish Discovered*, Ifold & District Local History Society, 1989.

Bruce, Pamela, *Northchapel, A Parish History*, Northchapel Parish Council, 2000.

Montgomery, John, *Abodes of Love, Chapter 13*, Putnam,1962

Sirgood John, *Religious Intolerance in the Rural District of West Sussex, Lawyer's Notice to a Shoemaker & The Shoemaker's Reply,* James Sirgood, Kennington, 1861. The author has copies of original letters, together with Mr Napper's unpublished reply,14 June 1861 - the originals in possession of Mr Donald Kitchener, Loxwood.
Sirgood, John, *Religious Intolerance in the Rural District of West Sussex, Notice from a Magistrate & A Working Man's Reply,* James Sirgood, Kennington, c1866

The Dependant's Hymn Book, Loxwood, 1958.

Unpublished Testimonies, etc

Testimony of Brother Benjamin Piper of Warnham (1868-1848), handwritten copy, 1936

A Short Account of the Life and Experiences of James Denyer (1842-1931) of Plaistow West Sussex, Elizabeth Denyer (1882-1975), handwritten copy, undated.

Rowland William Leswell (1906-1984), typescript copy,1982.

Mary Mitchell Farquhar (1912-1999), handwritten copy, undated.

Northchapel, The Late Mr S. Rugman: An Appreciation (Samuel David Rugman, 1881-1949), 1949.

Letter from 'One who knew Bro John' to Miss May Kenward, Northchapel Stores, Old Christmas Day [7 Jan] 1914, author's copy of original letter in possession of Mr Donald Kitchener, Loxwood.

The Stores (Combination) Loxwood, Sussex, Sarah Woods (1869-1951), typescript copy, 1947.

A Meeting with Mr Alfred Goodwin, handwritten interview notes, C. H. Bayley, May1989. An audiotape of Alf Goodwin talking about his life and the Dependants is in the possession of Mrs Marion Way – I have used notes made from this.

A brief account of a very glorious meeting at Lords Hill, 19 Feb 1917 (Charles Hackman Funeral), Elsie Piper (1898-2002), copied from her handwritten book of testimonies, letters and hymns in possession of Mrs Marion May, Shamley Green.

Periodical and Magazine Articles

Articles in periodicals, newspapers, magazines, referred to in Chapter 13 are too numerous to mention again (and more may come to light as newspaper collections are digitised and made available online), but the following are significant milestones:

Buckwell, John C., *Stories of Loxwood*, Sussex Archaeological Collections, Vol 56, 1914.

Homan, Roger, *The Society of Dependants, A Case Study in the Rise and Fall of Rural Peculiars*, Sussex Archaeological Collections, Vol. 119, 1981.
Homan, Roger, *The Sussex Cokelers,* 1981.

Turnour, Viscount, *The Cokelers: A Sussex Sect*, National Review, September 1904.
Earl Winterton, *The Cokelers: A Sussex Sect*, reprinted, Sussex County Magazine, Vol 5, November/December 1931.
Viscount Turnour became the 6th Lord Winterton, and, as an Irish peer, sat in the House of Commons as member for Horsham for 50 years.

MacAndrew, Donald, *The Sussex Cokelers: A Curious Sect,* Sussex County Magazine December 1942/January 1943.

The Petworth Society Magazine, ed. Peter Jerrome, various issues, including:
        No. 29, Sep 1982
        No. 64, Jun 1991
        No. 65, Sep 1991
        No. 67, Mar 1992
        No. 70, Dec 1992
        No. 78, Dec 1994.

Principal Primary Sources

Loxwood Burial Register (photocopy, original book survives in a safe in the chapel).
Loxwood Death Register (photocopy, original book may no longer survive).

Indenture, 24 May 1880, handwritten copy notebook, indenture signed 1883 (WSRO).

Aylward Smith & Co. Ltd, Loxwood, Minute Book, 1911-1973 (WSRO).

Brown, Durant & Co. Ltd Northchapel, Minute Book, 1910-1969 (WSRO, final pages missing).

ancestry.co.uk and findmypast.com – censuses; births, marriages, deaths; county
directories, telephone books, probate register, etc.

Acknowledgements

In Loxwood - The Loxwood History Society, for asking me to talk to their members and
guests in North Hall, which was the spur I needed to begin to write, and for some additional
photographs.
David and Rita Gumbrill, family friends and long-time residents of Loxwood, closely
connected with the Dependants through employment and family (respectively), guardians
of the Cokeler flame in Loxwood and Loxwood Chapel in particular, for conversation and
loan of a treasure trove of photographs, documents, etc.
Ray Noakes, Loxwood Emmanuel Fellowship, for showing me the chapel interior and
documents kept safely there.
Don Kitchener, Loxwood resident, for loan of original documents in his possession.

Marion May, Shamley Green, guardian of the Cokeler flame in Lordshill, for conversations
and loan of a huge quantity of original handwritten books, papers, notes, photographs, tape
recordings, clothing, and china, and for her redoubtable effort in mounting a well-attended
exhibition in Salters Gallery, Guildford in 2003. Author, The Story of the Cokelers.

Roy Taylor, Portslade, for correspondence about Warnham.

www.cokelers.living.org.uk, © Snow, Martin, 2003. Now removed from the internet.

Marion Woolgar, Bognor Regis, family historian, for information on Michael Woolgar, and
Felpham Chapel.

In South Norwood - John Hickman, local historian, South Norwood, for correspondence
including information from local directories, on the South Norwood Stores and chapels.
Dr Bruce Osborne for photographs and helpful comments about South Norwood
John Windell for helpful memories of South Norwood Stores.

Judy Middleton, local historian, Hove, for two images.

old-maps.co.uk for some of the © Ordnance Survey map extracts used in plates.

google.co.uk for some © map extracts and streetview images used in plates.

magic.defra.gov.uk/MagicMap for Ordnance Survey map extracts used in Appendix 3.

And finally,
to Doug Betts for editing and checking the text of the whole book, my huge thanks. Also, thanks to Trish Morgan for page setting.

The author wishes to apologise to anyone or any company whose images have been used without express permission. This is a small circulation not-for-profit book, and no document or map has been used unless in a small extract. If anything has been used without attribution, the mistake is unintentional.

Index, Chapter Subheadings

General Index

Selected people and places, etc. are indexed. Space forbids a complete index of every person and place, or of their every occurrence.